PAX

Also by Tom Holland

RUBICON:
The Triumph and Tragedy of the Roman Republic

PERSIAN FIRE:
The First World Empire and the Battle for the West

MILLENNIUM:
The End of the World and the Forging of Christendom

IN THE SHADOW OF THE SWORD:
The Battle for Global Empire and the End of the Ancient World

DYNASTY:
The Rise and Fall of the House of Caesar

DOMINION:
The Making of the Western Mind

TOM HOLLAND

War and Peace
in Rome's
Golden Age

PAX

a

abacus
books

ABACUS

First published in Great Britain in 2023 by Abacus

3 5 7 9 10 8 6 4 2

Copyright © Tom Holland 2023

Maps by John Gilkes

A CIP catalogue record for this book
is available from the British Library.

Hardback ISBN 978-1-4087-0698-5
Trade Paperback ISBN 978-1-4087-0700-5

Typeset in Spectrum by M Rules
Printed and bound in Great Britain by
Clays Ltd, Elcograf S.p.A.

Papers used by Abacus are from well-managed forests
and other responsible sources.

Abacus
An imprint of
Little, Brown Book Group
Carmelite House
50 Victoria Embankment
London EC4Y 0DZ

An Hachette UK Company
www.hachette.co.uk

www.littlebrown.co.uk

To Bill Heald: without whom the writing of this book would have been very much more of a challenge.

CONTENTS

ACKNOWLEDGMENTS

ACKNOWLEDGEMENTS

My chiefest thanks are to my brother, James Holland, who introduced me to Bill Heald. Bill, one of the world's great cancer surgeons, came to my rescue midway through the writing of the book, and pretty much personally ensured that I was able to finish it. I would also like to thank Amyn Haji, Andrew Emmanuel, Margaret Burt and all their teams at King's College Hospital for the meticulous care they have given me over the past year. As ever, I owe more than I can say to Richard Beswick and everyone at Little, Brown; to Lara Heimert and everyone at Basic Books; and to Patrick Walsh, the best of agents, and everyone at PEW Literary. My devotion to the staff of the British Library, the London Library and the Hellenic and Roman Library knows no bounds. Jamie Muir not only read the book in manuscript, but took the most wonderful photographs of my coins for me. Llewelyn Morgan, the kindest and most generous of scholars, assisted me with eunuchs and elephants alike. Sophie Hay, that tutelary guardian of Pompeii, allowed me to use some of her beautiful photographs. Matei Blaj not only invited me to Romania, but drove me all the way to Sarmizegetusa. Dominic Sandbrook and everyone at Goalhanger did all they could to stop me finishing this book – but to such enjoyable effect that I cannot begrudge them their many, many, many demands on my time. My beloved family – Sadie, Katy and Eliza – were, as they have ever been, the rock on which I build everything.

MAPS

PREFACE

In AD 122, the world's most powerful man arrived on the banks of the Tyne. The river – which flows through what today is the city of Newcastle – was the most northerly point that had ever been visited by a Roman emperor. Below it stretched lowland Britain, the fertile southern half of the island, which over the course of the previous eighty years had been conquered, pacified and tamed by the legions. Beyond it lay the wilds of the north, lands too savage and poverty-stricken to merit conquest. Such, at any rate, was the judgement of the visiting Caesar. Publius Aelius Hadrianus – Hadrian – was a man well qualified to distinguish between civilisation and barbarism. He had studied with philosophers, and ridden to war against head-hunters; lived both in Athens and on an island in the Danube. Prior to his arrival in Britain he had been on a tour of military bases along the Rhine, and given orders for a great palisade to be built beyond the river's eastern bank. Now, standing beside the grey waters of the Tyne, Hadrian had plans for an even more formidable marvel of engineering.

The boldness of the project was evident from the very presence of Caesar in Britain. It was not only his legions who needed squaring. So too did the gods. Sacrifices had to be made both to the Ocean, that immense and fearsome expanse of water in which Britain was set, and to the Tyne itself. Hadrian, a man punctilious in his dealings with the supernatural, knew better than to commission a bridge without assuaging the spirit of the divine that was manifest in every river. Pons Aelius, the structure was named: Hadrian's Bridge. This, for an obscure spot on the margins of the world, was a signal honour. Only bridges in Rome were normally named after emperors. In due course, a decade later, when Hadrian came to commission a huge mausoleum for himself on the far bank of the Tiber, and wished to provide ready access to it from the capital, Pons Aelius was the obvious, the only name for the resulting structure. There were now, with its completion, two very different bridges bearing the imprimatur of Hadrian's favour. The result, upon the distant outpost in Britain, was the bestowal of an even more solemn dignity.

It was not just the bridge over the Tyne that was called Pons Aelius, but the fort that had been constructed on the river's northern bank. This fort, in turn, was only one of a number of military encampments stretching in a direct line from one shore of the Ocean to the other. Joining them, and running for eighty miles, was a wall fashioned largely out of stone. Behind the wall ran a metalled road. Behind the road ran a ditch, dug so deep that it could only be scaled with ladders. Infrastructure of such an order, built on such a scale, was as awesome a memorial to Hadrian as anything he had sponsored in Rome. It proclaimed a degree of martial effort and a capacity for intimidation that had no rival anywhere. The emperor's visit to the Tyne had been fleeting, the merest way-stop — but he had left behind him the unmistakeable stamp of a superpower.

Not that many Romans ever saw the Wall. So distant was it from all that made for civilization — 'trade, seafaring, agriculture, metallurgy, all the crafts that exist or have ever existed, everything that is manufactured or grows from the earth'[1] — that it tended to serve them as, at best, a rumour. In time, they would come to forget that it was Hadrian who had built it at all. For a millennium and more after the collapse of Roman rule in Britain, its construction was attributed to another, later Caesar; and only in the mid-nineteenth century was the Wall conclusively proven to have been the work of Hadrian.

Since then, thanks to the labours of generations of archaeologists, epigraphers and historians, our knowledge of how and by whom it was built has improved immeasurably. The study of Hadrian's Wall is now 'littered with the bones of discarded hypotheses'.[2] Meanwhile, along its spectacular central stretch – a section which in 1600 had been so infested by bandits that the antiquarian William Camden was forced to omit it altogether from his tour – visitors today are greeted by interpretative signs, gift shops and toilet facilities.

Even so, a sense of the mysterious has not been banished entirely from Hadrian's Wall. In the early winter of 1981, when an American tourist by the name of George R. R. Martin visited it, dusk was closing in. As the sun set and the wind gusted over the crags, he had the site to himself. What would it have been like, Martin began wondering, to stand there in Hadrian's time, to be a soldier from Africa or the Near East posted to the very limits of civilisation, to gaze into the darkness and dread what might be lurking there? The memory stayed with him. A decade later, when he embarked on a fantasy novel called *A Game of Thrones*, his visit to Hadrian's Wall was to prove a particularly vivid influence: a wall, as he would later describe it, 'defending civilisation against unknown threats beyond'.[3]

In Martin's fictional world of Westeros, the 'unknown threats' prove to be the Others, pale demons formed of snow and cold who make slaves of the dead. The Roman frontier system is recalibrated in his novels as a seven-hundred-foot-high wall of ice, eight thousand years old and three hundred miles long. It has ancient spells carved into it. Every so often it gets attacked by mammoths. Martin's version of Hadrian's Wall, thanks to the blockbusting success both of his novels and of the TV shows adapted from them, has come to put the original somewhat in the shade. Yet it also demonstrates, perhaps, just how firm the hold of a particular understanding of Rome's empire remains on our collective imagination. There is never any question in *A Game of Thrones* that our sympathies lie with the Night's Watch, the soldiers who garrison the Wall, rather than with the Others. Martin, after all, when he stood on the northernmost limit

of Rome's empire, and gazed out into the dusk, had been imagining
himself a Roman, not a Briton. People visiting Hadrian's Wall rarely
identify with the natives. Novels and films that feature it invariably
adopt the occupier's perspective. To venture beyond the limits of
Roman civilisation, whether with a doomed legion or in search of
a lost eagle, is to venture into a heart of darkness. Rudyard Kipling,
the great laureate of the British Empire, cast the Wall itself as a monument to civilisation. 'Just when you think you are at the world's
end, you see a smoke from East to West as far as the eye can turn, and
then, under it, also as far as the eye can stretch, houses and temples,
shops and theatres, barracks and granaries, trickling along like dice
behind – always behind – one long, low, rising and falling, and hiding
and showing line of towers. And that is the Wall!'[4] Even today, in an
age infinitely less keen on imperialism than it was in 1906, when
Kipling published his stories about Roman Britain, it is possible to
cast the presence of soldiers on Hadrian's Wall from Morocco or Syria
as a cause for celebration. It was to emphasise this aspect of the Wall
that the BBC, in a recent film made for children about Hadrian's
arrival in Britain, amended chronology so as to portray the governor
of the province at the time as African.* The same Roman Empire that
built a wall across its most barbarous frontier, and ruled perhaps 30
per cent of the world's population, remains today what it has been
since the late eighteenth century: a mirror in which we feel flattered
to catch our own reflection.†

It was Edward Gibbon, in 1776, who originally cast the second
century AD as the most golden of golden ages. Famously, in the first
volume of *The Decline and Fall of the Roman Empire*, he defined the reigns
of Hadrian and of his immediate predecessors and successors as 'the

---

* Quintus Lollius Urbicus, who served as governor of Britain in the years
immediately following Hadrian's death, was a Berber. Quintus Pompeius
Falco, the governor who welcomed Hadrian to Britain, was the son of Sicilians.
† An estimated 20 to 40 per cent of the world's population was ruled by Rome
in the time of Hadrian. Certainty, of course, is impossible.

period in the history of the world, during which the condition of the human race was most happy and prosperous'. Everywhere from the Tyne to the Sahara, and from the Atlantic to Arabia, lay at peace. Lands that once, prior to the establishment of Roman rule, had been convulsed by internecine conflict – kingdom against kingdom, city against city, tribe against tribe – had come to lie 'under the guidance of virtue and wisdom'.[5] True, this commendation came with various caveats. Subtle and mordant, Gibbon was far too knowing to imagine that any period of history had truly been paradise. He was alert to the autocratic character of the Caesars' rule – and he knew, of course, none better, what was to come. Even so, to a man of his temperament – refined, tolerant, respectful of learning and commerce – the world ruled by Hadrian appeared immeasurably preferable to the barbarism and superstition that he identified with the Middle Ages. 'The frontiers of that extensive monarchy were guarded by ancient renown and disciplined valour, The gentle, but powerful influence of laws and manners had gradually cemented the union of the provinces. Their peaceful inhabitants enjoyed and abused the advantages of wealth and luxury.'[6] The tone of gentle irony with which Gibbon framed this account of the empire's prosperity implied no scorn for the Romans' achievement. Order was better than chaos, and the order brought by the Caesars to 'the fairest part of the earth, and the most civilized portion of mankind', was indeed a thing of wonder. Gibbon knew this because it had been a thing of wonder to the Romans themselves. They had marvelled at the spectacle of one-time enemies laying down their weapons and devoting themselves instead to the arts, so that cities everywhere were radiant with beauty, and the countryside like a garden. They had revelled in the scale of the shipping that crowded the seas, bearing treasures from as far afield as India. They had felt moved that the flames of sacrifice, previously dots of isolated fire, were now something inextinguishable, passing ceaselessly from people to people, always ablaze somewhere across the face of the world. Such, it might seem to a provincial raised in Hadrian's empire, were the fruits of the Roman peace: the Pax Romana.

Since the time of Gibbon, knowledge of how this peace functioned and was maintained has improved by quantum leaps. Archaeological sites have been excavated, inscriptions tabulated and evaluated, papyri and writing tablets dug up from rubbish tips painstakingly transcribed, and the immense mass of evidence synthesised to a degree that would have stupefied and delighted Gibbon. Confidence on the part of Western scholars that the empire ruled by Hadrian did indeed comprehend the fairest part of the earth was long ago qualified by an awareness that it was not the only superpower on the face of the Eurasian landmass. Today, comparative studies of Roman and Chinese imperialism are as cutting-edge a field of scholarship as any in ancient history. Nevertheless, the sheer scale and duration of the peace that was imposed on the western edge of Eurasia during the first and second centuries AD, a period when for the first time much of it constituted a single political unit, remains unparalleled. As in the 1770s, so today: no one can claim, as the Caesars proudly did, that the Mediterranean is exclusively theirs.

Even the prosperity of the Roman world — which is liable to seem, to twenty-first-century consumers, a good deal less dazzling than it did to Gibbon — is still perfectly capable of impressing economists. 'Living conditions', so the Gray Professor Emeritus of Economics at the Massachusetts Institute of Technology has calculated, 'were better in the earlier Roman Empire than anywhere else and anytime else before the Industrial Revolution.'[7] Inevitably — the lack of precise data being what it is — the size and efficiency of the Roman economy in the first two centuries AD remain topics of furious debate; and yet the resources that were available to cities across the empire are familiar not just to scholars of the period but to countless numbers of tourists. It is hard even for the most casual visitor to Ephesus or Pompeii not to feel impressed by the sights. Temples and theatres, baths and libraries, paving stones and central heating: all constitute ready markers of the Pax Romana. To this day, whether in films, cartoons or computer games, they serve as shorthand, not just for the heyday of the Roman Empire, but for civilisation itself.

But what did the Romans ever do for us? The answer: sanitation, medicine, education, wine, public order, irrigation, roads, fresh water systems and public health. Such a list, even as it flatters the Pax Romana, hardly sums it up, of course. If there was light, there was also darkness. The most famous of all Roman monuments, beloved alike of the Italian tourist industry and Hollywood, was a stage for the spilling of blood. The cross that once stood in the centre of the Colosseum may be long gone, removed by archaeologists in the 1870s, but the murderous entertainments staged in the amphitheatre — even if there is no hard evidence that Christians were ever fed to lions there — remain as much a focus for moral disapproval today as they did back when the site hosted a chapel and the Stations of the Cross. No one watching *Gladiator* sides with the emperor. In our instinctive sympathy for the victims of Roman blood sports, we show ourselves the heirs not of the Caesars but of the early church.

'I saw the woman, drunk with the blood of the saints and the blood of the martyrs of Jesus.'[8] So wrote Saint John in Revelation, the last book of the New Testament, some time during the late first century A D. John's vision ranks as an apocalypse, a parting of the curtain that veiled from mortal gaze events that were yet to come; but it is also the most vivid, the most coruscating, the most influential attack on imperialism ever written. The woman beheld by John was a whore, dressed in purple, bedecked with extravagant jewellery and sitting on a scarlet beast with seven heads and ten horns. Babylon was her name, and she ranked as the mother of all the world's depravities and abominations. An angel, speaking to the narrator, revealed the true identity of this monstrous prostitute: 'the great city which has dominion over the kings of the earth'.[9]

In Revelation, the power and the wealth of the world's capital serve only to heighten the relish John feels at the spectacle of her ruin. A voice from heaven informs him that in a time to come the kings of the earth will weep and wail when they watch her burn and merchants will mourn:

Alas, alas, for the great city
that was clothed in fine linen, in purple and scarlet,
bedecked with gold, with jewels, and with pearls!
In one hour all this wealth has been laid waste.[10]

Here, incubated by Rome's empire, was a prophecy of her downfall that was fated always to be the shadow of the memories of her greatness. Just as it was the age of Hadrian and of his successor Antoninus Pius that Gibbon hailed for having offered the world its fairest prospect of universal peace, so it was the spectacle of barefooted friars singing vespers in a pagan temple, in the very heart of Rome, that first prompted him to muse on her decline and fall. The ancient gods were not alone in having been humbled by Christ. Also brought low were the Caesars who had ruled the empire at its greatest extent. Today, in Rome, neither Hadrian's mausoleum nor the Pons Aelius commemorate the man who built them. They bear witness instead, on the summit of the mausoleum, to the appearance of the archangel Michael, who in Revelation is described as throwing down Satan to the earth. Meanwhile, on the triumphal column raised by Trajan, Hadrian's predecessor and the most fêted of all Rome's emperors, it is not Trajan himself who stands there, but Saint Peter, a humble fisherman. Christ had foretold all of it: 'So the last will be first, and the first last.'[11]

The notion that this was to be viewed as a positive, as a consummation devoutly to be wished, would have appeared incomprehensible to Trajan. To the Roman elite in this period, the beliefs and teachings of Christians were only dimly a matter of concern. They were a faint and only occasionally noted presence in the empire's urban fabric, like Mesozoic mammals in an ecosystem dominated by dinosaurs. Yet just as mammals were destined, in the long run, to inherit the earth, so, too, were the Christians. Indeed, so total was the revolution in values brought about by their triumph, and so utterly have we in the West come to take them for granted, that it can be hard for us today to appreciate just how profoundly influenced by them many of our assumptions remain. If Europeans and Americans have always looked back to Rome with admiration, then so also has that admiration – even during the heyday of Western imperialism – been clouded by suspicion. Christians, when they annexed the lands of other peoples, did so as the followers of a provincial who had been tortured to death on the orders of an imperial administrator. To take on the role of Pontius Pilate, then, might not sit readily or easily with their consciences. Enthusiasm for decolonisation is a very Western phenomenon.

The Romans, in their own displays of colonial violence, were more innocent. To them, a cross served not – as it did for Christians – as an emblem of the triumph of the tortured over the torturer, but rather the opposite: of the right they claimed for themselves to suppress insurrection as brutally and uncompromisingly as they pleased. No feelings of guilt shadowed their callousness. It was Christianity that first instilled those. Today, although church attendance in the West may not be what it used to be, our society remains as stamped as it ever was by the legacy of the early Christians' hostility to the Whore of Babylon. Historians of classical antiquity bear its imprint no less than everybody else. Certainly, enthusiasm for empire tends not to be a feature of contemporary classics departments. The martial qualities the Romans valued, which enabled them both to conquer and to uphold their immense imperium, to reap vast harvests of slaves, and to celebrate blood sports as entertainment, are rarely the toast of scholars in universities today.

It is one of the great paradoxes of ancient history, then, that the most influential legacy of the Pax Romana should have been a movement so revolutionary in its ultimate effects that today it requires a huge effort for us even to begin to comprehend the world as the Romans comprehended it. For now we see through a glass, darkly. Christianity, however, is not alone in having endured from the first and second centuries AD as a living tradition, nor is it the most radical in its hostility to the memory of Roman imperialism. In due course, after all, Caesars came to power who were themselves Christian, and the empire that previously had been drunk on the blood of the saints and the martyrs was reconsecrated to Christ. Even though Trajan, in the long run, did come to fall, the replacement of his statue on the summit of his triumphal column in Rome with one of Saint Peter signalled no condemnation of the emperor's memory. Just as the Romans themselves had hailed him as *Optimus Princeps*, the Best of Emperors, so did medieval Christians admire him almost as one of their own. Indeed, prompted by anxieties as to the fate of his soul, a remarkable story about him came to be told. It was claimed that a particularly saintly pope, impressed by the details of Trajan's life, distraught that such a paragon of virtue should have failed to gain entry to heaven, and moved to plead for his salvation, 'went to Saint Peter's Church and wept floods of tears, as was his custom, until he gained at last by divine revelation the assurance that his prayers were answered, seeing that he had never presumed to ask this for any other pagan'.[12] This was why Dante, in his great poem *The Divine Comedy*, felt able to place Trajan in Paradise. It was not only Christians, however, who speculated about the fate after death of Caesars who had ruled during the empire's pomp. So too did Jews. Not for them any fretting over the fate of emperors' souls. If rabbis could barely utter the name of Hadrian without cursing him − 'May his bones rot!' − then it was an earlier Caesar who attracted the most unsettling traditions. Titus, who had ruled briefly between AD 79 and 81, and was the second of a dynasty called the Flavians, had merited terrible punishment. A gnat, the smallest of God's creatures, had flown into his nose and entered his brain. There, for seven years, it had buzzed incessantly. When at last Titus died, and physicians opened his skull, they found that the gnat had grown to become a creature like a sparrow, with a beak of brass and claws of iron. The emperor's sufferings, meanwhile, were not at an end − nor would they ever be: for in hell, his reconstituted body was fated every day to be burned to ashes.

What had been Titus' crime? In AD 70, four years after the Jews had risen in revolt against Rome, an army under his command had captured the holiest building in the Jewish world, the Temple of

Jerusalem, and put it to the torch. Six decades later, Hadrian rubbed salt into Jewish wounds by ordering a pagan temple built on the site. Once again, the Jews rose in revolt. Once again, the Romans crushed them. This time, the work of pacification was to prove decisive. Jerusalem was rebuilt as a Roman city. The name of the Jewish homeland, Judaea, was changed to Palestine. The Jews, so a Christian scholar gloated, 'are the only people in the world to have been banished from their own metropolis'.[13] They had become a nation in Exile.

The impact of these fateful developments still reverberates today. The great rock where the Temple once stood is now a site sacred to Muslims as well as to Jews, surmounted as it is by the first master-piece of Islamic architecture, the Dome of the Rock, and Islam's third-holiest mosque. It ranks, in consequence, as a flashpoint as dangerous as any in the world. Meanwhile, Israel — a Jewish state established in what was once Judaea — has always drawn on the memory of the wars against Rome to consolidate its sense of national identity. Masada, a mountain south of Jerusalem where some time in the early 70s AD almost a thousand Jewish men, women and children were reported to have taken their own lives rather than surrender to the Romans, has become an emblem for Israelis of the courage and resolve that they, too, as a people surrounded by enemies, feel sum-moned to show. Such a sense of self-identification is founded upon a key principle: that Israel does indeed stand in a line of descent from the Judaean state that was first conquered and then obliterated by Rome. When, in 1960, recently discovered letters from the leader of the Jewish revolt against Hadrian were shown to Yitzhak Ben-Zvi, the president of Israel, they were described to him as 'dispatches written or dictated by the last President'.[14]

A joke — but not entirely a joke. The risk of anachronism in assuming that the inhabitants of the Roman province of Judaea were Jews in the sense that we use the word today is very great. So great, in fact, that I have opted not to take it. Just as the inheritance of Christian tradition can operate as a smokescreen, obscuring for us the contours of the Roman Empire in its heyday, so, too, can the inheritance of Jewish tradition. Much that makes what today we call 'Judaism' distinctive — the role played by rabbis, synagogues, the Talmud — constitutes less a preservation of what had existed before the wars against the Romans than an adaptation to its loss. Prior to the final destruction of their homeland by Hadrian, the *Ioudaioi* — as the Greeks called the inhabitants of Judaea — ranked as a people, an *ethnos*, much like any other. Yes, they might appear eccentric; but so did many other peoples. They were certainly not seen as belonging to a 'religion' called 'Judaism': for both words, which derive from specifically Christian theological propositions, would have meant nothing to the Romans, nor to the Greeks, nor to the Jews themselves. Just as the inhabitants of Athens were Athenians, and of Egypt Egyptians, so is it most accurate, perhaps, to term the inhabitants of Judaea Judaeans. The Roman Empire in its heyday was a world very different from ours, and it is perilous to write about it in a language such as English, one that has been shaped and weathered by over a millennium of Christian assumptions, without being alert to just how treacherous a medium it can potentially be. Just as I have sought to be true to the spirit in which the Colosseum was built by calling it in my narrative the Flavian Amphitheatre (this having been its original name), so also have I sought to guard against more insidious anachronisms: perspectives and assumptions that would have been incomprehensible to the people who are the protagonists of this book. Roman attitudes towards dimensions of experience that we might be tempted to view as universal — dimensions of morality, or sexuality, or identity — were, to our way of thinking, radically strange and unsettling. So unsettling, indeed, that some have preferred not even to recognise them as such. My goal in writing *Pax* has been at all times to show the inhabitants of the Roman world the respect due to all ancient peoples: by attempting to understand them not on our terms, but on their own, in all their ambivalence, their complexity and their contradictions.

Anyone attempting to fulfil such an ambition confronts an

obvious challenge. When, in 1960, letters from the dying days of the revolt against Hadrian were discovered in a cave in the Judaean desert, the excitement they generated was not due solely to Israeli patriotism. The find was stunning because it helped to fill – however incompletely – a yawning gap in the historical record. The conflict, momentous though it may have been, had left behind few written sources. While there are scraps of detail to be garnered from inscriptions, or from coins, or from the much later – and transparently tendentious – writings of rabbis and church fathers, the only narratives to have survived are sketchy in the extreme. Historians and archaeologists, over the past few decades, have sifted the rubble of the evidence to heroic effect; and yet still, despite the recent publication of a number of studies of the war, it has proven impossible to arrive at anything more than the barest outline of its course. The myths told about the Judaean death-struggle against Hadrian remain far more vivid than any narrative of it that a historian can hope to write.

True, there are other conflicts that we know even less about. There was an uprising in Britain during Hadrian's reign, for instance, that one Roman writer explicitly compared to the war in Judaea, and which presumably contributed to the emperor's decision to build his famous wall; but we know little more about it than that.* Conversely, the narrative that can be told of the revolt of the Judaeans against Hadrian is made to seem all the more ghostly by the fact that the original Judaean uprising – the one that culminated in the destruction of the Temple and the siege of Masada – left behind what ranks, by the standards of ancient history, as quite prodigious quantities of evidence. We have biographies of the two Flavians – Titus and his father, Vespasian – who commanded the legions in the conflict. We

* The Roman writer was Fronto, in a letter to Marcus Aurelius, who was his student at the time. A popular theory – and one that inspired a famous children's novel, Rosemary Sutcliffe's *The Eagle of the Ninth* – is that the Ninth Legion, Legio IX Hispana, was annihilated during the course of this war; but this has always been speculation.

have a scabrous survey by Tacitus, the greatest of all Roman historians, of everything that made the Judaeans appear peculiar to their neighbours. We have coins, and inscriptions, and friezes. Above all, we have a detailed narrative account of the revolt and its causes, written not by a Roman but by a Judaean – and a Judaean, what is more, who played a significant role in the conflict. Josephus' *Judaean War* is one of the supreme works of history to have survived from antiquity; and yet, remarkably, it is not the only narrative account of those fateful years that we have. Tacitus wrote one as well – albeit focused not on the Judaean revolt, but on the civil war that was simultaneously convulsing the Roman world, and which saw, in the year AD 69, no fewer than four Caesars rule in succession.

To tell the story of the period, then, is always to be alert to how the evidence for Roman history, sometimes blazing bright, sometimes non-existent, is a variable thing. The world portrayed in this book is illuminated much as a coastline at night might be illuminated by an immense battery of lighthouses. This way and that their beams sweep in irregular and untrustworthy patterns. Sometimes a stretch of rocks may be flooded by brilliant light. Sometimes the scene may be abruptly cast into darkness. Entire reaches of the shoreline may never be illuminated at all. So it is with the decades between the first Judaean revolt and the second, between the year of the four emperors and the accession of Antoninus Pius.

I emphasise this not to alarm the reader, but rather to explain the balance and the rhythms of the book. The range and focus of my narrative, the degree to which it moves from setting to setting and zooms in and out, is determined above all by the nature of the available source material and archaeological evidence. We may lack records for entire years at a time; but we can reconstruct the events of one particular year, the fateful one of AD 69, month by month, and often day by day. We may lack histories that focus on the doings of town councillors, or women, or businessmen, or slaves; but we have been left the remains of Pompeii and Herculaneum, in which the ghosts of many such people still haunt the streets. We may lack a biography of

Trajan, that most admired of all the Caesars; but we do have detailed accounts of what was happening under his rule in a very particular province. This is a story that begins and ends in Rome; but is about very much more than Rome. It is a story that embraces the entire Roman world, and beyond.

Although it has very much been written to stand alone, *Pax* is the third in a series of histories. The first, *Rubicon*, tells the story of Julius Caesar and his age; the second, *Dynasty*, that of Augustus, Rome's first emperor, and the line of rulers who claimed descent from him. *Pax* opens at a key moment in history: the suicide in AD 68 of Nero, Augustus' last male descendant. With his death, Rome's first dynasty of autocrats became extinct. What was to replace it? The attempt to answer this question brought a long century of civil peace to an end. In AD 69, four men in succession ruled as emperor. Soldiers slaughtered one another in the streets of Rome, and the capital's greatest temple was consumed by fire. The year of the four emperors served as a brutal reminder to the Roman people that all their greatness, all their prosperity, might be threatened by the very quality that had originally won them their empire and enabled them to ensure its security: their aptitude for killing. The capacity of the legions to exercise extreme violence was the necessary precondition of the Pax Romana. This is why, in a book about the longest sustained period of peace that the Mediterranean has ever enjoyed, the context should be provided by war.

A child alive when Nero committed suicide might well have attended the obsequies of Hadrian, the rites surrounding his death. The decades separating the two emperors witnessed a succession of episodes so dramatic that their fame endures to this day: the siege and destruction of Jerusalem; the eruption of Mount Vesuvius; the inauguration of the Colosseum. Conflicts, even once the mass of the Roman world had been restored to order following the year of the four emperors, still flared: in Britain, along the Danube, in Judaea. The legions carried their arms to the Persian Gulf. The Romans remained who they had always been: the heroes of a great drama marked by incomparable feats and ordeals. Yet most momentous of all was a process of change that, over the course of the period covered by this book, served forever to transform what was meant by the name 'Roman'. By the time Hadrian died, it had come to signify, in the words of one contemporary – a man close enough to the emperor to have swapped poetic witticisms with him – 'less a single people than the entirety of the human race'.[15] The empire was the wealthiest, the most formidable, the most terrifying state that had ever existed: a state that repeatedly, over the course of the decades described in *Pax*, made a show of its invincibility, so that even its enemies came to believe it could never be defeated. I have sought to portray the Romans in their imperial heyday, not as our contemporaries, not as straw men either to be emulated or condemned, but as a people who command our fascination, above all, by virtue of being different – unnervingly, compellingly different.

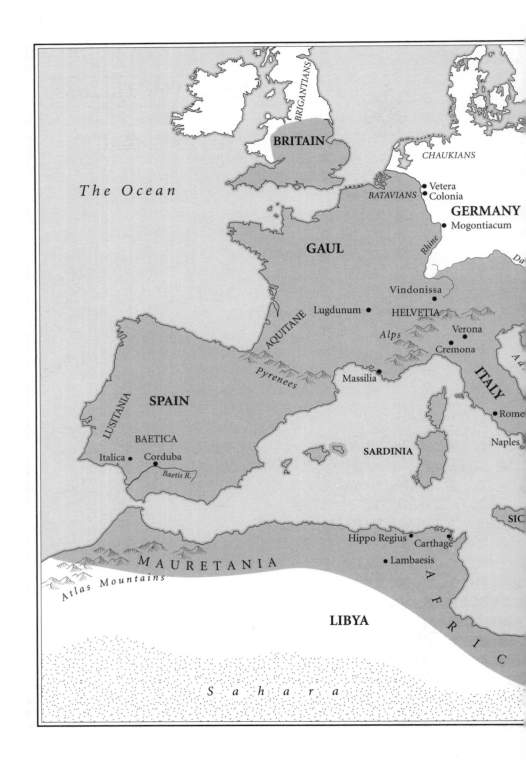

BRIGANTIANS

BRITAIN

The Ocean

CHAUKIANS

BATAVIANS

● Vetera
● Colonia

GERMANY

● Mogontiacum

GAUL

Rhine

Da

● Vindonissa

Lugdunum ●   HELVETIA

AQUITANE

Alps

Verona ●

Cremona ●

ITALY

Pyrenees

Massilia ●

A a

SPAIN

● Rome

LUSITANIA

BAETICA

SARDINIA

Naples

Italica ● Corduba ●

Baetis R.

SIC

MAURETANIA

Hippo Regius ● ● Carthage

Atlas *Mountains*

● Lambaesis

A
F
R
I
C

LIBYA

Sahara

The Roman World in AD 68

0   100   200   300   400   500 miles

0   200   400   600   800 km

Sarmizegetusa

DACIANS

Danube

M O E S I A

Black Sea

Caucasus Mts.

ARMENIA

MACEDONIA

Thessalonica

Byzantium

P O N T U S

BITHYNIA

GALATIA

COMMAGENE

Tigris

Carrhae

GREECE

Aegean

Pergamon

ASIA

Sardis

Athens

Ephesus

C I L I C I A

Euphrates

Antioch

SYRIA

Cythnus

Rhodes

Berytus

M e d i t e r r a n e a n   S e a

JUDAEA

Jerusalem

Cyrene

Alexandria

CYRENAICA

NASAMONIANS

EGYPT

Nile

ARABIA

Red Sea

Truly, it is as though the Romans and the boundless majesty of their peace have been bestowed by the gods upon humanity to serve them as a second sun.

PLINY THE ELDER

Where they make a desert they call it peace.

TACITUS

PART ONE

WAR

I

THE SAD AND INFERNAL GODS

A Golden Age

Sixty-five years after the birth of Christ, the most celebrated woman in Rome became a god. On earth, a sumptuous funeral was staged to mark her ascension to the heavens. Her corpse, stuffed with the most expensive spices that money could buy, was borne in solemn procession down the side of the Palatine, grandest and most exclusive of the city's famous seven hills. Choruses singing funerary hymns preceded it, and officials masked and costumed to look like the dead woman's ancestors; soldiers provided her with her escort. Down into the valley that ran between the Palatine and a second, smaller hill, the Capitol, the procession went. This valley – the Forum, as it was known – was a location splendidly appropriate to the occasion. Paved with gleaming marble, hemmed in by luxury shopping centres, and adorned with a veritable confusion of statues, temples and arches, it stood at the heart of the greatest city on earth.

'Rome, seat of empire, abode of the gods, surveys from her seven hills the circuit of the globe.'[1] So a poet, some fifty years earlier, had hailed the city. Rome's sway, in the intervening decades, had only expanded. Even Britain, a boggy land of milk-drinking barbarians beyond the Ocean, had been brought to acknowledge its rule. From Spain to Syria, all the Mediterranean was Rome's. There was no city on the shores of that ancient sea so wealthy, so beautiful, so renowned that it did not yield place to Rome. This greatness, as the dead woman was borne in sombre procession towards the cluster of structures in front of the Capitol, was manifest all around. To the right of the mourners, for instance, as they advanced along the Forum, lay a particularly spectacular sweep of temples and open spaces. The complex was barely a century old. It stood as a monument to conquest. The first stretch of it to be completed, a forum raised by a great statesman and warlord named Julius Caesar – a man of such transcendent achievement that he had ended up a god – had been built with the loot of Gaul. The second stretch, another forum, had likewise been funded by victories won across the sweep of the world. The man responsible for it had done more than any other Roman to expand his city's power. Augustus – 'a name signifying that he was something more than human'[2] – had been Caesar's great-nephew and adoptive son, and such was his glory that it had come to put even his father's in the shade. Augustus had made himself the ruler of Egypt, a land incomparably wealthy and fertile; completed the pacification of Spain; trampled down beneath his imperious tread the savages who lurked beyond the Rhine. He had won plunder on a scale fit to stupefy previous conquerors. Much of it he had spent on beautifying Rome. 'He boasted of having found it made of brick and leaving it made of marble.'[3] Fittingly, the most splendid of all the many buildings he had sponsored, a great temple in his forum adorned with statues and a gilded roof, was dedicated to Mars, the god of war. Behind distant frontiers, garrisoned by the most formidable fighting force that history had ever known, the peoples of the civilised world lived in peace. Augustus himself, his work once done, had duly ascended to join his father in heaven.

A city that reigned as the capital of the world was more than just a city. A century previously, a maze of narrow streets had stretched where the great marble complexes now stood. Apartment blocks, workshops, taverns: all had been swept away. Calm had replaced chaos; symmetry confusion. The dignity of the location had demanded nothing less. Not just the heart of Rome, it was the heart of all that lay beyond. The mourners, as they laid the dead woman on a marble-fronted rostra in the shadow of the Capitol, could see looming behind it a monument which rendered this particularly

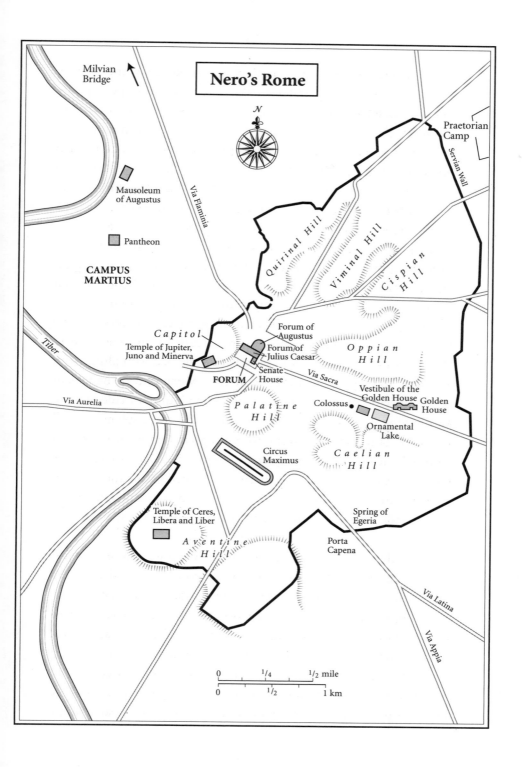

Milvian
Bridge

Nero's Rome

N

Praetorian
Camp

Mausoleum
of Augustus

Via Flaminia

Servian Wall

Pantheon

**CAMPUS
MARTIUS**

Quirinal Hill

Viminal Hill

*Cispian
Hill*

Capitol

Forum of
Augustus

*Oppian
Hill*

Temple of Jupiter,
Juno and Minerva

Forum of
Julius Caesar

Tiber

FORUM

Senate
House

Via Sacra

Vestibule of the
Golden House

Golden
House

Via Aurelia

Colossus •

*Palatine
Hill*

Ornamental
Lake

Circus
Maximus

*Caelian
Hill*

Temple of Ceres,
Libera and Liber

Spring of
Egeria

*Aventine
Hill*

Porta
Capena

Via Latina

Via Appia

0		1/4		1/2 mile

0		1/2		1 km

manifest. For eighty-five years it had been standing there: a giant milestone sheathed in gold. Augustus, the man responsible for its erection, had commissioned it to mark the spot from which distances across the empire were to be measured. Whether on the margins of the Sahara, or on the banks of the Rhine, or on the shoreline of the Ocean, a Roman could know with confidence where he stood. He was defined by his distance from the Forum. All roads led to Rome.

Yet the distant past, when wolves had stalked the Palatine and the Forum had been a marsh, was not forgotten. Poets delighted in picturing a time when cattle had roamed the future capital of the world, and when boats sailing up the Tiber had done so shaded by forests. It was not just in poetry, however, that the Roman people could find reminders of their city's beginnings. Immediately in front of the rostra where the pall-bearers had laid their burden there was to be seen a distinctive stretch of paving. This, black against the white of the low marble wall that surrounded it, was the Lapis Niger: the 'Black Stone'. Scholars disagreed as to what precisely it signified – but no one doubted that it was very ancient. Some claimed that it marked the final resting place of Romulus, a son of Mars who, 817 years previously, had founded Rome and given the infant city his name. Others insisted that Romulus, far from mouldering in a grave, had been taken up to the heavens in a thunderstorm, and that it was this – the moment when a Roman had first become a god – that the Lapis Niger commemorated. Either way, it served as a memorial to the first two centuries and more of the city's history: a time when the Roman people had lived not as citizens but as the subjects of a *rex* – a king.

Seven men in all, from Romulus through to a haughty tyrant by the name of Tarquin, had sat on the throne of Rome. Fabulously remote in time though these kings were, the Lapis Niger was not the only trace of them preserved in the fabric of the megalopolis that Rome had since become. On the Palatine, for instance, where Romulus, pondering whether to found a city, had looked up and seen twelve vultures flying overhead – an infallible sign that he should – visitors could admire his hut. Then, by taking the road that led south of the Palatine to the city walls, they could arrive at another sight. Next to a gateway called the Porta Capena, beside a dripping aqueduct, there stood a grove; and in this grove there bubbled a spring sacred to the memory of Rome's second king, Numa Pompilius. It was beside its waters that Numa, a learned philosopher, had been instructed in the ways of the gods by Egeria, a nymph. 'Egeria loved him, you see, and had communion with him, and this it was that endowed him with superhuman wisdom, and a life rich in numerous blessings.'[4]

Not every memorial to the kings was on public show. Some had been buried away – literally so. Beneath the Lapis Niger there lay an underground shrine; and within it stood a block of stone inscribed with enigmatic Latin. Barely decipherable, with clumsy lettering that looked almost Greek, it bore witness to a time when kings had stood guard over sacred groves and driven oxen to sacrifice. Conservators, nervous of its potency as an emblem of the ancient past, had stowed it with various other artefacts beneath the black paving stones: for they had known better than to destroy it. Writings from the beginnings of Rome's history might well carry a charge of the supernatural. The most dramatic evidence for this was to be found in a temple on the summit of the Palatine, where three rolls of prophecy, inscribed in antique Greek, were stored. Tarquin had bought them from the Sibyl, an aged priestess who stood guard over an entrance to the underworld outside Naples. Contained within the scrolls were remedies for every calamity, every fearsome warning from the heavens that was fated over the course of the centuries to afflict the Roman people. Access to this sensitive material was tightly regulated. Death was visited on anyone found copying them. They remained in Nero's time what they had always been: the ultimate secrets of state.

Unlike the Sibylline Books, the age of the kings had long since been consigned to the dung heap. In 509 BC, 244 years after the foundation of Rome, Tarquin had been expelled from the city. The monarchy had been abolished. No longer had its powers – what the Romans termed its *imperium* – been held by a single man. Instead,

7

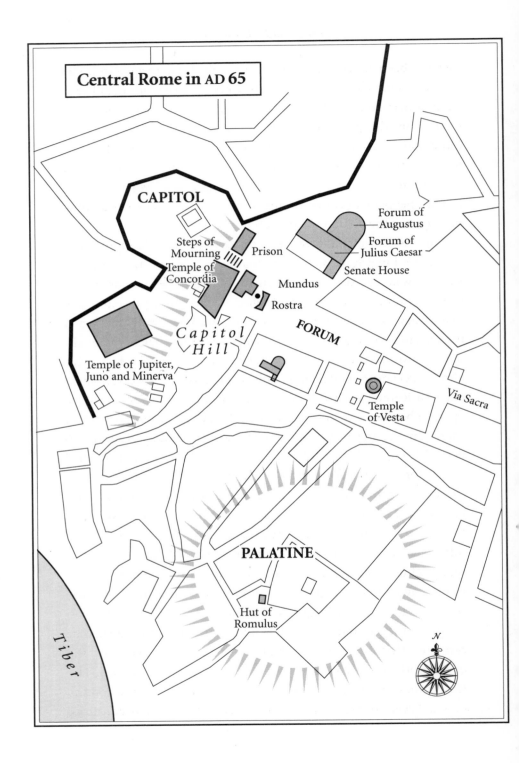

Central Rome in AD 65

they had been divided up among a range of elected magistrates. The most eminent of these – two in number so that each one could keep a watchful eye on the other – were named consuls. Annual elections to the consulship ensured that no man could hold the office for more than a year at a time. The intention had been very deliberate: to rein in the ambitions of anyone who might otherwise be tempted to aspire to monarchy. No longer the subjects of a single man, the Roman people had come to rank as *cives*: citizens. The word 'king' had become the dirtiest word in their language.

This did not mean, however, that the Romans disapproved of a citizen's longing to win glory for himself. Quite the opposite. Honour was regarded as the ultimate, the only test of worth. The limits set on a consul's term of office, even as they prevented the magistracy from serving as a stepping-stone to monarchy, had inspired in every high-reaching citizen the dream that he too might win a consulship. It was a dream that had never faded. This was why, almost six centuries after the expulsion of Tarquin, consuls still held office in Rome. Awaiting the funerary procession, they sat in the open air beside the rostra, before the full gaze of everyone. Alongside them, dressed in sober mourning attire, were ranked other members of Rome's elite: men from distinguished families, of certified wealth, or of worth decisively proven in a whole range of magistracies and commands. These were the *optimates*: the best class. Their authority reached back to the very beginnings of Rome. Romulus himself, it was said, had convened the hundred leading men of the infant city to serve him as a council of elders – a 'senate' – and formally acknowledged them as the fathers of the state. The fall of the monarchy had only confirmed them in their authority. It was the senate, in the wake of Tarquin's expulsion, that had led the Roman people in their struggle for independence; it was the senate, in the centuries that followed, that had guided them in their conquest of the world. Granted, the city's public affairs – its *res publica* – were the business of the people as well as of the senate of Rome; but no one had ever doubted who was the body and who the head. *Senatus*

Populusque Romanus: SPQR, the Senate and People of Rome. Such was the Roman republic.

And it had all begun with the spectacle of a woman's body laid out in the Forum. No senator, as he gazed at the rostra that summer day 573 years after the downfall of the monarchy, would have been ignorant of the story. Lucretia, nobly bred, nobly married, and a woman of impeccable virtue, had been raped by Tarquin's son. Summoning her father and her husband, she had told them of the outrage done her, and then she had stabbed herself to death. Her kinsmen, 'to whom the reason for Lucretia's suicide was a greater cause of shame and distress than the suicide itself',[5] had shouldered her corpse and borne it down to the Forum. There, drawn by the shocking spectacle, a crowd had begun to amass. Fury that a free-born woman had been treated as though she were a slave had swept the city. The Roman people, outraged and insulted, had risen in defence of their liberty. A stern precedent had thereby been set. A Roman, faced by servitude, had only two real options: either to take his own life or to kill the man who had made him a slave.

And now, in the very place where Lucretia's body had been exposed to public view nearly six hundred years earlier, the corpse of another woman lay before the gaze of the assembled people. What lesson did this second funeral teach? Certainly, the name of the dead woman – Poppaea Sabina – conveyed more than a hint of antique virtue. The Sabines, a rustic people inhabiting the fields and foothills which stretched north-east of Rome, had been early partners in the rise of the Roman people to greatness. Numa Pompilius, for instance, had been a Sabine. It was the dream of every jaded urbanite to retreat to a Sabine farm. *Sabinus* still served as shorthand for honest, peasant values. Poppaea's forebears, however, had long since left the barnyard behind. Her grandfather had held a consulship in the same year as his own brother. Her stepfather and half-brother had both likewise served as consuls. Poppaea herself – although ineligible, naturally, as a woman, to hold a magistracy – had ended up more famous than any of them. No less than her husband, she relished being talked about.

She was certainly a woman of many parts. 'From her mother, the most celebrated beauty of the day, she had inherited both looks and renown.'[6] She was formidably smart. Rich and well-bred, Poppaea had comported herself in public with the dignity appropriate to a Roman matron. This, however, had done nothing to stop her from becoming the object of feverish fantasy. Her habit of half-veiling herself in public was interpreted not as a display of modesty, but as a tease. The Romans were a people addicted to gossip, and Poppaea had given them a field day. She shod her mules with gold. She bathed in asses' milk. She was as promiscuous as she was proud. True or not, these rumours would never have taken fire as they did without the blaze of her charisma and sex appeal. Women wanted to be her; men wanted to bed her. And now she was dead. Brought in state to the Forum Poppaea may have been; but a new Lucretia she was not.

What, then, was she doing there, this woman who had been pro-claimed a god, eternally beautiful, Venus Sabina? The senators in their togas of mourning had assembled in the Forum that summer day not of their own volition, but in obedience to the wishes of her husband. For almost eleven years now, Imperator Nero Claudius Caesar Augustus Germanicus had been acknowledged by the Roman people as *Princeps*: First Citizen. The title had ancient roots. Crabbed and suspicious though the great men of the republic had invariably been, even so it was possible, when there could be absolutely no denying it, for a citizen of particularly formidable achievement to be acknowledged as princeps. This rank was never an official one, and would unfailingly generate bitter resentment. A citizen had to have saved the Roman people from some terrible foreign enemy, or secured them spectacular conquests, or served as a particular model of rectitude, to be given the title. Nero, however, had done none of these things. Deep-rooted though the assumption was among the Roman elites that responsibilities were properly the due of age, and that youth was not to be trusted, he had first been hailed as princeps at the tender age of seventeen. Senators, far from wrinkling their noses at this extravagant praise, had instead scrambled to vote him a whole raft of legal powers. Honours, prerogatives, priesthoods: Nero had been granted them all. The result had been to give him, in effect, the rule of the Roman world. 'Caesar is the republic.'[7] So it was said. When Nero decided to stage a public funeral in the Forum, it was a brave soul who turned down the invitation to it.

If all this sounded very like a monarchy, then so it was. Much had changed in Rome over the course of the preceding century. Senators in the Forum that day had only to look up at the hill above them to appreciate this fact. The Palatine, once crowded with the mansions of the republic's power brokers, was now the property of a single man: Nero himself. The ability of Rome's aristocratic clans to stamp their presence on the city's prime real estate had been systematically degraded to nothing. Even the senate house, a complex of chambers directly behind the Lapis Niger, bore the name of Julius Caesar. So, too, did the gleaming forum that stretched beyond it. The same Gallic loot that had funded Caesar's taste for *grands projets* had enabled him to put the whole republic in his shadow. Backed by legions steeled amid the killing fields of Gaul, he had brought the traditional structures of Roman government crashing down in ruin. Victorious in a bloody civil war, Caesar had ended up the master of Rome.

Inevitably, many of his erstwhile peers had found this unendurable. Conscious of themselves as the heirs of the antique heroes who had expelled Tarquin and his rapist son, they had felled Caesar beneath a hail of daggers. This desperate act, however, had done nothing to restore the republic. Instead, the Roman world had once again been plunged into civil war. For a decade and more it had raged. Warlord had fought against warlord. By the end of this murderous cycle of violence, only two had been left standing. One of them was Caesar's most formidable lieutenant, a seasoned veteran of great charisma and even greater appetites: Mark Antony. The other was Caesar's adoptive son and heir: the young man who would come to be known as Augustus. In 31 BC the two warlords had met in a great naval battle at Actium, a bay on the western coast of Greece. Antony had been defeated, and the following year he had committed suicide. It was Caesar's son, not his deputy, who had emerged triumphant in the great struggle for the world. The mass of the Roman people, rather than resenting his mastery, had welcomed it. They were weary of chaos and bloodshed. They craved peace. Better a monarchy than anarchy. The republic, to all intents and purposes, was dead.

Augustus, however, knew better than to rub the noses of his countrymen in that reality. As subtle as he was self-disciplined, he had no wish to end up, as his deified father had done, murdered by his fellow senators. Accordingly, he had done all that he could to veil his supremacy. He insisted that he had restored the republic. 'He always loathed "Master" as an accursed and dishonourable title.'[8] Certainly – for all that he had briefly contemplated naming himself Romulus – Augustus had no intention of ruling as a king. It was simply not worth the risk. He was interested in the reality, not the show, of power. Behind the façade of republican government – the debates in the senate house, the stately succession of consul by consul, the insistence on the sovereignty of the Roman people – he methodically gathered the reins of state into his own hands. The *imperium* that previously had been shared out among a whole multitude of magistrates was monopolised, to all intents and purposes, by a single man. It was to this regal scope of power that Nero, by becoming princeps, had succeeded. Not just Rome, but the entire world subordinated to Rome, was subject to his authority. Unsurprisingly, over the course of the decades that followed the lifetime of Augustus, the word *imperium* had gradually come to take on a subtle new shade of meaning. No longer just the powers wielded by a princeps, it signified as well the vast expanse of territory that was subject to these same powers. To rule as Nero did was to rule over an *imperium Romanum*: a 'Roman empire'. It was to rank as an *imperator*: an 'emperor'.

'Your destiny it is to live as in a theatre where your audience is the entire world': so an advisor was said to have warned Augustus.[9] It was not enough, however, for an emperor to be an actor. Unlike a king, unlike a consul, he did not have a script to follow. To make a success of his role, he had to write his own. No one, of course, had understood this more completely than Augustus; and no one had made a more resounding success of it. The emperors who followed him had swung to extremes. Augustus' immediate successor, a war hero and man of formidable accomplishment named Tiberius, might well, had he lived in a free republic, have been hailed as princeps by virtue of his own achievements; but those days were for ever gone. Heir to an autocracy that he secretly despised, Tiberius had proven himself a terrible actor, so contemptuous both of his own role and of the flatterers who surrounded him that he had ended up retiring for good to the island of Capri. Nero, by contrast, adored acting. He loved the big stage. The first princeps since Augustus to have adopted the title *Imperator* as his first name, he relished the thought that, as emperor, he could command the audience of the entire world. Already, he had adopted many roles. He had posed as Apollo, the radiant god of music. He had posed as Sol, the celestial charioteer of the sun. Not only had he played a lyre and driven a chariot, but he had done so before the public gaze. This, by the standards of conservative opinion in Rome, was a shocking betrayal of the dignity expected of any citizen, let alone a princeps; but many among the Roman people, members of the elite among them, had thrilled to it. Now, mustering all his taste for flamboyance, all his relish for grandiloquence, all his eye for spectacle, Nero was set to play a further role: that of bereaved husband.

Poppaea's corpse, stuffed with spices, had been mummified. Next to it, piled in unprecedented profusion, was incense from across the East: 'the spring produce of Cilicia, the flowers of Sabaea, the flame-feeding harvests of India'.[10] So much perfume had been imported from Arabia that the region's entire annual supply was said to have been exhausted. Poppaea richly deserved such tribute. Not merely a goddess, she had been pregnant with Nero's child. The loss of the boy – if indeed boy she had been carrying – was a tragedy not just for Nero, but for all the Roman people. The family of Augustus was a sacred thing, touched by the supernatural, numinous with the potency of the man who, by saving Rome from ruin, had proven himself worthy to reign eternally as a god. Augustus' heirs, who had ruled the world neither as kings nor as elected magistrates, had done so instead as members of his house: as Caesars. This was true even of those who had not shared in his bloodline. Tiberius, for instance, had succeeded to the rule of the world as the August One's adoptive son. Nero, by contrast, was the genuine article. Commending his dead wife to the senate and people of Rome, he did so as the great-great-grandson of Augustus. When they mourned Poppaea, they were mourning someone else as well: the stillborn infant Caesar.

The loss, as everyone knew, was a grievous one. Rome was fast running out of people who could boast the sacred blood of Augustus in their veins. The various branches of the August family, in the half-century since his death, had been relentlessly pruned. Tiberius, suspicious and resentful of anyone with a claim on the rule of the empire, had proven particularly murderous. Only a very few of Augustus' descendants had survived his reign. Of these, only one — a young man named Gaius, who ever since his childhood had been nicknamed Caligula, or 'Bootikins' — was qualified by gender to succeed to the rule of the world. His reign had not, for the *optimates*, been a pleasant experience. Indeed, they remembered it as a terrifying demonstration of 'just how far, when combined with supreme power, supreme vice might go'.[11] When, after four scandalous and sanguinary years, Caligula made the mistake of insulting one of his own guards, and ended up hacked to death on the Palatine, there were many in the senate who talked openly of restoring the republic. It was not just the trauma of all they had suffered at Caligula's hands that prompted them to push for this. It was also the fact that, in the wake of their tormentor's assassination, there was no man of the bloodline of Augustus available to succeed him. How could anyone who was not a Caesar possibly rule as emperor? The problem appeared insuperable.

Except that, in the event, it proved entirely superable. Too many powerful people had too much at stake in the system of monarchy founded by Augustus not to see it endure. Claudius, a nephew of Tiberius who, despite a nervous twitch and an unjustified reputation as an idiot, had at least been brought up in Augustus' household. The Praetorians, the military garrison stationed in Rome, hailed him as *imperator*, and the senators, impotent in the face of this démarche, duly bowed to the inevitable, voting to give Claudius the name of Caesar. The new emperor, much to everyone's surprise, proved a great success. He built aqueducts, sponsored the construction of a new port at the mouth of the Tiber, and embarked on the conquest of Britain. Even so, Claudius could never quite suppress a sense of imposter syndrome. Looking around for ways to fortify his regime, his gaze fell on a princess of the bloodline of Augustus: a sister of Caligula, formidable and imperious, by the name of Agrippina. That she was also his own niece gave him only momentary pause. Despite the disgust felt by his fellow citizens for incest, which they viewed as a repellent custom, appropriate perhaps to foreign despots but certainly not to a Roman, he did not hesitate to take her as his wife. The move promised him much advantage. It was not only his own legitimacy that was shored up by the marriage, but that of his two children by a previous wife: a girl named Octavia and a boy named Britannicus. Nor was that all. Agrippina was able to contribute even more to the prospects of the dynasty. She had a son of her own: older than Britannicus, of an age to inherit the rule of the empire, and with the blood of Augustus in his veins. That son was Nero.

It might have seemed, then, that Claudius had pulled off a masterstroke. In AD 53, when he married his new stepson off to Octavia, the redemption of the August family from extinction appeared complete. With Britannicus, his own son, soon to come of age, and every prospect that Octavia would shortly be giving him grandchildren, Claudius could look to the future with confidence. Yet his hopes were to be grievously disappointed. No sooner had Nero married his stepsister than death returned to stalk the August family. In

AD 54, Claudius died while at supper. So, too, the following year, did Britannicus. Rumour laid the blame for both deaths on Nero. Four years later, when Agrippina was cut down by a Praetorian hit-squad — stabbed, it was said, through her womb — the young emperor's responsibility was clear: for he openly acknowledged it. People claimed and believed that it was Poppaea who had urged him to matricide; and certainly, there could be no doubting her role in his next crime. In 62, impatient to marry the woman with whom he had become infatuated, and who was already pregnant by him, Nero divorced Octavia. Then, shortly after exiling his ex-wife to a tiny island off the Italian coast, he had her executed. The charge: adultery. Octavia's severed head was presented to Poppaea. Once again, the August family had been brought almost to extinction. Once again, its future was left hanging by a thread.

That it was Nero himself who bore the chief responsibility for this precarious situation helped to explain, perhaps, the titanic scale of his grief now that Poppaea too, and her unborn child with her, were dead. Who could say just how deeply his guilt ran? Gossip had it that his wife had nagged him for staying out late at the races, and that he had momentarily lost his temper, that he had kicked her in the stomach, and that she had died of the resulting miscarriage. Was the story true? Certainly, there was no crime so dark or terrible that Nero might not be thought by his enemies capable of it. Equally, however, it was possible to cast his bereavement in a very different light. Many found in it a theme fit to rival the tales of gods and heroes. It was Venus herself, so one poet wrote, who had arrived on the Palatine to claim Poppaea; the goddess would bear her away on a chariot, up into the heavens past shooting stars and planets, to a place of honour high above the northern pole. 'Downcast she was, and felt no joy in the favour done her. For she was leaving behind her husband, a man equal to the gods. Loudly, then, in her longing she moaned for him.'[12]

Just as he moaned for her. Heavy and stupefyingly expensive, the cloud of incense hung over the ranks of mourners. Even as Nero delivered his eulogy, it had begun to drift across the forum of

Julius Caesar, across the city walls, and across the expanse of monuments and parkland beyond the Capitol. This was the Campus Martius – the Field of Mars. In earlier times, it was where Rome's citizens, summoned to war, had gathered to take the oath that transformed them from civilians into soldiers. Now the Campus was a showcase for the arts of peace. It was where people came to exercise, or to picnic beside an artificial lake, or to indulge in some luxury shopping. There were bath-houses, and theatres, and temples. It was typical of the Campus that the most splendid of these, built back in the early days of Augustus' supremacy, should have been dedicated not just to one god, not just to a few, but to all the gods: the Pantheon.

No one touring the Campus could possibly forget that Augustus himself had come to be listed in their ranks. Everywhere stood monuments to his glory. Most sombre was a great circular mausoleum, adorned with cypresses and topped by a funerary temple, at the far end of the Campus. This, the tomb Augustus built for himself, was also where the ashes of Nero's predecessors had been laid: Tiberius, and Caligula, and Claudius. So too the ashes of the great women of the August family: from matriarchs to princesses. Augustus was not the only god whose mortal remains had been laid to rest in the mausoleum. Both his wife and Claudius had similarly been deified. Now, with Nero's speech ended, and pall-bearers shouldering the byre, all that remained on earth of another god was being brought to join them. Leaving the Forum, passing through a gate in the city walls, entering the Campus Martius, the funerary procession headed for the mausoleum. There, deep in the bowels of the complex, a chamber awaited them. A chamber fitted for the mummy of Poppaea.

To some, this came as a disappointment. 'The Roman way is to dispose of a body by burning it.'[13] Ever since the cremation of Augustus, when flame-edged theatricals had kept the assembled crowds entertained for hours, the funeral of a member of the August family had served the people as a guarantee of spectacle. Yet Nero,

18

showman though he was, knew that the enthusiasm of many in the city for fiery extravaganzas had recently taken a knock. The previous year, a devastating conflagration had swept Rome. Nothing on its scale had ever been witnessed before. For days the firestorm had raged. Between a quarter and a third of the world's capital had been left as blackened rubble. One year on, and the terrible scarring of it continued to disfigure the city. Buildings along the eastward summit of the Palatine had been destroyed, and ancient, much-loved trees. So too had a stretch of the Forum. Of other districts, where the streets had been cramped and the buildings made of wood, nothing was left at all. Vast numbers of people, left homeless by the inferno, had been reduced to squatting out on the Campus. The shanty town stretched for miles. Leaving behind the city walls, the funerary procession had no option but to pass the destitute masses huddled in their tents. Ahead of the mourners lay the paved area outside the mausoleum where cremations were conducted. Here, under normal circumstances, on a day when the funeral of a member of the August family was being celebrated, a pyre would have been erected. No pyre, however, awaited Poppaea. The pall-bearers continued into the cool of the tomb. The mummy vanished from public view. It was neither the time nor the place for pyrotechnics.

To rule as Caesar was indeed to drive the chariot of the sun. The horses had to be guided with the utmost care. Veer too far one way, and humanity would burn. Veer too far in the opposite direction, and all would be lost to ice. The Roman peace — the Pax Romana — did not sustain itself. Only a leader of divine quality could hope to preserve it. Nero, when he compared himself to Sol, was not indulging in vainglory. He was reminding the Roman people of what it took to rule the world. A touch of the reins here, a flick of the whip there, and all would be kept steady. Amid the infinite calamities to which mortals were heir, whether bereavement or the burning of a city, Nero could be trusted to keep the Roman people on a steady course. To keep them from ruin. To bring them, as though they were a phoenix rising from ashes, to a golden age.

The Rape of Proserpina

There were certain times, certain places, when the human and the divine, the earthly and the supernatural, would meet and become interfused. This was the assurance that Nero offered the Roman people. From the very beginning he had been bathed in gold. Born in December, the dead of winter, he had been greeted as he came into the world by the first rays of the dawning sun. Light from an invisible source had haloed him. As emperor, it had been his ambition to bring a similar radiance into the heart of the city. The great fire of AD 64 had provided him with his perfect opportunity. Four years on from the conflagration that had inflicted such devastation on Rome, the bodies and blackened rubble had all been cleared away. The emperor had appropriated entire swaths of the world's most valuable real estate, an area once crowded with mansions and apartment blocks. Beyond the Forum, in a valley stretching between two hills, the Caelian and the Oppian, Nero had commissioned an immense and improbable estate. Much of it was parkland. There was a lake, vineyards, woods, wild animals, even models of famous cities. Most spectacular of all, extending up the slope of the Oppian Hill, was a sprawling villa decorated with gems and pearls. It was adorned as well with great works of art, had some forty lavatories, and was sheathed all over with gold. The sun had only to rise in the sky for the blaze of this complex – the 'Golden House', as Nero called it – to dazzle the Romans who gazed upon its beauty. The emperor, taking possession of it, had joked that at last he could begin 'to live like a human being'.[14] In truth, what it offered was a god's-eye view of the world; or, to be more precise, a view of the world such as Sol, looking down from his golden chariot, might enjoy: for the Mediterranean, seen from such a distance, might indeed look like a lake, and the lands all around it like the stretches of a park. Nero, just to ram home the point, had even commissioned a giant bronze statue of himself, 120 feet high, crowned with the rays of the sun. When completed, it was to stand guard over the entrance to the

Golden House. Those who had seen it spoke of it in stupefied tones. They called it the 'Colossus'.

Not everyone was impressed. Surveyors mapping out Nero's new estate had done so over what, until recently, had been people's homes. 'An overweening stretch of parkland has robbed the poor of their dwellings.'[15] No wonder that there was resentment. Mutterings could be heard at every level of society. Senators, too, had lost homes to the Golden House. Nero's contempt for the *optimates* as a class had become, over the course of his reign, increasingly evident. He had mocked their sensibilities; offended their proprieties; rubbed their noses in the brute fact of their impotence. Unlike the mass of the Roman people, whom he had wooed with spectacle and entertainment, the traditional elites of the city had come to loathe him. An emperor who scorned to show the senate the respect that was its ancient due was, in the opinion of those who belonged to it, a bad emperor by definition. Even as the masses cheered Nero's name, the heirs of Rome's most distinguished families had begun, in whispered tones, to call him a tyrant. The Golden House had only confirmed them in this opinion. To the poor, at least – the plebs, as they were called – the spreading expanse of parkland in the very heart of the city offered relief from their cramped and noxious living conditions; but to senators it had become merely a reminder of just how very little they counted. 'All the city now has become a single house.'[16]

Naturally, there had been conspiracies. Nero, whose spies were everywhere, had crushed them all. Large numbers of senators had been variously executed, forced to commit suicide, or dispatched into exile. Even so, in the dying days of the year AD 67, some particularly unsettling reports had begun to reach the emperor. A major plot had been foiled in the capital itself. In Gaul, so his agents informed him, one of the governors was plotting revolt. Gaius Julius Vindex was a senator of formidable capabilities. 'Physically fit and mentally alert, seasoned in war and bold enough not to shrink from a perilous enterprise, he combined a deep love of liberty with immense ambition.'[17] Not only that, but he was descended from a line of Gallic kings. Even so, Nero, who – unlike his predecessors – had never led an army in battle, was not sufficiently alarmed to start mustering troops now: for there was a more effective way to combat incipient rebellions. Death squads, which he had employed to great effect against conspirators in Rome, could also be sent out into the provinces. Informed that Vindex had been in touch with the governor of Spain, a grizzled martinet by the name of Servius Sulpicius Galba, who had failed to report the treason, Nero duly gave orders for the governor's assassination. He had no reason to doubt that such measures would work. Apollo, the god of prophecy as well as of music, had personally sent him a message: 'Beware the seventy-third year.'[18] Nero, who was still only thirty, drew great comfort from this oracle. Clearly, he assured his friends, he still had decades of life and good fortune ahead of him. There was nothing remotely to worry about.

Nevertheless, with the passing of the old year and the beginning of the new, even Nero could not help indulging a certain mood of introspection. Solemn ritual marked 1 January. For two hundred years, it had been the day on which the two new consuls embarked on their term of office. It was not just for the Roman people to endorse their election; the heavens, too, had to give their approval. This was why, on the first day of the 820th year since the founding of Rome – the year that we commemorate as AD 68 – the consuls made sure to seek the backing of the king of the gods, the deity hailed by the Romans as *Optimus*, the 'Best': Jupiter. Senators in blindingly white togas accompanied them. Nero's own robe, embroidered with gold, was the most blinding of all. Other citizens in holiday finery swelled the lengthy train. Perfume hung in the air. Saffron crackled on lighted braziers. Attendants led two white bullocks, unbroken to the yoke, along the route of the procession. The path was a steep one, and so the animals, their hooves skittering on the flagstones, had to be urged up the slope. Ahead of them loomed a great crowd of temples. The Capitol, where in ancient times a giant and mysteriously well-preserved head, a *caput*, had been found, portending Rome's destiny as the head of the world, ranked as the most sacred of the city's seven hills; and on 1 January it was especially so.

Jupiter's temple, which stood on the very summit of the Capitol, was the most imperious in the city. Its roof, like that of Nero's new palace, was sheathed in gold. It boasted columns plundered from Athens. It dominated the Forum, which Jupiter shared with two other deities: Juno, his queen, and Minerva, his daughter. The view from the central chamber of the massive edifice, where the god had his throne, commanded all of Rome. Jupiter, the Romans knew, would never abandon such a seat: 'the finest and most splendid monument in the world'.[19] His temple was as close to an image of eternity as the city provided. It was impossible to imagine a time when it would no longer stand there, and when priests would no longer climb the Capitol to reach it. No wonder that bronze tablets from Rome's archives, detailing laws and decrees of the senate reaching back to the very beginnings of the city, were stored there: for where was more imperishable? The consuls who on 1 January made the first public sacrifice of the year to Jupiter knew themselves to be part of a tradition that reached both backwards and forwards through time.

So, too, did Nero. The consulship, once bestowed by the votes of the people, was now bestowed by the favour of Caesar. 'The majesty of the giver shines in the gift.'[20] Nero, as the man who had graced the new consuls with their magistracies, was no less anxious than the consuls themselves to know what signs of approval or disapproval – 'auspices' as they were known – might be given by the gods. It was the responsibility of the emperor himself to take them. The rituals that traditionally marked the new year had swelled since the time of Augustus by additional, more recent observances: oaths of loyalty sworn to Caesar; promises to uphold his legislation; the gifting to him of *strenae*, New Year presents. Such ceremonies were conducted across the immense span of the empire, in provincial cities and in legionary camps; but it was what happened on the Capitol that had the greatest heft. Nero, with magistrates and senators gathered round him in a great crowd, and priests, and citizens representing all the various classes of society, knew that he had the perfect opportunity to broadcast a message, not just to Rome, but to the world. Conspiracies were wasted effort. His rule was planted on solid foundations. The auspices were good.

Later, people would remember two things. The first was that no one had unlocked the doors to the temple of Jupiter, prompting a frantic search for the keys. The second was the *strena* presented to Nero by Poppaea Sabina. Two and a half years had passed since the death of Rome's most famous beauty. In his bereavement, Nero had sought such comfort as he could. A naturally uxorious man, he had turned for companionship to Acte, a freedwoman from Syria with whom he had conducted a passionate affair early in his reign, and still held fast in his affections. He had also married again. Statilia Messalina, although she might lack the glamour of Poppaea, was very much Nero's kind of woman: smart, witty, well-bred. Indeed, so devoted was he to her that he had forced her husband, a serving consul with a fatal talent for banter, to commit suicide. Yet Messalina, devoted to her though her new husband was, had one debilitating drawback: she did not look like Poppaea. So Nero – rather than live with the ache of his frustration – had sought to find someone who did. The search had been long but ultimately successful. A new Poppaea had been brought to the emperor's bed. Soft-skinned, auburn-haired, she seemed to all who saw her to be the ultimate manifestation of Nero's genius for transmuting fantasy into reality. Dressed in the dead empress's robes, arrayed in the dead empress's jewels, borne in the dead empress's litter, she was treated exactly as though she were the dead empress herself. Nero had even married her. First, though, prior to the wedding, the bride-to-be had been readied for her future as Caesar's wife. A surgeon had been summoned. Poppaea's doppelgänger, strapped onto the operating table, had been obliged to endure the loss of his genitals: testicles, penis and all.

Nero, making a joke of it, had nicknamed the mutilated boy Sporus: 'Spunk', in Greek. Yet the presence in his bed of a partner who not only looked like Poppaea, but answered to her name, and had legally become his wife, was no laughing matter. To Nero, and to all who saw her with him, it seemed that a great miracle had been achieved: that Poppaea had been brought back to life. So besotted was the emperor that he dreamed of moulding Sporus completely into a woman. An immense reward was offered to anyone capable of implanting a uterus within the eunuch. This, of course, even for a man of Nero's genius for bending reality to his will, was an ambition too far; but the sterility of the Poppaea he had fashioned for himself did not prevent her presence on the Capitol that January morning from carrying an unsettling charge. What Nero offered to the Roman people was the assurance that the mundane could be rendered fantastical, the predictable spiced up with the unexpected, and the world of the everyday fused with that of myth. This was why, when 'Poppaea' stepped forward to present Nero with his *strena*, she seemed to the assembled crowd a creature both more and less than human. It was also why, in the months and years that were to follow, the ring which she presented to her husband that morning on the Capitol as he was taking the auspices would itself come to seem a portent.

On the ring was a gemstone, and carved onto the gemstone was the image of a goddess. Libera did not have a shrine on the Capitol. If the great temple of Jupiter provided the king of the gods with a seat from which he could survey not just the limits of Rome, but the entire world beyond, then the setting of Libera's temple was altogether less grand. Beyond the Capitol, there stretched a flat and low expanse of land, bordered by the Tiber and, on the far side of the various apartment blocks and warehouses that crowded it, a second hill. The Aventine, unlike the Palatine or the Capitol, had never been home to winners. Instead, from the very beginnings of Rome, it had provided a refuge to those who had failed in the great race of life: to the poor, the immigrant, the down-at-heel. The temple of Libera, founded in the tenth year of the republic's existence, and rebuilt by Augustus after its destruction in a fire, stood on the northernmost slope of the Aventine, directly above the banks of the Tiber. There, it served the plebs as the great temple on the Capitol served the elites: as a focus of their supplications, their devotions, their hopes.

Just as Jupiter shared his sanctuary in Rome with Juno and Minerva, so did Libera share hers with her mother, Ceres, and her brother, Liber. The worship of Ceres reached all the way back to the time of Numa Pompilius – as well it might have, for she was the goddess who blessed the fields with harvest and put bread on the table, without which everyone would starve. Though the rustic days of Numa were long gone, her great festival, the Cerealia, was still celebrated every spring, at the start of the agricultural year. Its stage was the Circus Maximus, the largest stadium in the world, built by Romulus in the valley between the Aventine and the Palatine; incinerated during the first hours of the Great Fire; and already, thanks to Nero's patronage and energy, restored to its former glory. Whether, that coming spring, the festival would be celebrated in the traditional way, by releasing foxes with lighted torches on their backs into the arena, was obviously a sensitive question; but certainly, now that the renovation of the Circus was complete, there would be chariot races and all kinds of spectacles. Nero, a natural showman, would make sure of that. He perfectly understood how to keep the plebs entertained. Extravaganzas would also be staged a month earlier, to mark the Liberalia, the festival that honoured both Liber and Libera, and which, despite the enduring disapproval of moralists, had long been celebrated on the Aventine as a licence to cast off every kind of inhibition. *Liber*, after all, meant 'free'. Wine, sex, rampages through the streets: the Liberalia was literally a riot.

The ring, then, had been thoughtfully chosen. The reminder it gave to Nero as he stood before the temple of Jupiter surrounded by senators was a welcome one. The foundations of his power lay not just in the Capitol but in the Aventine. Rome was the largest city the world had ever seen. It contained a million mouths. Only one man could possibly keep such an immense population from starvation: Caesar. The message was one that Nero had made sure to stamp on his coins. On one of them Ceres was shown sitting in front of a woman holding a horn overflowing with the fruits of the harvest. This woman was Annona: the embodiment of the grain supply. It had long been the privilege of every citizen in Rome to receive from Caesar a monthly corn dole. The annexation of Egypt, which had enabled Augustus to fund the beautification of Rome, had enabled him as well to banish the spectre of famine from the city: for the wealth of the country had consisted of more than gold. The fields that bordered the Nile were the great breadbasket of the world.

Every year, hulking freighters loaded with corn would set sail from Alexandria. Meanwhile, others would depart Carthage, the capital of Africa: for this province too was famed for the fertility of its soil. These transport ships, for a long time, had been unable to head directly to Rome. Instead, because the waters at Ostia, the port which stood at the mouth of the Tiber, had been too shallow to receive them, they had been obliged instead to dock at Puteoli, a port on the Bay of Naples. Recently, however, Ostia had been given an upgrade. The Roman people, whose sway extended across sea as well as land, were not to be defied by mere reeds and silt. In a great engineering project begun under Claudius and completed under Nero, a deep-water port was constructed a mile or so north of the existing facilities at Ostia. The corn transported from Egypt and Africa still had to be unloaded at Puteoli; but it could now be transported onwards to the mouth of the Tiber in something approximating to bulk. From there, it could then be moved into the giant warehouses that, fortress-like, lined the river for sixteen miles, all the way to the Aventine. The plebs, long habituated as they were to receiving bread from Caesar, did not view this as charity. 'Every man gets his dole by virtue of being a citizen.'[21] Such, at any rate, was the maxim. The fire, however, had placed the imperial budget under terrible strain. Nero, even as he struggled to ensure the continued supply of corn to the city, had been obliged to suspend the dole itself. Poppaea, by giving her husband a ring stamped with the image of Libera, was reminding him of his responsibility to restore it. Headquarters for the distribution of corn was Libera's temple: the temple that she shared with Liber, and Ceres, her mother.

Libera, however, was not merely Libera. Just as the temple of Jupiter, following its incineration by a thunderbolt in 83 BC, had been rebuilt using material plundered from Athens, so had Libera, as the centuries had passed, become ever more Greek. Initially, she had been a shadowy figure – so shadowy, indeed, that it was debated by antiquarians whether she might not have been Liber's daughter rather than his sister. Increasingly, however, as Roman power expanded first across Italy and then into the eastern half of the Mediterranean, this had changed: for the more that the conquerors put the Greek world in their shadow, so the more had their gods come to be painted in the colours of the conquered. The Greeks, too, worshipped a goddess of the harvest. Demeter, they called her: the mother of a daughter named Persephone. The story told of this girl – Proserpina, as she was known in Latin – was a haunting one. That once, back in the early days of the world, when all had been eternal summer, she had been walking with her handmaidens across a meadow in Sicily; that Pluto, the god of the dead, had appeared suddenly in his chariot and abducted her; that her mother, plunged into grief and despair, had left the corn in the fields and the fruit on the trees to perish, and the earth to turn to ice; that finally, under the terms of a truce brokered by Jupiter, it had been agreed that, for six months every year, Proserpina should return to her mother, but that for the other six months, enthroned in the underworld as the queen of the dead, she should stay with Pluto; and that ever since there had been winters as well as summers. The story had become a familiar one to the Romans almost half a millennium before the time of Nero. Proserpina had long since been elided with Libera. Deeply embedded in the soil of the Aventine though her temple was, this goddess whose origins reached back to the very beginnings of the city hinted at mysteries – haunting, tantalising mysteries – that were not to be fathomed in Rome. Those who wished to learn them had to travel elsewhere: to Greece.

And it was to Greece, as it so happened, that the boy transformed into Poppaea, only a few months after the operation that had made him into a woman, had been taken by Nero. Borne in a litter appropriate to an empress, the new Poppaea had toured a succession of the festivals for which Greek cities were famed. Her husband had been in heaven. In the country that ranked as the home of the performing arts, Nero had felt himself appreciated at last. His singing had been greeted with rapturous applause. So, too, his performances as an actor. He had even raced in the Olympic Games. Risking unspeakable danger by yoking his chariot to ten horses rather than, as was customary, two or four, he had not only lived to tell the tale, but taken first prize. His delight had been off the scale. Imperious in his gratitude, he had remitted the taxes of the entire province. Even as he did so, however, he proclaimed that his true debt was not to the Greeks themselves, but rather to their gods. 'For both by land and sea they have ever looked out for me.'[22]

Many were the hills, the groves, and the shrines in Greece that, over the course of the centuries, had been hallowed by their presence. Well-educated Romans, schooled in the Greek classics as they were, tended to be no less aware of this than the Greeks were themselves. One sanctuary in particular haunted their imaginings. Ten miles outside Athens there stood a town named Eleusis. Here it was that Ceres had sat in mourning for her lost daughter; and here it was that the pair of them had been reunited. The mystery of what had happened in this holy place, the restoration of the earth to fertility and the triumph of life over death, was one that mortals, if they purified themselves sufficiently and swore a binding vow of secrecy, might have revealed to them. It was not only Greeks who were seduced by this promise. Rome's most learned men were intrigued as well. The mysteries taught at Eleusis were, in their opinion, Athens' greatest gift to the world. 'Thrice blessed', a tragedian had written back in the city's golden age, 'are those mortals who, having seen these rites, then descend into the underworld: for while everyone else passes into wretchedness, they alone have life.'[23] Here was a promise that anyone might welcome – even a Caesar. The image on the ring given to Nero while he was taking the auguries on the Capitol was a nod to this, for it portrayed the rape of Proserpina. Poppaea, who had only just returned from Greece with her husband, knew just how haunted by the story of Proserpina's abduction he had been – and just how haunted by his longing to visit Eleusis.

Yet he had never gone. The mysteries were not lightly penetrated, and Nero had good reason to fear them. During his tour of Greece, putting on the mask of a tragic actor, he had repeatedly played matricides: murderers who, commanded by oracles to commit the most terrible of crimes, had then been hounded by the Furies, fearsome goddesses armed with whips and blazing torches. Nero, by bringing to life ancient myth on the stage, had been performing the most audacious of manoeuvres: the presentation of himself as a hero of legend. Yet this had come with costs. Every year at Eleusis, before the rites of initiation began, a herald would warn away all criminals; and Nero, who confessed to being haunted in his dreams by the ghost of his mother, had particular reason to dread the admonition. True, he was notorious as a man contemptuous of the gods. Only one of them, a fish-tailed goddess from Syria, had ever truly commanded his devotion; and even her he had come to despise. So badly had he fallen out with her, indeed, that he had taken to relieving himself on her statue. Or so people claimed. Nero's relish for mocking convention, and the glee he took in making the eyes of prudes pop, made such rumours all too believable. Nevertheless, there were limits. Even Nero knew better than to desecrate certain mysteries. The gates that led to the realm of Pluto and Proserpina were not lightly opened. Nero, dreading to visit Eleusis, had never doubted it. This was because, only three years previously, he had opened the same gates himself.

The great fire had left Rome a city of the dead. Such had been its ferocity that untold numbers had been turned to ashes. There had been no prospect of recovering their bodies, or of giving them proper burial. The horror of this had lain like a shadow over the entire city. Naturally, then, Nero had turned for advice to the Sibylline Books.

The instructions he found there were clear. Various gods required propitiation. Chief among them were Ceres and Proserpina. There were rites to be performed at their temple on the Aventine and in the heart of the Forum, rites that reached back to the very origins of Rome. It was Romulus who had first instituted them. Next to where the senate house would one day stand, and where Nero, the year after the great fire, would deliver his funeral oration over the mummified body of the first Poppaea, he had dug a circular trench. In it he had placed the fruits of the harvest: everything that, 'sanctioned by tradition as good and by nature as necessary',[24] was sacred to Ceres. Yet this trench – which the Romans called the *mundus*, the 'world' – was a place of death as well as life. The black stone of the Lapis Niger, which lay within the *mundus*, had been carefully chosen. Great pains had gone into its sourcing. Brought to Rome from Cape Matapan, the southernmost tip of Greece, it had been quarried from beside a cave that led to the underworld: a place much haunted by the flickering and gibbering of ghosts.[25]

The Lapis Niger, however, was not the only emblem of death that stood within the *mundus*. There was also an ancient cypress, with roots so fibrous and grasping that they reached all the way to the forum built by Julius Caesar. No wonder, then, that the *mundus*, like Eleusis, and like the cave on Cape Matapan, should have ranked as a portal to the underworld. For most of the year it was shut; but there were times, shadow-haunted times, when it was made to stand open. On such days no business could be done, no battles offered, no marriages celebrated: 'For when the *mundus* is open, it is as if the gates of the sad and infernal gods are open.'[26] There was nothing, on such occasions, to stop the dead from visiting the realm of the living – nothing to stop those who had perished in the great fire from returning to the scene of their incineration. Nero, by acting in obedience to the Sibylline Books, and opening the *mundus*, had sought to give rest to their shades, to make up for their lack of a burial, to draw a line under the calamity of the inferno that had consumed them and reduced them to ashes.

But no line had been drawn. The gates of the underworld remained open. The shades of the dead still roamed the city unavenged. Such, at any rate, behind closed doors and in nervous huddles, was what Nero's enemies whispered. It was said, and believed, that the emperor had started the fire himself; that he had employed his agents to ensure its spread; that he had sung, as the city blazed, of the ruin of Troy. Nero, in the immediate wake of the disaster, had vowed to raise altars across the city to Vulcan, the god of fire; but these altars, three years on, were still nowhere to be seen. Small surprise, then, in the weeks and months that followed the new year, that the ring given to Nero at the New Year should have come to seem more and more ominous a sign. The emperor had many enemies, and events, it turned out, were slipping from his control. Out in the provinces, his attempt to nip rebellion in the bud had failed. The shadow war was over. In March, Vindex openly raised the banner of revolt. In April, Galba did the same. Nero, shocked into a sudden realisation of the peril of his situation, sought to rally such legions as he had with him in Italy. Simultaneously, he mustered reinforcements. Legions in the Balkans were commanded to rally to their emperor's cause. He also enrolled a legion from scratch, by recruiting marines from Misenum, a port on the Bay of Naples that constituted Rome's largest naval base. Nero's flurry of activity, however, had its limits: despite the fact that he was the first Caesar since Augustus to have had himself portrayed on coins in military dress, he remained reluctant to ride out at the head of his troops. Instead, he trusted them to a proven loyalist, a former consul and governor of Britain by the name of Petronius Turpilianus. Petronius headed north to rendezvous in northern Italy with the legions coming from the Balkans. Nero, meanwhile, waited in Rome. His mood, despite the sudden blaze of rebellion, remained positive.

But then, at the beginning of June, came ominous news. Vindex, defeated in battle by an army drawn from the German frontier, had committed suicide; but the triumphant legions, far from dedicating this victory to Nero, had promptly hailed their commander as emperor. The commander himself, a man of subtle and cautious temperament named Verginius Rufus, had refused the title; but Nero, shaken by the disloyalty of troops whose love he had until that moment taken for granted, was plunged abruptly into despair. It was less force of arms that made him fear for his throne than rumours and exaggerations. Even Petronius was reported – erroneously – to have defected. Nero, increasingly frantic, began to contemplate flight to Alexandria. Yet still he lingered in Rome. Only once he had finally convinced himself that all was lost did he abandon the capital; but not for Egypt. Instead, taking horse, he made for a villa on the outskirts of the city. With him went the boy transformed into Poppaea and his most trusted secretary, a freedman named Epaphroditus. It was to prove a fateful mistake. Brought news that the senate had formally condemned him as a public enemy and sentenced him to death, he prepared to commit suicide. For an hour he hesitated; but then, when he heard hoofbeats on the road outside, and realised that guards were coming to apprehend him, he summoned the assistance of the loyal Epaphroditus and slit his own throat. A centurion, hurrying into the villa, sought to staunch the wound with his cloak; but it was too late. 'So fixedly did his eyeballs bulge from their sockets that onlookers were filled with horror and fear.'[27] Nero was dead.

And Poppaea Sabina, that maimed and sterile parody of the woman he had loved and raised to the heavens, beating her breast, pulling at her hair, tearing her clothes, mourned the husband who, like Pluto, had raped her and borne her into a realm of shadow.

Back to the Future

The women who tended the tomb in the garden had no doubt that their lord was dead. They had personally arrayed his body in shining white vestments; and then, when all was ready, laid his physical remains to rest. Rejected as he had been by his own people, legally

PAX

condemned as an enemy of Rome, brought to a squalid and igno-
minious end, his defeat seemed total. What victory, then, could there
possibly be in the wake of such a death?

Acte, Nero's first great love, and his two childhood nurses, leaving the tomb where they had reverently deposited the emperor's
ashes in a porphyry sarcophagus, were not alone in feeling stunned.
Everything seemed to have happened so quickly. Few people in the
capital had been aware of the distant rumblings of insurrection.
'Nero had been toppled more by dispatches and by rumours than by
force of arms.'[28] The news of his suicide, then, had come as a general
shock. Rome had been at peace for more than a century. The prospect of civil war returning to the city's streets seemed grotesque, a
nightmare conjured up from the dark days of the republic's collapse.
Yet the portents which followed Nero's death were too ominous to be
ignored. Rivers had been seen flowing backwards. On the east coast
of Italy, an entire olive grove had uprooted itself and crossed a road.
In Rome itself, lightning had struck the temple built by Julius Caesar
in his forum, decapitating all the statues of the emperors placed
there. Now, in the Forum itself, the cypress which for centuries had
stood within the limits of the *mundus* abruptly died. The gates of the
underworld, it seemed, were open yet. The people who, in the wake
of Nero's funeral, bore flowers to his tomb, and lamented his passing,
were not merely mourning Nero himself. They were also mourning
the family of Augustus, that dynasty shot through with a sense of
its founder's immortality, and yet which now, with the death of its
last surviving member, had perished for ever. The vast mass of the
Roman people, looking to the future, felt a sense less of relief than
of trepidation. 'In their despondency, they were desperate for news.'[29]
Who was to rule in Nero's place? To maintain the peace that, for a
century now, had been general across the empire? To keep the city
supplied with bread?

In the senate house, they already had an answer to these questions. The same decree that had proclaimed Nero's condemnation
as a public enemy had proclaimed as well the award of all his

prerogatives, all his titles, to Servius Sulpicius Galba. To most senators, the governor of Spain seemed the obvious choice. No living Roman was more distinguished. Forebears of his had won the consulship long before Augustus' rise to power. This fact, however, had not prevented Galba from serving a succession of emperors loyally and well. Unlike most senators who came from ancient families, he had scorned to spend his days sulking on his estates, snobbishly resentful of the Caesars' supremacy. Instead, just as any ambitious nobleman would have done back in the heyday of the republic, he had sought to make a name for himself: as a magistrate, as a soldier, as a governor of major provinces. Breeding and public service: the combination was a rare one. Certainly, to senators weary of Nero's relentless mockery, the craggy and unbending Galba appeared the perfect candidate to serve as princeps: an antique hero sprung from the pages of a history book. Accordingly, taking ship, a delegation of *optimates* headed for Spain, there to press on him the name of Caesar.

Yet they were, of course, deluding themselves. Any notion that a would-be emperor with an army at his back might be dependent for his elevation to supreme power on the decrees of the senate was fantasy. That Galba himself, a confirmed conservative, paid lip-service to them as the source of his legitimacy did not render him any the less a usurper. 'A secret of state had been revealed: that a man might be made a princeps elsewhere than in Rome.'[30] Even in the capital, the ability of senators to influence events was limited. This was a lesson that Claudius' seizure of power had already taught them. Now they found themselves having to learn it all over again. The senate was not alone in sending an embassy to Galba. Also sailing for Spain were a squad of Praetorians. Far more than the senate house, it was their camp, a vast, brooding fortress on the north-eastern edge of Rome, that constituted the true foundation of an emperor's authority in the city. To command the Praetorians was to command a force that could make or break a Caesar.

This was why, ever since the original construction of their base back in the time of Tiberius, no senator had ever been appointed as their prefect. Only a private citizen of sufficient wealth and ability to qualify as an *eques* – a cavalryman – could aspire to that. The rank harked back to the distant days when membership of Rome's elite had been signalled by possession of a horse; but the equestrian order, over the course of the centuries, had evolved to become a very different beast. While it might never hope to rival the prestige of the senate, it did mark those enrolled in it as high achievers, talents worth watching, men on the make. Under Augustus, the equestrian order had provided aristocrats from obscure Italian towns, officers who had picked the winning side in the civil wars, and even, on occasion, the wealthy sons of former slaves, with a status that demanded respect. Senators might sneer at such upstarts; but not too openly. Increasingly, equestrians had come to provide what every Caesar needed: a reservoir of able and hard-nosed men capable of serving in a whole variety of administrative posts. Some of these posts were more important than others; and of them all, none was more important than the prefectship of the Praetorians. The Praetorians, after all, were not just any body of men to be commanded. They were soldiers with responsibility for the security of Caesar; which meant, in turn, that they were soldiers capable of swaying the very fate of Rome.

Nero, perfectly aware of what had happened to Caligula when he forgot this, had gone to great lengths to keep them sweet. He had lavished pay rise after pay rise on them, bonus after bonus. He had also made sure to split the command. Both the men he had installed as prefects had evil reputations. This was hardly surprising, for the pair of them had served as his enforcers. Both were notorious for their thuggishness; both were despised by their peers as blots on the equestrian order. One, Gaius Ofonius Tigellinus, had worked variously as a gigolo and a racehorse trainer before Nero, appreciative of the talents suggested by this curriculum vitae, had raised him to the command of the Praetorians; the other, Gaius Nymphidius Sabinus, was the son of a freedwoman rumoured to have sold herself for sex in the slave quarters on the Palatine. Tigellinus, although for long the senior partner, had recently been elbowed aside. His colleague, determined not to let a crisis go to waste, had moved with ruthless speed to capitalise upon the swell of insurrections in Gaul and Spain. Nymphidius it was who had convinced the Praetorians to abandon Nero; Nymphidius it was who, capitalising on Galba's reputation for fabulous wealth, had succeeded in winning their backing for him by promising them a bonus massive even by the standards of Nero's prodigality. The prefect, having staked everything on this throw, could be well pleased with how the dice had come to fall. Nero eliminated; Tigellinus put decisively in the shade; Galba's favour secured. Nymphidius was effectively the master of the capital.

Nevertheless, his situation remained precarious. Accordingly, even as the capital waited with trepidation for its new master to arrive from Spain, Nymphidius set to shoring up his position. He continued to court Galba. Simultaneously, he sought to bring Rome ever more under his thumb. Senators were alternately wooed and menaced. Sometimes Nymphidius would invite them to dinner; sometimes he would berate them for presuming to go behind his back. Naturally, as a man who would have been nothing without Nero's patronage, he made sure as well to harry agents of the toppled regime. When lynch mobs turned on them, crushing informers beneath fallen statues of the emperor or the wheels of heavily laden wagons, he did nothing to save his former colleagues. His pose throughout was one of high-minded patriotism. He had no wish, after all, to be thought a vulgar opportunist.

Yet even Nymphidius, the man whose treachery had served to doom his master, could not help but remain in thrall to Nero's charisma. In his house he kept the most outrageous of all the many souvenirs left behind by the dead emperor. To sleep with Sporus, the wretched boy transformed into the image of Rome's most beautiful empress, was to sleep with Poppaea Sabina. This was why, rather than allow her to accompany the other women to the garden when Nero's ashes were laid to rest, Nymphidius had seized her, and kept her as his own. A man taking such a trophy to bed with him might well dare to dream. The upstart prefect began to have it put about that he was the offspring, not – as people had previously believed – of servile parents, but of Caligula. If true, this would have meant that he had the blood of Augustus flowing in his veins. Already, Nymphidius had made himself the master of Rome. Why, then, amid all the confusions of the age, should he not aspire to the mastery of the world?

To own Poppaea was, perhaps, to be driven a little mad. She was, after all, a living, breathing embodiment of the great conviction to which Nero had dedicated his life: that there was no fantasy so impossible, no dream so implausible, no desire so shocking, that it might not be rendered real. Certainly, to transform a male into a female was a project better suited to a god than to a mortal. Only the boldest, the most self-assured were likely to attempt it. Nero might be dead; but the example of what he had achieved with Poppaea, the fashioning of a young boy into not merely a dead empress, but the most famous beauty in the world, still served as a memorial to his ambitions. Nymphidius, abducting her even as Nero's corpse lay on its pyre, had known what he was stealing. She was a symbol not just of imperial power, but of the daring required to reach after impe-rial power. Well might those who had moulded her, fashioning an empress out of a boy, think nothing beyond them.

Even women. Nero, wishing his creation adorned in a manner appropriate to her rank, had appointed as Poppaea's wardrobe-mistress a noblewoman notorious equally for her rapacity and for her role as 'his tutor in sexual depravity'.[31] Now, with her patron dead, Calvia Crispinilla had taken refuge in her native Africa.[32] There, with a startling display of initiative, she had persuaded the commander of the legion stationed in the province, a man named Lucius Clodius Macer, to raise the banner of revolt. First Macer seized Carthage, the provincial capital; then he halted the corn supply. He began to mint coins that signalled his intention to take Sicily – and to do so, what was more, as an agent of the senate. The aim, self-evidently, was to cripple Nymphidius' authority in Rome. Calvia, a woman with a track record in bending reality to her wishes, had shown that her talents were not confined merely to the dressing room. Just as she had transformed a mutilated boy into a shimmering vision of female glamour, so had she now wrought an even more startling metamorphosis: that of Rome's African breadbasket into a source of grievous danger, not just to Nymphidius, but to Galba as well.

Except that Galba, far from answering Nymphidius' increasingly frantic calls for assistance, showed himself flintily unperturbed by them. Rather than advance on Rome at speed, he spent a month after his elevation making sure of his rear. Only in July did he finally set out from Spain. Climbing the Pyrenees, he marked with contempt how the Praetorians sent to him from Rome were forever grumbling about the exertions of the march, the paucity of the rations, the strictness of the discipline. Sent furniture by Nymphidius from the Golden House, he scorned to use it. Crossing Gaul, he neglected to take the shortest route to Rome, but instead, striking inland, removed Verginius Rufus from his command; received the acclamation of various Gallic tribes; and then, taking a road that led not along the coast, but over the Alps, flogged the Praetorians over yet another mountain range. All this, from Nymphidius' point of view, was bad enough. But it was not the worst. Galba, although a perfectly well-meaning old man, was also a fond and foolish one. So Nymphidius' agent reported back. For all his breeding, for all his record of public service, for all his commitment to discipline, the new emperor was the creature of a gang of worthless favourites. Some were freedmen; some were senators on the make. Laziest and most venal of the lot was an officer named Cornelius Laco. Nymphidius' agent, in describing the new emperor's associates, had particular reason to dwell on Laco. Galba, after all, had just appointed him Praetorian prefect.

This was, to put it mildly, a bold piece of management. Rome was effectively in Nymphidius' hands, and the prefect – unsurprisingly – did not take the news of his replacement well. Deciding to gamble everything once again on a throw of the dice, he sought to strike against Galba as only a few weeks previously he had struck against Nero. His backers in the senate were squared. One of them – a consul designate by the name of Cingonius Varro — even wrote him a speech. Armed with this oration, Nymphidius headed at midnight to the Praetorian camp. His aim was to deliver it to the soldiers and then employ them to secure the city. When he arrived at the camp, however, it was to find the gates barred against him. The Praetorians — persuaded by one of their officers that Galba, as a man innocent of murdering his mother and performing as an actor, should be given a chance — refused to hear their prefect out. Even when the gates were finally opened to Nymphidius, it was only so that he might the more easily be cornered and slain. His corpse, dragged out from the camp, was put on public show, there to be gawped at by the masses.

Galba, brought news of this, could be well pleased. He had long experience in smacking down uppity officers. His fame as a martinet was richly deserved. The senatorial elite, in turning to him, had been turning as well to an image of Rome long nurtured by traditionalists: as a city made great by the iron-forged discipline of its people. Everyone knew the stories. Once, for instance, back in the heroic early days of the republic, a consul by the name of Manlius Torquatus, riding at the head of an army, had ordered that no one was to break ranks, no one to fight except in a line of battle. Shortly afterwards, his own son went out on patrol. Provoked by the taunts of the enemy, the young man engaged one of them in single combat, slew him, and then, bearing the corpse of his adversary, returned in triumph to the camp. Manlius, rather than praising his son, gave orders that he be executed on the spot. And so it was done. While Galba, who was childless, had never quite matched this edifying standard of severity, his reputation was very much that of a man who, only given the chance, would surely have taken it. Whipping flabby soldiers into shape was his particular forte. Once, sent by Caligula to improve standards of discipline along the Rhine, he had set the legions there a personal example by running alongside the emperor's chariot for twenty miles, all the while holding a shield. Now, summoned to the rule of a city long indulged and corrupted by Nero, he faced a similar challenge. It was not one that he intended to shirk.

The Roman people had grown soft. They needed toughening up. This was why, in Galba's opinion, the threat to the corn supply was nothing much to worry about. Certainly, he had no intention of restoring the corn dole: for what was a handout if not a menace to Rome's moral fibre? Likewise, just as Manlius Torquatus, in his commitment to discipline, had shown himself implacable, a man forged out of iron, so now did Galba, in his determination to return his fellow citizens to their traditional values, scorn to show either fear or favour. Entering Rome as its emperor, he aimed to make an example of worthless senators no less than of delinquent soldiers. Cingonius Varro, the consul designate who had written a speech for Nymphidius, was duly executed without trial. So, too, as a confirmed partisan of Nero, was Petronius Turpilianus. Even royalty was not spared Galba's grim resolve to punish insubordination: Mithridates, a king visiting Rome from the shores of the Black Sea, was put to death on a charge of having laughed at the emperor's baldness. Meanwhile, far from granting the Praetorians the bonus that Nymphidius, on Galba's behalf, had promised them, the new emperor left them empty-handed. Playing the antique hero to the hilt, he explained his reasoning in lapidary terms: 'I choose my soldiers, I do not buy them.'[33]

Most salutary of all, perhaps, was his treatment of the marines who, a few months earlier, had been promoted by Nero to serve as legionaries. As Galba, nearing the end of his long journey from Spain, was advancing through the outskirts of Rome, a large crowd of them had met him on the banks of the Tiber, beside the Milvian Bridge. There they demanded that the emperor confirm them in their new status and award them an eagle: for it was an image of this bird, 'the king and most fearless of all birds',[34] that served every legion as its standard. When Galba, impatient with these importunities, sought to brush them aside, the former marines began to riot. Some even drew their swords. Galba promptly gave orders to his cavalry to cut them down. Entering the capital, he did so along streets that were slippery with blood and echoing to the moans of the dying. Meanwhile, the survivors of the massacre were being rounded up and put under guard. Galba was not done with them yet. Back in ancient times, it had been the practice to inflict on mutinous legionaries a punishment known as decimation: the selection by lot of one man in every ten, who would then be put to death by his peers. No one had imposed this penalty for many decades – and certainly not in Rome itself. This, however, was hardly a consideration to perturb Galba. The punishment went ahead. The lesson it taught was a very public one. The Roman people, redeemed from the squalid indignities that had marked the rule of Nero, were being returned to their best, their noblest traditions.

Or were they? Nero, preparing to leave Rome on campaign against Vindex, had commissioned a wagon train to transport his various props to the front, and dolled his concubines up as Amazons. This, in its subversive theatricality, was everything that Galba most despised; and yet the truth was that, by inflicting a punishment so shocking, so self-consciously antique, he was staging a spectacle no less idiosyncratic than Nero's had been. Galba's enemies, rather than taking him at his own worth, might legitimately have pointed out that his actions, far from evoking the noble traditions of Rome's ancient past, were reminiscent instead of the very tyrant whose rule he had usurped. To execute distinguished senators without trial smacked all too uncomfortably of Nero's recent purges. So did the manner in which Galba dealt with Clodius Macer. Rather than set sail for Africa and confront him in open battle, as a hero from Rome's ancient past would surely have done, he had him murdered by an assassin.

Nero, posing as the charioteer of the sun, had not merely been gratifying a taste for fancy dress. He had also been making a serious point. To rule as emperor was to drive a chariot that threatened the world with danger even as it bestowed on humanity the blaze of its light. Galba, taking up the reins left hanging by Nero, had no choice but to yank on them hard, to jerk them this way and that, to struggle with horses that were, in their headstrong way, forever threatening to career off-track. No matter how sternly he might seek to define himself against his predecessor, he could not avoid the occasional compromise with Nero's legacy. Even the most sinister of the dead emperor's creatures, if they had something to offer, might flourish under Galba's rule. It was noted, for instance, that Calvia Crispinilla, far from sharing in Macer's ruin, had gone from strength to strength. Not only was she richer than ever, but she had succeeded in marrying a former consul. Why, people wondered, had the vengeful Galba spared her? Presumably because, behind the scenes, she had struck a deal. As to what the deal might have been, there was a possible clue in the fact of Macer's murder. That an assassin had ever come close enough to strike him down was a remarkable thing. Only someone he trusted, someone intimate in all his counsels, could have finessed it. Only someone, perhaps, who had encouraged him to become a rebel in the first place.[35]

Nero was gone, but there were still players in the great game of Roman politics who had known him, served him, and drawn inspiration from his style. Some, such as Calvia, operated in the shadows; others were public figures. Galba knew this perfectly well. Back in the formative days of his insurgency, before openly declaring his defiance of Nero, he had succeeded in winning the support of two key Iberian officials. One of them, a young man named Aulus Caecina Alienus, managed the finances of Baetica, the lush and mineral-rich region of southern Spain named after the river Baetis — the Guadalquivir, as it is called today — and governed from the wealthy city of Corduba. Of ancient family, as keen witted as he was towering, and ferociously ambitious to boot, Caecina yearned to cut a dash on the stage of the world. Unsurprisingly, he had leapt at the chance to elbow aside his elders and secure a promotion; otherwise, he might have had to wait for years. Sure enough, as reward for delivering the treasury of Baetica into the new emperor's hands, he was appointed to the command of a legion on the Rhine: evidence of the opportunities that might arise in a time of civil war.

Caecina, however, was not the most significant magistrate in the Iberian Peninsula to have swung behind Galba. Marcus Salvius Otho,

43

like Galba himself, was a governor. For a decade, he had administered the province of Lusitania – modern-day Portugal – and done so responsibly and well. This, to the sniffier among his contemporaries in the senate, had come as a surprise. Nothing good had been expected by his elders of Otho. Back in Rome, he had become a byword for both effeminacy and hooliganism. His beauty regime was a matter of scandal: for as well as depilating himself on a daily basis, he was darkly rumoured to wear a toupee. Simultaneously, he was notorious as the man who had served Nero as guide to the seamier reaches of the city. The pair of them, roaming the darkest back-alleys, were said to have amused themselves by beating up passers-by, and tossing them up and down in military cloaks. Whatever the truth of these stories, it is certain that Otho and the young emperor had grown inseparable. Or so it had seemed. Abruptly, it had all gone wrong. Otho, fallen out of favour, had been packed off by Nero to Iberia. Although officially it had ranked as a promotion, everyone – Otho included – knew the truth. He had been sent into exile. And so, for a decade, he had twiddled his thumbs in Lusitania.

Homesick for Rome and embittered by Nero's treatment of him, Otho enthusiastically backed Galba. First he donated all his gold and silver tableware to help fund the revolt; then, joining the new emperor on the road to Rome, he provided such excellent analysis and advice that the pair of them would often ride together for days at a time. Yet Otho, for all the grudging respect he had won from Galba, had not entirely changed his spots. He remained recognisably the man who had once roistered with Nero. As well as tableware, he had furnished the new emperor with slaves sufficiently educated in metropolitan etiquette to wait on a Caesar's table; soliciting the company of the Praetorians, he had made sure to distinguish himself from the crabbed and stern-faced Galba by expressing sympathy for their privations, and discreetly offering bribes. Even the scandal that had led to his exile, and rendered him a figure of notoriety among the respectable, lent him – among men inclined to be entertained by such matters – a certain raffish allure. So often had the story been retold that no one could be quite sure of the precise details; but everyone knew that it had revolved around Poppaea. Rome's most beautiful woman, before she married Nero, had been married to Otho. Some said that he had seduced her so as to facilitate Nero's cheating on Octavia, and then fallen in love with her himself; some that he had bragged about his wife's sex appeal once too often, and paid the price; some that there had been the souring of a *ménage à trois*. Whatever the truth, the fact remained that Otho, no matter how vital a role in Galba's revolt he might have played, offered to those bored of discipline and severity an authentic touch of Neronian style. He had, after all, slept with the dead emperor's wife.

Perhaps it was no surprise, then, that the moment he arrived in Rome, Otho moved quickly to claim a prize left ownerless by the murder of Nymphidius: the one-time freedboy who had been trans-formed into Poppaea Sabina.

Head-Hunters

Galba, on his return to Rome, found it a strange and unfamiliar place. He had been absent from the city for almost a decade, and in that time the combination of fire and Nero's taste for *grands projets* had served to transform the cityscape. The horizon was dotted with cranes. For four years, Rome had been the world's largest construction site. Stupefied by the sheer scale of Nero's ambitions, people claimed that he had been planning to rename it 'Neropolis'. True or not, Nero had certainly sought to transform the fabric of the city. Rome had long been a deathtrap. Away from the Campus, its streets were narrow, twisting, irregular, its various quarters lacking in even the most rudimentary firebreaks, its rickety apartment blocks raised up on timber lintels. Ugly and shabby Nero had found it. This, people claimed, was what had prompted him to burn it to the ground. Certainly, whether he was responsible for the fire or not, he had seized the opportunity to set the city on new foundations.

Rome had been given an airier, more regular street-plan, complete with open spaces and broad boulevards. Porticoes were added to the fronts of both townhouses and apartment blocks, 'so that fires might more readily be fought from their terraces'.[36] Vaults replaced timber beams. The result was the emergence from the ashes of a city unlike anything that had existed before: a city in which even the humblest structures were fashioned out of concrete and stone.

Not everyone appreciated it. People complained at the loss of familiar streets; at the lack of shelter from the sun; at the clamour and chaos which filled the entire city with dust. Galba, who rarely backed an initiative unless it had been superannuated for several centuries, was not a natural patron of innovative urban design. Yet he had nothing to offer in its place. Although there were entire quarters of Rome that had survived the fire, snarls of ancient streets, court-yards where pigs still rooted about in the dirt, garrets that seemed to teeter beneath the weight of the families crowded inside them, he was not the man to roam a slum. He lacked the easy familiarity with the more squalid reaches of the city that both Nero and Otho had come by. The shows of patronage with which he graced the Roman people were felt by the plebs to be grudging, niggardly, slight. Even though he might remind them on his coinage of the role he had played in upholding the supply of corn, he did not restore the dole. The treasury, after all the extravagances of Nero's reign, was exhausted. There was no alternative, Galba sternly insisted, to austerity.

Yet it was noted that the new emperor, even as he cut donatives and screwed money out of whomever he could, was not wholly lacking in funds. He certainly had enough to invest in the vast complex of warehouses that had long been owned by his family south of the Aventine, and which now, it seemed, needed enlargement. Few imagined it a coincidence that the warehouses, in addition to corn, were used to store oil and wine: commodities that were famously the specialities of Galba's erstwhile province of Spain.[37] Certainly, it did not take the Roman people long to deliver their verdict on the emperor. That November, shortly after his arrival in the capital, games were staged at which actors performed a farce. The play featured a character called Onesimus: a stingy, wrinkled, finger-wagging misanthrope. Gusts of laughter swept the theatre. When one of the actors embarked on a song about Onesimus, the entire audience not only joined in but sang it over and again. 'Even Galba's age, to a people accustomed to the youth of Nero, seemed something ludicrous and grotesque.'[38]

Once, before the rise to greatness of Augustus – who had first made himself consul at the point of a sword when only nineteen – the Roman people had set a premium on crows' feet and sagging jowls. The literal meaning of *senator* was 'elder'. Galba's age, in the first flush of his coming to power, had seemed a marker of his legitimacy. Not only had he met Augustus as a young boy, but the Princeps, pinching his cheek, had foretold that one day he would rule the world himself. Apollo, it was now apparent, had delivered a similar prophecy: for had he not warned Nero to beware 'the seventy-third year', and was not Galba seventy-three?* Yet even the new emperor's most devoted henchmen knew that he ranked as, at best, a stopgap. Not only was he elderly, but he had no surviving children. All the more essential, then, that he adopt an heir. For six months Galba had put off making a decision. He had lived long enough to appreciate that it was ever the way of men to abandon the setting for the rising sun. Yet he was also a patriot. He knew his duty: to look to the future, and think of the welfare of Rome. As the days shortened, and the turning of the year drew near, so Galba began to sift the candidates. On 1 January, he entered into his second consulship. As Nero had done the previous year, he went in stately procession to the Capitol, where he offered in sacrifice two white bulls. Ten days later, he summoned his closest advisors to a meeting. He had come to his decision.

A year had passed since Poppaea, the empress who had once been a boy, had given her husband the ring with its engraving of the rape

---

* Probably. The sources for the date of Galba's birth are contradictory. But he was certainly in his early seventies.

of Proserpina. This, people had come to see, had been an ominous portent. Much had happened since. One emperor had fallen; another had risen to take his place. Otho, by seizing the maimed parody of his former wife, had known full well what he was doing. Poppaea served as a totem. To own her was to signal a readiness to play the role not merely of a Caesar, but of a Nero. The six months of Galba's rule had demonstrated that there was no mileage for an emperor in attempting to rule the world as an antique hero might have done. The demands on a Caesar were too gruelling, too complex, too contradictory for that. The plebs had to be kept fed, the masses amused, the Praetorians sweet. Otho, by cutting a Neronian dash in the streets of Rome, did not intend to undermine Galba. Quite the opposite: he was looking to cement the emperor's rule. As the first provincial governor to have come out openly in the usurper's favour, he had no need to prove his loyalty. His only ambition was to demonstrate to Galba the full range of his talents. All were at Caesar's service. And then, in due course, once Galba was dead, Otho, his duly appointed heir, would become Caesar in turn, at the service of the Roman people.

His hopes, however, were to be cruelly dashed. Galba, informing his most trusted confidants of his decision, did not name Otho as his heir. 'The worst kind of people', he declared, 'will always miss Nero.'[39] There was to be no pandering to such base nostalgia. Rome had suffered enough already from playboys. It was not even as though Otho had a distinguished ancestry. His father had been the first of his family to become consul, his grandfather the first to become a senator, and his mother was darkly rumoured to have been a slave. Clearly, it was out of the question for such an upstart to be adopted by an emperor. Instead, pondering how to set the Roman people back on the straight and narrow, Galba did what he invariably did: he looked to the past. The great families who, back in the heroic days of the republic, had furnished Rome with magistrates for generation after generation, and led their city to the rule of the world, were not entirely extinct. Much diminished as a result of the murderous suspicions of the Caesars though they were, a few of them, a century on from the collapse of the republic, endured, like exotic beasts kept in a zoo. Galba, who was himself just such a beast, had never doubted that his city's interests would best be served by setting these legacies of a vanished age to roam free and proud once again. 'For here,' he declared, 'it is not as it is for people who are ruled by kings, where one family enjoys perpetual rule and everyone else is a slave.'[40] Such were the considerations which determined his choice of heir.

Lucius Calpurnius Piso Frugi Licinianus, a nobleman barely thirty years old, was pretty much as well-bred as it was possible for any Roman to be. He was linked variously by blood and by adoption to some of the most famous names in Rome's history. These included the only two men whom Julius Caesar had ever acknowledged as his peers. One of them, Gnaeus Pompeius Magnus – Pompey the Great – had swept the seas clear of pirates, conquered a vast swath of the eastern Mediterranean, and built Rome's first permanent theatre; the other, Marcus Licinius Crassus, had combined stupefying wealth with a reputation as the most formidable fixer in the history of the republic. Ancestral connections such as these, under the Caesars, had proven highly dangerous. Piso had lived his entire life beneath their shadow. Claudius had executed both of his parents and his eldest brother; Nero had put another brother to death; and Piso himself had spent much of his adult life in exile. Unlike Otho, he had no experience negotiating the political rapids. He had never gone drinking with an emperor; governed a province; held any magistracy at all. Nevertheless, as well as his descent from Pompey and Crassus, he could boast an upright character, old-school attitudes, and a manner seen by his admirers as dignified and by his enemies as stiff and sour. These attributes, in Galba's opinion, were more than sufficient to qualify him as a Caesar. So it was that the emperor introduced the young man to his closest confidants as his heir.

Who next to inform of the good news? Galba – after a brief moment of hesitation – decided to bestow the honour not upon the senate, nor upon the people, but upon the Praetorians. As thunder

PAX

rumbled overhead, and drizzle shrouded the city, the emperor travelled with his new son to their camp. There, delivering a speech that was as curt as it was lacking in any mention of donatives, he introduced Piso to the assembled ranks. Various officers responded approvingly. The rank and file said nothing. Galba, not pausing to wonder what might explain this surliness, then headed to the senate house. Again, he gave a short speech. Piso also delivered an oration. It was well received. Those senators who admired Piso were effusive in their congratulations; those who cared nothing for him even more so. The session went on late. Then, when it was finally over, the emperor and his son retired to the Palatine. An important step had been taken. Rome had a new Caesar. Everything had gone very well.

Or had it? Otho — to whom Galba's adoption of Piso had come as a complete shock — certainly did not think so. Neither did the power brokers who, seduced by his seemingly great expectations, had lent him vast sums of money; nor the Praetorians, to whom he had repeatedly promised lavish bonuses. When Otho, in the immediate aftermath of Piso's adoption, joked 'that it made no difference to him now whether he fell in battle at the hands of an enemy or in the Forum at the hands of his creditors',[41] he was not signalling the ruin of his hopes, but the opposite: his resolve to fight for them to the death. Too many people, he suspected, had too much invested in him to give up on his prospects now. And so it proved. Agents were recruited, bribes judiciously deployed, and large numbers of Praetorians recruited to his cause. Otho, his delight in the swelling scale of the conspiracy matched by his dread of leaks, waited impatiently for favourable omens to arrive. He did not have long to wait. The gods indicated their approval of his venture on 15 January. Otho promptly gave the signal for the coup to begin. Piso had been a Caesar for a mere five days.

That morning, Galba, too, was taking soundings from the gods. Otho joined him on the Palatine, where sacrifice was being made to Apollo. The seer consulted the entrails. The omens, he warned the emperor, were threatening. A conspiracy was gathering pace. There

50

was an enemy within the gates. Otho, listening to these words, kept a perfectly straight face. Then, a few moments later, one of his freedmen brought him a message. 'The architects are waiting,' he said.[42] Otho, making his apologies, explained that he was in the midst of a complicated property deal, and slipped away. Leaving the Palatine by a back route, he stole down the side of the hill. At its foot, met by his accomplices, he climbed into a woman's litter. He was then borne away at top speed to the Praetorian camp. After a while, noticing that the porters were flagging, he climbed out and began to run – but as he paused to re-tie his sandal, his companions lifted him onto their shoulders and hailed him as Caesar. Cheering soldiers surrounded him. The officer in charge, taken aback, failed to close the gates, nor made any attempt to disperse the swelling crowd of men. Since Laco, the prefect, was with his master on the Palatine, Otho and his accomplices found it a simple matter to secure the camp. To raucous cheers, a gilded statue of Galba was brought crashing down. Otho, saluting the soldiers and blowing them kisses, delivered a rabble-rousing speech. He then gave orders for the arsenal to be opened. By now, with both the Praetorians and I Adiutrix – the legion of former marines that had been decimated on Galba's orders – giving him their full and enthusiastic backing, he could afford to breathe a sigh of relief. His gamble had paid off. Rome was effectively his.

Meanwhile, on the Palatine, rumours of the coup were starting to percolate. The reports, however, were confused. Neither the emperor nor his advisors remotely grasped the scale of the crisis facing them. Piso delivered a worthy speech. Messengers were dispatched to rally troops that had already defected to Otho. A large crowd, senators among them, gathered to demonstrate their support and to demand vengeance on the rebels. Galba, ignoring advice from one of his closest confidants to lock himself up inside the palace, decided to send Piso to check on the Praetorian camp. But no sooner had the young Caesar gone than a fresh rumour eddied across the Palatine. Otho was dead, his followers slaughtered, the rebellion over before it had begun. A Praetorian displayed a sword dripping with blood and claimed personally to have cut down the usurper. The emperor, by now sufficiently mistrustful of these reports to have strapped on a breastplate, nevertheless allowed himself to be swept up by his supporters. Sitting in a chair, he was borne this way and that, swaying on their floodtide. All were cheering and chanting. And then, as Galba was carried into the Forum, he suddenly looked round and saw Piso.

The young Caesar was wild-eyed and out of breath. The news he brought, that Otho was very much alive and in command of the Praetorian camp, could not have come to Galba as more of a blow. As his closest advisors debated frantically among themselves whether to return to the Palatine, or barricade themselves on the Capitol, or take shelter behind the rostra, the emperor himself appeared befuddled by the shock of it all. Rather than attempting to take back control, he allowed himself to be borne still on the ebb and flow of the crowd. Then, abruptly, from the far edge of the crowd, he heard screams. Looking round, he saw a squad of horsemen. Their swords were drawn. Onwards they came. Across the Forum they galloped. All those in their path, even senators, were trampled down. Galba called out to the Praetorians who had been attending him to take up position. None of them did as they were told. Instead, one of the guards reached for the image of the emperor on their standard, tore it off and flung it onto the ground. Everyone now understood that Galba was doomed. His supporters sought to flee. Among those joining the stampede were the men who had been carrying the emperor in his chair. Galba was sent sprawling onto the flagstones as Otho's men surrounded him.

Differing accounts were given of the emperor's end. Some, those who hated him, claimed that he had grovelled before the Praetorians and promised them a pay rise. Most, however, were agreed that he perished bravely. His murderers, once he was dead, continued to stab and hack at his body. Others, fanning out across the Forum and beyond, hunted down his accomplices. Among the leading figures in Galba's regime to be butchered by the Praetorians was their own prefect — fit punishment, it might have been thought, for Laco's disastrous failure to maintain their loyalty.[43] Piso, who had taken shelter in one of the temples in the Forum, was cut down on the very threshold of the sanctuary.

The heads of all three men were delivered to the new emperor. The soldier who had decapitated Galba, prevented by the emperor's baldness from taking it by the hair, stuck his thumb into the dead man's mouth and carried it that way to Otho. Head-hunting was regarded by the Romans as a horrific and barbarous practice, beneath the dignity of a civilised people. Yet heads were now being harvested. The events of a day which had seen an emperor publicly murdered in the very shadow of the Capitol, beneath the looming and sacred immensity of its temples, had introduced into the city a strange fever of savagery. The world seemed turned upside down. Romans indulged in displays of barbarism that would have shamed a German or a Briton. Otho gloated over the head of Piso; Galba's head, stuck on a spear, was paraded by camp-followers around the Praetorian barracks. Only as the sun began to set was it finally handed over to the dead emperor's steward. Galba's burial that same night in his private gardens was the burial as well of an entire tradition in Roman public life. A scion of the ancient nobility had been given his chance to restore the city to its ancient ways – and he had failed spectacularly. The chance would never come again. 'Everyone had agreed how suited Galba was to rule – except that then he had ruled.'[44]

II

FOUR EMPERORS

Mutiny on the Rhine

Part of the bewilderment felt in Rome at the spectacle of Galba's downfall was that mighty convulsions in the affairs of the world rarely took place in January. The death of Nero, Galba's march from Spain, the establishment of his regime in the capital: these upheavals, seismic though they were, had at least happened during the time of year when great events were supposed to happen. Winter, by contrast, was a season for drawing breath. Soldiers kept to their barracks, ships to their harbours, and those who could afford to do so to their homes. Snow mantled the mountain peaks that fringed the capital, and trees strained beneath its weight. It was a time to stoke up the fire, bring out a jar of vintage wine, and leave the screaming of gales to the gods.

Such, at any rate, was the idea. In AD 69, however, things were to prove different. Otho, compassing the downfall of a Caesar, may have been the first in that fateful year to grasp after the rule of the world; but others would soon be doing the same. Not for a century had Rome been troubled by the tread of rival warlords. The Roman people had grown accustomed to peace. The blood spilled in the wars that had brought Augustus to power had long since dried, and the wounds had been bound up and healed. Senators in the capital, groaning under the rule of a Caligula or a Nero, may have learned to dread the hammering of Praetorians on their gates; but this had only ever been a tax paid on their rank. The vast mass of people, whether in Rome, or in Italy, or in the provinces beyond, had never had any cause to imagine that the days of civil war might return. The Pax Romana had held.

No wonder, then, barely two weeks after the turning of the year, that the murder of an emperor on the streets of Rome should have come as such a shock. Even in the farthest reaches of the empire, where barbarians might still endure as a lurking presence, swords were rarely drawn from their sheaths in the icy dead of the year. Chill though the streets of the capital might be in January, they could not compare for cold with more northerly climes. Winter was notoriously harsh on the banks of 'the icy Rhine'.[1] The barbarians themselves, of course, knew no better. 'The climate has habituated them to the cold.'[2] To anyone raised in Italy, however, the snow and sleet of a northern winter were bound to seem grimly appropriate to the wilds that stretched beyond the Rhine. There was nothing in Germany that anyone from a civilised land might envy or desire: only bristling forests and stinking swamps. Savage lands bred savage men.

Sixty years previously, in AD 9, a general named Quinctilius Varus had suffered one of the most humiliating defeats in Rome's history when he and some twenty thousand men, stumbling along the margins of a great bog, had been ambushed by German warbands and wiped out almost to the last legionary. The 'Varian disaster', as it was commemorated by the Roman people, had prompted an iron-forged response. This was a matter of course. The occasional reverse in battle might be forgiven; but defeat in a war never. No Roman could ever concede that. Vengeance on the tribes responsible for the Varian disaster had been murderous. Summer after summer, the legions had marched across the Rhine. Summer after summer, they had visited fire and slaughter on everyone in their path. Summer after summer, they had sent echoing into even the remotest reaches of Germany, into its most impenetrable depths, a rumour of the wrath and terror of Rome.

Eventually, however – once the point had been decisively made – a halt had been called to such operations. It was never a matter of policy for the Roman people to exterminate their adversaries.

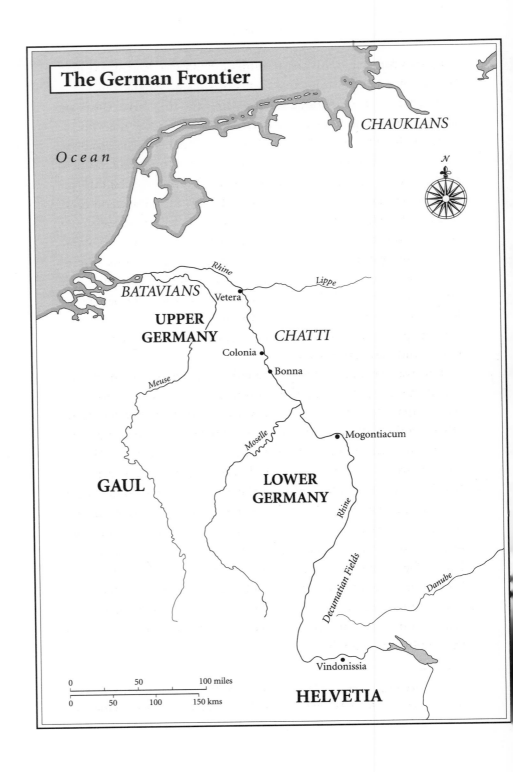

The German Frontier

CHAUKIANS

Ocean

N

BATAVIANS

UPPER
GERMANY

Rhine

Lippe

Vetera

CHATTI

Colonia

Bonna

Meuse

Moselle

Mogontiacum

GAUL

LOWER
GERMANY

Rhine

Decumatian Fields

Danube

Vindonissia

HELVETIA

0	50	100 miles
0	50	100	150 kms

Augustus himself, in his last testament, had rendered this explicit. 'When it was safe to pardon foreign peoples,' he noted graciously, 'my preference was to spare rather than to wipe them out.'[3] His own hope had always been to tame the Germans, to plant cities in their midst, to break them to the civilisation that came from being the *cives* — the citizens — of a settled community. The Varian disaster had put paid to that. By refusing to accept Roman rule, the Germans had shown themselves undeserving of its fruits. Better, a succession of emperors had concluded, to leave them to wallow in the sump of their own savagery. Yet this policy too had imposed demands on Roman arms. Barbarians, by their very nature, were shiftless, treacherous, migratory. The risk was always that, left to their own devices, they might attempt to force the Rhine, to spill into lands brought the benefits of Roman peace, to strip them bare. 'Always, whenever Germans cross into the provinces of Gaul, it is in pursuit of the same things: rape, riches, and a change of scene.'[4]

This was why, even though the bulk of Germany might not be worth the effort of conquest, there remained an obligation to stand sentry upon its flank. The mobility and aggression that traditionally were the hallmarks of Roman military power had come to be tempered. Twin military zones were established along the Rhine's western bank. The first of these, Lower Germany, ran from the North Sea to the confluence with the Moselle;* the second, Upper Germany, along the middle reaches of the great river. Here, in this narrow strip of land, had been invested a massive effort of engineering. No barbarian could miss it. Watchtowers loomed above the Rhine. Signal-stations dotted its length. Ships patrolled its waters. Lacking in cities the western flank of Germany may have been; but not in military infrastructure. Nowhere in the Roman world was the army so omnipresent. The aim was to render Gaul and the vitals of the empire impenetrable.

---

* Or perhaps the river Aar. The identity of the *Obringa*, the river that marked the southern border of Lower Germany, has not been definitively settled.

This buttressing of the Rhine did not, of course, imply any acceptance on the part of the Roman high command that there might be limits to their own reach. There was no word for 'frontier' in Latin. Valuable as the Rhine might be as a physical delineation of Roman power, the river did not mark its limits. Bridges spanned the swirling currents. Pastureland on the eastern bank was designated *prata legionis*: 'meadows of the legion'. No Germans were permitted to settle close to it. Those who made the attempt were unfailingly driven back. The Roman military authorities reserved the right to destroy their settlements, burn their crops, and enforce the transfer of entire peoples should the situation so require. To gaze from a watchtower on the Rhine to the far bank was to know that civilisation, rather than coming to an abrupt halt, faded gradually. The great charge of Roman arms was to keep the barbarism festering in the very darkest reaches of Germany, where men lived like animals, and possessed the limbs and bodies of wild beasts, forever at bay.

By definition, to serve on the banks of Rhine was to stand at a remove from the centre of things. To Aulus Caecina, the ambitious young man promoted to the command of a legion there after delivering the treasury of Baetica into Galba's hands, his reward had proven a form of torture. While Otho, over the second half of AD 68, had been able to stalk the corridors of power in Rome, to wine and dine senators, to take out loans and lavish bribes where they would most count, Caecina had been obliged to twiddle his thumbs in Upper Germany. What was a bog compared to the Forum, a dripping forest to the Palatine? The frustration of it all, at a time when the convulsions of the age were offering unprecedented opportunity to men on the make, was intense. When Caecina, looking to feather his nest, embezzled some public funds, it betrayed his impatience as much as his greed. Not that this had cut any ice with Galba. The emperor had always looked askance at peculation. He had duly ordered the young man brought to trial. Caecina's prospects seemed to have taken a terminal plunge.

Or had they? To command a legion, even one stationed on the outer limits of civilisation, was not, perhaps, to be as entirely removed from the heartbeat of power as it might seem. The army stood at the very centre of what it meant to be a Roman. So it had always done. Once, back in the early days of the republic, a legion – a *legio* – had meant simply a levy of the Roman people. Only in times of war had the city possessed an army at all. The Campus Martius, rich in monuments and pleasure gardens though it had come to be, preserved in its name a reminder of those ancient days. To assemble on the Field of Mars, to be sorted into a legion, had been for the Roman people to pass from one dimension of citizenship into another: to become a different order of man. The oath that every recruit was obliged to swear – the *sacramentum* – fashioned him anew as a thing of iron, for it bound him 'never to flee, never to desert out of cowardice, never to abandon the battle line'.[5] Discipline was all. This was the tradition that had inspired the story told of Manlius Torquatus and his son, along with a host of similar edifying tales. They reflected a time when the army had been a unitary entity: the Roman people in arms.

A time long gone, of course. Inevitably, as Rome's power grew, so it had become impossible to maintain the army as a single levy. Rather than one legion, there might be ten, or fifteen, or twenty, at any one time in the field. These, operating in various theatres of war, often for years at a time, had become, by the final century of the republic's existence, not levies but professional armies. Legionaries had come to owe their loyalty not to Rome, but to the commander at their head. Warlords, during the civil wars, had presumed to impose their own version of the *sacramentum*. Last and greatest of these warlords had been Augustus. The legions that were posted to various parts of the Roman world – to the Rhine, to the Danube, to Syria, to Egypt – were his legions. The men sent to command them were his deputies: his *legati*, his 'legates'. The *sacramentum* the legionaries swore every year at the beginning of January, fearsome as it was and hedged about by blood-curdling sanctions, signified their allegiance to him personally. Each Caesar who succeeded Augustus inherited this command. Such it was to be an emperor. To lose the armies – as Nero had discovered – was to lose the rule of Rome.

No less than the capital itself, the forces camped out along the distant Rhine were indelibly stamped by the great revolution in the affairs of the city that had shattered the republic for ever and brought the Caesars to power. Caecina, arriving in Upper Germany, had been taking command not just of a legion, but of a living link to the age of Augustus. Originally recruited by Julius Caesar during the civil war that had brought him the mastery of Rome, IV Macedonica had never failed, following Caesar's assassination, in its loyalty to his adoptive son. Again and again, it had proved its devotion. Bloodiest and most heroic of its battle-honours had been a titanic engagement fought in Macedonia, in northern Greece, which had seen Caesar's murderers defeated once and for all, and provided the legion with its name. Augustus, rather than disbanding it once the civil wars had been brought to an end, and his own supremacy securely established, had opted instead to keep it in service. For a decade, completing a conquest of the peninsula that had dragged on for two centuries, it had fought in Spain. There, for another sixty years, it had remained as a garrison. Then, replacing a legion transferred by Claudius to take part in the conquest of Britain, it had been posted to Upper Germany. Its base was a camp named Mogontiacum: modern-day Mainz. By the early autumn of 68, when Caecina took up his legateship, IV Macedonica had been stationed on the Rhine for almost three decades. An entire generation recruited to the legion had known no other home.

Never before in history had there been a standing army of this order: IV Macedonica had over five thousand legionaries, and yet it was just one of thirty such armies. Some of these gloried in a record of campaigning that reached all the way back to Caesar's conquest of Gaul; others – such as I Adiutrix, the legion which Nero had raised in the last, desperate weeks of his life, and which Galba had decimated on his way to Rome – had been in existence for barely a few months. To serve as a legionary was not just to feel a ferocious *esprit de corps*, but to view other armies with a certain contempt. Resentments that in certain cases reached all the way back to the civil wars might be nurtured down the generations. IV Macedonica, for instance, was not the only fourth legion in service. A second one, IV Scythica, had been recruited by Antony, and even after its founder's death had refused to give up its number. Rather than risk stoking the legion's resentment, Augustus had ceded the point. It was in a similar spirit of compromise that he had permitted no fewer than three third legions to coexist. This was why an army required a name as well as a number to be properly distinctive: III Gallica had been recruited by Caesar in Gaul; III Cyrenaica had originally been stationed in Cyrene, a city in Libya; III Augusta commemorated Augustus. Of the two sixth legions, one was named Ferrata – 'Ironside' – and the other Victrix, 'Victorious'. In the name awarded to I Adiutrix – 'Helper' – there was to be found an assurance that, despite their bruising introduction to life as legionaries, the erstwhile marines might yet do good service.

There was, then, no one Roman army – just a range of armies. Even when legions shared a base, they would jealously guard their distinctiveness. On the Rhine, which had the heaviest concentration of troops anywhere in the empire, seven legions in all, there were two such headquarters. One, Vetera, stood in Lower Germany; the second was Mogontiacum. Both had been founded some eighty years previously; both, over the course of the decades, had been repeatedly expanded, strengthened, rebuilt. Together, they played a key role in maintaining Rome's offensive capabilities: for both commanded access to navigable rivers which, joining the Rhine on its eastern bank, reached like dagger thrusts deep into the bowels of Germany. It was along the line of one of these rivers, the Lippe, that Varus had marched on the fateful expedition that culminated in the annihilation of his three legions; and it was in the wake of the Varian disaster that Vetera, the fortress to which the three legions had been returning when the ambush took place, had been massively upgraded. Sixty years on, it bristled with freshly constructed stone fortifications. It also boasted barracks sufficient to accommodate not one but a pair of legions.

The senior of these, V Alaudae, had perhaps the most distinctive

name of any legion: for *alaudae*, 'larks', was not a Latin word, but a
Gaulish one. Julius Caesar had paid for the legion out of his own
funds as the conquest of Gaul was nearing its climax, and its soldiers – like those of III Gallica – had been recruited entirely from
Gallic warriors. They had made a point of wearing feathers on the
sides of their helmets, giving them, so the joke had it, a resemblance
to the crested lark.[6] This, more than a century on, was precisely the
kind of detail that any legionary serving with the Alaudae was bound
to treasure. Bragging rights were of particular importance to soldiers
obliged to share their base with another legion – and at Vetera there
could be no doubt which of the two armies outranked the other. The
other legion stationed there, XV Primigenia, named after the goddess
of fortune, had been in existence a mere thirty years, and its creator,
the notorious Caligula, could hardly compare in the annals of fame
with Julius Caesar. So it was that the Larks occupied the right-hand,
more prestigious side of the base: for pedigree, on the limits of civilisation just as in Rome, was never to be disrespected.

A point insisted upon by IV Macedonica as well. Just like the Larks,
they shared their base with a legion created by Caligula and named
Primigenia: in this case, XXII Primigenia. Here at least, for a man as
desperate to climb the slippery pole of advancement as Caecina, was
something to cling to. As commander of the legion that occupied the
position of honour in Mogontiacum, he ranked as the most senior
officer in the entire camp. To be sure, there was no getting away from
the brute facts of his situation: that he was stuck in a German winter.
To stand on the ramparts of the military base, to gaze down towards
the Rhine, to watch sentries on the great bridge that spanned its currents stamping their feet and blowing on their hands to keep warm,
was to have that rubbed brutally home. But it was also to appreciate
something else. The settlement that had grown up at the base of the
fort, and which reached all the way down to the river, was not an
entirely barbarous place. It had monuments to dead Roman heroes;
a bath-house; a gilded statue of Jupiter mounted to imperious effect
on a column, so that whenever the winter sun broke through the

clouds the god would blaze, and seem fashioned out of golden fire. Though it was raw and muddy, and to anyone familiar with Rome irredeemably provincial, yet it served too as a reminder of a time when Rome itself had been provincial. Back in the heroic early years of its existence, after all, the city that now ruled as the mistress of the world had been obliged to stand constant sentry against its foes. As Mogontiacum was now, so had Rome herself once been.

Such a reflection, perhaps, came naturally to a man with the command of an army. Professional though the legions were, and drawn though they tended to be from recruits who were most unlikely ever to have visited Rome, they aspired to be as hard and martial as soldiers in the early days of the city had been. 'The virile progeny of rustic warriors, youths taught to turn the soil with Sabine spades'.[7] this was how poets celebrated the ancestors of the Roman people. Sadly, however, the days when men of such quality might be found in Rome itself, and summoned to serve with the legions, were long gone. The fruits of peace had proven too enervating. What did the plebs know about turning the soil with Sabine spades? Men softened by the pleasures and perks of urban living could hardly be expected to display the backbone required of previous generations. Galba was not the first emperor to have fretted about this deterioration. 'Quite without the traditional courage and steel.'[8] Such had been the damning verdict of Tiberius on recruits drawn from towns across Italy. The result was a paradox. Where, moralists might well ask themselves, was one likeliest to meet men possessed of the spirit that had first, back in the early centuries of Rome's existence, enabled the city to embark on its rise to greatness? Not in the Forum, not in the Campus Martius, that was for sure. Rather, in places so distant from Rome that antique heroes such as Manlius Torquatus most likely had never even heard of them. In places, it might be, like the Rhine.

'Military discipline – that is what underpins the Roman state.'[9] Four hundred years and more had passed since Manlius, arraigning his son on a charge of disobedience, had delivered himself of this ringing maxim. What in the metropolis might seem rebarbative and almost comically out of fashion did not seem so in Germany. There, everyone knew what was owed to the habit of obedience. The Gauls might have been more numerous, the Germans taller, the Spaniards physically stronger, the Africans more practised in the arts of treachery and bribery, the Greeks more cunning and intelligent; but only the legions had the *disciplina Romana*.[10] This it was that had enabled them to conquer the world. Four centuries on from the age of Manlius Torquatus, and the steel shown by legionaries in battle was of a kind that might have startled even the stern old consul. No longer, as their ancestors had done, did they advance in loose formation, chanting and pounding their weapons on their shields. Such wild behaviour was now left to barbarians. Instead, slowly and steadily, maintaining tightly serried ranks, a Roman army walked in silence towards its foe; and only at the very last moment, once the enemy was within range, would the legionaries break their silence with a great battle cry, hurl their spears, and break into a run. Self-control of this order was impossible without years of rigorous training – which was why only a Roman army could master it.

Nevertheless, a legion was not some mere killing machine. A Roman officer wanted more than blind obedience from his men. To be sure, punishments for the rank and file might often be brutal, and no one sentenced to them had any right of appeal. Nevertheless, the scarring that many soldiers bore on their backs, entire fretworks of welts, did not mean that they were ever to be compared with slaves. Quite the opposite. Only citizens were allowed to serve with the legions. Slaves, if they were found to have volunteered, would invariably be sent to the mines. This was because a legionary, even as he had to be broken to discipline like a horse or a hunting dog, also had to exercise the *virtus*, the manly quality that was properly that of a citizen. He had to show initiative as well as obedience; ardour for glory as well as self-restraint. If this risked paradox, then so had it always done, right from the earliest days of the republic. The genius of the Roman people had long lain in their ability to square two seemingly contradictory instincts: a yearning to excel, and a deep suspicion of vainglory. The republic might be long gone; but there still remained, in a base like Mogontiacum, just a ghostly hint of its paradoxes.

'What is a camp to a soldier? Why, it is like a second Rome.'[11] This conviction, that no legion, not even when it was on the march, should ever submit to spending a night in the open, but rather should fashion a camp for itself, one commensurate with its dignity as an army of citizens, had been a constant for many centuries. Indeed, it was what had first brought home to the Greeks that the Romans were not merely barbarians. Foreign observers, even those familiar with the workings of the legions, could never entirely shake their sense of wonder at the ability of a Roman army to construct a camp complete with ramparts, neatly spaced blocks of tents and a forum in a matter of hours. 'It is as though a town has sprung up from nowhere.'[12] Between a marching camp and the great military bases that studded the length of the Rhine there were differences of degree rather than of kind: for all the German legionary camps had originated as makeshift winter quarters. The Romans themselves compared them to beehives: geometric, perfectly ordered, a dimension in which everyone knew his place and the collective was all.

Not just a second Rome, then, but a model of what, in an ideal world, Rome might have been. The Roman people had always been great enthusiasts for evaluating and calibrating where they stood on the social scale. Back in the early days of the city, when citizens would gather on the Campus Martius in preparation for military service, each man would be ranked according to his wealth and status, and then, based on this ranking, receive assignment to a 'century'. So satisfying had everyone in the city found this system to be that it had provided the basis not just for the structure of the army, but for elections too. Throughout the entire existence of the republic, the Roman people had voted in centuries. Only with the coming to power of Augustus had this constitutional arrangement finally ended: for would-be magistrates, no longer dependent on the votes of their fellow-citizens, had come to compete instead for Caesar's favour. Even so, old habits died hard. A sense persisted that Rome could only properly be Rome if detailed records were maintained of precisely who held citizenship. This is what had prompted Claudius, in the year 47, to conduct a census. Evidence had been taken from one end of the empire to the other. The total number of citizens had been recorded with an impressive degree of exactitude: 5,984,072. Claudius himself had publicly acknowledged just how gruelling the effort of arriving at this figure had been. The truth was that Rome had become too vast, and the reach of the empire too immense, for a ready track of her citizens to be maintained. Only in military bases was it different. Only there could the traditional enthusiasm for calibration still be given free rein.

As a result, there were few institutions in the world quite as bureaucratic as a legion. Every recruit had his own personal dossier. Details of his character, his distinguishing features and his military record were kept permanently on file. 'To rank as soldiers men must first be entered on the records.'[13] This was simple common sense. Without records, after all, how could any legionaries know their proper place? Every soldier served in a century. Every century was commanded by an officer — a 'centurion' — whose responsibility it was to keep his men in order, and who had himself, most likely, been promoted from the ranks. Six centuries formed a cohort; ten cohorts formed a legion. The first century in every cohort, and the first cohort in every legion, ranked as the most senior. All of which, in a manner true to the most venerable and noble traditions of the Roman people, instilled in every soldier a hunger, a passion for honour. There was no legionary so humble that he might not dream of becoming a centurion, just as there was no centurion who did not dream of promotion to the command of a more senior century. The pinnacle of every soldier's ambition was to lead the first century in the first cohort, the most distinguished century of all: for then he would rank as *primus pilus*, the legion's chief centurion. Those who despaired of Rome's moral character had only to look to the Rhine for reassurance that an ancient maxim still packed a punch. 'Its

66

venerable customs, and the quality of its men: these are what enable the Roman state to endure.'[14]

Obedience was the first duty of every soldier; but loyalty to the traditions and best interests of Rome was just as important. The *sacramentum* was sworn to the emperor; but so, too, was it sworn to the Roman state. What if these two obligations should come into conflict? This, in the opinion of many in the legions stationed along the Rhine, was not a merely abstract question. Galba's rise to power had brought it sharply into focus. The new emperor did not have the blood of Augustus in his veins. He could claim no line of descent from a god. Nor was he remembered fondly on the Rhine. His term of command there had been a savage one. It was not enough for a general to be a disciplinarian; he also had to win his soldiers' love. This Galba had signally failed to do. The events of the past year had only confirmed the German legions in their suspicion of the upstart Caesar. He had failed to reward them for suppressing Vindex's revolt. He had dismissed Verginius Rufus, their much-respected com- mander, from office. He had persistently treated them with disdain. So it was, on 1 January, that many along the Rhine hesitated to swear the *sacramentum* to him. In Vetera, it was true, this mood of resentment did not blaze into open mutiny: the legionaries in Lower Germany were persuaded by their officers to swallow their doubts and swear the oath. In Mogontiacum, however, it was a different story. There, it was not the rank and file who took the lead in repudiating Galba. It was their legate.

Caecina's stage as a mutineer was the Principia. This great complex of courtyards and buildings standing at the very heart of the base served as his legion's headquarters. The most impressive building of all was an immense hall lined with columns, one half of which had been built by IV Macedonica, and the other half by XXII Primigenia.[15] Each half contained a shrine, and each shrine a gilded eagle. Every legion had one. To lose it — as the three armies wiped out in the Varian disaster had done — was the worst disgrace imaginable. This was why Galba, by refusing to grant an eagle to I Adiutrix when he first entered Rome, had precipitated a full-blown riot. It was also why the statues of the emperor that stood next to an eagle in its shrine possessed, for the soldiers of a legion, a rare and awful potency; and it was why, for any legionary who had sworn the *sacramentum*, the thought of smashing them was a blasphemy too shocking to contemplate. Equally, the refusal of the soldiers stationed in Mogontiacum to pledge their loyalty to Galba was a signal, that first day of the year, to send them toppling onto the floor. Incited by Caecina, IV Macedonica took the lead; after some initial hesitation, XXII Primigenia followed. Four centurions who tried to stop the mutiny were arrested. The fateful step had been taken. The die had been cast.

The oath the legionaries swore that day was not to any individual, but to the Senate and People of Rome. This did not, however, imply any ambition to restore a republican form of government. Rather, it reflected the awkward fact that the mutinous legions had not yet settled on their own candidate as Caesar. Caecina, for all his ambition and restlessness, was not so headstrong as to imagine that he might take Galba's place. Only a man with sufficient rank and pedigree could hope to do that. The obvious choice for Caecina and his fellow conspirators was the governor of Upper Germany, a former consul by the name of Hordeonius Flaccus; but he was widely despised, and not even the most optimistic mutineer could seriously imagine him as emperor. Fortunately, Flaccus was not the only high-ranking official stationed on the Rhine. The neighbouring region, too, was a military zone. Its commander stood at the head of formidable resources of manpower. Accordingly, even as Caecina was rousing his own soldiers to mutiny, he had already factored in the need to win over the legions of Lower Germany to his side, and to persuade their commander to take a fearful step: claim the rule of the world.

The headquarters of Lower Germany lay some ninety miles downriver from Mogontiacum, in a settlement that over the course of the preceding century had emerged to become the single most impressive Roman foundation anywhere on the Rhine. Originally it had been called Altar of the Ubians, after a German tribe that had transferred from the eastern bank back in the time of Augustus and settled in the region. The Ubians, however, in honour of Nero's mother, had renamed themselves the Agrippinians, while Claudius, in a gracious show of patronage, had raised the settlement's status to that of a *colonia*: the highest honour to which any city could aspire. To rank as a colony was to stand in a tradition that reached back to the distant days of the monarchy: to plant such settlements in pacified territory had always been a favoured method of the Roman people for ensuring that a territory stayed pacified. The inhabitants of a colony – whether retired legionaries or favoured natives – enjoyed privileges beyond the dreams of those in the surrounding countryside: for exclusivity was precisely the point. The Colonia of Claudius and the Altar of the Agrippinians – Colonia, as it came to be known, or Cologne – served as the true capital of the north. From here the governor of Lower Germany commanded no fewer than four legions: the two based at Vetera and two others, I Germanica and XVI Gallica. Colonia itself had no need of legions to endow it with a martial air. As well as a formidable fleet, it boasted as its most precious relic the sword of Julius Caesar. It was, in short, a seat not inappropriate to a would-be emperor. Caecina certainly trusted that this was so. No sooner had the statues of Galba been sent toppling at Mogontiacum than he was dispatching a trusted officer to Lower Germany. The officer left at top speed. So hard did he ride that he arrived in Colonia that same evening. He went straight to the commander's headquarters. There, without waiting for the morning, he hurried through halls of sumptuous magnificence. His ambition: not just to report news of the mutiny, but to summon the commander of Lower Germany to the rule of the empire.

Aulus Vitellius was at supper.[16] This, to gossips back in Rome, would have come as no surprise. Vitellius was notorious as a glutton. Like Otho, he trailed a reputation for viciousness and depravity that reached all the way back to his youth. A favourite of both Caligula and Nero, he had shared the passion of both men for racing chariots at furious speed, until a spectacular crash had left him with a permanent limp. He had also gambled prodigiously, and — so it was darkly rumoured — prostituted himself. There was no need, however, to assume that he had slept his way to advancement. Vitellius' record was more impressive than the slanders of his enemies might suggest. His father, although a latecomer to the senate, had ended up reaching heights dizzying even by the standards of the very grandest senator. Not only had he held the consulship three times and served as Claudius' colleague in the conduct of the census, but upon his death he had been granted a public funeral and awarded a statue on the rostra. Dignities such as these counted for much. Vitellius' pedigree, even if it could hardly compare with Galba's, let alone Nero's, was not entirely worthless. Nor was his record of public service. As governor of Africa he had been highly praised for his integrity; as Galba's appointee to the command of Lower Germany, he had shown himself, in the space of only a few months, to be both competent and personable. He had rescinded injustices, introduced reforms, and displayed a common touch that, although dismissed by his fellow senators as vulgar, delighted the rank and file. Louche he may have been — but there were worse qualities, in the opinion of those who had experienced Galba's term of command, for a Caesar to possess.

Still, Vitellius hesitated. His doubts about the course of action being urged on him by the mutineers ran deep. He had no wish to embroil the Roman people in a civil war, nor any certainty that he had what it took to rule the world. Yet to refuse equally threatened disaster. It would leave Vitellius with little choice but to suppress the mutiny — and how confident could he be that the soldiers under his own command would consent to that? The answer was not long in coming. On 2 January, the elderly legate of I Germanica, Fabius Valens, came galloping into Cologne. He had ridden from Bonna — Bonn — where his legion had its base. Notorious for his mastery of the darker political arts, he was, much like Caecina, a man in a hurry, impatient for promotion. The two legates, perhaps unsurprisingly, detested one another. Just as Caecina had done, Valens urged rebellion. The following day, all the armies along the Rhine, in Lower and Upper Germany alike, hailed Vitellius as emperor. Rather than show their respect for the constitutional proprieties by informing the senate, they prepared instead to march on Rome. That the traditional start of the campaigning season was still several months away worried Caecina not a jot. Ever impatient, he had no intention of waiting for spring before seizing the initiative. Nor did Valens want to be left in the starting blocks. Both men were set on bringing war to Italy as fast as they possibly could.

So all along the Rhine, amid the snow and sleet of a German January, the legionary bases echoed to the preparations for war. Meanwhile, as though to escape dwelling on the crisis that had overwhelmed him so abruptly, and out of dread at what the next months might bring, the would-be ruler of the world was sinking into a sozzled torpor. 'Wallowing in luxury and hosting lavish banquets, so that by midday, bloated with food, he would slump into a drunken slumber: such were the preparations of Vitellius for becoming emperor.'[17]

A Very Peculiar People

News of the mutiny on the Rhine was greeted with horror in Rome. Otho was not the only one to be appalled. So, too, were the city's elite. Vitellius' failure to inform them of his change of circumstances was noted with indignation. This slight, however, was not the worst. Civil war now threatened. The flooding by the Tiber of the corn market, and its destruction of Rome's oldest bridge, were ominous portents of the ruin that was plainly to come. As Otho and Vitellius, despite the winter season, both readied themselves for the looming death struggle, many in the senate expressed a longing, albeit under their breath, to see both men lose. It seemed to them a cruel twist of fate that Nero should have been toppled only for the empire to be fought over by a pair of his cronies: 'the two men in the world most notorious for shamelessness, indolence and extravagance'.[18]

Not that Otho agreed, of course. The sneering of his critics only steeled him to prove them wrong. For all the murderous circumstances of his accession, he had no relish for bloodshed. He behaved with a notable leniency towards Galba's followers, and did his best, in the opening weeks of the conflict, to arrive at terms with Vitellius. He also made sure to tickle the tummy of the senate. Prominent senators exiled by Nero were recalled; appointments to the consulship respected; a concern for constitutional proprieties flaunted. Even so, it was a treacherous tightrope that Otho had to walk. Galba's brief term as emperor had left many in Rome nostalgic for his predecessor; and Otho, anxious to portray himself as heir to the house of Augustus, knew that his youthful friendship with Nero might well, among certain constituencies, be played for advantage. Funds were duly made available to complete the Golden House; statues of Poppaea restored to their plinths; Sporus maintained in his finery. Otho had a talent for the nod and the wink. When the plebs and the Praetorians hailed him as 'Nero Otho', the new emperor made sure not to acknowledge the title; but neither did he repudiate it.

Meanwhile, Nero himself had come back from the dead. Such, at any rate, was the news that began to sweep Greece. The appearance on Cythnus, a small island in the Aegean, of a man who not only looked like Nero but could sing and play the harp provoked wild excitement. The emperor's name still exerted a potent magic. 'Many, eager for change and hating the state of the world as it was, felt its pull.'[19] Only the fortuitous stop-off on the island of a provincial governor en route to take up his command enabled the uprising to be nipped in the bud. The imposter, apprehended by the governor's escort, was put to death, and his corpse sent on a tour around the Aegean. Its bulging eyes and the ferocity of its expression provoked general astonishment. Then, once it had been made clear to everyone in Greece that Nero was well and truly dead, and that he had not, after all, cheated the sad and infernal gods, the body was sent on to Rome.

Yet the incident was more ominous than many in the capital cared to acknowledge. The enthusiasm of the Greeks for Nero's memory was hardly surprising. He had, after all, remitted their taxes. Anxiety that this policy might soon be reversed was widespread – and justifiably so. Yet any nostalgia the Greeks felt for Nero was double-edged. Just as he was the emperor who had lifted their tax burden, so it was he who had originally crushed them beneath its weight. Golden houses, after all, did not come cheap. There was an entire capital to rebuild. Tax-collectors, in provinces untouched by Nero's generosity, swarmed like flies over joints of meat. Misery in the face of ceaseless exactions fused with yearning for a brighter day. Across the eastern half of the empire and beyond, assorted prophecies of a new and impending age of justice swirled, shimmered and coalesced. Nero, in these, often had a starring role. In some he was a figure more than human, who had escaped his persecutors, and would soon come again to reign in majesty. In others he was a monster, who had fled Italy 'like a runaway slave unseen and unheard'.[20] Invariably, in all these fantasies there glimmered the same vision: of a world torn to pieces, and Rome's empire drowned in blood.

Otho, however, had other priorities. Focused as he was on the threat from the Rhine, he had no time to worry about the seething mood of discontent in the eastern provinces. It had been a long time since the Greek world had presented any military threat. The age of Alexander the Great, whose conquests had reached as far afield as India, was four centuries past. The eastern Mediterranean, once ruled by various dynasties descended from Alexander's henchmen, was now a Roman lake. Famous cities – Antioch in Syria, Alexandria in Egypt – no longer served as royal capitals, but as the headquarters of provincial governors. Their wealth, their scale, their splendour, far from serving to intimidate the Roman elite, tended instead to inspire in them a mild contempt. The peoples of Asia, for all the dazzle of their many achievements, were naturally fitted to be slaves. This was no idle prejudice. Greek philosophers, wise in the ways in which the climate affected the human constitution, had long ago proven it to everyone's satisfaction. Just as the cold weather of northern Europe bred men who were spirited but stupid, so did the enervating heat of Syria or Egypt breed men who were brilliant but soft. The happy medium, those who were simultaneously spirited and brilliant, were the people who occupied 'the mid-position geographically'.[21] The Greeks, with their customary conceit, had identified this with their own cities. A comical error. History did not lie. The 'mid-position geographically' was patently, self-evidently Rome.

Fitted by nature, then, for rule, the Romans had found it a far more profitable business to subdue the peoples of the Orient than the barbarians of the North. Whereas in Germany or Britain the infra-structure required to extort taxes from a subject population needed to be created from scratch, in Egypt or Syria it had been in existence for centuries. Governors sent from Rome to the great capitals of the East ruled as the heirs of toppled royal dynasties. Whether in Alexandria or Antioch, they lived in palaces, relied on bureaucracies, and commanded structures of patronage inherited from Macedonian kings. There were, however, many ways to shear a sheep. Direct rule was not the only way to fleece subject peoples, and the Roman authorities had no objection in principle to sponsoring monarchies. What mattered was to be pragmatic.

Certainly, a king petty enough never to present a military threat, but armed with sufficient tax-collectors to raise appropriate tribute, might prove a valuable servant. As a result, the fabric of Roman rule in the Near East had always been a patchwork. Provinces alternated with kingdoms; legates with dutifully subservient monarchs. All were dependent on Caesar. Just as a governor who overstepped the mark or failed in his responsibilities might expect a recall, so did the threat of deposition hang over every king who ruled as a Roman client. Augustus, redrawing the lines of provinces or kingdoms as circumstance demanded, had set an example followed by every sub-sequent emperor. What mattered was not consistency but whether the coffers were full. That Nero had emptied them only made the task of replenishing them the more urgent. Everything hung upon it. Without taxes, after all, how were the soldiers to be paid? And without pay, how were the legions to be maintained? And without legions, what prospect of maintaining peace in the world?

Yet there was always, shadowing Rome's voracious appetite for revenue, a parallel danger. If the tax-collectors pushed their extortions too far, they might well end up undermining rather than buttressing Roman power. Nero's reign had provided dramatic evidence of this. In Britain, a recently invaded and precariously stabilised province, the natives had been pushed into open rebellion. Led by a warrior queen named Boudicca, they had gone on a murderous rampage. Three Roman settlements had been left as smoking rubble. Only in the very nick of time, courtesy of a crushing victory won against overwhelming odds, had the provincial authorities managed to claw the situation back from the brink. Perhaps, bearing in mind the character of the Britons, the rebellion should not have come as a surprise. Barbarians that they were, and only recently conquered, they were not accustomed to tax-collectors. The same could hardly be said, however, of a second people who had erupted into revolt during Nero's reign. These were the inhabitants of a small but strategically vital region midway between the ancient lands of Egypt and Syria, whose experience of conquest by foreign powers was a venerable one, reaching back many centuries: the Judaeans.

For a hundred years and more – ever since the storming of Jerusalem, their ancient capital, by Pompey – they had been under the thumb of Rome. Like most other peoples of the Near East, they were habituated to the use of money, to tax-collectors, to the demands of mighty empires. Indeed, prior to Pompey's arrival, the Judaeans themselves had behaved as an imperial power, assimilating their southern neighbours to their way of life, and waging a brutal war of extermination against their neighbours to the north, a people called the Samaritans. So successfully had they prosecuted this that in 112 BC, half a century before Pompey's arrival in the region, they had captured both the holiest shrine in Samaria and its capital city, 'destroying it utterly, and enslaving its inhabitants'.[22] Despite these twin calamities, the Samaritans had succeeded in preserving their identity against the Judaeans' resolute attempt to destroy it; and the coming of the Romans had obliged the rival peoples, however reluctantly, to cease their hostilities. Nevertheless, the mutual hatred between them was undiminished – and certainly much greater than the resentment either felt towards their new overlords. The Romans, old hands at dividing and ruling, had naturally made sure to take full advantage.

The Judaean elites in particular had proven ready collaborators: for the Roman authorities, far from undermining the local primacy of Jerusalem, had consistently sought to buttress it. This was why, far from anticipating trouble, they had felt able to govern Judaea with a notably light hand. No legion was stationed there. Such garrisons as did exist were small. Even when the peculiar customs of the Judaeans required them to assemble in Jerusalem in vast and teeming numbers, the Roman authorities – habitually nervous of large provincial congregations – made no attempt to ban them. There seemed no need for such measures. Certainly, nothing in the century and more of Rome's engagement with Judaea suggested trouble. Rather, it seemed that the Judaeans could be relied upon to play by the rules: to pay their taxes, and avoid doing anything foolish. But then, abruptly, this conventional wisdom had been turned on its head. In AD 66, while Nero was in Greece, touring the country's festivals and soaking up the applause of the crowds, startling news had reached him. The Judaeans were in revolt.

The blaze, it seemed, had been sparked by a distant fire. In 64, Rome had gone up in flames. That same year, Nero had sent out a new official to administer Judaea. Gossips claimed that Gessius Florus had secured his appointment thanks to his wife's friendship with Poppaea; but it was not long before he had begun to demonstrate a qualification that might have recommended him to Nero even more. 'He stripped bare whole cities; he ruined entire communities.'[23] Wherever there were funds to be extorted, Florus would extort them. Depredations on this scale were something new. Barely a year into

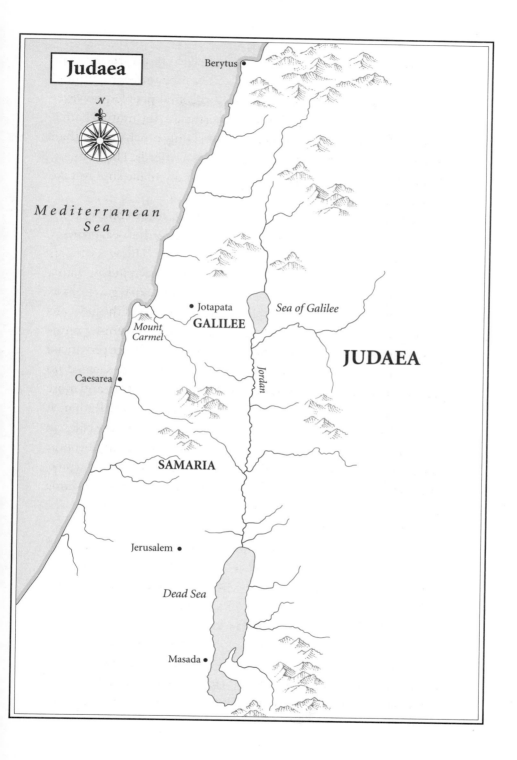

Judaea

N

Mediterranean
Sea

Berytus •

Jotapata •
GALILEE

Sea of Galilee

Mount
Carmel

JUDAEA

Jordan

Caesarea •

SAMARIA

Jerusalem •

Dead Sea

Masada •

Florus' term of office, a vast demonstration was staged against him in Jerusalem. The occasion was the visit to the city of Cestius Gallus, the governor of Syria, and Florus' immediate superior. Cestius, listening to the protestors, had given them solemn assurances. Florus would be reined in. His exactions would be eased. Yet Cestius was in no position to meet these promises. Florus was answerable not to him, but to Nero. What Nero wanted Nero got — and what Nero wanted in the wake of the great fire was large amounts of money. So it was that Florus had continued with his depredations; and so it was, a mere two years after his appointment to the province, that Judaea had exploded.

Yet this, perhaps, was not the entire story. Even analysts who could recognise how badly the Judaeans had been treated, and 'how patiently they had endured their oppression',[24] could recognise as well that they were a most unusual people. If, like the Egyptians or the Syrians, they had been shaped by their experience as the subjects of a long succession of monarchies, then so also, in many of their customs, did they more closely resemble the barbarians of the north. Like the Germans, they counted it a crime to expose unwanted babies; like the Germans, they were renowned for their suspicion of foreigners; like the Germans, they refused to put up statues to the gods. Even these comparisons, however, only hinted at the behaviour that rendered the Judaeans most truly distinctive. 'Everything we hold sacred they scorn as superstition, and practices which we abominate they uphold.'[25] That the origins of the Judaean way of life went very far back in time — and were certainly more ancient than Rome itself — even the most hostile witnesses agreed. Broadly understood as well were some of the more curious details of the Judaeans' history: that their distant ancestors had lived in Egypt; that they had been led to what became their homeland by a man named Moses; and that this same Moses had instructed them in a most novel form of worship. The precise details were too obscure to merit close study; but the outline was clear enough. The Judaeans believed that there was only one god, 'almighty and eternal, inimitable and without end'.[26]

Various laws had been given by this god to Moses. The Judaeans were obliged to circumcise themselves; to sit around every seventh day – the 'Sabbath', as they termed it – in indolence and idleness; never to eat pork. No matter where they might live – whether in Judaea itself, or in Alexandria, or in Rome – they were all required to follow these prescriptions. Outlandish, of course; but obedience to the law given by Moses had at least enabled the Judaeans, in a world where they were vastly outnumbered by other, more powerful peoples, to preserve their identity. 'Whether at table or in bed, they exist as a people apart.'[27]

Even so, despite their many peculiarities, the Judaeans were not notably more alien or sinister than numerous other peoples who, over the course of the centuries, had likewise been brought under Roman rule. They did not, for instance, as the Britons did, practise human sacrifice. They did not, as the Egyptians did, worship gods in the form of animals. They did not, as the Syrians did, castrate themselves. A few Romans, indeed, far from scorning the worship of the Judaean god as folly and superstition, rather admired it. Learned scholars might identify him with Jupiter. Philosophers might praise Moses for his wisdom, and salute the Judaeans as 'philosophers by race'.[28] Men about town, somewhat improbably, might recommend the house of prayer built in Rome by the Judaeans of the city – the 'synagogue', as it was known – as a place to pick up girls. Even Poppaea, that very epitome of fashion, was known by the Judaeans to be a *theosebes*: a woman who respected their god. It was not necessary actually to attend a synagogue, or to give up pork, or to keep the Sabbath, for Roman trendsetters to recognise in Judaean customs and beliefs something daringly countercultural, something edgy and chic.

'So far have the practices of this detestable people spread that they have been adopted across almost the entire world.'[29] This – a complaint that conservatives in Rome were prone to levelling against any foreign cult they might find in the city – was a wild exaggeration. Judaea was far too distant, far too insignificant, to have much of a public profile. Its people nevertheless did have a certain talent for punching above their weight. Synagogues were to be found in all the great cities of the empire: not only Rome, but Alexandria, and Antioch, and many others besides. The Judaeans were an ancient people; and antiquity, so the Romans had always believed, merited honour. Claudius – citing Augustus as his witness – had pointedly issued a warning to anyone who might think otherwise. 'The customs used by the Judaeans in the ritual of their god demand respect.'[30]

Such a declaration – coming as it did from Caesar – brooked no argument. Mobs in Alexandria tempted to turn on the Judaean community in the city were to remember that its presence there was almost as old as the city itself. Soldiers in Judaea who insulted the writings of Moses by ripping them up or tossing them on a fire might expect to be beheaded. Officials tempted to curry favour with an emperor by erecting statues of him in Jerusalem or minting coins with his head on them had only to recall the reverse suffered by a governor named Pontius Pilate. 'A vindictive man with a monstrous temper',[31] Pilate had permitted legionary standards to be brought into the city; but when the Judaeans, falling to the ground and baring their throats, had cried out that they would rather die than break their law, he had been left with little choice but to order the eagles removed. The lesson was one that the Roman authorities had made sure to absorb: there was no point in offending Judaean sensibilities just for the sake of it. Pilate, indeed, rather than bearing a grudge against the provincials who had forced him into retreat, had shown himself, over the course of his lengthy term of office, to be a consistent patron of their interests. He had worked closely with the Judaean priests. He had graced Jerusalem with an aqueduct. He had harassed and bullied the Samaritans – so much so that, in the end, it had led the governor of Syria to send him home.

The Roman people had won the rule of the world not only by force of arms, but also by mastering the arts of peace. Jerusalem, the

ancient capital that was, in the opinion of the Judaeans, the very holiest place in the world, had flourished under the rule of the Caesars. It
was, so Roman gazetteers freely acknowledged, 'the most famous city
of the East'.³² The Temple itself, once shabby and nondescript, had
been spectacularly renovated. Immense blocks of gleaming white
stone; fittings of a sumptuous splendour; courtyards vast enough to
host the thousands of sacrifices offered up day by day: here were spectacles that even visitors who were not Judaean freely acknowledged
to be one of the great sights of the empire. The Temple, that great
monument to the devotion of the Judaeans to their god, was a monument as well to Roman order. Without pilgrims travelling from every
corner of the world to Jerusalem, bringing with them rich offerings
of tribute, the city would have been a miserable shadow of itself; but
equally, without the peace maintained by Roman arms, the roads
kept free of bandits, the shipping lanes kept free of pirates, the flood
of pilgrims would have diminished to a trickle. Most Judaeans – and
especially those who lived beyond Judaea – perfectly appreciated this.
'An empire so vast in scale could never have come into being except
with the help of God.'³³ This, to the Judaeans of Rome or Alexandria,
appeared self-evident. It was why, in their synagogues, they did not
hesitate to make offerings to the emperor. In the Temple, too, among
the hereditary priests who constituted the Judaean ruling class,
there was no quibbling over the regular sacrifices made on Caesar's
behalf. Certainly, to the provincial authorities, these had appeared
a perfectly acceptable expression of loyalty: a demonstration that
there need be no contradiction between rendering unto Caesar and
rendering unto the Judaean god.

But then had come Florus' term of office. In 66, looking to make
up a financial shortfall, he had confiscated a large sum of money
from the Temple. An incendiary move. This was not least because
the garrison at his back had been recruited from the Judaeans'
bitterest, most inveterate rivals: the Samaritans. Outrage had
blazed across the city. Rioters had taken to the streets. Florus had
responded with savage reprisals. Given licence to make the streets

of the city flow with blood, the Samaritan garrison had needed no second invitation. Over three thousand people – women and children as well as men – had been cut down. Eminent Judaeans had been arrested, scourged, tortured to death. Every level of society had been left scarred. How, though, were the Judaeans to be rid of their tormentor? As crowds of the poor bayed for action, there had been many among the priests who urged the traditional course of circumspection: appeals to Cestius, appeals to Caesar. Others, however, had scorned such equanimity as feebleness and cowardice. A faction of militants, keen to ride the mood of insurrection in the city, had seized control of the Temple. From there a young priest named Eleazar, bold, charismatic and impetuous, had announced a fateful measure: the banning of all gifts from foreigners. The implications had hardly needed spelling out. No more sacrifices on behalf of Caesar. No more gestures of loyalty to Rome. A declaration of war.

To defy the world's greatest power was a fearsome step. There were plenty of Judaeans who thought it suicidal. 'Do you imagine you are taking on Egyptians and Arabs here? Only contemplate the immensity of Rome's empire, and then how feeble by comparison you are.'[34] What, though, the insurgents demanded, if their god were on their side? Certainly, their initial actions had met with miraculous success. Efficiently if brutally, Eleazar and his men had eliminated the two major sources of opposition to their rule of the city: the garrison of soldiers recruited by the Romans from Samaria, and the Judaean peace party. The Samaritans had been lured out of their fortress by a promise of safe passage and promptly massacred; the leaders of the peace party were burned to death in their own opulent homes, or else hunted down, dragged out from where they had been hiding, and murdered. Among the victims had been Eleazar's own father. A few weeks later, when Cestius arrived from Antioch at the head of the inevitable reprisal force, a series of seemingly miraculous events had only confirmed the rebels in their conviction that their god was on their side. First, just as he seemed on the point of capturing the Temple, Cestius had abandoned his siege; then, attempting an orderly withdrawal, he had suffered a series of ambushes in the narrow defiles that led from Jerusalem. The withdrawal had fast become a rout. The corpses of over five thousand Romans had ended up littering the road. Catapults, battering rams, artillery: all had been lost. So too an eagle.[35] The disgrace of it could hardly have been any worse.

The legion that had lost its eagle – XII Fulminata, 'Thunderbolt' – was a famous one: originally levied by Caesar, and with many battle-honours to its name. How, then, could it possibly have been defeated by a ragtag posse of Judaean rebels? Moralists were in no doubt. For decades, ever since the time of Augustus, XII Fulminata had been stationed in Syria. Anxiety about the debilitating effect of service in the East ran deep among the Roman high command. The same climate that rendered the peoples of Asia effeminate was bound, so disciplinarians fretted, to soften legionaries as well. Unlike on the Rhine, where the legions served at a safe distance from the distractions of civilisation, those in the eastern provinces were stationed in close proximity to teeming cities. In Egypt, two legions shared a base just outside Alexandria; in Syria, the province's legions were billeted in towns around Antioch. Small wonder, then, that seasoned generals, arriving to take over postings in the East, should often have despaired of the men under their command. For a decade prior to the outbreak of the Judaean revolt, the most celebrated of all Rome's soldiers – a stern, charismatic and formidably able man named Gnaeus Domitius Corbulo – had been busy whipping the flabby garrisons of the eastern frontier into shape. Legionaries rousted out of the fleshpots of Antioch had been marched up into the mountainous wilds of Armenia, and there obliged to spend an entire winter under canvas. Sentries had frozen to death at their posts. 'One soldier, indeed, was seen carrying a bundle of firewood, and so frostbitten were his hands that they actually dropped off, still attached to their load.'[36] Such it was to be a Roman, and a man. Corbulo's methods had proven resoundingly effective. Nothing had better illustrated their success than the record under his command of X Fretensis.* This legion, like XII Fulminata, had been stationed for many decades in Syria, but unlike XII Fulminata it had been honed by Corbulo to a formidable degree of proficiency. Battles had been won, cities stormed, uppity foreigners brought to sue for terms. The ferocity of the legion had proven more than worthy of its standard: a wild boar. The Tenth had deserved well of Caesar. So, too, had Corbulo.

Except that in 67 Nero had summoned the great general to Greece, charged him with treason, and instructed him to kill himself. Corbulo, ever obedient to orders, had briskly fallen on his sword. His downfall had served as a warning to ambitious men everywhere: the reward for high achievement, in an autocracy such as Rome had become, might very well be death. It is unlikely, however, that a man such as Cestius Gallus — appointed as he had been to the command of various legions by a suspicious and vengeful emperor — had needed such a lesson. Why, with Jerusalem at his mercy, had he embarked on his disastrous retreat? The capture of the Temple would certainly have nipped the insurgency in the bud; but it might also have secured for Cestius a fatal nimbus of glory. Rather than risk that, it may be that he had aimed simply to demonstrate Roman prowess to the insurgents, and then, his mission accomplished, discreetly withdraw. If such had indeed been his plan, then it had signally failed. The loss of an eagle had set the seal on a disgrace that there was no option but to avenge. As in Germany after the Varian disaster, so now in Judaea: honour demanded an unstinting, an annihilative vengeance.

This, as Nero's regime imploded, as Galba rose to the rule of the world and then fell, as Otho and Vitellius prepared for civil war, remained a sacred obligation laid upon the Roman people. Three years on from the outbreak of the Judaean revolt, the back of the insurgency appeared broken. Jerusalem remained in arms, as did a

* During the civil wars that brought Augustus to power, the legion had served the future emperor by guarding the straits — the *fretum* — of Messina: hence its name, *fretensis*, the legion of the straits.

few other scattered fortresses; but otherwise Judaea had been pacified. The campaign bore witness to Nero's eye for talent: for just as he had not hesitated to eliminate able commanders if he felt menaced by them, so also had he been perfectly ready to promote them if they presented him with no threat. Titus Flavius Vespasianus was a man ideally suited to the Judaean command. A veteran of both the Rhine frontier and the conquest of Britain, he was a soldier of great ability: brave, strategically astute, and popular with the men he had commanded. He was also – no less germanely to Nero's purposes – quite without pedigree. Raised in a small Sabine hamlet some fifty miles from Rome, he came from a family, the Flavians, who, in the opinion of high society, 'lacked even the slightest distinction'.[37]

Even so, they were definitely on the make. Vespasian's elder brother, Sabinus, was a man of notable ambition who had succeeded in serving as a consul, a provincial governor, and finally as the magistrate charged with keeping order in Rome: the prefect of the city. Vespasian, bobbing along in his brother's wake, had likewise managed to secure a consulship, likewise managed to secure a governorship; but he remained, even so, to his high-achieving brother, something of an embarrassment. His accent was rustic; his sense of humour coarse; his expression – 'like a man straining to have a shit',[38] as one wag put it – that of a peasant who had spent too long in the sun. Perennially short of money, he had been reduced, prior to the Judaean command, to mortgaging all his property to Sabinus, and investing in the mule-trading business: a humiliation that had led him to be nicknamed, inevitably, 'the muleteer'. War, however, was a lucrative business – and Vespasian, as the conqueror of the Judaeans, could look forward to a rosy future. At his back now, after all, he had three battle-hardened legions. One of them, under the command of a stern and able senator from Baetica named Marcus Ulpius Trajanus, was none other than X Fretensis. The other two legions as well could boast a formidable fighting record. It was a fine thing at any time to enjoy the command of such an army; but especially so when civil war threatened, and the world itself seemed in play.

Not that Vespasian, throughout his term of office, had behaved with anything other than exemplary propriety. Conscious that with Nero's death his command stood in abeyance, he had paused military operations against the Judaeans. He had sent his eldest son, Titus – a dashing young heart-throb who was with him in Judaea as a legate – to serve as his ambassador to Galba; and then, when the news of Galba's murder came through, and Titus, uncertain what to do, turned back mid-journey, thrown in his lot with Otho. Vespasian had certainly dropped no public hint that he might be 'brooding on private hopes'.[39] Yet in the dimension of the supernatural, where the patterns of the future might be read by those skilful enough to trace them, Vespasian had found good reason to nurture high ambition. Despite his provincial upbringing, portents of good fortune had long shadowed him. An ox had once knelt before him and bowed its neck; a stray dog had brought in a human hand and dropped it at his feet. Evidence enough, it might have been thought, that he was destined for very great things indeed.

There was more, however, to come. Vespasian's appointment to the Judaean command had brought him to a land celebrated across the world as one of the great homes of prophecy. Poppaea's fascination with Judaean lore had been due in large part to this reputation – just as it might be reported, in the stories told of Nero's second coming, that he was fated to appear in Jerusalem, where he would sit in the Temple, 'proclaiming himself to be God'.[40] Vespasian knew better than to heed such ravings; even so, he could not help but ponder a couple of prophecies that he personally had received. The more the world seemed to totter on its foundations, so the more he found himself haunted by them; and the more he found himself haunted by them, so the more he dared to dream.

Back in the early summer of 68, as Nero's doom was becoming apparent, Vespasian had travelled to the border of Judaea with Syria. Here there rose a mountain named Carmel; and on its summit, in an ancient shrine 'without image or temple, but only an altar',[41] there was a priest named Basilides. Skilled as he was in the art of deciphering the future, this priest had inspected the sacrifice offered by his visitor and read in it startling news. All Vespasian's dreams, no matter how soaring they might be, were destined to come true. So Basilides had revealed. The news had spread like wildfire among the legions billeted in Judaea. Entrails, however, were not the only place where Vespasian's destiny might be read. There was Judaean scripture as well. Visions of the future, recorded by ancient prophets, now seemed transparently on the verge of fulfilment. 'The time had arrived, according to a belief as venerable as it was well-established, and which had become general across the East, when men were fated to come from Judaea to rule the world.'[42]

The Judaean insurgents, rising in revolt against Rome, had assumed that this prophecy referred to them; but at least one of the rebels, captured by the Romans and brought in chains before Vespasian, had acknowledged the error of his ways. Yosef ben Mattityahu was a man of distinguished family: a priest from Jerusalem, learned in the scriptures of his own people, but familiar as well with Rome, a city to which he had travelled as a young man, and where – as he proudly let everyone know – he had 'become known to Poppaea, the wife of Caesar'.[43] Following the defeat of Cestius, he had been appointed by the insurgents to the command of Galilee, a region north of Samaria long racked by tensions: between Judaeans and their neighbours, between rich and poor, between towns and countryside. Since Vespasian's base lay in Syria, it was Galilee that he had first invaded, and Yosef's command that he had first sought to crush. Yosef himself, cornered in a fortress named Jotapata, had managed to hold out for two long months; but the walls, as they were bound to be, had eventually been stormed. A large band of Judaeans, Yosef among them, had hidden in a cistern. There they had agreed to a suicide pact; but Yosef – 'whether by good fortune or divine providence, who can say?' – had managed to survive the mass slaughter. Taken prisoner, he had been hauled in front of Vespasian, Titus and the rest of the Roman high command. Painfully aware that he risked either execution or being sent as a prisoner to Rome, he had requested a word in Vespasian's ear. Then, when granted it, he had announced that he spoke as a prophet, a messenger of God. 'You, Vespasian are Caesar and emperor – you and your son. So load me with your heaviest chains, and keep me as a prisoner here. My master though you may be, you are the master as well of much more: of the land, and the sea, and all humankind.'[44]

Almost two years had passed since this dramatic revelation; and if Vespasian, in that time, had kept the self-proclaimed Judaean prophet close beside him, and granted him certain favours – the company of a woman, gifts of clothes – then so also had he made sure to keep Yosef in chains. Private hopes were private hopes, after all; and Vespasian, having pledged his loyalty to Otho, was resolved to keep his word. Yet with Vitellius preparing to advance on Italy, and all the world hanging in the balance, who could say for certain what might happen?

So it was that Vespasian, mulling his prospects, kept his counsel, and waited to see what the news might be from Rome.

The Sweetest Smell

Meanwhile, far from Judaea, Valens and Caecina were waiting for nobody. Their strategy was a simple one: to seize Rome as early in the year as they possibly could. It was this that had determined the date of their departure: for the passes into Italy generally became useable in April, and it was a long march from the Rhine to the foothills of the Alps. Two separate columns had embarked on the winter offensive. The first, under the command of Valens, had been drawn from the armies of Lower Germany: principally V Alaudae, but also the two legions stationed at Vetera. Much excitement, on the day of their departure from Colonia, had greeted the sight of an eagle flying ahead of them along the road: a certain portent of success. Caecina, meanwhile, was busy recruiting his own force from the bases of Upper Germany. Heading down the Rhine from

Mogontiacum, he arrived at the most southerly of the German legionary headquarters: a stone-clad settlement near the headwaters of the great river named Vindonissa. Home to the menacingly named XXI Rapax – 'Predator' – the base constituted a key strategic crossroads, for it controlled access to the Danube as well as the Rhine. More to Caecina's purposes, however, it also served as a gateway to Rome: for beyond it loomed the two highest mountains in the Alps, and between the two mountains a road that, soon enough, would enable him to make the crossing into Italy.

In the meantime, however, rather than kicking his heels as he waited for the snows to melt, Caecina decided to pick a fight with the local Gauls. Helvetia was a land celebrated in the annals of Roman martial achievement. Natives of the Alpine valleys, the Helvetians had once been a restless and aggressive people. Back in the time of Julius Caesar, it was their attempt to burst out from their mountainous homeland, and seize more fertile lands to the west, that had provided the conqueror of Gaul with his first taste of military glory. The tendency of barbarians to go crashing into lands where they were not wanted had long been the stuff of Roman nightmares. Ever since a horde of Gauls, back in the early days of the republic, had erupted across the Alps, swept southwards, and briefly occupied Rome, the city had been steeled by a grim resolve never again to endure such a humiliation. This was why Caesar had been able to cast his conquest of Gaul as a campaign conducted in self-defence. The natives had needed to be brought the fruits of Roman dominance. The days when entire tribes might load up their wagons, and embark on mass migrations, had been brought to a decisive end. Redounding to the benefit of the Roman people, it had all been for the good of the Gauls as well.

'Wars were rife, and your country fractured into a multitude of petty kingdoms, until you accepted Roman rule.'[45] What Gaul could possibly dispute this? Brutal though the original conquest might have been, its fruits had been those of peace. The blood of the million natives said to have been slaughtered by Caesar's legions had served to fertilise an entire new civilisation. Once, the great men of Gaul had

worn trousers and checked cloaks, held court on hills behind palisades topped with severed heads, and dripped gravy from their long
moustaches. No longer. The descendants of Gallic kings now draped
themselves in the stately robes appropriate to the senate house. They
lived in great stone palaces complete with mosaic floors and central
heating. They enjoyed luxuries sourced from across the Roman
world, scorned head-hunting as repellent barbarism, and were never
less than impeccably clean-shaven. Not everyone, of course, ranked
as an aristocrat; but even in the most backward reaches of Gaul, be it
in the depths of the countryside or along the margins of the Ocean,
markers of Rome's rule were never far away. They might be found in
the agricultural labours of those whose ancestors had been 'forced
to lay down their weapons and take up farming';[46] in a style of cheap
pottery familiar across Italy; or in altars raised to gods with Roman
names, and inscribed in rudimentary Latin. Roads, great gashes of
stone scored across the landscape where previously there had been
only muddy tracks, ensured that nowhere in Gaul lay beyond the
reach of provincial officials and tax-collectors. Even on the very edge
of the world, in Armorica, as Brittany was known, there were settlements laid out on neat grid patterns, and buildings with red tiles
for roofs, and monuments that aped those of distant Rome. People
in these towns might jingle coins stamped with the head of Caesar,
cook with olive oil, and wash themselves in baths. It was hardly
sophistication; but neither was it barbarism.

Even so, the venerable Roman dread of the Gauls had never
entirely been exorcised. Back in the time of Tiberius, a tribe named
the Aedui, the inhabitants of what today is Burgundy, had risen in
open revolt, in the conviction that their ancient glory and independence were destined to be restored. Only with difficulty had the
rebellion been suppressed. The Roman authorities, impatient with
any hint of subversion, had cracked down hard on anyone predicting
that their rule might not be eternal. As in Judaea, so in Gaul: the traditions of prophecy were both venerable and distinctive. Yet unlike
the priests of the Judaeans, whom Roman governors had customarily

treated with punctilious respect, those of the Gauls had met with escalating persecution. 'Druids', they were called: magicians who in the depths of dark forests were reported to harvest mistletoe, burn their victims alive in great wicker cages, and feast on human flesh. Both Augustus and Tiberius had sought to rein them in. Then, under Claudius, had come outright repression. 'It is impossible to overestimate the debt that is owed the Roman people for their having put an end to these monstrous rites.'[47] Such was the consensus of all civilised people. Just as marshes bred sickness, so did the wild places of Gaul breed superstition, savagery and insurrection. The peace brought to them by Rome could never entirely be taken for granted. The legions of the Rhine, even as they stood sentry over the barbarians beyond the river, were always conscious of a certain need to guard their backs.

Caecina, by embarking on a brisk but bloody campaign against the Helvetians, was making play with what remained, among the soldiers under his command, a deeply held conviction: that the Gauls, no matter how civilised they might seem, and no matter how loyal to Rome they might pretend to be, were never entirely to be trusted. The Helvetians, rather than acknowledging Vitellius as emperor, had gone so far as to detain one of his centurions: insult enough to the legions from the Rhine. Even without this justification, however, they would still have been primed to embark on an Alpine war. Their defeat the previous summer of Julius Vindex, the governor who had first raised the banner of revolt against Nero, had been, they felt, insultingly rewarded. Far from seeing Vindex as he had seen himself, as a Roman patriot, they had viewed him with contempt as merely the latest in a long line of Gallic trouble-makers. That he had been joined in his revolt by the Aedui, those perennial malcontents, had merely confirmed the legions of the Rhine in their conviction that they had preserved Gaul from a full-blown insurgency. Galba's refusal to acknowledge this, let alone permit the legions to plunder the homelands of the rebels, had been a key factor in their mutiny. Unsurprisingly, as Valens led his column past Aeduan territory,

the tribesmen went out of their way to avoid giving him even the slightest pretext for attacking them. Every demand for money or arms was met with cringing promptitude; supplies of food were handed over unprompted. The fate of the Helvetians demonstrated just how sensible these precautions had been. Brief though the war in the Alpine valleys was, thousands were slaughtered, thousands more taken as slaves. As Caesar had once dealt with the Helvetians, so now had Caecina. The Romans, it seemed, were the Romans still; the Gauls were still the Gauls.

Or were they? In truth, the devastation visited on Helvetia, far from affirming how distinctive the two peoples remained, demonstrated something very different: just how blurred the boundary between them had become. Identity in Roman Gaul was a shifting, deceptive, and treacherous thing. Just as Julius Vindex might seem, depending on perspective, either a senator or an insurgent, so it was not immediately clear, as Caecina's legions slaughtered and enslaved the Helvetians, who should rank as the barbarians. Long gone were the days when the tribesmen of the Alps had been among the most obdurate enemies of Rome. Their failure to put up even the most token resistance to the armies of Upper Germany demonstrated that Gauls, no less than Italians, might be softened by long years of peace. It was not arms they relied upon to defend themselves, but rather a mastery of Latin. Sent by Caecina to Vitellius for judgement, a leading Helvetian succeeded in reducing even hardened legionaries to tears with his oratory, thereby securing a triumphant acquittal. Meanwhile, it was a Roman officer of ancient family who had led an army of warriors down from the Rhine; who had stripped a defence-less and sedentary people bare; and who was now poised to cross the Alps and descend into Italy, just as barbarian invaders had done long centuries before. Spring that year arrived early. Caecina, rather than delaying, decided to steal a march on both Otho and Valens by taking the mountain road in early March. Though the snows were still deep, up and over the pass he went. Down into the rich plain of the Po Valley he swept. Riding at the head of his column, he was dressed in the trousers and patterned cloak of a Gallic chieftain. By his side, mounted on a war-horse, rode his wife. The dash he cut was less that of a Roman magistrate and more — so it seemed to his enemies, at any rate — that of some barbarian warlord.

Unsurprisingly, then, the news of his Alpine descent reverberated across Italy like the echo of a very ancient story. Otho, alerted that war had come to the Po, was steeled in his resolve to play the part of a traditional Roman hero. Just as in the early days of the republic a barbarian incursion would prompt consuls to muster an urgent levy, so did Otho, scorning a multitude of baneful omens, move with impressive speed. No time now for his beauty regime. Instead, leaving Rome, he did so unshaven, marching on foot, wearing the iron armour of a common legionary. Ahead of him he had already sent his main force, led by figures redolent of antique virtue: a former consul, an erstwhile legate, the general who had defeated Boudicca. In a council of war, this officer openly dismissed the elite forces arrayed against them as 'Germans'. Adopt a holding strategy, he urged Otho: for the legionaries from the Rhine, he argued, would find the heat of an Italian summer unendurable. 'Should we manage to protract the war, they will prove physically incapable of coping with the climate. The sun will be too much for them.'[48]

Otho, however, knew better than to clutch at such straws. No less than Vitellius, he was dependent on the support of legions from the barbarous reaches of the empire: even though, advancing from Rome, he had the Praetorians and I Adiutrix at his back, the bulk of his manpower consisted of armies summoned from the Balkans. Legionary was doomed to fight with legionary; citizen with citizen. Like some flesh-hungry corpse risen from the dead, the spectre of civil war, long banished to the history books, had returned to put Italy in its shadow. There was no prospect now of confining the conflict to the provinces. Although Caecina had met with rebuffs since crossing the Alps, he had succeeded in his primary goal: to seize and fortify a formidable bridgehead. Cremona, a colony founded three centuries previously beside the waters of the Po, had served Rome originally as a bulwark against invasions from beyond the Alps; then as a base for the conquest for Gaul; then as one of the largest and most prosperous cities in northern Italy. Now, with Otho gathering his strength some twenty-five miles along the line of the Po to the east, and Valens fast approaching from the west, it had been restored to its role as a military stronghold. Whoever held it held the key to Italy.

Otho understood this as well as Caecina did; and when, on 10 April, Valens and his column finally arrived in the city, all three men knew that the moment of reckoning had arrived. Certainly — no matter what his generals might advise — Otho could not afford to sit on his hands. Vitellius, he knew, was already on his way from the Rhine with a mass of reinforcements. Soon Otho and his men would be decisively outnumbered. A flying column would find it a simple matter to bypass him and capture a defenceless Rome. He had no choice but to force a battle. Sure enough, four days after Valens had rendezvoused with Caecina, Otho ordered his legions to march on Cremona. Two days later, after an agonisingly slow advance through vineyards and over irrigation channels, they blundered into the enemy. Both sides scrabbled desperately to take up position. Raggedly, then increasingly murderously, battle was joined.

That evening, news of the result was brought to Otho. Rather than joining the fighting, he had opted to remain in his base to the rear. This decision had been dictated by common sense, not cowardice, for any victory his legions won would have been wasted if it came at the cost of his life. As it was, however, the victory had not gone to Otho's men. Long and hard though they had fought, in the end they had proven no match for the steel and greater numbers of the legions from the Rhine. The slaughter had been terrible. Thousands upon thousands of corpses lay heaped in tangled piles across the fields of Cremona. Those of Otho's men who had succeeded in extricating themselves from the battle were weary and demoralised. Even so, the emperor's cause was not wholly lost. Reserves and survivors remained to him, and there was the prospect of further reinforcements arriving from the Balkans. The Praetorians, who had remained by Otho's side in his camp, urged the man they had raised to the rank of Caesar to keep fighting. 'Certainly, no one can doubt that it would have been possible to continue with the war, brutal though it was, and the cause of terrible misery, for still the victory had not gone decisively to either side.'[49]

Yet Otho, ignoring the appeals of the Praetorians, had no intention of continuing. It was now, in defeat, that he prepared to demonstrate to the world that all his role-playing as an antique hero, which ever since his usurpation had constituted the keynote of his behaviour, had not been merely role-playing. Even as a private citizen, the civil wars that destroyed the republic had always filled him with a particular horror; nor, with thousands of his fellow citizens already littering the soil of Italy, was he willing to be the cause of further bloodshed. 'Am I the man to allow the flower of Rome again to be winnowed, all these famous armies again to be mown down and lost to the service of the state?'[50] That night, answering his own question, Otho retired to his tent. He wrote a pair of letters: one to his sister, one to Statilia Messalina, Nero's widow. Rather than gorging on a final meal or drowning his sorrows in wine, he contented himself with a single glass of water. Then he went to sleep. When he awoke, he picked up a dagger from under his pillow, placed its point over his heart, and ran it through with a single thrust. And so he perished, that the Roman people might not.

Nothing in Otho's life became him like the leaving of it. His men greeted the news of his suicide with extravagant displays of grief: they rained kisses on his corpse, and several of them gathered around the blaze of his pyre and immolated themselves. Most of the defeated legions, it was true, consented to swear the *sacramentum* to Vitellius: yet this, for the victorious emperor, was not entirely the triumph it might have seemed. Everyone knew that Otho had killed himself in the hope that the wounds of civil war might be bound up: and so the spectacle of his soldiers laying down their arms redounded to the glory of the dead emperor quite as much as it did to that of Vitellius. The truth was that Otho had laid a lethal trap for his successor. In death, a man who in life had been viewed as effeminate, selfish and dissipated had shown himself manly, patriotic and sober. Even the great crime that had brought him to power came to be seen, in the wake of his suicide, in a better light. 'It was widely asserted that he had toppled Galba, not to win power for himself, but in order to give back Rome her freedom, and to restore the republic.'[51] Otho, with the gaze of his fellow citizens fixed upon him, had passed his last and greatest test. How – now that he seemed to have the stage of the world to himself – would Vitellius perform?

News of the victory his legions had won reached the new emperor only shortly after his departure from Colonia. Out on the open road as he was, there was no platform immediately available to him appropriate to his new standing. Fortunately, it did not take him long to reach one. Lugdunum – modern-day Lyon – was the metropolis of Gaul. No administrative capital north of the Alps boasted a larger population or more impressive monuments. Roads led out from it in every direction like the spokes of a wheel. An altar raised to Rome and Augustus had been a focus of loyalty for all the various tribes of Gaul for eighty years. Taking up residence in the city, Vitellius could be confident that he was among friends. The people of Lugdunum, vehement in their loyalty to the house of Caesar, had barred their gates to Vindex, and suffered for it under Galba. The welcome they gave to the commander of the German legions was a joyous one. Vitellius, much buoyed as a result, felt confident enough to signal the founding of a new dynasty. Already, back in Colonia, he had declined the title of 'Caesar'. Now, before an assembly of his legions, and with Caecina and Valens flanking him on either side, he proclaimed his six-year-old son his heir. The name he bestowed on the child: 'Germanicus'.

Yet if the new emperor's dynasty was to be raised on firm foundations, it could not rely solely on the legions of the Rhine. His support base was perilously narrow. How best to buttress it? Vitellius, torn between the rival options of clemency and severity, veered between the two. The Praetorians who had backed Otho in his coup were pensioned off, the centurions who had constituted the backbone of his army executed. The generals who had opposed Caecina and Valens at Cremona were pardoned, but Galba's closest relative, a man whom Otho had banished from Rome but otherwise left alone, had his throat slit in a roadside tavern. The effect of these mixed messages — which contributed to an already widespread sense of the new emperor as a man too indolent and lacking in self-discipline to hold to consistent policies — was further compounded by a series of public relations disasters. Vitellius' journey from Lyon to Rome might almost have been designed to burnish Otho's posthumous fame. No simple glass of water for him. Perhaps only a very ostentatious sobriety might have redeemed him from his reputation as a glutton; but Vitellius was in no mood to make such a display. As a result, there were prodigious stories told of his greed: that the imperial gullet was insatiable; that entire cities had been ruined by the need to keep it filled; that wagons bearing delicacies and titbits for the emperor were making the whole of Italy shake. Vitellius, intimate of Nero though he was, had never mastered the art of reading a crowd. Unlike Otho, he had failed to learn how to craft his image. His every attempt to strike a pose proved maladroit. Arriving in Cremona, where the fields beyond the city were still strewn with corpses, rotting in the summer sun, he scorned to retch. 'A dead enemy smells sweet,' he declared, 'but an enemy slain in a civil war sweeter still.' A memorable aphorism — but one which prompted widespread revulsion. Visiting Otho's tomb, Vitellius mocked it for its meanness; presented with the dagger with which his rival had committed suicide, he sent it to Colonia, there to be dedicated to Mars. Such behaviour, simultaneously petty and vindictive, did not help to win him golden opinions.

Not that anyone in Rome cared much either way. With Nero dead, and his two successors toppled in quick succession, there were few in the city who felt a strong sense of identification with the new dynasty proclaimed by Vitellius. The recent dizzying round of murders and battles had become, for the Roman people, merely a fresh form of entertainment. Fittingly, news of Otho's defeat at Cremona had reached them as they were celebrating the Cerealia in the Circus Maximus. When Flavius Sabinus, Vespasian's elder brother, stood up to proclaim Vitellius the new emperor, his words were applauded rather as a victory in the races might have been. That Vitellius had, in his youth, been a celebrated charioteer only enhanced the sense of him as a man whose ascent was a wild and startling sports result. Certainly, his entry into the capital seemed – in its fusion of artifice and jeopardy, of novelty and dazzle – precisely the kind of pageant that might have graced the Circus. The eagles of the legions, the decorations worn by the centurions, the serried ranks formed by the soldiers: it was, everyone agreed, 'a splendid show'.[52]

It was also, so people whispered, not entirely what it seemed. Vitellius, parading through the streets of the capital, was robed appropriately in the toga of a Roman magistrate; but only because his friends, seeing him cross the Milvian Bridge dressed in armour and with a sword at his side, had frantically advised him not to look as though he had conquered the city. It was noted as well that Vitellius' vanguard, which had entered Rome before the emperor, had worn not their parade armour but cloaks made of animal skins. They might as well have been a pack of wolves. Meanwhile, even as soldiers like these roamed the city, Vitellius was lavishing money he did not have on the exhibition of wild beasts. Between the criminal savaged by a bear or a lion and the spectator in his seat, cheering on the bloodshed, the boundary was normally absolute. That summer, it seemed very different: as though all of Rome had been given over to predators.

Vitellius, in his awkward, clumsy way, knew perfectly well whose example he was following. On the Campus Martius, he made public sacrifice to the shade of Nero; at banquets, he would demand that musicians play compositions by the man he termed simply 'the Master'.[53] Yet even Vitellius might hesitate, on occasion, to follow where other admirers of Nero had led. Otho's death had left him as a spoil of war the wretched boy who had been transformed into the likeness of Poppaea Sabina. Rather than using his prize as

Nymphidius and Otho had done, as a private perk, he proposed a different, more beneficent course: one that would enable him to pose as a crowd-pleasing friend of the people. Let Poppaea, who had given Nero a ring engraved with the image of Proserpina, now play the role of Proserpina herself. Let her be brought onto a public stage for the entertainment of the masses, 'and be raped just as Proserpina had been raped'.[54] Here at last, Vitellius might have thought, was a gesture that could not fail to redound to his credit: a public relations triumph. But it was not to be. Poppaea, unable to endure the shame of what was being proposed, committed suicide. The spectacle had to be cancelled. The sad and infernal gods had mocked the hopes of yet another emperor.

The Fourth Beast

That July, as Vitellius was nearing Rome, and rumours were swirling that yet another convulsion in the affairs of the world was imminent, an officer came to find Yosef ben Mattityahu. Still weighed down by chains, as he had been ever since his capture at Jotapata two years before, the Judaean was led before Vespasian and his staff. The general greeted his prisoner warmly. He issued a command, and a man stepped forward with an axe. Then, with a single blow, he severed the chain. Vespasian had already made clear to his companions that he had good reason for setting Yosef free: 'For it is unacceptable to see treated as a prisoner a man who is a mouthpiece of God, and has prophesied my rise to greatness.'[55]

For months Vespasian had been mulling over what fate might have in store for him, and what he should be doing to embrace it. Cautious and canny, he hesitated to take a step that he knew, were he to stumble, would prove fatal, not just to himself, but to all his family. Still, behind the scenes, he had been making plans. Even as he publicly pledged his loyalty to a succession of emperors – Galba, Otho, Vitellius – he had been in secret negotiations with a pair of other key players in the Roman East. One, a former consul by the name of Gaius Licinius Mucianus, was the new governor of Syria: replacement for the hapless Cestius. A man of feline character, snobbish and elegant, he was as celebrated for his literary talents as he was notorious for his private proclivities, but seasoned as well both as a magistrate and as a commander. Initially, his relationship with Vespasian had been a scratchy one, for Mucianus, who had served with Corbulo in Armenia, rated his own military capabilities highly, and had not cared to cede the limelight to a Sabine bumpkin. The governor of Syria, however, was nothing if not a shrewd judge of character, and he had soon come to recognise Vespasian's qualities. The two men, alert to the opportunities opened up to them by the gathering convulsions of the age, had buried the hatchet. Charmed by Titus' youthful charisma, impressed by Vespasian's potential as a Caesar, Mucianus had privately committed both his three legions and his own prestige to the Flavian cause. This was an alliance such as senators in the dying days of the republic might have recognised: a compact made between warlords in the hope of deciding the fate of the world.

Yet it was the measure of how distant the age of Caesar, Pompey and Crassus had become that the other key figure in Vespasian's calculations, the man without whom he could never hope to challenge Vitellius, was not even a senator, not even from Italy. Tiberius Julius Alexander, the prefect of Egypt, was a native of Alexandria – and a Judaean. His family was a distinguished one, with a notable record of service to their people. Alexander's father, a fabulously wealthy businessman, had paid for the gates of the Temple in Jerusalem to be overlaid with gold and silver; his uncle, a philosopher admired even by Greek intellectuals, had written pioneering studies of Judaean law. Alexander himself, however, had opted for a career that was altogether more Roman. Drive and ability had combined to demonstrate just how high, a mere century after the conquest of Egypt, a provincial might climb the rungs of advancement. Alexander had served as governor of Judaea; as an officer under Corbulo; as an ambassador to the court of a barbarian king. Entry into the senate, it was true, had proven a step too far; but it was precisely this lack of senatorial status that had enabled Alexander, even as the bushfires of revolt were starting to blaze in Judaea, to set the crown on a brilliant career: appointment to the rule of neighbouring Egypt.

Some posts, after all, were simply too sensitive to be granted to senators. Indeed, so wealthy was Egypt that they had been banned, ever since the days of Augustus, from so much as setting foot in the province. Alexander's only rival as the highest-ranking equestrian in the empire was the commander of the Praetorians. With his two legions and his ability to throttle Rome's corn supply, the prefect of Egypt was a key player in the great game that Vespasian aspired to play. No one could hope to become Caesar without Alexander's backing. But which way would he jump? On 1 July he announced his decision. Travelling to the great legionary base outside Alexandria, he instructed the two legions stationed there to repudiate their oath of loyalty to Vitellius. Alexander himself, the legionaries under his command, the crowds in Alexandria: all committed themselves with full-throated enthusiasm to a new emperor. The same name was heard on everybody's lips: Vespasian.

Two days later, when news of what had happened in Egypt reached Judaea, and the legions stationed there began to join in the acclamation, there was no longer any need for Yosef ben Mattityahu to remain in chains. The prophecy that he had discerned in the scriptures of his people, and which Vespasian had for two years been brooding over, could be broadcast at last to the world. The one-time rebel against Rome was now the servant of a Caesar. Yosef, a man skilled at tracing the patterns of God's plans in the rhythms of history, knew full well in whose footsteps he was following. Once, in the great city of Babylon, there had been a Judaean by the name of Daniel; and such had been Daniel's talent for reading the future that it had won him his freedom from captivity and the ear of a king. The record of his visions had been preserved in Judaean scripture. In a dream, he had seen a horned beast rise up out of a storm-tossed sea;

and this beast was 'terrible and dreadful and exceedingly strong; and it had great iron teeth; it devoured and broke in pieces, and stamped the residue with its feet'. Ten in number were its horns; but then, as Daniel gazed at them, 'there came up among them another horn, a little one, before which three of the first horns were plucked up by the roots'.[56] Haunting indeed: for what could the vision possibly signify but the very crisis even then convulsing Rome's empire, that great beast, which had devoured and broken all the other kingdoms of the world into pieces? Since the time of Pompey, ten men had claimed its rule; and of these, in the course of only a year, three had followed in quick succession. Who, then, could doubt that Vespasian was destined to triumph over all his foes, that his victory was written in the book of the future, that he was none other than the eleventh horn, 'before which three of the first horns were plucked up by the roots'?

All that summer, the sense of a great reckoning in the dimensions of both the mortal and the divine was palpable. In mid-July, Vespasian met with Mucianus for a council of war. The venue for their meeting, the *colonia* of Berytus – modern-day Beirut – was the most Roman city in the entire East. Settled by generations of retired legionaries, it boasted everything that might make a visitor from Rome feel at home: baths, amphitheatres, a population speaking Latin. Where better for a would-be Caesar to plot a march on the capital? The planning at Berytus that July was for a titanic military effort: a summoning to war of legions from across the Roman world. Mucianus, it was agreed, would lead a task force from Syria and make the provinces he passed through 'ring from end to end with the preparation of ships, troops, and arms'.[57] He would also soak the provincials for cash. Simultaneously, the Balkan legions were to be roused to mutiny. All was to be readied for an invasion of Italy the following year. Vespasian, meanwhile, would remain in the East. Specifically, he intended to winter in Egypt. Here he would prepare for what he trusted would be his final reckoning with Vitellius in the spring. A cool and measured strategist, he saw no point in snatching too rashly after the rule of the world.

Alexandria, the largest city in the empire after Rome itself, was a seat not unworthy of Vespasian's ambitions. Wealthy, sophisticated and touched by the enduring glamour of its founder, Alexander the Great, it ranked as the undisputed capital of the East. From his base in the city, Vespasian could ensure that no corn ships sailed for Rome; that no barbarians menaced Syria; and that no rebels caused undue trouble in Judaea. But he could also benefit from something else. In Alexandria, he could burnish his stature as a man who was more than human. Crude and earthy though Vespasian might be in private, he did not disdain the nimbus of the divine that had begun to attach itself to him. When he went alone into the greatest of all the city's temples, the gods granted him a vision of the prosperity that was to be his. The natives hailed him as a man marked out by destiny as the heir of Alexander. Yosef, brought in his train to Egypt, continued to preach the good news: that the scriptures of his people were being fulfilled, and that a man had emerged from Judaea to claim the rule of the world.

Not that Vespasian was alone in identifying his cause with supernatural purposes. The more that crisis roiled Rome's dominions, so the more did prophecies of a new order threaten to slip his grasp. Everywhere it was being whispered that the gods, who for so long had bestowed their blessings upon the Roman people, had withdrawn their favour. If to the Roman people themselves the prospect of their downfall was naturally a dreadful one, then so it inspired many others, both in the provinces and beyond, to dream wild and fantastical dreams. Back in April, for instance, outside Lugdunum, a Gaul of humble background by the name of Mariccus had won thousands of followers by claiming to be a god. The presence of Vitellius in the city, far from giving him pause, had only encouraged him to preach that the age of Roman rule was at an end. When the Aeduan authorities, alarmed by the spread of this message among their people, had him arrested and handed over to the imperial authorities, he was condemned to be eaten by wild beasts; but the animals would not touch him. True, Vitellius had then had the self-proclaimed king of the

Gauls executed in his own presence; but the readiness of large numbers of provincials to believe that Mariccus had indeed been a god, and had conquered death itself, was an ominous straw in the wind.

Meanwhile, beyond the immediate reach of Roman power, the winds were blowing even stronger. In Germany, for instance, there was no controlling the swirl of prophecies. Many of these were borne specifically on the gusts of the civil war. Rome's agonies had not gone unnoticed on the far side of the Rhine; nor had the withdrawal of large numbers of legionaries from the various bases along the river. On the banks of the Lippe, in the valley that stretched eastwards from Vetera, there stood a tower; and in this tower there lived a seeress. So formidable was her reputation that many of the natives viewed her as divine; and even Romans, who referred to her as Veleda, might well be in awe of her powers. Perched as she was high above the world, she was practised at hearing the future whispered on both gales and breezes. The long years of humiliation suffered by her people were at an end. War was coming to the Rhine. The great bases of the legions were fated to be wiped out from the face of the earth. Such were Veleda's prophecies. Few were permitted to approach her, but this only added to her mystique. Far and wide her words were reported. They were heard deep in the eastern forests of Germany, by peoples who prided themselves on having cast off the Roman yoke; but they were heard as well along the Rhine, in regions where the natives had long since been habituated to Roman ways, where the goods they produced all went to Roman markets, and where young men enlisted as a matter of course in the Roman military.

Auxilia, these soldiers were called: auxiliaries. Even the legions, incomparable as heavy infantry though they were, could not function without the support of cavalry, archers, and lightly armed skirmishers: and so it had long been the practice of Roman commanders to recruit such additional troops as might be needed from among native allies. Augustus, impatient with this ad hoc process, had brought his customary genius for organisation to the task of regularising them. His achievement had been typically subtle. The auxiliaries had been fashioned into a fighting force that complemented the legions without ever rivalling them. Like legionaries, they were professional; but at a third of the rate of pay. Like legionaries, they were arranged into units; but these were each a tenth of a legion's size. Like legionaries, they were well-trained; but not so formidably that they might not, should the state of a campaign require it, be sacrificed to the cause of preserving the legions from danger. To serve as an auxiliary was always to be conscious of a certain inferiority; and this, to be sure, might easily provoke resentment. Certainly, it had never been forgotten by the Roman authorities that the greatest disaster to befall their arms in Germany – the annihilation of Varus' three legions – had been masterminded by a one-time auxiliary commander. Nevertheless, the shadow of this precedent did not fall as darkly as it might have done. Mutinies among auxiliary units were few and far between. The Roman authorities were alert to the hatreds that might exist among their various subjects, and did not hesitate to capitalise on them: this was why the cohorts Florus had commanded during his time in Jerusalem had consisted of Samaritans. Nor was the opportunity for weight-throwing the only perk of service an auxiliary enjoyed. The reward for completing a term of duty was a precious one: Roman citizenship. Its benefits were such that they extended down the generations. Any sons of a barbarian broken to civilisation by service with the auxiliaries would be eligible to serve in the legions. They might gain promotion, become centurions, and retire as people of great eminence. Their sons, in turn, might aspire to even higher status. The perks of rank, the pleasures of wealth: all might very well be theirs. Why, then, should anyone think to jeopardise such a prospect?

In times of peace, there were many incentives for provincials brought under Roman rule to identify with their conquerors. The horizons of a global empire were broad. Peasants might toil in the fields to satisfy the demands of tax-collectors; farmers might dread the confiscation of their pack-animals by passing soldiers; prophets might preach visions of Rome's downfall, and of how the last were destined to be first, and the first last. But these, by the classes who, in provinces across the empire, flourished under Roman rule, and whose prosperity was dependent on its continuance, might easily be ignored. Now, though, in a time of chaos and upheaval, matters were different. Obedience to Caesar was all very well – but what if there were numerous Caesars? Everything then became a gamble. One man's loyalist, after all, was another man's rebel. The welter of assassinations and suicides that, in barely a year, had claimed emperor after emperor, the spectacle of legion slaughtering legion, the sense that the entire fabric of Rome's dominion might be groaning and buckling, threatened to scramble everything. A disorienting possibility had opened up. What if the empire was not, after all, eternal? 'It is the doom of the legions to be wiped out.'[58] Such was the message delivered by Veleda from her tower. She was not alone, of course, in issuing such a forecast. Variations on the theme had been circulating in the eastern provinces of the empire for decades. Never before, though, had they seemed quite so urgent. The more that people were tempted to believe in such prophecies, the greater the likelihood of open rebellion; and the greater the likelihood of open rebellion, the more the local elites were obliged to wrestle with split loyalties. Should they stick with a Roman order that had long buttressed their own fortunes, or throw caution to the winds, and seek to carve out a new status for themselves? The stakes could hardly be higher. It was, for everyone, a fearsome choice.

Any who doubted this had only to look to Judaea. There, three years on from the onset of the great revolt, there were still men and women who hoped to square their identity as Judaeans with their loyalty to Rome. Vespasian, heading to Berytus for his council of war with Mucianus, had summoned the highest-ranking of them all to join him. Marcus Julius Agrippa was – despite his Roman name – the great-grandson of Judaea's most celebrated king. Herod the Great, a brutal but slippery survivor much admired by both Antony and Augustus, had richly deserved his renown. Seventy years after his death, Judaea remained stamped by his relish for showy building projects. Herod it was who had rebuilt the Temple in Jerusalem, a decades-long programme of construction designed to showcase his piety, rally Judaean support for his regime, and immortalise his name. Simultaneously, he had displayed a rare talent for collaboration. He had raised temples to Augustus; graced Jerusalem with a theatre, a hippodrome, and various other monuments fit to impress any visiting Roman; and commissioned a stupefying harbour which he had named — with typical smoothness — Caesarea. No reach of Judaea was so lonely that it might not bear the mark of his genius for reconciling the Judaean with the Roman. Deep in the badlands south of Jerusalem, for instance, on the summit of a sheer mountain, there stood a fortress named Masada; and inside this fortress Herod had built two palaces. The interior decoration of these twin complexes was a pointed fusion: mosaics adorned with fruits and flowers, symbols of the divine favour that had graced the Judaeans with their homeland, paired with wall-paintings that would not have disgraced the Palatine. Certainly, no one could have doubted, visiting Masada, that it was possible for a Judaean ruler to serve both his god and Caesar.

Yet it was the measure, perhaps, of just how skilfully Herod had walked a tightrope that no one, in the wake of his death, had been found to replace him. The Roman authorities, slicing and dicing his kingdom, had never quite been able to decide how it should best be administered. Even as its central core had been reconstituted as a province, ruled directly from Rome, so had various other portions been divided up between Herod's heirs. The authority of Agrippa — who ruled a patchwork of lands to the north and east of Judaea — was, compared to that of his great-grandfather, a spectral thing. Although he had been vested by Claudius with responsibility for ensuring the proper management of the Temple, he had never had any troops stationed in Jerusalem, nor had the city been a part of his sovereign kingdom. Chains of command, as a result, had become hopelessly entangled. Nothing quite like the confusion of it existed anywhere else in the empire. It had long seemed, in Jerusalem, that the city had not one but two masters: the Roman governor and Agrippa.

It was the king, in the febrile, fatal months before Judaea exploded into open revolt, who had taken the lead in attempting to broker a compromise between Florus and the radicals pushing for insurrection. Or rather, it had been his sister, Berenice: a much-married princess darkly rumoured to be the mistress of Agrippa himself, but whose presence in Jerusalem had been due reflection of her piety and devotion to the god of her people. Barefoot and at risk of her own life she had stood before Florus, begging him to show restraint, but in vain. Agrippa, joining his sister in Jerusalem shortly afterwards, had also sought to reconcile his countrymen to the continuance of Roman rule; but they had only stoned him and proclaimed his banishment. Leaving the city for the last time, Agrippa had done so in tears. 'Only with the help of God can you possibly hope to win – and that will never come, since it is evident, from the sheer scale of their empire, that He is already on the side of the Romans.'[59]

This prophecy, uttered a year after Nero's suicide, was one that many Judaeans could legitimately doubt. To people praying for a miracle, the spectacle of the rulers of the world tearing themselves to pieces had a particular resonance. Vespasian, whose repression of the revolt had initially been so remorseless, had not only halted his campaigning, but actually left Judaea for Egypt. In Jerusalem, in Masada – where refugees had fled in the earliest days of the uprising – and in a couple of other fortresses still in rebel hands, people raised their prayers and dared to hope. In the sky, ghostly armies dazzled onlookers with the blaze of their weapons; in Jerusalem, the Temple periodically seemed lit by heavenly fire. No one doubted that these wonders portended a mighty reckoning. The prophecies that Yosef ben Mattityahu had interpreted as applying to Vespasian were understood very differently by the rebels. Repeatedly in their scriptures, Judaeans could read of an age when a kingdom of righteousness was destined to emerge, and when the foreign rulers, in all their arrogance, would be smashed like a potter's vessel. God's Anointed, a prince, was destined to come: his 'Messiah'. This *Christos* (so Greek-speaking Judaeans translated the title) would be no Caesar.

Rather, he would restore Jerusalem to the status it had enjoyed back in ancient times, when the Temple had first been built and the city had ranked as the capital of a mighty kingdom: Israel. 'With justice he will give decisions for the poor of the earth. He will strike the earth with the rod of his mouth; with the breath of his lips he will slay the wicked.'[60]

Assurances like these had long furnished Judaeans with hope. Many, unsurprisingly, yearned to believe that their fulfilment was at hand. As in Gaul, so in Judaea: self-proclaimed prophets had arisen and won themselves many disciples. One, 'a charlatan named Theudas', had told his followers to follow him to a river named the Jordan, on the promise that he would part its waters and lead them to the far side; another, a man known as 'the Egyptian', had emerged from out of the desert at the head of several thousand supporters, and sought to bring down the walls of Jerusalem with a single word of command. Neither had caused the provincial authorities undue alarm. Both had been easily routed; both had been briskly put to death. Not that it was only the Romans who despised such men as frauds. So too did many Judaeans. Priests in particular were deeply suspicious of men from beneath their own class who modelled themselves on ancient prophets, set themselves in opposition to Roman rule, and claimed a particular closeness to God. They were charlatans, magicians, frauds. Yet what, in the final reckoning, had the revolt against Rome been, the uprising against the terrible and dreadful beast with its great iron teeth, if not the expression of a belief very similar to that held by Theudas or the Egyptian? Agrippa, warning the people of Jerusalem that without divine assistance their rebellion was doomed, had been speaking from the heart. Unless, indeed, the appointed time was at hand, when all the peoples of the world were destined to be brought under the yoke of the God of Israel, and the new wine to dry up, and the leopard to lie down with the goat, then nothing would be sufficient to spare their city from annihilation.

This was why Yosef, even as his former comrades reviled him as a traitor, never doubted that by serving the cause of the Romans he was serving the cause of his own people as well. During his term of command in Galilee, he had experienced for himself just how bitterly divided the region's inhabitants were. There were many, out in the wilds of the countryside, who profoundly resented foreign rule, who feared the spread of alien customs, who might go so far as to boycott Roman plates, or cookware, or lamps; but there were others, particularly in Sepphoris, Galilee's largest city, who had offered their surrender to Vespasian even before his army had taken the field. Local landowners, eager to exploit the chaos of the times, had raised private armies, showing themselves quite as ready to turn on one another as on the Romans. The boundary between freedom-fighter and bandit repeatedly seemed to blur.

Even before the arrival of Vespasian's legions in Galilee, the fields had been littered with corpses. Smoke had drifted above burning farms. Then the Romans had come. The horror of it still lived with Yosef. Although his time in the countryside had been miserable, he had not been oblivious to its beauties, and had marvelled at how, along the banks of the lake in the heart of Galilee, 'the soil is so wonderfully fertile that not a plant there fails to flourish':[61] walnuts and palms, figs and olives, grapes and wildflowers. Even the Sea of Galilee, however, had ended up a butcher's shambles. Fugitives from the legions, taking to fishing boats and rafts, had been hunted by the Romans; and such was the slaughter that the blood and viscera of the slain had come to dye the entire lake red. The beaches had been strewn with swollen carcasses, clammy and rotten in the sun. The stench of it had reached to the heavens.

That such a fate might be visited on the Temple was a prospect not to be borne. Vespasian, for all that his gaze was fixed on Italy, had not forgotten Judaea. The prosecution of the war against the Judaeans had been entrusted to Titus, his able, ambitious and smoulderingly charismatic son. The force at his back was a formidable one, for in addition to the army his father had previously commanded, Titus had been given XII Fulminata, 'a legion which hungered to avenge

the defeat it had previously suffered at the hands of the Judaeans'[62] –
and a host of other forces besides. There was little reason to doubt
that the Romans would treat the rebels in Jerusalem, should they fail
to surrender, just as they had treated the rebels in Galilee.

Yet this did not mean that the Temple was doomed to burn.
Yosef himself, devout in the worship of his god even as he followed
in Titus' train, could offer himself as living evidence that there was
no necessary contradiction between being a Judaean and submitting
to Caesar. He could point as well to the intimate links between the
Roman high command and Agrippa. Julius Alexander, who had
been appointed to serve Titus as his deputy, had once been Berenice's
brother-in-law. Berenice herself had embarked on a passionate affair
with Titus. Intimacy between Judaeans and Romans was certainly
possible. Yosef, clinging to this assurance, felt no shame at his role as
a collaborator with the Romans. It was the devout, the patriotic, the
properly Judaean thing to do. Only the rebels' submission, after all,
would enable the Temple, and Jerusalem with it, to be spared. The
empire might indeed seem to be tottering; but Yosef, that battle-
scarred veteran of the war for Galilee, still had no doubt that the
Judaean revolt was doomed. The fundamental law which for so long
had governed relations between the peoples of the world still held.
No peace was ever on offer except a peace on Roman terms.

III

A WORLD AT WAR

We Who Are About to Die

Autumn in Italy was a time of ease. The fields were harvested, the apples picked from the orchards, the vats filled and foaming with the juice of sun-warmed grapes. 'Ripe and mellow, the season no longer blazes with the passions of youth: for now that autumn has come, the year is poised midway between youth and old age, and its hair is streaked with grey.'[1] Farmers could spend their time singing, dancing, enjoying the fruit of their labours. Oxen could rest in their stalls. Soldiers, as the evenings drew in and the south wind brought squalls of rain gusting across fields and hills, could afford to relax: for the campaigning season was over.

Or was it? Ever since the first proclamation of Vitellius as emperor, the times had been in disorder. The rhythms of the year were out of kilter. Caecina, who had raised the banner of mutiny on the very first day of January, who had led his troops to war in the depths of winter, who had crossed the Alps while the passes were still covered with snow, had blazed a particularly notable trail. In the Balkans, where the legions seethed with loathing for Vitellius, most of the officers had been content to follow the recommendation of Vespasian: that they should await the arrival of Mucianus and his task force, and prepare to invade Italy in the spring. One legate, however, impatient with this advice, had been eager to emulate Caecina and risk a winter campaign. Marcus Antonius Primus had been appointed by Galba to the command of VII Galbiana: a legion recruited only the previous year by Galba himself. Fiercely devoted to their imperial patron, the

113

soldiers of VII Galbiana had accompanied him from Spain, done much of the killing that had accompanied his entry into Rome, and then, one month later, been posted to a station of honour on the Danube. Unsurprisingly, their loyalty to Galba's successor was shaky in the extreme. In their legate they had a commander more than ready to take advantage of their resentment and urge on them the course of insurrection.

Antonius, a beak-nosed aristocrat of commanding presence and imposing physique, was ideally suited by his talents to a time of crisis. Peace had seen him sent into exile as a convicted fraudster; war had seen Galba award him his Danubian command in the province known by the Romans as Pannonia. Like Caecina, he was ferociously ambitious; like Caecina, he had a fondness for cutting corners; like Caecina, he yearned to cut a dash on the great stage of the world, and not to moulder for ever on the banks of some distant and barbarous river. A natural demagogue, he had found it a simple matter to override the reservations of his fellow legates. By late August, he had come to stand at the head of a host of legions drawn from across the Balkans; by September, he had launched a full-scale invasion of Italy; and by early October, he had seized control of Verona, a city which – no less than Cremona – constituted a key strategic hub. Caecina, dispatched northwards by a frantic Vitellius to oppose this onslaught, could hardly help but be impressed. As he advanced from Rome, all the reports reaching him cast Antonius as a commander cut from his own cloth.

Certainly, the contrast with Vitellius seemed a marked one. Caecina, after months spent in the company of the man he had done so much to raise to greatness, had come to share in the emperor's own self-estimation: that he was simply too torpid, too indecisive for the job. His entire regime was rotten with a lack of purpose. Assorted favourites pandered shamelessly to their master's appetites, squandering fortunes that the treasury could ill afford. Valens, Caecina's partner in the great venture that had brought Vitellius to the throne, and his bitterest rival, lay sick. Even the legionaries, as they marched northwards to confront Antonius, lacked the steel-forged discipline that had been their hallmark on the Rhine: a summer spent scattered across the capital had badly impaired their cohesion and morale. To Caecina, as he advanced on Verona, met the enemy south of the city, and clashed with them indecisively, it seemed that he was facing the man he himself had been, and the army he had led, only a few months before. The reflection plunged him into despair. It also decided him on a fateful course. Twice already he had betrayed a Caesar. Now, ever ready as he was to cast off his loyalties, and contemptuous of the emperor he had left behind in Rome, he prepared to do so once again.

On 18 October, Caecina sent the various legions under his command out of the camp on manoeuvres. Only the senior centurions, and certain hand-picked legionaries, were ordered to stay behind. Summoned to Caecina's headquarters, these men listened in astonishment as their commander urged them to abandon their oath of loyalty to Vitellius, jump ship, and side with the Flavians. No matter that their camp was well protected by marshes on its flanks and a river in its rear, that they had eight legions in the field, that they were yet to lose so much as a skirmish, Caecina succeeded in winning his audience round. The portraits of Vitellius were sent toppling. The name of Vespasian was inscribed on the standards. Then, towards evening, V Alaudae returned. Contemptuous as the Larks were of the forces ranged against them, and proud of their own long and distinguished record of service, they reacted with fury to any suggestion that they should merely go over to the enemy. An eclipse that stained the moon the colour of blood seemed a fitting image of their commander's treachery. Still sufficiently respectful of Caecina not to put him to death, they nevertheless loaded him down with chains. Then, with the backing of the other legions, the Larks picked their own legate as his temporary replacement and prepared to evacuate the camp. The plan was to withdraw to Cremona: that mighty stronghold of their cause, and a city to which Caecina had already sent two legions as an advance guard. There they would be able to await the arrival of Valens: for Caecina's great rival, alerted to his erstwhile colleague's treachery, was reported to have roused himself from his sickbed and left Rome with reinforcements. So it was, breaking the bridges behind them as they went, that the Vitellians made for a destination calculated to stiffen their morale: the site of the crushing victory they had won only six months before.

Meanwhile, in Antonius' camp, there were soldiers who could also find inspiration in their memories of the battle. The men of XIII Gemina nurtured a particular grudge. The emblem of their legion's record of service — one that reached all the way back to Caesar's conquest of Gaul — was the lion: that fiercest and most kingly of beasts. Yet their punishment, in the wake of Otho's defeat, had been a humiliating one. Lions had been treated as donkeys. Caecina, rather than cashiering them or sending them back to Pannonia, had set them to work as builders. True, there was, for a legion, nothing inherently degrading about this. Soldiers were supposed to be handy with tools. 'Picks win wars' — so Corbulo had put it.[2] Camps and roads did not just materialise by magic, after all. The men of XIII Gemina, however, had not been put to building a camp or a road. Instead — as the citizens of Cremona, jeering the soldiers as they laboured at their task, had taken great pleasure in pointing out — they had been put to improving the civic amenities of the city. Specifically, they had been put to building an amphitheatre.

Any Roman city with pretensions to greatness had to have one. The word — 'a space that can be viewed from both sides', it literally meant — derived from Greek, but the design was all Italian. No other style of monument was more distinctively Roman. To have one was to boast a stage fit for a Caesar. Vitellius, travelling through Gaul from the Rhine, would never have used Lugdunum to proclaim his dynastic ambitions had it been the kind of city to lack an amphitheatre. *Spectacula*, the Romans had originally called such a structure: a place for putting on a spectacle. The spectacle itself was twofold. There was the show staged in the arena; and there was the show provided by the sponsor of the entertainments, a demonstration of splendour and munificence calculated to stupefy all who beheld it. Spectaculars, of course, were expensive, just as the infrastructure necessary to host them was expensive: which was why, across most of Gaul, amphitheatres were few and far between. Equally, it was why in Lugdunum, a city that cast itself as the capital of all the Gallic provinces, tribal leaders had been desperate to build one. The man who had paid for it, an aristocrat from Aquitaine, had been a priest of the altar to Rome and Augustus; and in AD 19, when the amphitheatre was inaugurated, he had made sure to let everyone know it. No structure in the whole of Gaul was less provincial; no structure in the whole of Gaul more truly Roman. Vitellius, though still many days distant from the capital when he arrived in Lugdunum, had been able to stage shows in the city's arena and feel that, by doing so, he was introducing himself to the world. A spectacular indeed.

True, it was the nature of live entertainment that it might some-times go wrong. The refusal of wild beasts to touch Mariccus, the Gallic rebel sentenced to the arena, had been a particular embarrass-ment. Jeopardy, however, was precisely what made the experience of attending an amphitheatre so thrilling. The less a show was scripted, the more exciting spectators were likely to find it. Executions – for all the civic lesson that they taught – were the least popular of the attractions staged in an amphitheatre precisely because they so rarely served up surprises. Entertaining though it might be to watch lions or bears devour a criminal loaded down with chains, how much more so was it to watch them pitched against huntsmen. Even this, however, tended not to be the biggest draw. Top of the bill was invariably the pairing of warriors, the one against the other. Nothing provided more drama, nothing generated more excitement, than spectacles of armed combat. When fans flocked to an amphitheatre, it was above all to watch contests between well-trained and proficient fighters, stars at the very top of their game, men sworn by their own ferocious version of the *sacramentum* to endure fire, chains, the whip and the sword: gladiators.

The origins of the obsession were venerable. Bouts between armed men had first been staged in Rome as *munera*: offerings to the shades of the departed. Over the course of the centuries, the funerals of distinguished men had come to be marked by fights between ever greater numbers of pairs of gladiators. The makeshift amphitheatres erected in the Forum to host these *munera* had grown in size and extravagance. Caesar, staging games to propitiate the ghost of his father, had set 320 pairs of gladiators to fight one another, all of them arrayed in silver armour. His enemies, painfully aware how likely this was to boost his appeal, had sought to regulate such displays of extravagance as tightly as they could; but the effort had been hopeless. The collapse of the republic had made sure of that. Once Augustus was secure in his supremacy, he had been free to stage extravaganzas beyond the dreams of previous generations. No expense had been spared 'to fill the hearts and eyes of the Roman people with unforgettable spectacles'.[3] One in particular, jaw-dropping in its scale, had featured ten thousand gladiators. *Munera*, once staged to keep the dead at bay, had come to serve as an essential prop of the new regime. The Roman people, greedy for ever more eye-popping entertainments, had looked to the emperor to provide them; and the emperor, in his role as benefactor to his fellow citizens, had made sure to oblige. Nero, unsurprisingly, had raised the bar to particularly stupefying heights. Even men 'doddery with age, hoary-headed, grown old in the city',[4] had confessed themselves amazed by his games. This was why, for Vitellius, the staging of *munera* at Lugdunum had been quite as important a demonstration of his new rank as the parading of his victorious legions or the proclamation of his dynasty. No one could lay claim to the rule of Rome and fail to serve up gladiators.

Even so, an emperor had to tread carefully. To stage games before the gaze of the world was potentially a perilous business. Pitfalls lurked everywhere. This was especially so in a time of civil war. Vitellius, travelling from Lugdunum to Cremona, had arrived there to find its amphitheatre freshly completed. Naturally, he had made sure to inaugurate it: a mark of gratitude both to the people of Cremona and to Caecina, who had furnished the gladiators. Yet the setting had been as haunted by the spirits of the dead as the very first *munera* had been all those centuries before. Games were not normally staged next to a battlefield littered with the corpses of legionaries. Indeed, moralists approved of gladiatorial combat precisely because it reminded citizens softened by peace, unfamiliar with arms, far distant from scenes of war, of what it took for Rome to rule the world. Unlike theatrical entertainments, which were self-evidently corrupting and enfeebling, *munera* served to harden those who watched them. Yet Vitellius, listening to the roar of the crowds, sharing in their sense of excitement, had drawn the wrong conclusion. It was presiding in the amphitheatre that had inspired him to visit the scene of carnage beyond the city; and there, rather than reflecting with sorrow on the vast numbers of his fellow citizens who lay rotting in the summer heat, he had behaved as a fan might have done at the games, giddy with delight at the slaughter. Vitellius had signally failed to propitiate the shades of the dead. Instead, he had offered them only insult.

And now, six months after their dispatch to the realm of the sad and infernal gods, the time was nearing, perhaps, for them to claim vengeance. Unbeknown to the Vitellians, the Flavians were heading for Cremona too. Antonius, informed that the enemy force camped south of Verona had abandoned its base, and was nowhere to be found, had decided – rather than go blundering around northern Italy in search of it – to target a different adversary. The two legions Caecina had sent to garrison Cremona had seemed too tempting a quarry not to hunt down, isolate and eliminate. Accordingly, riding at the head of four thousand cavalry, five legions and assorted cohorts of auxiliaries, Antonius had left Verona. Like Caecina, he was a man forever in a hurry. The pace he set was a furious one. After two days of hard marching, he and his men arrived at a village called Bedriacum, some twenty miles east of Cremona. This, six months previously, was where Otho's legions had made their base; and it was where the Flavians now set up camp. The legionaries dug ditches, threw up ramparts, and raised palisades; then caught their breath. Not Antonius, however. At the head of his horsemen, he went for an exploratory canter down the road that led to Cremona. Here it was – to the mutual surprise of both forces – that he blundered into the Vitellians. Like the Flavians, they had made remarkable speed. Like the Flavians, they were startled to discover that all along they had been in a race. Now, at last, the two adversaries were face to face. The contest, long brewing, had come to a head.

It was the morning of 24 October. As the sun climbed in the sky, so the rival vanguards clashed. The fortunes of battle swung this way and that. First, Antonius and his horsemen were stampeded back towards Bedriacum; then, making a stand beside a river, they succeeded in blocking the enemy advance and forced the Flavian cavalry in turn to retreat. Meanwhile, both sides had been summoning reinforcements. By late afternoon, all the Vitellian legions – the two originally stationed in Cremona included – had taken up position in the fields outside the city. Opposite them, the Flavian legions, marching up the road from Bedriacum, were also massing. Among them was XIII Gemina. The same legionaries who had toiled at building the amphitheatre for the people of Cremona now stood before the city of their tormentors, spears and swords at the ready, braced for combat. The Cremonans had wanted to stage great spectacles of slaughter. Now they were to get their wish: a spectacle of slaughter that threatened not just the rival combatants, but the audience as well.

Already, to astute observers, it was becoming clear that soldiers and gladiators, in a time of civil war, might easily seem indistinguishable. Back in the spring, during the first round of fighting at Cremona, one of Otho's partisans had employed a force of two thousand gladiators against Caecina; Vitellius, approaching Rome with his victorious legions, had sought 'to bulk them up as though they were fighters in the arena'.[5] Never before, however, had the elision between the gladiator and the legionary, between the arena and the battlefield, between entertainment and the terrifyingly serious business of warfare, appeared quite so unsettling as it did that October evening to the people of Cremona. All of them understood the stakes. Standing on the walls of their city, they could see the watch fires of the rival armies. It was as though the entire world had become an amphitheatre – and they, like the soldiers preparing for battle, were trapped in the arena.

The sun set. A couple of hours passed. Clumsily at first, falteringly, but then with escalating savagery, the rival legions engaged. Gladiators were not permitted to refuse combat; nor, in similar manner, had the Vitellians taken the sensible option of retreating into Cremona for the night, and leaving the Flavians to shiver out in the open. Instead, swept with confused alarms of struggle and flight, the fields beyond the city became a hellish scene of slaughter. There was no one battle, just a succession of ragged but murderous engagements. The Vitellians had various advantages: numbers that were more than a match for the Flavians; lethal artillery; supplies that could be brought to them throughout the night by the women of Cremona. Yet the Flavians refused to yield. The moon blazed in their rear, magnifying their shadows and disconcerting their opponents; a suicide mission took out the Vitellian artillery; Antonius, making his way from legion to legion and tirelessly urging them on, proved far more effective a commander than the makeshift generals on the other side. The hours passed. The sky to the east began to lighten. Antonius, alert to the mood of his adversaries, sensed that their morale was fraying. Then, as the sun rose, so too did a rumour: that Mucianus and his legions were approaching. Antonius seized his chance. Hurling his last reserves into the fray, he hit the enemy with everything he had; and at last the Vitellians broke.

Even now, however, the rout was not total. Although many of the fugitives fell on the road that led back to Cremona, many did not. Some reached the legionary base on the eastern flank of the city; others took shelter within the city itself. Like a gladiator brought to his knees, but resolved not to bare his throat to his adversary, the legionaries who had sworn the *sacramentum* to Vitellius, and fought so hard to win him the rule of the world, now refused to abandon him. The officers felt less commitment to their oath. Once the legionary base had finally been stormed, after a desperate and pulverising struggle, and the Flavian artillery began to target the city walls, they knew the game was up. Their opponents, if they did not surrender, would be given licence by the rules of war to storm the city, level it to the ground, and slaughter all its defenders – and where was the profit in that? The men on both sides of the terrible conflict were, after all, fellow citizens. The ideals of peacetime still counted for something. That this was so had been evident even amid the confusion of battle: there were some among the Vitellians, brought food by the women of Cremona, who had shared it with friends of theirs in the Flavian ranks, crying out in distress, as they did so, 'What are we doing here, why are we fighting?'[6]

Once the members of the high command had resolved to lay down arms, their first port of call was Caecina. Releasing him from his chains, they begged for his help in negotiating with the Flavians; but Caecina, smug as only a man proven to have made the right call could be, turned them down. Left with no choice but to offer an unconditional surrender, the Vitellian commanders duly hung olive branches from the battlements; then, once the artillery fire had ceased, they marched out disconsolately through the city gates. At first they were jostled and jeered by the Flavians, but it did not take long for emotions of fellow-feeling to assert themselves. Terrible dispatches had been received from the front. Worst was the story of a legionary from VII Galbiana who had cut down a man from XXI Rapax during the rout that followed the battle, but who then, gazing at the dying soldier, had realised, to his horror, that it was his own father. The news of this, for all the lamentations and curses it provoked among the Flavian ranks, had done nothing to check the violence of the fighting. Now, however, with the surrender formalised, a great yearning to see the wounds of civil war bound up swept both sides. Even Caecina, whose role in the recent cycles of slaughter had been such a prominent one, helped contribute to the healing process – for when he emerged from Cremona, resplendent in the finery of his office, surrounded by guards, and confident in the service he had done the Flavians, he was roundly booed by both sides. Antonius, stepping in to keep him from being manhandled, sent him onwards to Alexandria, there to report the news of the battle to Vespasian and claim his reward for jumping ship. Caecina, with his gambler's instinct, had made another winning bet.

That the horrors of fratricidal strife might work to the advantage of those bold and ruthless enough to profit from them had never been forgotten. Although Augustus' regime had ended an age of civil war, it had been bred of it as well. Over all the convulsions of the past year, all the upheavals that had seen emperor succeed emperor, and the fields of Cremona fertilised by blood, an ominous question had hung: what if a new Augustus were never to emerge? Fires once started might not easily be put out. Dread of this possibility, that Rome might be turned to ashes, and horsemen strike the city with clattering hooves, had long been stamped on the Forum itself. At the base of the Capitol, there rose a flight of steps known as the Stairs of Mourning; and next to these steps there stood a temple to the goddess Concordia. She it was who had enabled the Roman people to live in harmony with one another during their rise to greatness and to win themselves the rule of the world. Always, though, they had understood that she had her shadow. Discordia had no temple, for she existed only to destroy. Given the chance, she would shatter the iron-covered doors that kept strife otherwise immured; let violence rule the streets; unleash civil war. Once already, in the terrible decades that had preceded Augustus' reign, she had done this; and only by a titanic effort had the doors been barred again. Now, with Discordia loose a second time, there was a desperate need for one of the warlords competing to rule as Caesar not just to triumph, but to triumph by stamping out all the flames of war. For otherwise the whole world might burn.

After Antonius received the Vitellian surrender, he went to the bath-house, as though to wash away the filth and blood of war. Stepping into the water, he complained that it was tepid. 'Not to worry,' he added, 'it will soon be hot enough.'[7] And so it would be.

Soldiers in his train, hearing Antonius' comment, took it to mean what they wanted it to mean: that Cremona should be put to the torch. Word spread, and the legions began to force their way into the city. Neither Antonius nor any other officer was able to restrain them. The hunger for gold, sex and vengeance was too great. Only after four days of plundering, rape and slaughter had the legionaries finally had their fill. By that time, nothing remained of Cremona save a single temple. A city that had stood for 286 years, and long served the Roman people as a bulwark against their foes, had been wiped from the face of the earth. Its very soil was left so polluted that the legions had to abandon the site. The shame felt by Antonius and the rest of the Flavian high command did nothing to bring the city back. Rather, it highlighted the mortal danger in which Rome and its empire now stood: that a commander might urge his men to sheathe their swords, and still the swords would flash.

Batavian Foam

There was no reach of the Roman world so remote that it might not be touched by the shocks of the age. Even on the shores of the northern sea, where everything was mud, their impact could be felt: a great sucking pull, like the brown and icy tides that daily retreated from the mouths of the Rhine delta. Just as the line of the river marked where civilisation and barbarism met and mingled, so were the plains that bordered its lowest reaches neither truly land nor water, but an indeterminate dimension comprising both. Cattle cropped grass amid estuaries so broad that they might as well have been the sea. Lakes were dotted with oaks torn up from the shore during floods, 'sailing upright through the water, with huge islands of soil trapped between their roots'.[8] Here was a glimpse of the chaos that had once existed before the separation of the elements: a reminder of the confusion that awaited humanity were civilisation to collapse.

Roman efforts to order this watery and barbarous realm had been strenuous. Corbulo had led them. Prior to his appointment to the command in Armenia he had served as governor of Lower Germany. Predictably, he had set his men to digging. A canal was excavated, joining the Rhine to the river Meuse some twenty miles to the south, 'thereby sparing people the risks of making the journey by sea'.[9] New roads were constructed, new forts. Just as the drear flatlands required taming, so too did the barbarians who lurked among them. North of the Rhine, settled around a great inland lake, were a people called the Chaukians, who seemed, to a degree startling even to seasoned observers, closer to creatures of the sea than to men. They lived on stilts or artificial mounds perched above the high-water mark, 'so that when the tide sweeps over the surrounding land, they look like seafarers, and when the tide withdraws, like ship-wrecks'.[10] They dug mud with their bare hands, drank nothing but rainwater, and subsisted on seals and the eggs of seabirds. Periodically, setting sail in ships made from dug-out tree trunks, they would launch raids on the coast of Gaul, until Corbulo, employing a mixture of armed force and targeted assassinations, succeeded in pacifying the whole area. The lesson once taught, he had pulled his forces back to the Rhine. Where was the value to Rome, after all, in ruling a wasteland of mud?

Nevertheless, the peoples of the northern sea were not without their uses. Settled on a great island in the Rhine delta were the Batavians: a Germanic people who, since their transplantation there back in the early days of Roman rule, had come to enjoy a special renown. In part this was due to the popularity of their hair products: for 'Batavian foam', a soap compounded of ashes and fat, not only cleaned hair but — to the delight of fashion-setters back in Rome — lightened it. Chiefly, however, the fame of Batavia was due to a quite different export: its young men. Subject to Roman rule though the Batavians might be, they were spared the humiliation of paying taxes. Instead, to a degree unique among the various Germanic peoples who lived on the western banks of the Rhine, they had been encour- aged to maintain their fondness for battle, and to serve the Romans just as weapons or armour served them: 'as tools of war, and nothing else'.[11] The Batavians, unlike other auxiliaries, were commanded by their own chieftains; and these, for all that they ranked as Roman citizens and sported Roman names, maintained a pride in their native traditions that had long since faded among the aristocracies of Gaul. Like bulls bred for the arena, the Batavians exhibited a strain of wildness that, in the opinion of their Roman patrons, was precisely what rendered them so distinctive and valuable.

Fit, in fact, to protect a Caesar. There had been no more striking measure of the reputation the Batavians enjoyed than their employment as bodyguards by Augustus and his successors. Only with Nero's death had this tradition finally ended – for Galba, suspicious of the Batavians' loyalty to the extinguished imperial dynasty, had disbanded them and sent them packing. Service in the capital, however, was not the only opportunity they had to demonstrate their worth. Their record on campaign was viewed even by seasoned legionaries with awe. There was no one quite like a Batavian for crossing a swollen river with his horse and in full armour. A recent battle, during the invasion of Britain, had won them the particular admiration of Vespasian, for their prowess as swimmers had enabled them to ambush an army of natives on the far bank, establish a bridgehead, and assist the legate in securing a decisive victory. Nor was even this the limit of their talents. A favourite trick was to shoot an arrow, and then, 'while it hung in the air, hit and split it with another'.[12] Martial ferocity, an ability to swim like frogs, and expertise with firearms: here were capabilities rarely combined. The Batavians were the auxiliaries that every Roman commander wanted in his ranks.

All of which, in the early months of the civil war, had been good news for Vitellius. The Batavians, already alienated by Galba, had rallied to his cause. That spring, eight cohorts of them had played a key role in the defeat of Otho's legions at Cremona, holding the right wing and outflanking I Adiutrix. This contribution notwithstanding, however, they were not popular with their comrades. Ever since the beginning of the campaign to make Vitellius emperor, they had been rubbing the legions the wrong way. The chains of command

The sad and infernal gods: Pluto, the king of the dead, flanked on the left by Proserpina, the goddess he raped and abducted to the underworld, and on the right by Ceres, Proserpina's mother. (linari/Bridgeman Images)

Soldiers from the Praetorian Guard, the military garrison stationed in the capital. Responsible as they were for the security of Caesar, they repeatedly showed themselves capable of swaying the very fate of Rome. (Tom Holland)

Four emperors ruled in the fateful year of AD 69: Galba . . .

. . . Otho . . .

... Vitellius ...

... Vespasian.

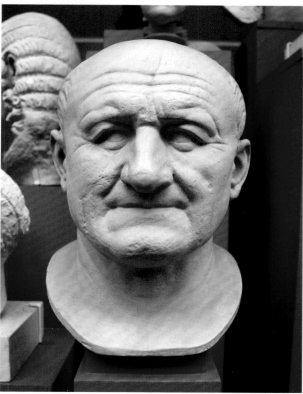

The tombstone of a centurion. He is shown wielding a vine rod, the symbol of his authority over the men under his command. Discipline, the Romans knew, was what had enabled them to conquer the world. (Archaeo Images/Alamy Stock Photo)

A coin issued by Otho and then, after his death, stamped with Vespasian's mark. (Tom Holland)

Legionaries in battle. The relief dates from the Flavian period, and featured on a pedestal erected in the great military base of Mogontiacum (modern-day Mainz), on the Rhine. (GDKE-Landesmuseum Mainz (Ursula Rudischer))

The death of Vitellius. (Wikipedia (Creator: Georges Antoine Rochegrosse))

The Temple of Jerusalem: part of a scale model of the city besieged and destroyed by the Romans in 70. (Wikipedia Creative Commons)

The great menorah looted from the Temple and paraded through the streets of Rome during the triumph celebrated by Vespasian and Titus. (Zev Radovan/Alamy Stock Photo)

IUDAEA CAPTA. Flavian propagandists never wearied of harping on the victory won by Vespasian and Titus over the Judaeans. (GRANGER - Historical Picture Archive/Alamy Stock Photo)

Pompeii. Vesuvius looms in the background. (Sophie Hay)

The tomb of Gnaeus Nigidius Maius, the grand old man of Pompeian politics. Erected just outside one of the city gates, it boasted an inscription listing in detail his many achievements and benefactions. (Sophie Hay)

Gladiators in the arena, as portrayed on Maius' tomb. (Sophie Hay)

that under normal circumstances served to maintain the military pecking order, and in particular the subordination of auxiliaries to legionaries, had started to fray. Naturally prone to bragging, the Batavian cohorts had become increasingly bumptious. Vitellius, who originally had been planning to take them to Rome, was appalled to discover the full scale of their unruliness. Concerned as well to replenish troop numbers on the Rhine, he had duly ordered them home. The wisdom of this decision was made clear during an incident in Turin, when the Batavians had got into a brawl with the fourteenth legion, and the entire city had only narrowly avoided being burnt to the ground. Deep were the sighs of relief among the members of the Vitellian high command when the Batavian cohorts were reported to have arrived in Mogontiacum. There, at least, on the margins of the world, they could do little harm.

But then the Flavian onslaught had begun, and Vitellius, in a panic, had sent a frantic message to the Batavian cohorts, ordering them back to Italy. They had set out, but they were destined never to arrive. Messengers from the Rhine brought news to the capital that, devastating though it was, would not, perhaps, have come as a total surprise to fashionistas and their hairdressers. Every woman who used Batavian foam knew the score. There was always the risk – an exceedingly slight one, but a real one, nevertheless – that the soap, rather than dyeing the hair a fetching shade of blonde, might singe it, and destroy it, and leave the user bald. Now, to the consternation of Vitellius and his command, it seemed that the military authorities on the Rhine were facing an analogous disaster. The Batavians, it was reported, had risen in revolt. Forts along the Rhine estuary had been put to the torch. An entire fleet, manned by Batavian rowers, had deserted to the rebels. The remnants of V Alaudae and XV Primigenia, all the legionaries stationed at Vetera who had not marched earlier in the year to Italy, had been defeated in open battle. Vetera itself lay under siege. And how had the rebels come by sufficient manpower to bottle up an entire legionary base? The answer to that particular question hit Vitellius like a punch to his ample stomach. Prominent among the forces camped out around Vetera were none other than the reinforcements he had been banking on to come to his rescue: the eight cohorts of Batavian auxiliaries.

Here, for anyone nervous that civilisation might sink, its great battle lost, was yet another lurching development. The fortresses, the watchtowers, the naval stations, everything that had adorned the otherwise featureless skyline of Batavia: all had been swept away. The Batavians themselves, who for decades had benefited from the rare favour of Caesar, and the discipline that only service alongside the legions could instil, appeared to have reverted to the savagery that was the natural condition of barbarians. Their commander, a nobleman with the impeccably Roman name of Julius Civilis, had vowed, so reports had it, to dye his hair the colour of blood, and never to cut it until he had destroyed the Larks and XV Primigenia once and for all. Just as a dyke, if it failed to be maintained, might start to crumble before the surging of the sea, so had stripping the legions from the Rhine and the Danube left the provinces adjoining them alarmingly exposed. In the Balkans, bands of menacing tribesmen named Dacians had begun to cross the lower reaches of the Danube and flood into Moesia, the province that bordered the Black Sea; and only the fortuitous arrival of Mucianus at the head of his task force had enabled their tide-surge to be blocked. Meanwhile, along the Rhine, German warbands in their canoes had taken to its waters in growing numbers. Plunder was their immediate object; but the prophecies of Veleda, who had pronounced the doom of the great legionary bases, were much on their minds as well. A desultory attempt to storm Mogontiacum was easily repulsed; but at Vetera, where the Batavians had already settled down for a lengthy siege, the growing number of forces under Civilis' command were not so easily dispersed. The legionaries too had heard Veleda's pronouncements. Huddled behind their ramparts, shivering through the lengthening nights, listening to the drunken chants of German tribesmen from around the watch fires, they dreaded that the prophetess was right, and that all Rome's efforts to redeem the world from savagery, all the legionaries' efforts to hold the line against it, were fated to melt into ruin.

The perspective was one that came naturally to soldiers who might well have spent their entire careers serving among the garrisons along the Rhine. There was, however, another way, a very different one, of understanding Civilis' purposes. The Batavian commander, prior to leading his cohorts against Vetera, had not pledged them to the overthrow of Rome. Quite the opposite. The Batavian cohorts, marching to war against the Larks and XV Primigenia, had done so as soldiers of Caesar. Not of Vitellius, it was true – but of Vespasian. In early autumn, even as Antonius was leading the Balkan legions into Italy, the Flavian commander had written to Civilis reminding him of his shared service with Vespasian in Britain, and urging him to prevent any reinforcements from reaching Vitellius from the Rhine. Civilis, restless and ambitious, had needed no further persuasion. That he had betrayed the man to whom he had sworn the *sacramentum* was true enough; but his truest oath of loyalty was not to a usurper, but to Rome.

This, in a time of civil war, was an argument that provided many officers with a justification for treachery. Civilis was certainly not the only officer to have stabbed Vitellius in the back. If Caecina's had been the most flamboyant example of treachery, there was another as well, altogether more underhanded, and for that reason perhaps more effective. Hordeonius Flaccus, the commander of Lower Germany, had not departed with Vitellius for Rome. Elderly and unwell, he was as notorious for lethargy as Caecina was for dash. This reputation, in the early weeks of the Batavian insurgency, had provided him with the perfect screen for collaborating with Civilis: for all along he had been in correspondence with Vespasian. As the weeks went by, Flaccus' failure to combat the rebellion came to seem to the troops under his command ever more obstructive. No less than the vast mass of the legions in the Rhine who had marched on Italy under Caecina and Valens, the legionaries left behind in Germany were solid in their loyalty to Vitellius. Demands by Civilis, prior to his march on Vetera, that they abandon it, and swear allegiance to Vespasian, had been rebuffed with indignant contempt. The longer the siege of Vetera dragged on, the more the suspicions of Flaccus festered. Caught red-handed with a letter from Vespasian, he was only able to stave off a mutiny by having the messengers who had brought it arrested and sent to Vitellius. Meanwhile, back in Vetera, the defenders gazed out at the totems that bristled along the enemy positions, the carvings of beasts the Germans had carried from their forests, and the standards the Batavian cohorts, those seasoned veterans of service to Rome, had brought, and wondered what kind of siege they were engaged in: a struggle against barbarians, or a civil war? 'And they could not make up their minds.'[13]

The garrisons on the Rhine were not alone in their sense of confusion. As the days shortened, and autumn turned to winter, so shadow seemed to be lengthening over the world. From the shores of the northern sea to the fields of the Po Valley, chaos threatened everywhere. Charred stumps marked where Roman forts had once stood; rubble was all that remained of a famous Italian city. Who could say where it would end? Discordia was the most terrible of goddesses. To a people long grown accustomed to peace, the speed with which she had staked her claim to the rule of their empire was bewildering. 'The centre cannot hold. Good sense is banished. Force rules the day.'[14] The legionaries trapped inside Vetera were not alone in their perplexity at how rapidly the boundaries between civilisation and barbarism had come to blur. If the dramatic events on the Rhine barely registered in the capital, then it was because its people, wrapping their cloaks around them against the gathering chill of winter, faced threats much closer to home. By demonstrating just how uncontrollably the passions of civil war might blaze, the news from Cremona had taught them to dread the worst. They were facing the very real prospect of fire and slaughter in the heart of Rome.

Rather than risk that eventuality, Otho had chosen to commit suicide. Vitellius, however, was cut from different cloth. Brought the news from northern Italy and the Rhine, he had scorned to fall on his

130

sword. His instinct had always been to block his ears to bad news; and he still had reason enough for optimism. Valens, who had left Rome too late to join the hostilities at Cremona, was still at liberty, and presumed to be heading to Germany, there to bring the Batavians to heel, and to raise reinforcements. Fresh cohorts of Praetorians had been recruited, loyal to their emperor as only soldiers whose throats were stuffed with gold could be. So, too, a legion raised, as I Adiutrix had been, from marines. Accordingly, rather than acknowledging the bad news from Cremona, Vitellius sought to hush it up. First he would interrogate spies who brought him news from the Flavian camp; then he would have them executed. Finally, in a spectacular gesture, a Praetorian officer who had been given a personal tour of the battlefield at Cremona by Antonius himself, and then, on his return to Rome, found his report doubted, committed suicide: 'in order', as he put it before running himself through, 'to demonstrate that I am to be believed'.[15]

By mid-November, with Antonius advancing steadily southwards, it had become clear even to Vitellius that simply sitting tight in Rome and hoping for Valens to turn up with reinforcements was no longer a viable policy. Accordingly, the emperor sought to put on a show of martial vigour. As large a force as he could muster was sent to block the Flaminian Way, the road that led from the Adriatic coast to Rome, and which Antonius was bound to take. The emperor even ventured out to their camp himself. His presence there did not greatly boost morale. Twitchy and indecisive, Vitellius responded to every piece of alarming news by getting drunk. When he addressed his troops, he found himself menaced by a flock of sinister-looking birds. When he sought to make sacrifice, the bull stampeded and impaled itself on a spike. Shortly afterwards, when news reached Vitellius of a mutiny at Misenum, the great naval base in the Bay of Naples, he was thrown into panic, and hurried back to Rome. Here, conscious that it was unlikely to be his for long, he finally accepted the name of 'Caesar'. Meanwhile, support for his regime continued to ebb away. Senators began to show him open disrespect. Across

Italy, ever more cities declared for Vespasian. Finally came the cruellest, most fatal cut of all. In Narni, the hill-town overlooking the Flaminian Way, to which the Vitellian forces had retreated following their emperor's own withdrawal to Rome, sentries saw a detachment of Flavians crossing the plain below them. They were carrying an object on a spike. It did not take the Vitellian forces long to recognise it, and to realise that their last hope was gone, that reinforcements would not be coming, that the war was effectively over: for the object was Valens' head. The Vitellians, acknowledging that the game was up, sued for terms. Soon afterwards, arrayed in full battle order, they marched down from Narni. It was Antonius who accepted their surrender. He spoke to them kindly, then dismissed them from service. The road to Rome lay open at last.

But not Rome itself. Vitellius still had troops in the city. This, even amid the collapse of all his fortunes, was sufficient to provide him with leverage. Each side, anxious to avoid visiting the fate of Cremona upon the capital of the world, had already been sounding out the other's terms. Vitellius, a reluctant emperor from the outset, had not the slightest wish to make a heroic last stand. 'So plunged into despondency was he that, had others not kept in mind he was an emperor, he would himself quite have forgotten it.'[16] Such criticism, however, was harsh. Torpid and indecisive though Vitellius may have been, he prosecuted his negotiations with all the vigour he could muster. The sudden death of his mother, to whom he had been deeply attached, only confirmed him in his resolve to keep the lines of communication to the Flavians open: for his hopes were vested above all in keeping his wife and children alive.* Granted, these lines of communication risked becoming confused. Antonius was not the only Flavian in the

---

* Suetonius reports two rumours: one – wholly unbelievable – that Vitellius starved his mother to death; the other, marginally more credible, 'that she was so depressed at the state things had come to, and so anxious about how matters might turn out, that she asked her son for poison: a request which he readily granted her' (*Galba*: 14).

game. Even as he closed in on Rome, so Mucianus was closing in on him. Vespasian's plenipotentiary, deprived by Antonius of glory that he felt should rightfully have been his, had not the slightest intention of allowing any further impairment of his authority. The victor of the battle of Cremona could not be permitted to claim Vitellius' surrender as well. Accordingly, when Antonius wrote promising the hapless emperor a dignified retirement in exchange for his abdication, Mucianus made sure to do the same. Vitellius himself, besieged by friends who scorned the very idea that the Flavians might permit him to live, was left all the more paralysed by indecision. His dilemma was very real. Who, at this terrible moment of crisis, with his own life, and the fate both of his family and of Rome itself hanging in the balance, could he trust to speak for Vespasian?

Fortunately, there was an obvious person to hand: none other than Vespasian's elder brother. Despite the guards Vitellius had appointed to keep watch over him, Flavius Sabinus was still the city's prefect. The fact that he had not been removed from the post stemmed in part from the emperor's high regard for him; but it was also partly due to the emperor's desire to veil his status as a hostage. Vespasian's younger son, an eighteen-year-old by the name of Domitian, was also in Rome; and he, like his uncle, had opted to trust to the forbearance of his captor rather than risk an escape. Accordingly, as all Vitellius' hopes crumbled and the limits of his dominion tightened in around him, he could look to a Flavian faction within the city itself. Already, in the early weeks of December, he and Sabinus had come together for a number of private meetings. At the last of these, held in the awesome setting of a temple that Augustus had raised on the Palatine, terms had finally been agreed. Only two witnesses were present to hear them; but onlookers reported that Vitellius seemed cowed and depressed, while Sabinus looked less triumphant than full of pity. On 17 December, the news from Narni reached Rome. That evening, addressing the Praetorians who stood guard over him on the Palatine, Vitellius informed them of his intention to lay down the rule of the world. It seemed that the civil war was over at last.

Yet the emperor, in his negotiations with Sabinus, had failed to take into account the interests of his most militant backers. The Praetorians, appalled by the prospect of losing their patron, and dreading that it would result in their own extermination, were outraged by Vitellius' plans. Indeed, so voluble were their protests that the emperor did briefly waver – but not for long. The next morning, he had himself dressed in dark robes and proceeded to the Forum. With him came the members of his household and his little boy, carried in a tiny litter, 'as though to a funeral'.[17] The crowd greeted him with cheers, the Praetorians with an ominous silence. Vitellius, determined not to be blown off course by either, proclaimed to the Roman people that the civil war had ended. The city was to be handed over to Sabinus. No opposition was to be offered the Flavian legions advancing along the Flaminian Way. Vespasian was to rule as emperor: 'I abdicate for the sake of peace, for the sake of our country.'[18]

But Discordia, fell and bloodthirsty, was not to be baulked so easily of her prey. Beyond the senate house, at the foot of the Capitol, stood Concordia's temple, Rome's greatest monument to civic harmony; and here it was that Vitellius, after first hugging his children, commending them to the Roman people, and bursting into tears, sought to head. His intention was to present the goddess with his sword, which he had already unstrapped as a symbol of his abdication, and thereby signal to the Roman people that civic peace had been restored at last; but Discordia had no intention of letting him reach her rival's shrine. Already the consul, offered the sword by Vitellius, had refused to accept it; and now, rather than allow the emperor to proceed with his abdication, the crowds blocked his passage, so that he found himself with no option but to return to the Palatine. Meanwhile, as Vitellius was retreating from the Forum, Sabinus was trying to reach it. Infuriated by the reports of what had happened, he was determined to seize back control of the situation, and spell out to the crowds exactly what had been agreed. He had not reckoned, however, on the gathering mood of violence. As he and his supporters headed down to the Forum, they were surprised by a posse of

Praetorians. The attack was beaten off; but Sabinus, thinking better of his original plan, decided that the safest course of action would be to retreat to the nearest fortifiable position. And so this is what he did. He and his companions climbed the Capitol.

No place, of course, was more redolent of patriotism. If Rome was the head of the world, then the Capitol was the head of Rome. The great temple on its summit, its roof sheathed in gold, its profile sharp against the sky, was what joined the rule of Jupiter in the heavens to the rule of the Roman people on the earth. It proclaimed the blessings of the gods on Rome's dominion to the entire world. By seizing control of the Capitol, Sabinus was making a defiant and very public statement about the legitimacy of his cause. That night, as gusts of icy rain blew across the city, he sent for his children and his nephew, Domitian. The Praetorians, lax in their sentry duty around the hill, failed to keep them from slipping through. Sabinus also managed to smuggle out a messenger to Antonius, alerting him to what had happened, and a centurion to the Palatine, there to upbraid Vitellius and demand that he rein in his supporters. All to no end. As the sky began to lighten, so it became apparent to Sabinus that he was trapped. Antonius was still a day's march away; and Vitellius proved powerless to help. 'No longer an emperor, he served his men merely as a justification for continuing the war.'[19] The Praetorians, all too bitterly conscious of what a new emperor was likely to mean for them, certainly had no intention of surrendering to the forces of a rival emperor. Discordia had triumphed over her sister.

Almost a year had passed since the murder of Galba; now, once again, the heart of Rome became a scene of conflict. As determinedly as though they were assaulting some barbarian stronghold, some distant capital held by inveterate rebels, the Praetorians advanced up Rome's most sacred hill. Sabinus and his followers, pelting their opponents with tiles and blocking their advance with toppled statues, frantically sought to keep them at bay, but in vain. The defenders were too few; the assailants too resolute; both sides too careless of the sacred ground they were treading. Who first torched the Capitol would subsequently be much disputed – but not the consequence. Flames were soon licking Rome's holiest building, flickering up its colonnades, then blazing through its gables, bringing its roof crashing down. 'And so the temple of Jupiter, undefended, unplundered, its doors locked shut, was burned to the ground.'[20]

Back in April, when proclaiming Vitellius emperor, Sabinus had done so in the Circus Maximus, the largest and most famous stadium in the world. Now, eight months on, he found himself the chief actor in a spectacle more awful, more heart-stopping, more stupefying than anything staged in the Circus. Shocking though the slaughter of the past months had been, it could not compare for sheer horror with the incineration of Jupiter's temple. Confusion had made his masterpiece. Yet this masterpiece – unlike the destruction of Cremona – was not one that threatened to engulf its audience. The crowds in the Forum, gathering to watch the Capitol burn, might as well have been sitting in the stands, gawping at splintered chariot wheels and mangled limbs. The din of battle mingled with the blazing of the fire. Then the slaughter began. Although some of the defenders – Domitian included – managed to slip away and escape the inferno, large numbers were cut down. Sabinus himself, scorning to offer resistance, was taken prisoner, loaded with chains, and dragged to the foot of the Palatine. There he was greeted by Vitellius, who sought to spare his life, but in vain: for the emperor had badly misjudged the mood. The crowd wanted blood. Boos and catcalls began to ring out. Then a host of daggers flashed. Sabinus crumpled to the ground. His body was slashed and hacked about, his head brandished as a trophy. Finally, when the mutilators of his body were done, what remained of his corpse was dragged across the Forum and dumped on the Stairs of Mourning. Above it, on the crown of the Capitol, the fire continued to blaze, while below it, at the foot of the steps, the temple of Concordia stood in the sombre and heavy shadows cast by the billowing smoke.

The murder of Sabinus was merely an appetiser for the entertainment that was to follow. That evening Rome seemed at peace, but the calm was deceptive, and everyone knew it. The city lay midway between dread and expectation. Sure enough, well before dawn, Antonius and his legions arrived on the outskirts of Rome. Alerted to the siege of the Capitol by Sabinus' frantic message, they had been hurrying all day and night to the rescue; now, learning that they were too late, Antonius called a pause. Curtly he dismissed the envoys sent by Vitellius to negotiate terms, informing them that there was no longer any deal to be made; then, summoning his troops to an assembly, he proposed making camp beside the Milvian Bridge and waiting for daybreak. But his men refused to halt. First in the cramped streets that lined the city walls, and then on the Campus Martius, the people of Rome woke to the din of combat. 'Like spectators watching gladiators clash for their enjoyment, they flocked to watch the fighting, cheering and applauding now one side, and now the other.'[21] This relish for the fury and bloodshed of battle was less a reflection of irresponsibility than a shrewd estimation that the result had already been decided. And so it proved. Only from behind the walls of the Praetorian camp did the Vitellians manage to offer sustained resistance; and even they, once Antonius had succeeded in bringing his overwhelming force of numbers to bear, were soon overwhelmed. The massacre, as the Praetorians had always feared it would be, was total. The camp was left a butcher's shambles. The din of battle ceased. Rome returned to calm.

A calm, it seemed to Vitellius, like that of the grave. The emperor, rather than joining with his troops in their last stand, had been fretting and vacillating, and scurrying this way and that. First he had headed for his wife's house on the Aventine; then, hearing a rumour that terms were agreed with Antonius, he had returned to the Palatine. The complex lay abandoned. Everyone – officials, soldiers, slaves – had fled. How long Vitellius paced the empty corridors, trying locked doors, starting at every sound, there was no one present to witness; but in the end, so it would later be reported, he had hidden himself in a porter's lodge, barricaded himself inside the room with a bed and a mattress, and chained up a dog next to the entranceway.* There he had waited: Vitellius Caesar, the heir of Augustus, the man who had laid claim to the rule of the world. And there, in due course, once the soldiers of his victorious opponent had climbed the Palatine, occupied it, and begun fanning out through its corridors, he was found.

Some would later report that the soldiers who dragged him out from his bolthole failed to recognise him. If so, his identity did not remain a secret for long. His clothes were ripped from his body, his hands tied behind his back, a rope tethered around his neck. Out from the palace he was dragged into the Forum. There, where only two days previously a great crowd had gathered to cheer him and prevent his abdication, he was mobbed by hissing, spitting people. Some tugged on his stubble; others prodded his protuberant belly and mocked him for his gluttony; still others pelted him with filth. When he lowered his eyes out of shame, a soldier held the tip of a sword to his chin, so that he had no choice but to meet the gaze of his persecutors and watch his statues being toppled from their plinths. Up the Stairs of Mourning he was hauled. There, fleetingly, he attempted to assert his dignity, suddenly retorting, to an officer who had been abusing him, 'And yet I was your emperor.'[22] His last words. As Sabinus had done the day before, he fell beneath a rain of blows. Then, as though his body were a joint of meat presented on a silver platter to the imperial table, his flesh was sliced with delicate precision from his bones. Finally, a hook was jammed into the roof of his mouth, and what remained of his body dragged away and dumped into the Tiber.

By now it was evening. As the crowds dispersed, so Domitian emerged from hiding. He presented himself to Antonius and the rest of the Flavian high command. The legions cheered him, hailing him as Caesar. Then, leading him through the darkening streets, they escorted him to his father's house: the house of Vespasian, emperor of Rome.

———

* The report is from Suetonius (*Vitellius*: 16). According to Dio (64.20), Vitellius hid in a kennel, and was savaged by dogs as he cowered there.

Not One Stone Shall Be Left

In Alexandria, the arrival of the news from Italy detailing the downfall of Vitellius was accompanied by great wonder. It happened one
day that Vespasian, as he sat in public, dispensing justice to the people
of the city, was approached by two men. One was blind; the other
a cripple.[23] Both men claimed to have been visited in a dream by a
god. 'Ask the emperor to spit on your eyes,' the god had instructed
the blind man. 'Ask the emperor to touch your leg with his heel,' he
had instructed the cripple. And so it was that both men, obedient
to the god's commands, had come to stand before Vespasian. The
emperor, torn between the scepticism that came naturally to a bluff
Roman military man confronted by Egyptians telling tall stories, and
a yearning to believe that they might just conceivably be true, hesitated. Only when his friends assured him that no one would blame
him for making the attempt did he do as the god had commanded. At
once the blind man could see. At once the cripple could walk. News
of the feat swept the city. Never before in Alexandria, city of wonders
though it was, had anyone witnessed quite such a miracle of healing.

Yet an infinitely greater one was needed from the new emperor.
The world, from the northern seas to the eastern deserts, was bleeding. Rome's dominion, grievously wounded as it had been by revolts
and civil wars, was still in a critical condition. Jerusalem remained in
rebel hands. Provinces from Britain to the Black Sea were wracked by
insurgencies and barbarian incursions. Most ominous of all was the
continuing chaos along the length of the Rhine. There, far from con-
ceding that the civil war was over, the legions had refused to accept
the new emperor.[24] When Flaccus sought to impose the *sacramentum*
in Vespasian's name, he was dragged out of his bed and murdered.
The mutineers were not alone in their continued loyalty to Vitellius'
memory. Some of Gaul's most distinguished senators, men who had
been serving him in a range of senior posts, also refused to accept
the new regime. This, of course, presented them with an obvious
problem. Who, if not Vespasian, were they to acknowledge as Caesar?

One of the Vitellians, a Gallic senator by the name of Julius Sabinus, proposed a radical solution. His grandfather, so he revealed, had been the illegitimate son of none other than Julius Caesar: meaning that he had a better claim to the imperial office than any upstart muleteer. Even though nobody in Gaul was naïve enough to imagine that this would play well south of the Alps, it was sufficient, among the Vitellian diehards, to consolidate support for what they termed an *Imperium Galliarum*: a 'Gallic Empire'. This was no declaration of independence from Rome, but something altogether more paradoxical: a claim to embody the legitimacy of its rule more authentically than Rome did itself.

Grotesque though this conceit inevitably appeared to the Flavian high command, the assumption underlying it was one that they could not entirely dismiss. The temple that since the distant days of the monarchy had stood at the heart of the city was gone. Its eternity had been taken widely for granted, and the shock of its destruction was felt far beyond Rome. What else could the disaster possibly have signalled if not the anger of the gods? This conviction, which had steeled the Gallic senators in their defiance of Vespasian, was one that nagged as well at many in the capital itself. To gaze up at the charred summit of the Capitol was to dread that perhaps the death of Vitellius had marked only a brief pause in the murderous cycles of civil war, and that the empire of the Roman people was doomed to be shattered beyond all hope of repair, reduced to blackened ruin just as their most sacred temple had been. Certainly, the news from the north seemed to suggest this. The Gallic senators, viewed from Rome, appeared to be rebels, plain and simple. The legions on the Rhine, by rallying behind Julius Sabinus and his cronies, had disgraced themselves 'by preferring submission to foreign masters to the rule of Vespasian'.[25] Then, still lurking in predatory fashion on the margins of Vetera, there were the Batavians. Ever more Germans from beyond the Rhine were reported to have swelled their numbers. The boundaries constructed with such effort by generations of legates and provincial administrators, between order and chaos, between civilisation and barbarism, seemed to be on the verge of total collapse. Treachery had come to be cast as loyalty, and rebellion as a defence of Roman values. It was, in short, a mess.

Yet in Rome itself — the head from which the rest of the world had for a year and more now been rotting — there were signs of hope. Swords had been sheathed; soldiers ordered off the streets; all traces of blood scoured from the Stairs of Mourning. Nothing about this had been inevitable. The scope for continued violence in the wake of Vitellius' murder had been considerable. The Flavian legions had already, after all, put the people of Cremona to the sword, and Antonius, their commander, was a man notorious for snatching after his own ambitions. Yet he, and all the other jackals around him, had proven no match for Mucianus. One day after the murder of Vitellius, with Rome still full of marauding soldiers and the streets piled high with corpses, senators had cautiously re-emerged from their hiding places. Convening in the senate house, they had listened as letters from Vespasian and Mucianus were read to them. They had then voted to grant Vespasian a great package of powers and titles: everything that had come to constitute, over the course of the previous century, the rank of emperor. One clause, however, was a novelty. With Vespasian absent, so it was decreed, the senate should be guided 'according to his will or authority'.[26] The hand of Mucianus — Vespasian's great partner and plenipotentiary — was unmistakeable. Sure enough, no sooner had he arrived in the capital at the head of his legions than he was taking full advantage of the licence granted him by the senate. Armed as he was with the imperial seal, 'so that he was able to transact any business that he wished without the emperor's specific approval', and settled on the Palatine, he ruled as the master of Rome.[27]

Yet Mucianus, imperious though he might be, was possessed of a certain selflessness as well. A man of deep subtlety and sophistication, he was perfectly content for Vespasian to serve as the public face of the new regime. He had recognised in the no-nonsense Sabine an instinctive and rugged conservatism of a kind that the Roman people, bruised by the upheavals of the past year as they were, had come to crave. Respect for tradition; obedience to proprieties; an unembarrassed commitment to Rome's primordial virtues: these were what the times demanded. Other qualities as well, however, were required by the circumstances of the age – and here Mucianus himself was content to step in. No dynasty could hope to establish itself without a certain measure of ruthlessness. What option was there, for the victors in a civil war, but to ride roughshod over the occasional civic norm, to betray the occasional deserving ally, to sponsor the occasional crime? Sure enough, senators who objected to Mucianus' high-handed behaviour were obliged to swallow their resentment, and flatter him as assiduously as they had once flattered Nero. Antonius, garlanded with empty honours, could only watch impotently as VII Galbiana, the legion he had personally commanded, was packed off back to the Danube. Various relatives of Piso, the blue-blooded unfortunate adopted by Galba, were discreetly eliminated. So, too, was Vitellius' brother, and Germanicus, that little boy who had been the great object of all the dead emperor's fondest ambitions. Mucianus, adept as he was at weighing up costs and benefits, was also content to shrug off the resulting blots on his reputation: for setting the new order on foundations as firm as he could make them was his one priority. And meanwhile, far from the capital, Vespasian maintained his own reputation for honesty and bided his time.

Not until the entire world had been set in order did he intend to set sail for Rome. Confident though he was in Titus' ability to bring the Judaeans to heel, he did not wish to depart from Egypt until their reduction was at least imminent. Jerusalem, after all, was the city that he had originally been mandated to capture; and only with its fall would he be able to return home trailing the requisite clouds of glory. Equally, but for diametrically opposed reasons, he was anxious not to head for Rome until operations north of the Alps had been satisfactorily concluded. There was nothing to be had there for

Vespasian but embarrassment. The refusal of the legions in Germany to swear the *sacramentum* to him made a mockery of his claim to enjoy the universal approbation of the Roman people. Clearly, there was no option but to launch a campaign of pacification along the Rhine. Clearly, too, it would require the most careful framing. Otherwise, it risked rubbing home a most awkward fact: that the civil war, no matter the claims of Flavian propagandists, was in reality far from over.

In the event – by a paradox worthy of the confusion of the times – it was the Germans who came to Vespasian's rescue. In early spring, Veleda's prophecy that the legionary bases along the Rhine were destined to fall had appeared fulfilled when the starving garrison of Vetera finally opened its gates to the Batavians. The siege had lasted, on and off, for many months, and the soldiers of V Alaudae and XV Primigenia had been reduced to eating grass. By the terms of the agreement negotiated with Civilis, the Batavians took possession of the base and all its contents; the legionaries were granted safe passage, despoiled of everything but their lives. Even these, however, were soon to prove forfeit. Eight miles from Vetera, the German warbands that had flocked to Civilis' banner ambushed the Roman column. One of the two legionary commanders was taken captive and sent as a human trophy to Veleda.* Some of the other officers were kept as hostages. Everyone else was left as food for crows. Civilis, indignant that the Germans had contravened the oath he had personally sworn, condemned them as criminals; but he did not choose to forgo their support. Instead, in acknowledgement of the vow he had made the previous summer, that he would exterminate the legionaries who had held Vetera as their base, he very publicly cut the hair he had let grow long. The remaining Vitellian forces in Lower Germany, granted their lives by Civilis on similar terms to those granted the troops at Vetera, did succeed in completing their evacuation, but at the cost of deep and public humiliation. Each

---

* It was perhaps his good fortune to be murdered on the way.

base, once its garrison had departed, was stripped bare and set on fire. Only two — Mogontiacum and Vindonissa — were left in Roman hands. Otherwise, of the great chain of strongholds built with such effort and implacability along the length of the Rhine, not a single one remained.

All of which, for the Flavian high command, came as a godsend. The annihilation of a legionary column by Germans, the torching of military infrastructure: here were horrors risen from the very depths of Roman nightmares. When the news from Vetera reached the capital, it cast the war zone north of the Alps in a stark and glaring light. Any acknowledgement that Civilis had originally attacked the base in the name of Vespasian, or that Sabinus had laid claim to the empire as a Caesar, or that Gallic senators, when they rode out on campaign, did so at the head of legions, arrayed as legates, in the cause of a Roman empire, was utterly banished. Mucianus, plotting the final defeat of the Vitellian cause, could represent the crisis on the Rhine as merely another round in a timeless struggle: between order and anarchy, between civilisation and savagery, between Roman and barbarian. Only with a titanic effort, such as had been displayed in the wake of the Varian disaster, could the situation hope to be resolved. And now, with the termination of hostilities in Italy, such an effort was indeed made possible. Vast and overwhelming force could be brought to bear hard on the problem.

As the months passed, so ever more legions were committed to the great labour of pacification. By the summer, no fewer than nine were operating along the Rhine. So, too, were vast numbers of auxiliaries — among them a unit of Batavian cavalry commanded by Civilis' own nephew, a veteran of numerous campaigns in Britain by the name of Julius Briganticus. By August, when Briganticus fell in battle, bravely defending a fortress on the banks of the Rhine against a surprise attack by his uncle, the war was effectively over. Sabinus, the would-be Caesar, had already vanished from the scene: brought to defeat, he had retired to his villa, which his slaves, following his suicide, had then incinerated to serve him as a pyre. Civilis, altogether more obdurate, managed to continue the fight into early autumn, breaching dykes in an attempt to halt the advance of his opponents, pursuing guerilla tactics against their garrisons, capturing their flagship and towing it up the Lippe to provide Veleda with yet another trophy. All this, however, had been by way of shoring up his negotiating position. Sure enough, with winter closing in, and a vast invasion force poised to bring ruin to his homeland, Civilis sued for peace. He and his adversaries met on the banks of a Batavian river. Prior to their arrival, workmen had demolished the central stretch of a bridge; and now, stepping onto what remained of it, the two negotiating teams communicated with one another by yelling across the gap: 'I have always shown Vespasian the utmost respect,' declared Civilis, 'and been known as his friend.' His conquerors, in implicit acknowledgement of this, were content to spare his life, and to grant his people the same terms of service they had previously enjoyed.* A telling offer. No matter how assiduously Flavian propagandists might cast the Batavians as rebels against Rome, the leniency shown them hinted at just how complex, and ambiguous, their role in the conflict had actually been.

Certainly, Vespasian owed his plenipotentiary a great deal. Mucianus had played a difficult hand cunningly and well. The glory of it redounded not only to Rome, but to the new imperial house. Quintus Petillius Cerialis, the man Mucianus had entrusted with command of the great campaign of pacification, had married into Vespasian's family, and as such could be reckoned a Flavian. Like Sabinus and Domitian, he had been held as an effective hostage by Vitellius; unlike Sabinus and Domitian, he had made a dramatic escape from Rome, disguised as a peasant. His enthusiasm for adventure was unquenchable. On occasion – as during Boudicca's revolt, when he had advanced impatiently against the rebels at the head of a single legion – this might result in disaster; but in general it enabled him to provide excellent copy. Certainly, his dispatches

---

* The ultimate fate of Civilis is unknown.

from the front were vivid with colour and excitement, contributing to a sense in Rome that the Flavians might be something more than mere usurpers: that they could be trusted to provide the city with glory as well as peace.

This was why Mucianus, far from resenting Cerialis' successes, was content to wait until the war was almost won before himself arriving in Gaul with reinforcements. With him he brought Domitian, moody, testy, ambitious to ride at the head of troops as a Caesar – and therefore not remotely what the situation required. Mucianus, rather than slapping the young prince down, opted instead to hug him close. The campaigning, he assured Domitian, was not worthy of his efforts: 'He should abstain from trifling risks, so that he would then be ready to take on greater ones.'[28] Rather than to the front, Mucianus sent him instead to Lugdunum. There, appearing before the people who only a year previously had been cheering Vitellius so rapturously, Domitian played a valuable role in reconciling the Gauls to his house. Vespasian, informed of his younger son's performance, was sufficiently impressed to make a joke of it: 'Thank you, my boy,' the emperor wrote, 'for allowing me to remain in power, and for granting me some time yet on the throne.'[29]

The joke was all the more pointed, of course, for the fact that Domitian did not even rank as his father's heir. Vespasian's younger son had never been left in any doubt as to his place in the pecking order. That summer, especially, there was no forgetting it. Impressive though the feats of arms performed north of the Alps might be, they could not compare for sheer drama with the great war of vengeance that at last, four years after the eruption of Judaea into revolt, had reached the walls of Jerusalem. The true measure of manhood, so the Romans believed, was the capacity to endure grim ordeals of exhaustion and blood; and Titus, by that reckoning, was proving himself a hero equal to any from their city's past. The Judaeans were not, like the Batavians, mere creatures of bog and marsh. They were an ancient people, inveterate in the pride they felt in their ancestry, and resolute in their conviction that they were the favoured ones of a jealous and demanding god. Rebels in Judaea, unlike those in more barbarous lands, might aspire not just to throw off Roman rule, but to purge themselves thoroughly of every last hint of Rome itself.

In looking to the future, the leaders of the Judaean revolt looked as well to the past. Coins now proclaimed the revival of the ancient realm celebrated in their scriptures and their prophecies: Israel. The script used by the moneyers was an archaic one, redolent of the distant age when the Temple had first been built. The calendar employed by scribes dated years not from the accession of a Caesar, but from what they termed the redemption of Jerusalem. No insurgents had ever before attempted such a thoroughgoing repudiation of Rome's claim to rule the world; and although Vespasian, town by town, village by village, had succeeded in stamping out resistance across most of the province, so impregnable to the revels did their capital appear that the majority of them continued to trust in the future of Israel. Certainly, the pause in the Roman offensive had not been wasted. The walls, already bristling, had been made to bristle even more. The city heaved with rival factions, all of them armed to the teeth. Titus, arriving before Jerusalem's gates in the spring of AD 70, had found himself confronted by a task such as no general had faced in over two centuries: a siege fit to challenge the legions to the very limits of their capability.

'The will of the immortal gods it is that the Roman people should rule over every nation.'[30] Faith in this venerable maxim, which had steeled generations of legionaries never to surrender, never to leave a defeat unavenged, had recently, of course, come to be badly shaken. First the collapse of the empire into civil war, and then the destruction of Jupiter's temple on the Capitol, had caused many to wonder if the will of the immortal gods was quite all that it had been. As in Gaul, so in Judaea: it was the responsibility of the Flavian house to repair the damage done to the self-confidence of the Roman people. So it was that Titus, right from the beginning, made sure to prosecute the siege with a ferocious energy. Rather than content himself

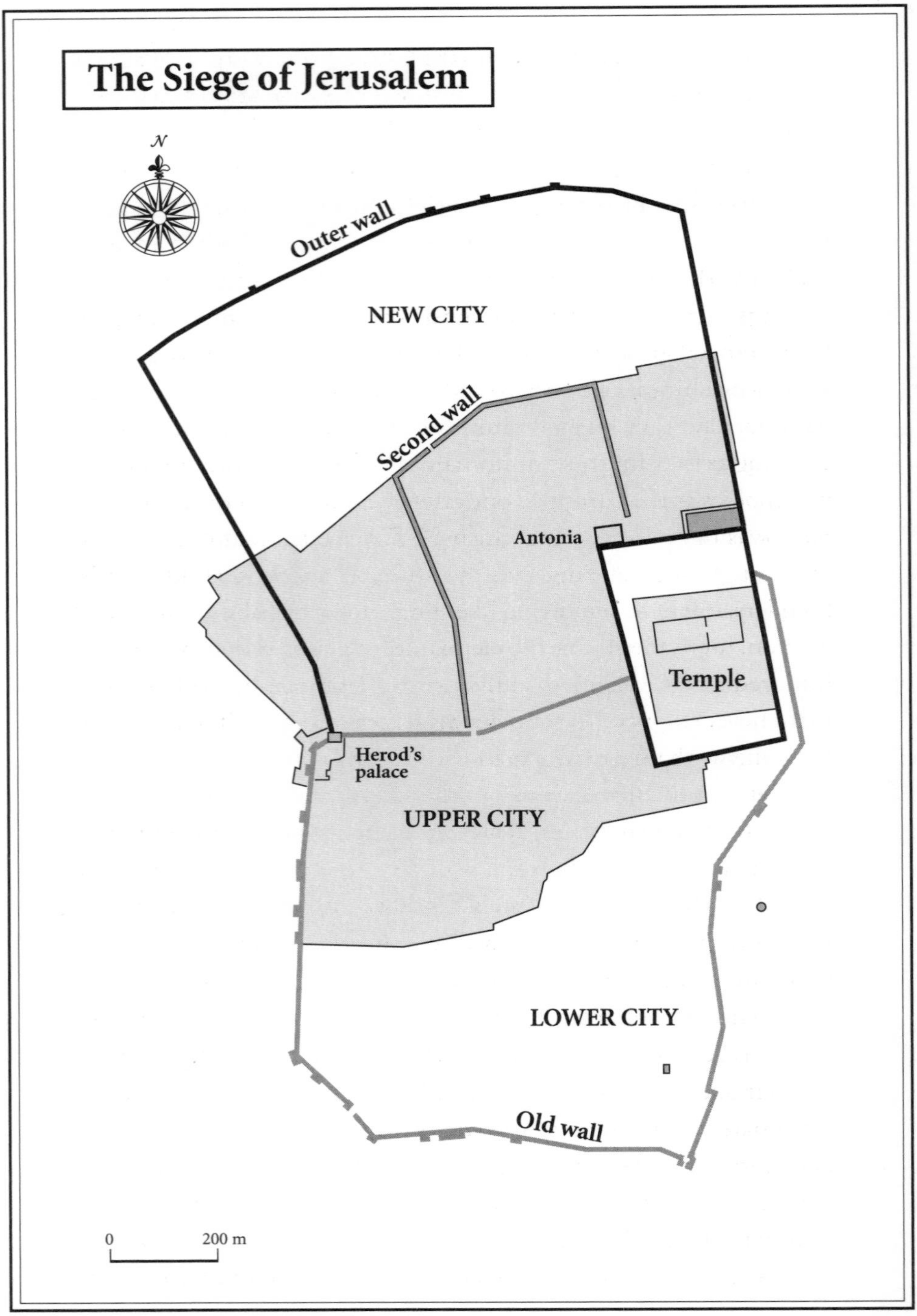

The Siege of Jerusalem

N

Outer wall

NEW CITY

Second wall

Antonia

Temple

Herod's palace

UPPER CITY

LOWER CITY

Old wall

0   200 m

with starving Jerusalem into surrender, he looked to storm it. The object of his initial assault was a wall which protected the northern suburbs of the city, and which, unlike the defences along its craggier reaches, could be approached across level ground. Like termites, the legionaries spread through the neighbouring woods. Three great towers were built from the harvested timber. Sheathed in iron, topped with battlements, these monstrous structures enabled the Romans to rain down death on the defenders. Meanwhile, from platforms ranged along the base of the wall, the legions deployed their killing-machines. The very sound of the artillery, hour after hour, day after day, was a kind of trauma: the screaming of the missiles; the crashing as they hit stone or human flesh; 'the constant thudding of dead bodies as they dropped one after the other from the rampart'.[31] Such was the velocity with which a bolt travelled that it might pass in through one defender and out through another. Heads, hit by boulders, might be sent flying like sling-shot. The baby of a pregnant woman, hit in the stomach by a missile, might be borne by it several hundred feet.[32] Relentless, pulverising, nightmarish, the bombardment never stopped. To the defenders, the assault on the city seemed to be the work less of men than of demons.

Then, on the fifteenth day of the siege, a Roman battering ram finally succeeded in forcing a breach. It did not take the legions long to come flooding through the wall. Yet even as his men occupied the suburb that lay beyond it, Titus knew the siege still had a long way to go. Beyond the outer wall lay two inner walls; and beyond them, in the ancient heart of Jerusalem, a brilliant cityscape of palaces, mansions and towers. Most stupefying of all — an image, so the Judaeans believed, of the universe itself, the place chosen personally by their god for his seat, the one building in the world that ranked legitimately as his sanctuary — there loomed the Temple. Its wonders were celebrated far beyond Judaea. A place of mystery, in which rituals quite unlike those of other lands were strictly veiled from all outsiders, it was also a place of incomparable beauty. 'To strangers approaching from a distance, it appeared like a mountain covered in snow: for all those stretches of it that were not plated with gold were a dazzling white.'[33] Such a prize was one worthy of a Caesar.

Self-regard, however, was not the only motive Titus had for wishing to take possession of the famous building. Already, he was looking to the future. Once the rebels among them had been eliminated, the Judaeans would have to be reconciled to his father's rule. The Temple could serve them as an emblem of Roman order, just as it had in times past. Agrippa, who had loyally accompanied him to war, was its patron, after all. A priesthood restored to the king's supervision would be a priesthood willing to offer sacrifice once again on behalf of Caesar. With Jerusalem taken, and the necessary reprisals completed, everything could return to normal. Yet this would only be possible if the city submitted quickly. The risks otherwise were very great. Five months had passed since the burning of the Capitol; and who was to say, should the rebels continue their fruitless resistance, what calamity might not come to engulf another famous temple? Accordingly, once the legions had breached the second wall, and occupied the stretch of the city that lay between it and the third wall, Titus called a temporary halt to the siege. The artillery fell silent. The rebels were granted a chance to surrender.

'To impose the works and ways of peace, to spare the vanquished and to overthrow the haughty by means of war':[34] such was the peculiar genius of the Roman people. Titus knew that many Judaeans were still keen to play their part in Rome's global mission. Some of them — Agrippa, Julius Alexander, Yosef ben Mattityahu — were in his train. One of them, Berenice, was in his bed. Others, however, were trapped in Jerusalem. Not everyone in the city was a rebel. Many — men as well as women and children — yearned desperately to submit. Even the rebels themselves, split as they were into various factions, offered nothing like a unified front. There was opportunity, so it seemed to Titus, to work on their divisions and doubts. It was time to put on a parade.

The fusion of magnificence with menace came naturally to the

Romans. Titus, a natural showman, knew how to make it pack a punch. As defenders on the unbreached city wall massed to gawp at the spectacle, he marshalled the four legions under his command, the twenty cohorts of auxiliaries, and the eight cavalry units in a display of dazzling intimidation. Dressed in mail, arrayed in formation, the world's most lethal fighting force stood on full parade; 'and such was the brilliance of the armour, such the perfect discipline of every man, that even the boldest rebel was filled with dread'.[35] Still, however, the gates remained bolted. The days passed. The city seethed with mingled despair and defiance. By night, slipping past the sentries, deserters began to flee the city; and when they had made it into the hills beyond the city they would squat, empty their bowels, and scoop out from their excrement the gold coins they had swallowed before making their escape.

These fugitives, however, were men who had always dreaded that rebellion against Rome would lead to disaster; and those who thought otherwise, putting their trust in their god, scorned to change their minds. So, too, did other rebels in the city: warlords who knew themselves to be beyond any hope of forgiveness, and who preferred to go down fighting rather than to submit to the vengeance of the Romans. These were the men who had seized the commanding heights of the city, and they had no intention of ceding them. When Titus, anxious to undermine their morale any way that he could, sent Yosef to address them from a safe distance – to paint in lurid colours the full scale of Roman might, to assure the rebels that they were fighting not only the legions but their own god as well, who had condemned them for their crimes and taken the side of Caesar – the resolve of the defenders was only stiffened. One of them, catching Yosef by surprise, knocked him out with a brick. His claim to be a prophet, acknowledged by the emperor himself, and self-evidently proven by events, was answered by howls of execration.

To abuse a friend of Caesar was, of course, to abuse Caesar himself. Titus, ordering his men to resume the siege, had no need to urge them to the fight. The insults done Rome by the Judaeans were manifold and grievous. Clearly, they demanded payment. One legion more than any other felt this with a raw and anguished intensity. The soldiers of XII Fulminata, men who had lost their eagle during Cestius' retreat from Jerusalem, had now, under Titus, been given the chance to redeem themselves. That the shame of defeat might be purged by iron-forged courage, by superhuman effort, and by a commitment to displays of pitiless terror was an enduring theme in Rome's annals. The legionaries of the Twelfth, summoned to storm Jerusalem, could feel themselves participants in a dimension of legend. Massive were their labours, heroic their resolve. Ever more trees were felled, until for ten miles all around there was nothing to be seen of the beautiful woods and parks that had once framed the city but a great desert of stumps. Vast platforms, vast ramps, vast towers were built; and when the Judaeans, who had mined them, set the tunnels on fire and brought everything crashing down, the men of the Twelfth doggedly set to work again. First, with the other legions, they constructed a wall around Jerusalem, nearly five miles long, and completed – to the astonishment and horror of the watching defenders – in only three days; then they returned to the city, and to the scene of their recent disaster. The object of their efforts was a great fortress named the Antonia: built by Herod, and named after Mark Antony, Titus had no choice but to storm it, for it served as the key to the Temple. And so, stinking in the summer heat, drained by the demands of their labours, resolute in their determination to prove themselves worthy as soldiers of Rome, the men of XII Fulminata toiled on; and week by week the platforms rose.

With all four legions labouring on the siege-works, the din of war around the Antonia was especially deafening. As well as the hammering and sawing, there was also the ceaseless crump of artillery fire, louder now than at any point since Titus' arrival before Jerusalem. The Judaeans, when they routed Cestius' expeditionary force, had captured large quantities of siege equipment; but they had found it a challenge to master the unfamiliar machines. Two months had passed, however, since the start of the siege: time enough for the defenders to become proficient. As the Romans raked the walls of the Antonia, so the Judaeans fired at the legionaries toiling away below them. The thud of the rival batteries of artillery, angry and desperate, pounded as though it were the heartbeat of the city. Yet away from the beleaguered fortress, in the streets, the courtyards, the marketplaces of Jerusalem, there was a stillness deep and death-like enough to muffle everything; and this, too, was the sound of the siege. Famine had come to stalk the city. Such supplies as remained were commandeered by the various bands of fighters. The rest of the population, out of options, began to starve. 'No one wept, no one mourned, for hunger had exhausted all their passions. With dry eyes and rictus grins those who lingered on alive gazed at those who had already perished.'[36] The starving, their bellies grotesquely extended, haunted open spaces like shadows, and when they fell lay untended, piling up in the streets. The rebel commanders, revolted by the stench, first sought to have them buried, and then, when all the available space in the city had been exhausted, flung from the city walls. Yet the corpses still piled up; and increasingly, rather than continue with the fruitless effort of clearing them, the fighters simply trod them underfoot.

The sacrilege of it shocked Titus. Coming across a great pile of bodies dropped into a ravine, he groaned and raised his hands, assuring the gods of his horror at what he was seeing. Likewise, when it was reported to him that various auxiliaries were slitting open the stomachs of refugees, in the hope of discovering gold inside them, he indignantly condemned it as a crime. Rome's greatness was not to be compromised by trampling on the laws of gods and men. Yet these scruples, it went without saying, implied no sympathy for the rebels. Slaves who rose against their masters merited nothing but the most brutal repression. It was not enough to punish them; their punishment had to serve the entire world as a lesson. This was why, in the arena, criminals were thrown to beasts, or put to death in a whole range of humiliating ways: to provide a public entertainment.

Cheaper, however, and easier, was just to hang an infractory slave from a cross. This, in the early weeks of the siege, when bands of rebels were still sallying out from the walls to launch raids or forage supplies, was precisely what the legionaries had done with all those they took captive. A great forest of crosses had sprung up before the city walls. 'The soldiers, giving vent to the anger and hatred they felt for the Judaeans, made a mockery of their victims by nailing them up in a variety of poses.'[37] Not just the rebels but Jerusalem itself had been made into a spectacle.

And soon it was to be made even more of one. The hopes originally entertained by Titus of bringing the siege to a speedy resolution were exhausted. The refusal of the Judaean rebels to surrender left him with no choice but to pulverise their every last holdout. Ten weeks had passed since the start of the siege – and now, at last, the Judaean defences were starting to crumble. On 3 July, the facing wall of the Antonia abruptly collapsed. An initial assault on the breach was beaten back; but two days later, under cover of darkness, a small band of legionaries crept up through the rubble, slit the throats of the Judaean sentries, and sounded a trumpet from the ramparts. The Judaeans, panicking, withdrew through the entrances that joined the fortress to the Temple; the Romans, storming up the toppled wall to take possession of the Antonia, sought to follow their retreating adversaries. They were repulsed, however, after a savage struggle; and the Judaeans, sealing the entrances off, were able to secure the entire perimeter wall of the Temple. So massive were its outer walls, so colossal the building blocks used for its construction, that it constituted, in effect, another fortress: a citadel 'on which more care and effort had been lavished than all the rest'.[38]

Not that Titus was daunted. Great feats, after all, required great effort. Again, he summoned his men to a draining display of labour. Broiling though the heat was, and terrible the stench and the dust, they succeeded in levelling the Antonia in the space of only a week. Then they set once again to the building of ramps, this time against the walls of the Temple. Four were raised from the foundations of the Antonia; four, most exhaustingly of all, from the base of the Temple itself. The resistance, meanwhile, was as ferocious as it was desperate. Traps were set in which large numbers of legionaries were burned to death. An attempt to climb the walls was repulsed with a massive loss of Roman life. The walls proved impervious to even the mightiest of battering rams. Yet Titus, grim and implacable, refused to pause. He knew that the Temple, for all his setbacks, was almost in his grasp. And so it proved.

Over three months had passed since the start of the siege, and Titus' plans for Jerusalem were no longer what they had been. Even now, his preference was to spare the Temple destruction if he possibly could – but not at the cost of further Roman casualties. Shortly after the failure of his frontal assault on the Temple's outer wall, he gave orders for its gates to be torched. The gold and silver plates donated by Julius Alexander's father began to melt, and drip, and hiss; the wood underneath them caught fire; the colonnades that framed the outer courtyard of the Temple burst into flames. The Judaean defenders, surrounded by a great wall of fire, retreated to the inner courtyard, within which stood the massive edifice of the sanctuary itself. Beyond that stood the last surviving stretch of the colonnade; and here many thousands of people from the city below, men, women and children, had sought refuge on the assurance of a prophet that they would receive there from their god 'miraculous signs of their deliverance'.[39] But the prophet had deceived them. They, and everyone on the heights where the Temple stood, were beyond deliverance. And now the reckoning was at hand.

It was 10 August. Two days had passed since the torching of the gates. Huge numbers of legionaries were camped out before the walls of the inner court. The day before, the Judaean fighters had sought to clear the enemy from the outer court; but in vain. Now, as the sun rose above the eastern hills, they returned to the attack. Again they were beaten back. A legionary, pursuing them to the walls of the inner court, picked up a blazing piece of wood, climbed onto the shoulders of one of his comrades, and hurled it through an aperture in the wall. Beyond the window lay one of the rooms that framed the inner courtyard. Its timber beams and tapestries were bone dry. The fire caught. The Judaean fighters, when they saw it, raised a terrible animal howl of anguish. They had no thought now of holding their positions. Their only concern was to extinguish the fire. But it was too late. The flames were out of control. Black smoke, billowing up from the blaze, was already pluming high above the Temple, drifting over Jerusalem, proclaiming to Judaeans across the starving city the news of a horror almost too great for them to compute: the ruin of the sanctuary they held to be the holiest place on earth.

And the news of it, soon enough, would spread across the known world. The burning of the Temple set the seal on a conclusion that had surely already, over the course of that long and terrible summer, come to stare Titus in the face. There could be no returning to the order that had existed prior to the revolt. The primacy of Jerusalem in the region, long upheld by Roman favour though it had been, was finished for good. Instead, the city was to serve the world as a symbol of the might, of the terror, of the invincibility of Rome. Not for two centuries and more had the legions inflicted such a fate upon a famous city. Perhaps, as the flames began to lick the Temple, Titus did regret that the option of returning it to the guardianship of Agrippa had once and for all been closed off; but certainly he shed no tears over its fate.[40] Terror visited on a recalcitrant foe was nothing to be ashamed of. Quite the opposite. Ruin and slaughter were what the legions had been trained to inflict. Surging into the inner court of the Temple, the legionaries fought not as wild beasts, but as soldiers joined by a common citizenship, men forged by unyielding discipline to feel no pity, no revulsion at the spectacle of blood. Thousands fell. Viscera, slipping out from stomachs slit open by Roman swords, slithered around the altar and spilled down the sanctuary steps. 'The heights on which the Temple stood, enveloped in one great blaze of fire as they were, appeared to be boiling up from their very foundations. And yet the sea of flame was nothing to the ocean of blood, nor the death-squads of legionaries to the legions of the dead.[41] And when the slaughter was done, and the Temple complex had been stripped bare of all its treasures, and the Temple itself was crashing down in ruin, the legions brought their standards into the court opposite the eastern gate, and there they set the eagles up and offered sacrifice to them; and then, with a thunderous acclamation, they hailed Titus as *imperator*.

The Judaeans, notorious though they might be for their customs and their powers of prophecy, had never been taken seriously by the Romans as a military threat. Back in the days of its independence, their kingdom had always ranked as a second-class power, and their revolt, when it broke out, as a provincial uprising of a thoroughly familiar kind. Now, four years on, the capture of their capital served the emperor and his son as a battle-honour glorious beyond anything that Galba, Otho or Vitellius had remotely been able to boast. When, a month after the incineration of the Temple, Titus succeeded in capturing the very last redoubt of the rebels in Jerusalem, the great palace built by Herod, and there was no one left in the city for his men to plunder, rape, enslave or kill, he gave orders that it should be razed to the ground. Only a single stretch of wall and three towers were spared: 'the wall to provide protection to the garrison left on the site, and the towers to demonstrate to posterity just how proud and mighty a city had once stood there, until vanquished by Roman courage'.[42] No longer a contemptible people, the Judaeans had been transfigured into adversaries worthy of a Caesar, and their capital into a city fit to stand comparison with any in the annals of warfare. Thanks to its annihilation, Jerusalem now mattered to an emperor in Rome as it had never done while it stood. Vespasian, leaving Egypt shortly before the final completion of combat operations in the Judaean capital, could return home knowing that his family's otherwise undistinguished reputation was now burnished to glorious effect.

The infant imperial dynasty owed a great deal to the Judaean rebels.

The Prince of Peace

No one knew how to celebrate a victory quite like the Romans. It was Romulus who had shown the way. Returning home after slaying a Sabine king with his own hands, he had paraded his booty through the streets of Rome. His troops, ranged in their various units and singing rude songs as they went, had marched alongside it. Romulus himself, 'dressed in a purple robe and wearing a crown of laurel on his head',[43] had ridden in a splendid chariot drawn by four horses. All through the city the procession had wound. Then, at the end of it, Romulus had climbed the Capitol and made sacrifice to the gods. The trail that he had thereby blazed was one that many subsequent generations of warlords had followed. Pompey, Caesar, Augustus: all of them had celebrated what the Romans termed a *triumphus*: a triumph.

Increasingly, however, since the time of Augustus, the custom had fallen into abeyance. Emperors, suspicious of the glory that triumphs bestowed on those awarded them, had come to reserve the honour for themselves. The most recent, staged by Claudius to celebrate his conquest of Britain, had been rendered considerably less glorious than it might otherwise have been by the fact that, as everyone knew, Claudius himself had spent barely two weeks on the island. No one, however, could accuse the new emperor and his son of any lack of heroism. Both had sustained injuries on the field of battle: Titus had actually had a horse killed under him, and sustained permanent damage to his shoulder. The senate – whose responsibility it was to adjudicate on such matters – duly decreed that both men should celebrate a triumph; Vespasian and Titus, breaking with tradition, but in a manner calculated to warm traditionalist hearts, opted to share the honour. The result was a spectacle such as the Roman people had not witnessed for a long while: one that transported them back to an age when every year, it seemed, had brought them news of fresh victories, fresh conquests, fresh triumphs. Time-honoured elements of the ritual, familiar to younger spectators only from history books, were thrillingly and flamboyantly resurrected. It was as though ancient history had come alive.

Vespasian and Titus rode as Romulus had once ridden, in splendid chariots, and Domitian on an equally splendid horse. Great quantities of loot – gold, silver and ivory; carpets dyed the rarest purple or else embroidered with vividly lifelike scenes; pearls and topazes set in dazzling crowns; exotic animals of every kind – were paraded past the cheering crowds. So too were prisoners: seven hundred in all, 'the tallest and most handsome'[44] of those taken captive after the fall of Jerusalem, together with their two most prominent generals. When the procession reached the Forum, guards trussed one of the commanders up, knocked him to the ground, and then lashed the flesh off his bones as he was hauled across the flagstones to an underground cell. Meanwhile, Vespasian and Titus had climbed the Capitol. There they waited on its summit. The news they had been expecting soon arrived: the Judaean commander was dead. A great din of joy erupted across the Forum. It was time to complete the day's celebrations, to offer sacrifice, to make dues to Jupiter. Axes swung over kneeling oxen, and blood spattered the rock of the Capitol. Entrails were inspected. The omens proved good. Smoke rose to the heavens, and the perfume of roasting meat drifted across the city, where sumptuous banquets had been prepared for the Roman people. The triumph was done.

From war had come peace. The victory won by Vespasian had not been solely over the Judaeans, of course. Everyone knew this; no one mentioned it. The notion that a Roman might celebrate a triumph over a fellow citizen was a repellent one, and Vespasian certainly had no wish to draw attention to the means by which he had emerged as emperor. Yet his triumph, although over barbarians, could not help but make play with the civil war as well. It reminded spectators of the conflict that had so recently engulfed the capital – and reassured them that such violence was now banished for good. The evening before their triumph, the emperor and Titus had met beyond the traditional limits of Rome, on the Campus Martius, and passed the night there: for it was an ancient law of the Roman people that only on the very day of a triumph might a general and his army be permitted to enter the city. Nowhere was it proclaimed, as the legionaries swaggered along the processional route, that the days of soldiers running amok in the streets were over; but every formalised detail of the triumph proclaimed it even so. In a similar manner, when Vespasian made sacrifice at the climax of the procession, no one watching could forget the inferno that had so recently engulfed the Capitol: for Rome's most sacred hill still bore the scars of the flames.

Already, however, the emperor had set to healing them. He had personally begun the clearance work, picking up a blackened lump of stone and carrying away a load of rubble on a hod. He had ordered a search for documents that might replace the three thousand bronze tablets, many of them dating back to the very beginnings of Rome, destroyed when the public record office on the Capitol had burnt down. He had already commissioned the construction of a new temple of Jupiter, as splendid and imposing as the old one, on the foundations of the vanished structure. *Roma resurgens*: such was the slogan stamped on his coins. 'Rome is back.'

Nero, of course, in the wake of the great fire, had proclaimed the same message. The comparison was not one to which Vespasian cared to draw attention. Unlike Otho or Vitellius, he had nothing to gain from affecting a Neronian pose. Quite the opposite. Vespasian's image – rough-hewn, no-nonsense, leery of extravagance and show-boating – had already done much for the Flavian cause. Rather than apologise for his lack of pedigree, he made a show of it. 'A warrior line, nourished on Sabine berries':[45] so one poet, stuck for anything better to say, celebrated Vespasian's ancestry. Ostentatious in his modesty, he spurned the echoing halls of the Palatine for life in the suburbs or – during the heat of summer – on his Sabine farm. Certainly, he had no intention of settling down in the Golden House. Workmen who under Nero had been employed to build the most fantastical complex ever constructed in Rome were employed by Vespasian on an equally showy project of demolition. The outer reaches of the estate were returned to their original purposes. When the Colossus, finally completed a decade after its original commission, was hauled up into position by the side of the road that led into the Forum, it wore the face not of Nero, but of the Sun. Most dramatic of all was the fate of the ornamental lake that had stood at the very heart of the park. Drained and filled with concrete, it might as well never have existed. Vespasian, however, was keen to build as well as to erase. Shrewd as ever, he had spotted a glaring gap in the capital's infrastructure. While other, smaller cities might boast amphitheatres built of stone, Rome did not. The only one that had ever existed in the city — a small and antiquated structure on the Campus Martius — had been destroyed in the great fire.* The solution, then, appeared obvious: devote a site notorious as the pleasure-garden of a single man to the pleasure of the entire Roman people. Build an amphitheatre on it. 'Restore Rome to itself.'[46]

Such a project of construction enabled Vespasian to present himself doubly as an *imperator*. No one in the city could doubt, watching as surveyors mapped out the vast space that was to constitute the arena, gawping at the sheer sweep of the seating area, marvelling at the sumptuous beauty of the fittings, that the new emperor was sponsoring a structure beyond the dreams of any previous Caesar. Even the memory of Nero, that great entertainer, was put in its shade. As row after row of seating went up, and storey after storey, so the full scale of Vespasian's ambition became evident: to provide a space in which the entirety of the Roman people might assemble. Yet Vespasian was not building his amphitheatre solely to provide the plebs with entertainment. His aim was to educate them as well: to remind them of what the word *imperator* had originally meant. Over the course of Rome's history, many generals had been saluted with

---

* Nero had built an amphitheatre out of wood, also on the Campus Martius, that may still have been standing when work began on the Colosseum — although it, too, may have been consumed in the great fire. The evidence is ambiguous.

the title on the field of battle. Titus, hailed by his legions amid the rubble of Jerusalem, had been only the most recent. Until its appropriation by Augustus, the word had been used primarily to describe a commander victorious in war. A structure massive on the scale of the Flavian Amphitheatre could only ever have been funded by a city victorious in many wars. Vespasian was not, as Nero had been, a man without experience of combat. He knew what it was to sleep on hard ground, to spill the guts of a barbarian, to watch flies swarm around an open wound. It was as such a man that he had commissioned his amphitheatre. It was as such a man that he aimed to raise it as a monument to Rome's rule of the world.

Yet Vespasian, too, was an actor. No less than Nero, he had a genius for fashioning Rome into a stage-set. His amphitheatre, massive though it might be, was simultaneously a thing of smoke and mirrors. Emperor and son, by celebrating a triumph, had ensured that no one would be left in any doubt, watching the Flavian refurbishment of the capital, as to precisely how it was being funded. The Roman people, after all, had seen with their own eyes the wealth of Judaea paraded through their streets. And not only that. Also included in the triumph had been vast billboards illustrating particularly dramatic moments from the war — the annihilation of Judaean phalanxes, the storming of wealthy cities — together with 'a large number of ships'.[47] Few in the crowd would have appreciated the truth: that the Judaeans had been far too few in numbers to meet the legions anywhere except from behind walls; that the only wealthy city stormed in the course of the war had been Jerusalem; that there had never been any naval battles, just the hunting after fugitives across a lake, and the odd skirmish with pirates. The new emperor and his son, riding through the streets of Rome, were not merely celebrating a triumph; they were also staging a fraud.

No one watching them, of course, would have presumed to point this out. Yet it was evident to anyone with even the vaguest awareness of the background to the Judaean revolt. Time-hallowed tradition decreed that only the conquest of fresh territory merited a triumph. The suppression of a rebellion did not suffice. Titus, it was true, while still in Judaea, had made a point of treating it exactly as though it were recently annexed territory: stationing his most formidable legion, X Fretensis, to garrison what remained of its capital, and constituting the region formally as a province. This was why the triumph had to take the form it did. Vespasian had no choice but to pose as the conqueror of a previously unconquered land, rich in pearls, ivory and embroidered carpets. Titus, veering even further into fantasy, claimed to have stormed a capital that had never in its history been stormed before. 'The city of Jerusalem, either attacked in futility or left entirely untried by all the leaders, kings, or nations before him, *he* destroyed.'[48] So it was proclaimed on a great arch erected in the Circus Maximus. Similar messages, whether chiselled onto monuments across the capital or composed by admiring poets, were everywhere. Year after year, coins were minted with the image stamped on them of a woman bowed in mourning, and the slogan *IUDAEA CAPTA* – 'Judaea has been taken captive.' The message was clear: Vespasian and Titus had succeeded in subduing a barbarous land previously beyond the limits of Roman rule.* No such feat of conquest had been witnessed since the days of Augustus. The glory of it bathed the Flavians – and the entire city of Rome with them – in a nimbus of purest gold.

The greatest actors did not draw attention to the fact that they were acting. Nero might never have understood this – but there was a Caesar who had. Augustus, the founder of the autocracy to which the Flavians were now heir, had also come to power after wading through Roman blood. Subtly and seductively, he had sought to mask the circumstances of his rise to dominance. Rather than focus on the civil wars that had left him unrivalled as Rome's master, he had dazzled his fellow citizens with the brilliance and splendour of his victories

---

* Intriguingly, a single coin has been found bearing the message *IUDAEA RECEPTA*, or 'Judaea has been recovered' – evidently the product of a mint that had failed to receive the correct propaganda briefing.

over foreign foes; rather than draw attention to the authentic basis of his supremacy, he had posted his legions to the outer limits of the empire, where no one in the capital could see them. Vespasian had studied the lessons of Augustus' career well. The more he promoted Judaea as a source of infinite treasure, the more he was able to disguise the true source of his wealth; the more he vaunted the role played by Flavian armies in the capture of Jerusalem, the more he was able to blur the memory of the sacking of Cremona. The war fought by Vespasian and Titus against the Judaeans, a campaign that originally had seemed merely a routine police operation, the suppression of a rebellion much like any other, now qualified as something very different: the foundation stone around which the Flavians had constructed their entire claim to legitimacy. It was, as a feat of image-building, one that even Augustus might have admired.

The wealth paraded by Vespasian in his triumph and lavished on his amphitheatre did not – in the main – come from Jerusalem. Rather, he and Mucianus, the two warlords who between them had triumphed in the civil war, had extorted it from across the provinces of the East. Even once Vitellius was dead, and the civil war brought to an end, the new emperor had continued to turn the screws. Sailing home from Alexandria, he had combined a leisurely tour of the Aegean with the imposition of swingeing tax demands. Some peoples had their obligations doubled, while others, previously exempt, were obliged to start paying tribute. Among the latter were the Greeks, who – to their impotent fury – had Nero's grant of freedom to them rescinded: this on the grounds that, as Vespasian drily put it, 'they had forgotten how to be free'.[49]

Elsewhere, the new emperor was obliged to tread more carefully. In Gaul and Germany, Vitellian sympathies still smouldered. Along the Rhine, where much of the military infrastructure had been reduced to fire-blackened stumps, the scarring was particularly visible. Vespasian, however, was not a soldier's soldier for nothing. He knew how to whip a potentially mutinous army into shape. Various legions – IV Macedonica among them – were cashiered; the

Larks were dispatched to the furthest reaches of the Danube; XXI Rapax and XXII Primigenia were transferred from Upper Germany to stations farther along the Rhine. Two new legions – both of them pointedly given the name 'Flavia' – were formed out of discharged Vitellians. The various legionary bases destroyed by the Batavians were rebuilt. Vetera was relocated altogether. Then, once the restoration work had been completed, the legions stationed in Lower Germany embarked on a series of punitive raids across the Rhine. Reprisals on the barbarians who had presumed to massacre the garrison of Vetera were predictably brutal. Just as the Judaeans had been punished for their criminality by the destruction of their temple, so were the Germans obliged to endure the loss of their great prophetess. The Romans, no less than their adversaries, stood in awe of Veleda – 'that tall maiden whom the Rhine-dwellers worship, shuddering at the thunderings of her golden voice'[50] – and they knew better than to risk the anger of the gods she served by putting her to death. Instead, once they had taken her captive, they dispatched her to Italy. There, in a town some twenty miles south of Rome, she was installed as a temple servant. The woman who from the summit of her lonely tower had prophesied the doom of the legions now served the interests of her conquerors: mediating between the gods and the Roman people.

Meanwhile, in Upper Germany, military control had not merely been restored, but advanced: the new emperor, keen to integrate the Rhine defences with those of the Danube, ordered the annexation of the Black Forest, the region known to the Romans as the Decumatian Fields, and which linked the upper reaches of both rivers. Briskly, efficiently, and to formidable effect, Vespasian had succeeded in reconstituting the entire empire north of the Alps. Nevertheless, he remained wary of potential trouble. When, to universal astonishment, Julius Sabinus, the self-proclaimed Caesar of the 'Gallic Empire', turned out not to have been cremated in his villa, but rather to have been kept in hiding by his wife, the emperor refused to share in the general mood of admiration for this display of marital devotion. Not even the revelation that Sabinus, on one occasion, had accompanied his wife to Rome disguised as her slave, all in a vain attempt to secure a pardon, was sufficient to spare them both execution. Decades later, Vespasian's insistence on putting such a self-evidently devoted couple to death was still remembered as a disgrace. 'Never in his entire reign did he commit a more cruel and savage act.'[51]

A claim that was, in its way, a compliment. Vespasian – certainly by the standards of previous Caesars – was not a man greatly given to cruel and savage acts. By doing his dirty work for him, Mucianus had enabled him to keep his hands clean. The elimination of Vitellius' young son while Vespasian was still absent in the East had left the stage clear for the emperor, on his arrival back in Rome, to make an impressively generous gesture: the arrangement of a splendid marriage for his dead rival's daughter. Not merely a display of beneficence, this had signalled to the Roman people that he was not a man to bear a grudge. In Vespasian, so his fellow citizens were delighted to discover, they had an emperor who rarely took serious offence, no matter what abuse might be levelled at him. Jokes, liberties, insults: all bounced off him like arrows off a shield wall. Vespasian had been wounded enough in the course of battle not to fret over a bit of mockery. He knew, as someone who had served both Caligula and Nero, to what dark ends paranoia might lead. This was why, when friends warned him that a senator was predicted by astrologers to become emperor, he promptly made the man consul, assuring his friends, 'He will not forget the favour.'[52] Even the practice of frisking visitors approaching the imperial presence, routine since the time of Claudius, was abolished. Vespasian, a man who all his life had shown himself as indomitable as he was contemptuous of flummery, had not become emperor merely to start at shadows.

Not that this rendered him any the less an autocrat. Supreme power was supreme power, and Vespasian made no apologies for it. Pointedly and deliberately, he rubbed the noses of senators tempted to look down on his regime in the brute fact that the commanding heights of the Roman state were now his to do with as he pleased. Ten years he ruled as emperor, during which time he held eight consulships, Titus seven, and Mucianus three. Nor was Vespasian any the less assiduous in monopolising control of the security apparatus. Rather than entrusting command of the Praetorians to an equestrian, he broke with all precedent by giving the command to Titus. The appointment was as cynical as it was shrewd. The conqueror of Jerusalem, who had already more than demonstrated his readiness to crush opposition, could be trusted to maintain the new regime as a family business. After all, he was due to inherit it.

Vespasian might scorn to display paranoia; but Titus, if he were to succeed his father to the rule of the world, could not afford to be so relaxed. His glamour, in the years that followed his triumph, was touched by more than a hint of the sinister. His fingerprints were suspected on two particular crimes: the execution of Helvidius Priscus, a senator celebrated for his stern and republican cast of virtue; and the murder, after one of Titus' own dinner parties, of Caecina. In both cases, it was true, there were extenuating circumstances. Helvidius, who had refused to grant Vespasian the titles that were a Caesar's due, had consistently been so rigid in his devotion to the traditions of the republic that he might as well have been courting execution; while Caecina, despite almost a decade of dutiful service to the Flavian cause, remained notorious as someone who had only to pledge his loyalty to betray it. Certainly, for all that Vespasian, as emperor, bore the ultimate responsibility for the deaths of both men, the blame did not attach to him. Even the severest moralists were inclined to give him the benefit of the doubt. 'He alone, out of all those who became emperor, was changed by it for the better.'[53]

A decade after launching his bid for power, Vespasian could be well pleased with all that he had achieved for the Roman people. Their empire stood on renewed foundations; their city, to a degree unparalleled since the age of Augustus, had been burnished and beautified. On the Capitol, the familiar silhouette of the temple of Jupiter was well on its way to being restored to the skyline; beyond the Forum, in what had once been the grounds of the Golden House, the Flavian Amphitheatre already rose three storeys high. Neither monument, however, served as the truest memorial to Vespasian's remarkable achievements. That was to be found instead just beyond Caesar's great marble forum, in what, until the great fire, had been Rome's central meat market, but was now, following its redevelopment, the site of an enormous temple to Pax: Peace.

Many were the paradoxes to which this building gave form. Dedicated to peace, it glittered with trophies to war. The centrepiece of its great collection of treasures was the plunder taken from the Temple in Jerusalem, and which, in the triumph celebrated by Vespasian and Titus, had been the only objects paraded through the streets to have come unambiguously from Judaea. Golden ornaments that once had pandered to the superstition and conceit of the Judaeans, a great table and a peculiar-looking lampstand with seven arms — a 'menorah' — now redounded to the glory of Caesar. Not that the spoils of Jerusalem were the only treasures to do so. Statues and paintings looted by Nero from across the Greek world, and originally installed in the Golden House, might now be admired by any citizen who cared to pay a visit to the Temple of Peace. The spectacle of masterpieces garnered from across many provinces, and all assembled in a single place, could not help but hint at a further paradox: that Rome, the mistress of the world, was no longer solely a Roman city.

'A building as beautiful as any in the world.'[54] Such was the verdict of Vespasian's contemporaries on the Temple of Peace. It was an astonishing legacy for the man once derided as the Muleteer to have fashioned for himself. The blend of meanness and shrewdness that the Roman upper classes commonly associated with Sabine peasants was certainly nothing of which Vespasian ever felt ashamed. Even as the Temple of Peace served as a monument to his supreme mastery of war, it bore witness to his unfailing eye for the bottom line. When Titus, alerted to the fact that his father had put a tax on urine, complained that the policy was a vulgar one, Vespasian held up a coin, shoved it under Titus' nose, and demanded to know if it stank; then, when Titus shook his head, answered, 'But it comes from piss, all the same.'[55] True or not, the anecdote bore witness to qualities that even the haughtiest of Vespasian's contemporaries, no matter how much they might look down their noses at the upstart emperor, could not help but privately admire: wit, lack of pretence, and an unflinching commitment to the service of the Roman people.

Duty was a concept that Vespasian had always held dear. Unsurprisingly, then, when he fell sick in the summer of 79, he continued to attend to his responsibilities as emperor, even going so far as to receive embassies while lying in bed. It was clear that he did not have long, for in the skies, an infallible marker of change, a fiery-tailed comet, was seen. At the end, Vespasian insisted on facing death like a soldier: on his feet. Propped up by his servants, he breathed his last in their arms. 'Poor me,' he had murmured at the onset of his illness. 'I think I am becoming a god.'[56] He had not been wrong. Like Caesar, like Augustus, like Claudius, Vespasian was raised after his death to the heavens. His achievements had been manifold, and his legacy would prove an enduring one. The terrible year in which no fewer than four Caesars had reigned, and civilisation itself seemed lost to chaos, had not, after all, proved fatal to the empire of the Roman people. Vespasian, just as the prophets of the East had predicted, had set the world on new and strong foundations. He had shown himself a prince of peace indeed.

PART TWO

PEACE

IV

SLEEPING GIANTS

Concrete Facts

In ancient times, so it was said, the greatest of all Greek heroes had visited Italy. The story was a favourite among the Romans. Hercules was the son of Jupiter — a paternity that had thrown Juno, the queen of the gods, into a towering rage. So irate was she at her husband's adultery that she had sent a mist of madness down upon Hercules. His insanity had driven him to commit a terrible crime: the murder of his wife and children. For this deed the gods had sentenced him to a series of supposedly impossible labours — which, being a hero, and the strongest man of all time, he had duly completed. The first of the labours had provided him with his signature look: the hide of a ferocious lion which he had throttled with his own hands, and worn ever afterwards as a cloak.* Another labour, the tenth, had been more demanding. It had required Hercules to travel to a distant island beyond the setting of the sun, to kill a three-headed giant, and then to drive the monster's cattle back all the way to Greece. It was in the course of completing this feat that he had arrived in Italy. Reaching what would one day be Rome, he had built a bridge over the Tiber and slain the local giant. Then, heading southwards, he had arrived in Campania, the rich and fertile land stretching inland from the Bay of Naples. Here he had found himself confronted not by one giant, but by an entire race of them. Never a man to duck a challenge,

---

* Though some claimed that it was a different lion, which Hercules had killed as a teenager.

he had fought the whole lot at once. The clash had made the earth shake – but Hercules, aided by his divine father, had finally emerged triumphant from the battle. The defeated giants, their wounds still fiery from the impact of Jupiter's thunderbolts, had been chained and imprisoned by the victorious hero beneath the great mountain that rose above the Campanian plain: Vesuvius.

Hercules' feat had been much commemorated by poets and scholars. To celebrate it, so they recorded, he had led a triumphal procession – a *pompe*, in Greek – along the lower slopes of Vesuvius. Then he had founded a pair of cities. One of these, Pompeii, stood at the very foot of the mountain, and commemorated in its name the hero's triumph. The other, Herculaneum, was situated on a promontory jutting out into sea, and was famed for its cooling breezes. Whether Hercules had truly founded these two cities might, perhaps, be doubted by sceptics. Yet even if he had not, and even if he had never been anywhere near Campania, the stories told of his battle with the giants reflected something about Pompeii and Herculaneum that was indisputably true: they were both very old.

This hint of the antique, along with its Greek patina, had always been a part of the appeal of the Bay of Naples for Rome's movers and shakers. Campania – 'that most blessed of plains'[1] – was a landscape numinous with myth. Nymphs had once swum in its waters and sirens sung from its islands. The Sibyl, bearing her books of prophecy, had travelled to meet Tarquin from its shores. Cumae, her home, contained what was widely agreed to be a portal to the underworld. Like Naples, which lay a few miles east from it along the coast, the city had been founded back in the mists of time by Greek settlers; and it still, centuries on, provided tourists from Rome with what they fondly liked to imagine was a touch of ancient Greece. Fantasy, in a setting as desirable as Campania, with its perfumed streets and its vine-clad slopes, its fields of wildflowers and its incomparable oyster beds, had long proven irresistible to those with the wealth to invest in it. Only in the more exclusive neighbourhoods of Rome were

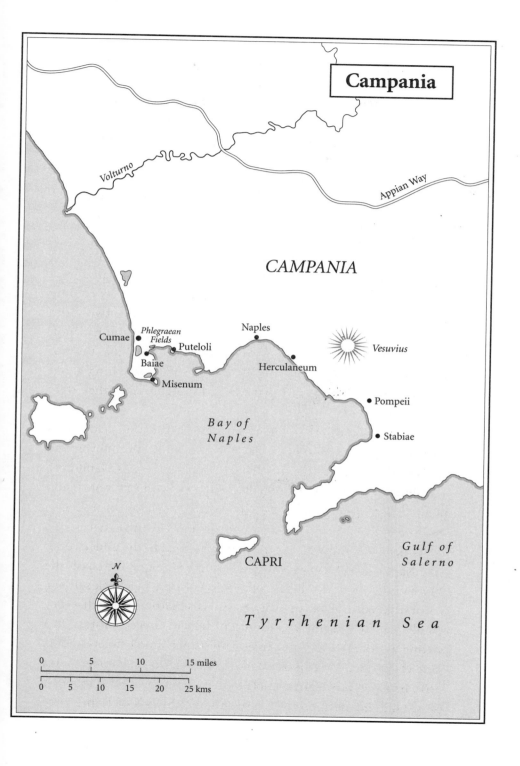

Campania

Volturno

Appian Way

CAMPANIA

Phlegraean Fields

Naples

Cumae

Puteloli

Vesuvius

Baiae

Herculaneum

Misenum

Pompeii

Bay of Naples

Stabiae

Gulf of Salerno

CAPRI

T y r r h e n i a n   S e a

N

| 0 | 5 | 10 | 15 miles |
| 0 | 5 | 10 | 15 | 20 | 25 kms |

properties more expensive. Otherwise, the Bay of Naples ranked as the priciest real estate in the world.

A sea view was especially prized. The most spectacular locations, those on rocky promontories or in other particularly beautiful spots, had originally been developed back in the final century of the republic; and already, by the time of Augustus, the sheer number of villas lining the coast had come 'to give the impression of forming a single city'.[2] These estates were not working farms, like those on the outskirts of Pompeii, an inland city, but palaces, vast complexes of colonnaded porticoes and landscaped gardens adorned with libraries, paintings and antique bronzes. Outside Herculaneum, for instance, there stood a villa originally commissioned by Julius Caesar's father-in-law, filled with philosophical texts and statues ransacked from the Greek world, that might as well have been transplanted from Alexandria. When he had built the Golden House, Nero had consciously been attempting to recreate the ambience of such an estate: its artificiality had been precisely the point. Villas along the Bay of Naples had long since ceased to draw sustenance from the towns and farms that existed beyond their walls. Everything that had originally attracted the super-rich to Campania — mythology, culture, beauty — had been privatised. Petronius, a senator obliged to commit suicide by Nero, and famed both as an arbiter of fashion and as a pathologist of decadence, had mocked the trend: 'Once, with my own eyes, I saw the Sibyl at Cumae hanging in a jar; and when the boys asked her, "Sibyl, what do you want?," she answered, "I want to die."'[3]

The coastline, however, was not exclusively a playground for the super-rich. It boasted quarries as well. Between Naples and Cumae the landscape had a peculiar quality: for here the giants imprisoned by Hercules lay sufficiently close to the surface that their fiery wounds scorched the earth and made water boil and bubble. The vapours were often toxic; and yet so fertile was the soil that in spring the perfume of the wild roses growing in the Phlegraean Fields, as they were known, was sweeter by far than that of roses in a garden. How to explain this? Scholars had arrived at what appeared to be the conclusive answer: once, long ago, the whole region had been on fire. This was evident from even the most cursory examination of the fields — and of the slopes of Vesuvius too. In both regions, the rock — 'although cold now for many long years'[4] — was black and porous, as only rock could be that had been burnt right through. 'Pompeian pumice', it was called; and rain, percolating through the soil, was retained by it, 'and kept like a warm kind of juice'.[5] So life-giving was this juice that it sustained the sweetest-smelling roses in the world, and the fairest orchards and vineyards, and no fewer than three harvests every year. Campania was a land perpetually in bloom.

Yet fertility was not the greatest gift the Phlegraean Fields and the slopes of Vesuvius had bestowed upon the region. The flames which once, back in ancient times, had scorched and blackened it had also turned the earth to 'a kind of sandy dust endowed with wonderful qualities'.[6] Mix this dust with lime, so engineers had discovered, and the result was the world's strongest and most adaptable con-crete. Remarkably, it even hardened under water. Transported far and wide, it had been used in cities ranging from Spain to Judaea. Unsurprisingly, however, it was in Campania itself that the frontiers of town planning had been pushed back to most innovative effect. What happened on the Bay of Naples served to shape the look of the world.

For a century, those who wanted a glimpse of the future had only to head for the coastline south of the Phlegraean Fields. Here was to be found the achingly chic spa town of Baiae, a place so celebrated for its delights that even Vespasian, after a decade spent sternly boycott-ing the resort, had at last, in the final year of his life, succumbed to temptation and paid it a visit. Beach parties, yacht parties, seafood, courtesans, scandals: Baiae had it all. In designing a townscape appro-priate to this fabulous place of pleasure, architects had exploited its ashy sands to the full. So many concrete piers had been thrust out into the bay that, as one joke had it, the very fish were cramped by them. Even more striking was a feature that had come to serve as a particular emblem of Baiae: the dome. Perhaps such a bold novelty could only have been developed in such a location, for nowhere else did engineers have concrete of sufficient quality to render it practicable. Set amid terraced gardens beyond the beach, the domes of Baiae, raised over sulphur baths and swimming pools, presented a sight like nowhere else. Well might poets hail the town as a princeps among seaside resorts. Nero, a lifelong participant in its delights, had been inspired by it to break with all convention, and commission a dome of his own for the Golden House. The sincerest form of flattery – and due reflection of the fact that still, a full century after their construction, Baiae's domes remained thrillingly cutting edge. 'Golden shore of happy Venus': so one visitor described the resort.[7] The goddess, it was clear, had come to love a bit of concrete.

Not that domes were the limit of what might be achieved with Campania's miracle substance. Far from it. Even as the strains of music and laughter filled the streets of Baiae, and waiters scurried along colonnades bearing oysters on golden dishes, and billionaires swapped gossip in the shade, there was constantly to be seen out at sea, beyond the glittering of gilded piers, ship after ship, oars churning the waters, gliding to and fro. Puteoli, a mile or so down the coast from Baiae, remained what it had been long before the development of Ostia by Claudius and Nero: an indispensable shrine to Annona, the goddess of the corn supply. Well might the sandy ash used to make hydraulic concrete have come to be known as 'Puteolian powder': 'for the harbours of Puteoli, by means of which the port has become an emporium like no other, are entirely man-made'.[8] Every summer, when the corn ships from Alexandria were first spotted on the horizon, the people of the city would rush to the docks, and there, crowded onto great artificial moles, celebrate that Rome had been spared starvation for another year. The Bay of Naples, for all its show of pleasure, was fundamental to the security of the capital. The events of the civil war had served doubly as a reminder of this fact. Just as Vespasian's occupation of Egypt had demonstrated how easily the shipment of corn to Puteoli might be throttled, so had the role played in the conflict by a second town visible from Baiae, the great naval base of Misenum, proved a wake-up call. Marines — whether recruited by Nero to serve as legionaries, or rising in mutiny against Vitellius — had played a key role in the conflict. Rather than disband I Adiutrix and post its men back to Misenum, Vespasian had sent the legion to the Rhine; but he had no desire to see others from the base get ideas above their station. Command of the fleet, then, was a crucial appointment. A firm hand was needed on the tiller. A hand that could be trusted not to jerk it this way and that wildly. A hand, in short, with grip.

Gaius Plinius Secundus — Pliny — was a man who had demonstrated grip all his life. Amiable, stout and asthmatic, he was simultaneously the very model of a go-getting equestrian. His promotion by Vespasian to the command of the fleet at Misenum had set the seal on a career of exemplary public service. Born in Comum, a beautiful lakeside town below the Alps, Pliny had never been a man to stay in one place for long. As a young officer he had held a range of posts along the Rhine, seeing active service, and making some exceedingly useful contacts. In his first posting, he had served under Corbulo; in his final posting, alongside the teenage Titus. It had taken time, however, for these associations to bear full fruit. Under Nero, Pliny's career had stalled. Retiring to Comum, he had devoted himself to writing books: on history, on oratory, on the vagaries of the Latin language. But then, with Vespasian's unexpected accession to power, his situation had dramatically improved. His term of service under Corbulo, that friend and patron of the great Mucianus; the time he had spent in a tent with Titus: both had marked him out as a natural favourite of the Flavians. Sure enough, Pliny had been entrusted by the new regime with a succession of prestigious posts. From province to province he had gone, administering the finances of each one with a display of competence and assiduity very much after Vespasian's heart. Duly appointed to the command of Misenum, Pliny had continued to impress. The time he spent on the Bay of Naples did not cut him off from the ultimate source of patronage: for he was frequently required to travel to Rome. There, he had capitalised on the fact that both he and Vespasian were early risers, regularly calling on the emperor before dawn. A man who under Nero had seemed doomed to provincial obscurity had emerged, thanks to the convulsions of civil war, an associate of Caesar himself. Pliny, under Vespasian, had reached as high as any equestrian could reasonably hope to go.

Even so, exhausting though his duties and responsibilities might be, they were not, in Pliny's own opinion, exhausting enough. Despite his return to public service, he had scorned to lay down his pen. Even the hardest working among his associates were stupefied by his stamina. 'His indefatigability was beyond belief, his powers of application exceptional.'[9] Here were the same qualities that Corbulo, Pliny's old commander, had identified as the prerequisites for success: the essential requirements for the projection of Roman power. Only by submitting to an iron-forged discipline could the legions hope to maintain the rule of the world; only by committing to a relentless programme of research could a scholar hope to catalogue everything in the universe. Pliny was not just looking to continue writing, but to write a book on a truly epic scale, one that might serve his readers as an all-round education: an *encyclopaedia*. It was, as he proudly acknowledged, an unprecedented ambition – 'for not even a Greek has attempted such a massive project single-handedly before'.[10] Perhaps this was because only a Roman could ever have conceived it: for it was only the Romans who had the world in their hands.

To look out from Misenum across the Bay of Naples, to track the freighters as they sailed past on their way to Puteoli, to marvel at the wealth and beauty on display along the shore, was to comprehend just what it meant for the whole world to be bound together in a single order. 'For who would deny,' Pliny demanded, 'now that the greatness of Rome's empire enables opposite ends of the globe to communicate with one another, that life is improved by the interchange of commodities, by a partnership in the blessings of peace, and by the general availability of things previously kept concealed from us?'[11] He was not alone in marvelling at how Roman rule had served to shrink the world. The crowds in the capital who gathered to gawp at Vespasian and Titus' triumph had been doing the same. Whether it was exotic blooms transplanted to adorn the gardens of senators, or dyes harvested from shellfish in distant seas, or rare materials mined from the very bowels of the earth, there was little that Roman consumers could not obtain. Naturally, they had to be wealthy enough to afford them; but this, in the opinion of even the sternest moralist, was precisely what rendered luxuries such as purple or gold acceptable as markers of honour. The risk, of course, was always that they might end up in the hands of people who did not merit them — upstarts, parvenus, social climbers — or, perhaps worse, that they might come to sap the character of those who did. Even as Pliny hailed the fruits of the Roman peace, he was not oblivious to the risks they might present to the Romans themselves: 'of all the many peoples on the face of the earth, the worthiest and the most upstanding'.[12]

Nowhere was this danger more evident than in the kitchen. Back in the early, heroic days of the republic, when even senators were to be found at the plough, the Roman people had subsisted on a plain, manly diet, the produce of their own fields, fertilised by their sweat. Greeks, meanwhile, they had dismissed as effeminates, fussing over cookery books. The Roman conquest of the world, however, had come to change all that. Exotic foodstuffs, fantastical recipes, celebrity chefs: all had been imported to their city. Now, in the age of the Caesars, it was the dinner parties of Italy, 'luxurious and improvident',[13] that provoked the envy of the Greeks. Even so, there remained deep within the Roman character a lurking suspicion of cookery. Vitellius had been despised not merely as a glutton but as an epicure. His most notorious accoutrement, a dish so wide as to resemble a shield, was said to have been laden with delicacies sourced from the very limits of east and west: 'the livers of parrotfish, the brains of pheasants and peacocks, the tongues of flamingos, the entrails of lampreys'.[14] Pliny, a man who was certainly not oblivious to the pleasures of good food, viewed all such extravagances with distaste. It repelled him that gourmands might eat the skin of an elephant's trunk, munching on it not because it was tasty, but because it enabled them to feel that they were dining on ivory. The wonders of the world merited respect. This was the conviction to which Pliny had devoted a superhuman degree of effort. The true value of Rome's empire lay not in the opportunities it provided for profit, or for ransacking previously inaccessible reaches of the world, or for stimulating jaded palates, but in something altogether nobler: its success in pushing back, to a degree never achieved before, the frontiers of knowledge.

To comprehend the world in its full richness and wonder it was necessary to travel. Not everything could be transplanted to Rome. There were plants that could only put down roots in certain soils; animals that could only survive in certain environments; rivers, lakes, deserts and mountains that had no equivalent in Italy. Most notable of all was the astonishing diversity of human custom. 'The sheer range of it is beyond computation – being almost as broad as the range of human groupings themselves.'[15] Pliny, who had served in many provinces, and who as admiral of the Misene fleet commanded men recruited from across the Mediterranean, knew from first-hand experience just how various were the peoples brought under Roman rule. He had seen for himself how, even as Italy had imported the produce of the world, it had also, like a loving mother gathering in her children, enabled distant lands to share in a common home: 'For she has joined together scattered empires, softened barbarous customs, brought a quite astonishing number of nations (all of them speaking inharmonious and savage languages) to converse in a common tongue, endowed humanity with civilisation, and become, to sum things up, the native land of peoples across the span of the entire world.'[16]

The implication was startling: that everyone in the empire was destined to become, in the long run, a kind of Roman. Not only that: Rome's conquests rendered the barbarians who lived beyond the limits of Caesar's rule, who had failed to benefit from its ameliorating influence, only the more barbarous. Pliny wrote as a man who, during his term of service on the Rhine, had seen for himself how the Chaukians lived. Why, then, should he doubt that on islands in the northern sea there were to be found people born with horses' hooves or giant ears, or that in Africa, beyond the Atlas Mountains, there might be a tribe that lived in caves, subsisted on snakes, and conversed entirely in squeaks? Even the farthest reaches of the world were not wholly beyond his gaze. Studying travellers' reports, he could read, for instance, that it was possible to sail southwards from the Persian Gulf and arrive in Spain, and that north of Britain, beyond a mysterious island named Thule, all the ocean was ice. The more brilliantly the blaze of Roman civilisation shone, the more it illuminated what had previously lain in darkness. This it was that had made possible Pliny's astonishing project: 'to cover everything in the entire world'.[17]

Knowledge was power. The mission to comprehend the world was not some eccentric flight of fancy, some idle amusement, but one heroically appropriate to the dignity of the Roman people. The Flavians, no less than Pliny, were committed to this principle. When Vespasian and Titus, shortly after coming to power, conducted a census, the resulting information had naturally served the emperor as a basis for his fiscal reforms; but it had also been something more, a public signal that the chaotic days of civil war were over, that anarchy was banished, that everything was restored to order. To fathom the rhythms and patterns of the natural world, too, was a duty that it would have been irresponsible for an imperial people to shrug aside. Mucianus, that subtle bulwark of the Flavian regime, had not hesitated, while serving in distant lands, to record everything wonderful, everything unexpected that he happened to see. Whether an immense plane tree beneath which he and a dozen companions had enjoyed a picnic; or the source of the river Euphrates; or monkeys playing chequers; or an old man, aged 104, who had grown an entirely fresh set of teeth: all lay within a Roman's purview. Pliny, detailing the great man's reminiscences, had made sure to supplement them, whenever he could, with reminiscences of his own. Just as Mucianus, visiting Greece, had met a man who originally, before sprouting a beard and muscles, had been a woman, so had Pliny, while in Africa, witnessed a bride on the very day of her wedding turn into a man. Hints of a universal order might be found in even the most incredible occurrences. Only in a global empire, however, was it possible to trace them. Such was the supreme achievement of the Roman people: to have fashioned a dominion that could reveal to humanity the fundamentals of the cosmos.

These fundamentals were evident less in the convulsions that had brought the Flavians to power than in the peace they had brought to the world. This was not to say, of course, that unanticipated disasters might not happen. Pliny, listing the vagaries of celestial phenomena, had recorded the death over a century previously of a man from Pompeii: killed by lightning from a clear blue sky. Fleetingly, throughout his encyclopaedia, he would make reference to cities only recently destroyed: he noted that Jerusalem was no more, and that in Cremona, just before its annihilation, a previously unknown species of bird, looking much like a thrush, had appeared (the bird itself, Pliny noted, was 'delicious'[18]). Yet who could doubt, surveying the glorious spectacle of the Bay of Naples – its harbours filled with shipping from across the world; its hinterland rich in vineyards, orchards and olive groves; its shoreline adorned with concrete – that the good times were here to stay: that the arc of the universe did indeed bend towards prosperity?

Big Fish, Small Ponds

Once, before the coming of the Romans, the mountains that loomed to the east of Campania had been home to a people despised and feared in equal measure by all who lived along the Bay of Naples. The Samnites, hardy warriors who wore collars of solid iron and shaved their pubic hair in public, had proven themselves adversaries as flinty and unyielding as the soil from which they scratched a living. Three grinding bouts of war it had taken the Romans to subdue them;

and still, almost four centuries on from their final subjugation, they served the super-rich along the Bay of Naples as the very epitome of peasants. Naturally, the days when the Samnites would descend from their mountain fastnesses to bring fire and slaughter to the soft lands below them were long gone, for they had come to rank as Roman citizens more than a century and a half before. Even so, reminders of the distant age when they had lived as a free and independent people were not completely banished from Campania. Their language, Oscan – once widely spoken along the Bay of Naples – was still to be heard on the streets of Puteoli or Pompeii, or seen inscribed on faded monuments, or glimpsed as scratched graffiti. More dramatic, however, was their enduring influence on the theatrics of the arena. Fighters dressed as antique Samnite warriors, complete with brimmed helmets, bobbing crests and short swords, had long been fan favourites; and even though, now that the people of Samnium ranked as Roman citizens, it was viewed as impolitic to refer to such gladiators as 'Samnites', their style of fighting remained far too popular to phase out. To attend *munera*, and to gawp at heavily armoured warriors, was to be reminded not just of how ancient gladiatorial combat was, but of another, no less striking fact: that its origins lay in Campania.

The Campanians did not begrudge Rome's appropriation of their most distinctive cultural export. It had worked to their benefit. Their gladiator schools were internationally renowned, their facilities beyond the dreams of other lands. Capua, an ancient city bordering Samnium, was home both to the most elite gladiator school of them all and to an amphitheatre that for a century had ranked as the world's largest. In Puteoli, which already had a perfectly serviceable stadium, Vespasian had commissioned the building of a second, almost as large as the one in Capua. More provincial towns also bore witness to Campania's obsession with *munera*. The amphitheatre in Pompeii, for instance, was the oldest to have been built of stone anywhere; but equally telling was the fact that for much of Nero's reign it had been empty of gladiators. This had not reflected any lack of enthusiasm for blood sports on the part of the Pompeians – quite the opposite. So fanatical were they in their support that in AD 59 they had become embroiled in a fight with fans from a neighbouring city. The senate, determined to crack down on such hooliganism, had not only imposed exile on the more eminent citizens involved in the brawl, but banned the city from staging gladiator fights for an entire decade. This punishment, as well as denying the Pompeians an entertainment to which they were addicted, had struck a wounding blow to their sense of self-esteem. Twenty years on, the shame of it was still felt as something raw.

Pompeii – like Colonia, like Cremona, like Berythus – ranked as a colony. It was not the foundation of the city by Hercules that sustained the conceit of its people, but its privileged relationship to Rome. True, the process of becoming a *colonia* – involving as it had the planting in Pompeii of two thousand retired legionaries, and the systematic erasure of Oscan culture – had been a brutal one; but all that was now ancient history. Pompeians did not just rank as Roman citizens, but as the citizens of a version of Rome. To live in a colony was to be as susceptible to the changing rhythms of life in the capital, to its fashions, its tensions, its upheavals, as the Ocean was to the phases of the moon. This was why the punishment slapped on the Pompeians by the senate had stung so painfully; and it was why, rather than enduring it uncomplainingly, they had sought to have it reversed. Several days' travel from the capital though they might be, Pompeians still had friends in high places. Poppaea Sabina, that most glamorous of patrons, had both roots and property in the region; and sure enough, a year before her death, she had persuaded Nero to relax the ban on gladiators. The emperor himself, visiting Pompeii and bringing with him from his wife lavish offerings of jewellery and pearls for Venus, the city's divine patron, had been greeted with wild enthusiasm. Factions defining themselves as 'fans of Nero' and 'fans of Poppaea' had come to dominate the city. Wherever there was chanting to be done, or space on the walls to scrawl graffiti, they had made sure to let everyone know their devotion to the impe-rial couple: a bandwagon which various local politicians, sniffing opportunity, had been quick to jump upon. Every year in Pompeii elections were held to determine who would have responsibility for the city; and these elections, in the wake of the relaxation of the ban on gladiators, had been won by candidates running on an obvious ticket. Collectively, they had been known as the Neropoppaeenses: 'the fans of Nero and Poppaea'.[19]

In Pompeii, then, as in Rome, Nero's downfall had come as an earthquake. Although the aftershocks had not been as severe in their effects on Campania as they were on northern Italy, they had not been negligible either. The region — boasting as it did Rome's largest naval base and its greatest port — was a key prize. In the wake of Vitellius' murder, the Flavian high command had duly dispatched their fastest cavalry unit to secure it. Capua, a hotbed of Vitellian sympathies, had been garrisoned all that winter by a legion from Syria. Visiting Pompeii, Mucianus' men had enjoyed the theatre, forced themselves on the local women, and scratched their names on various walls. While most had written in Latin, some had done so in a peculiarly strange and indecipherable script: Arabic.* Here, for any Pompeians who happened to observe the graffiti, was a striking measure of just how convulsive the civil wars had been: that they had brought soldiers from the outer limits of the world to the very heart of their town.

The mood of crisis, even once the period of direct military occupation was over, had persisted. Regime change in Rome had precipitated regime change in Campania. In Pompeii, the Neropoppaeenses had found themselves frozen out of government. A legate personally mandated by Vespasian to put the city's affairs in order, Titus Suedius Clemens, had made sure of that. Suedius was a man robustly and pointedly ignorant of Pompeii. A centurion whose record on the Danube had been sufficiently distinguished to win him appointment as *primus pilus*, he had served as one of Otho's

---

* Specifically in Safaitic, a script that records a dialect of Arabic spoken in the Harrah, a desert spanning what today is southern Syria and northern Saudi Arabia. See Helms.

leading officers and briefly commanded the Misene fleet. His record in the civil wars, although not as glorious as it might have been, was precisely what had recommended him to Vespasian: for it had won him a reputation for pugnacity and intemperance. The new emperor had need of such a legate in Pompeii: a man ready to ride roughshod over the subtleties and snobberies that had always characterised the city's politics, who could ensure victory for candidates favourable to Flavian interests, who was willing to put about a bit of stick. Grandees in Rome, distant from cities like Pompeii, might sneer at them as provincial; but not Vespasian. The emperor had been raised in the Sabine countryside, and he knew that one could not rule effectively in the capital without securing the support of the whole of Italy. Bruisers like Suedius could be relied upon to do the proper thing. To sweep up the rubble of the toppled order. To clear away the debris. To patch things up, so that in time no one would even know there had been an earthquake.

In Pompeii, however, the task of setting the city back on proper foundations was peculiarly challenging. It was not enough merely to secure the election of reliable magistrates. Earthquakes in Campania were something more than a metaphor. In AD 62, a tremor had shaken the region so violently that large stretches of both Pompeii and Herculaneum were reported in Rome to have collapsed altogether. This, perhaps, had been an exaggeration; and yet the damage had been severe enough. In Pompeii, the temple of Jupiter – which, as in Rome, loomed over the Forum – had been brought crashing down in ruin. Bath complexes across the city had been put permanently out of action. Great mounds of debris, swept up from the streets, had come to loom beyond the northern wall of the city. The plastering and the painting had never stopped. Suedius, arriving in Pompeii a decade after the great earthquake, had found the city still in a frenzy of reconstruction. Such a frenzy, in fact, that it had become a playground for chancers. Vespasian, impatient with displays of greed unless they served the public good, did not approve of such a free-for-all: for it had been reported to him that communal areas in Pompeii,

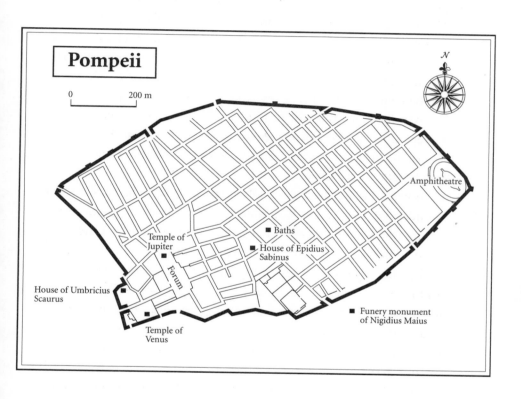

spaces that properly belonged to the people, or to the emperor, or to the gods, were being encroached upon by private speculators. The official charge laid on Suedius was to rectify this: to deal with predatory developers as he had once dealt with insubordinate legionaries. Such was the measure of the crisis in which Pompeii found itself: that it had led to the imposition on the city of a form of martial law.

But only a form. The very qualities that had recommended Suedius to Vespasian – his military cast of mind, his relish for a fight, his status as an outsider – had simultaneously set a limit on his usefulness. The emperor – as he had shown by giving licence to Mucianus, in the early days of his rule, to eliminate pretenders and browbeat the senate – had a talent for commissioning agents to do his dirty work for him; but equally, he had no wish to see them go too far. Suedius' official mission, his role in 'restoring places appropriated by private citizens to the republic of the Pompeians',[20] might be proclaimed on stones erected around the city, but nothing more than that. This was because – for all his success in strong-arming Pompeians into voting for candidates approved by the new regime – the truest responsibility for setting the city back on its feet lay not with Suedius, but with the candidates themselves.

Politics in Pompeii was properly political. The notion that any Caesar, even one as dutiful as Vespasian, might waste his time micro-managing local elections was, of course, a ludicrous one. Quite aside from anything else, he had no wish needlessly to insult those who were running for office. Vespasian, more than any emperor since Augustus, was alert to the ideals, the ambitions and the sensitivities of the Italian ruling classes. The balancing act that he had set himself, as a man who had risen to power on the back of a civil war, was a treacherous one: to whip civic elites across Italy into line while at the same time co-opting them as partners in his regime. Fortunately, the challenge was one to which Vespasian was well-suited. He knew, as a countryman himself, the surest way to foist radical change on the regions: by casting it as a return to tradition.

Pompeii was not merely a version of Rome, but a version of Rome as the city had originally been. Just as legionary bases, in their own distinctive way, bore witness to traditions and patterns of behaviour that derived ultimately from the vanished republic, so too did *coloniae*. Established as a colony more than half a century before Augustus' rise to supremacy, Pompeii preserved continuities with the past that had long since been extinguished in Rome. In the capital, no one could attain the consulship without Caesar's approval; nor could any resolution of the senate be passed without his say-so. In Pompeii, however, it was different. Suedius' intervention had been very much the exception that proved the rule, for even he had been obliged to get his way in the city by directly meddling in elections.

To become a *duumvir* — one of the two magistrates who served every year as the municipal equivalent of a consul — required votes. Securing votes, in turn, required a candidate to canvass his fellow citizens, to marshal heavyweight backers, to plaster walls with posters: everything that originally, back in the days of the republic, had characterised elections to the consulship. Admittedly, the *duoviri* — the 'two men' — did not, as the consuls had done, lead armies or sway the fate of nations. Their responsibilities were more circumscribed: decreeing the erection of statues, supervising public funerals, appointing contractors to renovate temples. Additionally, every five years, a particularly distinguished citizen would be elected quinquennial duumvir: a magistracy that, much like the censorship in Rome, required the man who held it to evaluate the moral and financial standing of his fellow citizens, and to calibrate their status accordingly. He it was who decided the eligibility of Pompeians to vote in the annual elections; he it was who determined membership of the city council — the Order of Decurions, as it was termed. To be enrolled as a decurion was to rank as one of the hundred movers and shakers of the city: an official and incontrovertible member of the urban elite. Such a status, viewed from Rome, might not seem much to boast about; and yet it was amplified by a hunger for honour no less intense for that. The duoviri could know, at the very least, that they served as magistrates directly elected by the people. No consul could any longer say as much. The prestige a duumvir enjoyed was, within the walls of his city, no mean thing. A big fish in a small pond was, after all, still a big fish.

'More than any other nation, the Romans have sought out glory and been greedy for praise.'[21] So Cicero, Rome's most celebrated orator, had declared back in the dying days of the republic. His own greed for praise had seen him enshrined as Rome's supreme exemplar of social mobility: for he had risen from the obscurity of Arpinum, a one-horse town south of the capital, to become the first man in his family ever to win the consulship. His speeches in the law courts and to the senate had provided schoolboys ever since with both their syllabus and a source of inspiration. 'His fame, his eloquence, that is what they pray for.'[22] No wonder that Pliny, in his encyclopaedia, should have lavished Cicero with particular praise: the equestrian from Arpinum, to the equestrian from Comum, had provided an obvious role model. Even though Pliny himself, despite his success in climbing the rungs of advancement, had failed to reach the very top of the ladder, he could always vest his hopes in his heir. He had no son; but he did have a nephew whom he valued as a son. The younger Pliny, a student of eighteen in the summer of Vespasian's death, had already imbibed from Cicero's example dreams of scaling heights that his uncle would clearly now never attain: fame as a wit and an orator, rank as a senator and a consul. Fresh out of the schoolroom though he might be, his horizons were already global in scale. He was no more content to spend his life in Comum than he would have been to settle down in Pompeii. The limits of municipal politics had already come to seem to him a kind of claustrophobia. A small pond, to the younger Pliny, might as well have been a prison.

Yet if Cicero served as a model, so he also served as a warning. His genius had brought him undying renown, but it had also doomed him. Murdered in the aftermath of Caesar's assassination on the orders of Mark Antony, an adversary whom he had relentlessly savaged in his speeches, he had perished a martyr for liberties that were themselves on the verge of vanishing. Under the heirs of Augustus, the greed for praise that Cicero had hailed as the birthright of every Roman had become, for those at the very summit of achievement, a perilous thing. To outshine a Caesar was to court death as well as glory. The ancient families who, over the course of the republic's history, had provided Rome with consul after consul, and woven their names into the very fabric of their city's history, had been remorselessly winnowed. Increasingly, they had seemed fabulous monsters, living out of time. The convulsions of the civil wars had pushed them even further towards extinction. Galba was not the only scion of a venerable dynasty to have perished amid the bloodshed. By the time Vespasian came to power, even the most distinguished of the nobles — men such as Marcus Cocceius Nerva, a senator whose great-grandfather had served as consul, whose grandfather had been a friend of Tiberius, and who himself had been a literary mentor to Nero — could trace their inheritance of high office only as far back as Augustus. Vespasian, respectful of tradition as he was, had duly recruited Nerva into his inner circle, and in 71 the two men had shared a consulship.[23] But the senate, under the Flavians, no longer embodied the full sweep of Roman history. That link to the deep past was gone for ever.

Many senators, indeed, were now not even from Italy. Typical was Marcus Ulpius Trajanus, the high-achieving senator from Baetica in Spain, who, after his term of service in Galilee, had been promoted by his former commander to serve as governor of Syria: as distinguished a post as any in the empire. Others, talent-spotted by Vespasian, had been fast-tracked into the senate from the provinces, either directly or under cover of the census. Most of these men hailed from the southern reaches of Spain or Gaul, where the *coloniae* — cities such as Italica, the birthplace of Trajanus — were centuries old; but there were senators too now from the eastern provinces. Here, for diehard conservatives, was a most unsettling development. The presence of men who spoke Greek as their first language in the great cockpit of the ancient capital, where Cicero, and Caesar, and Augustus had all held the floor, could hardly help but raise conservative hackles.

Certainly, for those who believed that Roman magistrates should properly come from Rome, it was all most discombobulating. The city, to the more disgruntled class of reactionary, seemed increasingly given over to foreigners. Indeed, it seemed barely to be Roman at all.

How very different things were in Pompeii. There, no one had succeeded in provoking the suspicious envy of a Caesar. The severest fate visited on those Pompeians who had fomented trouble – whether by stirring up riots or by parading their devotion to Nero – had been exile. The city's leading families were far too insignificant to have merited persecution. Some, as a result, could trace their ancestry back generations. Marcus Epidius Sabinus, a duumvir who swept to victory in 77 thanks in large part to the unsubtle backing of Suedius, was heir to a particularly ancient dynasty. His house, a spacious mansion next to the city's original bath complex, was one of the oldest in Pompeii and incorporated features dating all the way back to the Oscan era. Simultaneously, however, Epidius had made sure to swim with the times. A painting on the wall of his household shrine portrayed him and his father, solemnly arrayed in togas, waiting to sacrifice a bull to Vespasian.[24] Venerable ancestry, ostentatious loyalty: the combination was a winning one. Epidius, not content with victory in the duumviral elections, now had his gaze fixed on greater things. There was always the quinquennial duumvirate, of course; but even that was not the ultimate attainment. To rank as the most distinguished dignitary in Pompeii, the father of his city, it was necessary to serve as *flamen Vespasiani*: the priest of Vespasian. The person elected to this post mediated between his fellow citizens, the emperor, and the dimension of the supernatural: a truly awesome charge. Even as Vespasian, after returning from a trip to Campania, lay dying in his Sabine villa, Epidius was preparing to take the role on. He knew he had Suedius' backing. He knew as well that the priesthood would soon be vacant: for Vespasian, that summer of 79, was not the only man on his deathbed.

'In Rome, if you want high office, you can have it – but in Pompeii it is more of a challenge.'[25] Cicero, the man who had famously left the obscurity of his own town to become a senator and a consul, had been joking when he made the comment; but his tongue, even so, had not been entirely in his cheek. There was, indeed, as conservatives in Rome often acknowledged, a dignity to be had in local politics, an opportunity for service that might bring its own form of glory. This, under the rule of Augustus and his heirs, was even more the case than it had been back in Cicero's time. In Rome, there was no longer any opportunity for ambitious noblemen to do as their forebears had done, and lavish their fortunes on beautifying the city, or entertaining the people with games. Both activities were exclusively the prerogative of Caesar. In Pompeii, however, it was different. There, magistrates were not only permitted but expected to be models of generosity. Election to office in Pompeii brought opportunities to spend one's own money for the public good. A citizen who served his duumvirate by providing public benefactions was a citizen who had served his fellows well. This it was, in Pompeii, truly to merit praise and commemoration.

The living proof of this, as he had been for many decades, was the city's most distinguished and influential figure: Gnaeus Alleius Nigidius Maius. Of venerable ancestry, fabulously wealthy, the owner of a whole range of high-end rental properties, Maius could look back with satisfaction, that summer of 79, on a career of immense achievement. Every office that it was possible for a Pompeian to win, he had won: duumvir, quinquennial duumvir, priest of Caesar. His daughter, too, just for good measure, served as the most eminent priestess in the city. Even Maius' peers on Pompeii's council, a class of people not naturally immune to envy, were content to acknowledge him as *princeps coloniae*: the princeps of the colony.[26] Such admiration was due not only to his benefactions — lavish though these had certainly been — but to something more: the subtlety and generosity of spirit with which he had helped his fellow citizens navigate what had been, for the entire city, an exceptionally turbulent time. In the wake of a famine, Maius had subsidised the bread supply for four years. After the ban on gladiators, he had kept up Pompeian spirits by staging

195

such entertainments as were still permitted: hunting displays, athletic shows, fights with wild beasts. Following the earthquake, he had sponsored the refurbishment of public buildings. In the wake of Nero's downfall, he had stepped forward from the shadows to which the Neropoppaeenses had temporarily confined him to hail the Flavians, and to help smooth over any hint of lingering sympathies in the city for the toppled regime. Inaugurated as the priest of Vespasian, Maius had celebrated in the manner for which he had become famous: by staging *munera*. The occasion had been enjoyed by one and all. Awnings had kept the seats in shade; the water had been scented; gladiators had thrilled the crowds. It had served as a masterclass in keeping the people happy. No wonder Epidius had taken Maius as his model.

But now the grand old man of Pompeian politics was facing the final curtain. It would hardly have been surprising if people in the city, brought news of Vespasian's death, had thought to compare the achievements of the dead emperor with those of their own ailing princeps. Both had laboured to heal a city shattered by disaster; both had invested heavily in the entertainment of the masses. Although Maius, unlike Vespasian, was not raised to the heavens when he finally breathed his last, his fellow citizens honoured him as best they could. Immediately next to the city gates, beside the road that led southwards from Pompeii to a seaside resort by the name of Stabiae, his ashes were laid to rest in a particularly sumptuous tomb. Encased in marble, topped by a vaulted roof, the monument was designed to preserve the memory of Maius' accomplishments for all eternity. Friezes showed gladiators variously parading into the arena, engaging in combat and kneeling in the sand; an inscription listing the dead man's achievements proclaimed that he had once staged a spectacle comparable to anything that might be seen in Rome: '416 gladiators participated!' the eulogy breathlessly proclaimed.[27] Details such as this, garnishing the account of Maius' career, were designed to stay in the mind. Pompeii might not be Rome – but it offered its own kind of fame. So long as the city continued to flourish, and travellers took to the Stabian road, so the name of Gnaeus Alleius Nigidius Maius would be preserved, and the record of his benefactions recalled. It was, so the Pompeians might reflect, a kind of immortality.

Snakes and Ladders

The Roman who at the end of his life could take pride in duties fulfilled, ambitions met, the admiration of his fellows secured, was a Roman who had proved his *virtus*: his worth as a *vir*, a man. Naturally, the world being what it was, achievement was capable of inspiring jealousy as well as admiration. Pliny, aware that his young nephew was ambitious to elevate himself from equestrian status, to become a senator and attain the very summit of rank, liked to illustrate the potential snares and pitfalls that might await him with a particular story. The episode had taken place shortly before Pliny's appointment to the command of the Misene fleet, while he had been on service in one of the Spanish provinces, administering its finances. Even then, he had been well on his way to accumulating the twenty thousand noteworthy facts, sourced from one hundred authors, that were to provide him with the material for his encyclopaedia. The governor of the province, a man by the name of Larcius Licinus, wished to purchase his subordinate's notebooks. Approaching Pliny, he had offered to pay a vast sum. Pliny, deeply offended, had refused. His life's work was not for sale. Set on getting his own back, he had bided his time. Sure enough, once his term of office in Spain was done, he had recorded in his encyclopaedia an entertainingly embarrassing anecdote: how Licinus, while eating a truffle, had bitten on a coin and bent a tooth. Then, just for good measure, Pliny had recorded a second story: how, when Licinus went to inspect the source of a river in northern Spain, the waters had promptly dried up. This, so Pliny had noted with satisfaction, was 'a terrible omen'.[28]

The insult to his honour had been twofold. First, by offering as payment a sum that was exactly equivalent to the minimum property qualification required to rank as an equestrian, Licinus had pointedly been rubbing home the much greater wealth that he, as a senator, by definition enjoyed. Second, by insinuating that Pliny might have been conducting his researches for mercenary reasons, the governor had sought to cast his subordinate not as a scholar and a patriot, but rather as a grubbing drone, little better than a tradesman. The shame of such an aspersion was not to be borne. 'Any form of commercial exchange, when done on a small scale, must be reckoned vulgar,'[29] Cicero had ruled. Only when business interests spanned the world might they be reckoned a worthy source of income – and even then they could never compare in dignity to land. Smoke drifting from the roofs of tenant farms; vineyards and orchards laden down with succulent fruit; herds of cattle lowing softly in the deepening twilight: these, because they were timeless, were the most acceptable markers of Roman wealth. 'No better source of income than these, none more profitable, none more delightful, none more appropriate to those who rank as free.'[30]

That standards like these were exclusionary was, of course, precisely the point. Many millions of people lived within the Roman Empire; but no more than a thousand, perhaps, could lay claim to estates sufficiently vast, or businesses sufficiently international, to qualify for membership in the senate.* Below them ranked another ten thousand or so of the super-rich, men who were entitled by their wealth and standing to membership of the equestrian order. These gradations of status, rooted in the distant past, reassured Rome's elite that, for all the chasm of difference that might separate them from their forebears, they still maintained their traditional genius for social calibration. Nevertheless, as the masters now of an empire full of many cities, they had recognised a need to diversify their ranks. This was why, in addition to senators and equestrians, a third order

---

* The senate numbered around six hundred. Perhaps another four hundred men who qualified by income and status to become senators would have opted to remain equestrians.

had come to be accepted as belonging to the upper classes. It was not only in Pompeii that men could become decurions. Equivalents of Maius or Epidius were to be found in cities across the empire. In Gaul and Greece, in Spain and Syria, magistrates conformed themselves to the exacting standards both of their fellow citizens and of Roman snobbery. The blaze of a visiting senator — a legate or a governor — did not necessarily dazzle such men. To be sure, in the great firmament that was the world ruled by Caesar, decurions hardly ranked among the most impressive of celestial bodies. No one would think to compare them to the sun, or the moon, or the planets, or a comet. What was the member of some provincial city council, in comparison to a senator, but a tiny and delicate pinprick of silver? Better, however, to glimmer faintly as a star than not to glimmer at all. Between the three ruling orders and every other class the contrast was as profound as that between the Milky Way and the darkness that framed it. Rich and poor, honourable and contemptible, distinguished and invisible: these, in the final reckoning, were the divisions in society that truly mattered.

Such, at any rate, was the opinion of the imperial elite. Not everyone concurred: there were plenty of citizens who scorned any notion that their superiors' disdain for them might define their value. 'Vulgar and sordid':[31] this had been Cicero's withering opinion of, among many other classes of tradesmen, fishmongers. Yet there were plenty of seafood retailers who, far from feeling embarrassed by their trade, positively gloried in it. The fame of Pompeii's garum — a distinctively pungent condiment manufactured out of fermented fish guts — was a source of great civic pride. In between noting the value of the sauce as a salve for crocodile bites and the peculiar insistence of Judaeans on only eating it when it was made from a particular kind of fish, Pliny listed the city as one of the best in the world for the delicacy. Those who had grown rich on the back of the trade were perfectly happy to celebrate the source of their wealth. Showcase for this sense of pride was the house of the city's most successful dealer in fish-based sauces. Selling them across Campania, and even as far afield as southern Gaul, had brought Aulus Umbricius Scaurus considerable wealth. His mansion, fashioned out of two separate properties, stood on one of the most exclusive streets in the city and enjoyed splendid views out across the sea. It also boasted some highly distinctive mosaics. The visitor who entered the house was greeted in its hall by an unapologetic display of advertising: the image, at each of the floor's four corners, of a jar full of garum. 'Top class', read the inscription on one; 'the flower of garum', read another.[32] Scaurus' own name appeared on three of the jars. Quite as much as any senator, he knew his worth. He certainly scorned any notion that his business might be either vulgar or sordid.

It helped, of course, when defying the snobbery of the elites, to be rich. It was not, however, essential. Paid work, the very thought of which made senatorial noses wrinkle uncontrollably, provided identity to people a long way down the social scale. No one in either Rome or Pompeii needed any reminders as to just how important a role craftsmen had to play in repairing a cityscape devastated by fire or earthquake. Builders would advertise their workshops with signs that lovingly illustrated the tools of their trade: chisels, hammers, trowels. There was no profession so humble, perhaps, that it might not serve as a source of dignity. In Pompeii, when a woman named Clodia Nigella was commemorated, her career was emblazoned on her tombstone as a badge of honour: 'public pig-keeper'.[33] The poor no less than the rich had their pride. 'There is no condition so humble that it cannot be touched by the sweetness of glory.'[34]

This, in their very heart of hearts, was something that the elites were prepared to acknowledge. Just as Pliny, humiliated by his superior, had bided his time before exacting his vengeance, so might a carpenter or a potter, if shamed by a nobleman, scrawl abuse about him on a temple wall, or catcall him at the games, or defecate on his statue. In Rome, where senators no longer depended upon votes for advancement, this was a truth that mattered less than it did in a city like Pompeii, where the magistracies and priesthoods won by a luminary such as Maius had owed much to his popularity with the people. In the capital, there was only one member of the elite who still needed to pay close attention to the vagaries of the plebs, to court them, to flatter them, to parade for them his high regard – and that man, of course, was Caesar. Vespasian, shouldering the rubble of the Capitol onto a hod, had been demonstrating his respect not only for the gods, but for the city's workmen. That he valued their labour, and respected the dignity it brought them, was illustrated by a story much repeated. An engineer, so it was claimed, had invented a device that would enable columns to be transported to the summit of the Capitol at minimal cost; but Vespasian, although intrigued by the invention, refused to employ it. His explanation was a telling one. 'I have a duty to keep the masses fed.'[35]

Due tribute to Vespasian's popularity with the Roman poor – but a most improbable story, even so. Emperors were indeed committed to keeping the masses in the capital fed (that, after all, was what the corn dole was for); but none ever felt any obligation to maintain them in work. Even in Rome, the supply of free bread might prove insufficient to preserve the unemployed from starvation. The fate of those so wretched that they were reduced to huddling by one of the city's bridges, flapping their rags against carrion birds and hungry dogs, was common enough that poets might wish it on their rivals. Beyond the limits of the capital, where no one was given free bread, unemployment was even more to be dreaded. Sometimes, it was true, a grandee ambitious to win the affection of his fellow citizens would do as Maius had done in Pompeii, and offer his fellow citizens some form of aid; but never on a regular basis. The rhythms of the seasons, the demands for labour, were too fluctuating for that. Even philosophers – for all that they might feel 'commanded by nature to do good to every human being'[36] – never thought to channel this sentiment into anything remotely approaching poor-relief. Why should they have done? The poor, far from leading more wretched lives than the rich, often seemed much happier than their betters: they had less to worry about. Such, at any rate, was the opinion of the wise. 'No one finds poverty – inconvenient though it may be – a heavy burden, unless one is minded to do so.'[37] This, of course, was to cast the complaints of those on the verge of starvation as simple malingering: a point of view that it was hardly necessary to be a philosopher to hold. Citizens at the bottom of the pile were generally held to have brought their misfortunes on themselves. Poverty was due to moral failings. Here, in a society where every Roman knew himself to be defined by an exacting and relentless process of calibration, was a ready source of reassurance to everyone who stood above the breadline. It was not enough to succeed; others had to fail. Not only that: they had to be seen to fail. A message scratched anonymously on a wall in Pompeii spoke for many: 'I hate the poor. Anybody who asks for something free is crazy; pay the price and get the goods.'[38]

The judgement of fellow citizens was the only standard by which a man could truly measure himself. In the competition for honour which always, ever since the founding of Rome, had animated Roman society, there were necessarily losers as well as winners. Not everyone could have prizes. The destitute served their superiors, in effect, as a looking glass. Prosperity and glory were nothing without the reflection provided them by poverty and shame. Yet it was the glory of the Roman people that even the very poorest among them – the day labourer rejected for work by a foreman, the peasant scratching vainly at a patch of barren soil – could know themselves citizens still. The spirit of liberty animated them, guaranteeing at least a shred of dignity. There were fates, after all, worse than starvation: to be without a family or a homeland; to have no legal recourse against beatings or sexual abuse; to serve as a living embodiment of vileness and degradation; to rank as the very lowest class of human being. It needed no great effort for the Romans to imagine such an existence. This was because, serving as the shadow of their city's greatness, it was manifest everywhere they looked.

'The primary distinction in the law of persons is this: that all men are either free or slaves.'[39] So it had always been. Just as day was unimaginable without night, so was liberty without servitude. Freedom, in the opinion of the Romans, was distinctively their birthright. It was this conviction, in the days of their rise to greatness, that had steeled them to overcome every obstacle, to shrug aside every setback, to pursue the course of victory at all costs. The consequence was evident in the fulfilment of their city's destiny, divinely appointed as it was: to rule as the mistress of the world. Conversely, by failing to fight to the death, and preferring submission to annihilation, the peoples brought to acknowledge Roman dominance had shown themselves fitted for servitude. Touring Syria in the wake of his capture of Jerusalem, Titus had obliged his prisoners to act out their own defeat for spectators: a dramatisation both of the invincible quality of Rome's greatness and of the reasons why the Judaeans, by contrast, had forfeited every right to freedom. A moral lesson indeed.

Vast numbers of captives from Judaea had duly glutted the markets of Italy. Their feet chalked white, as an indicator to would-be purchasers that they were imports, they had stood on the *castata*, the platform on which auctions were performed, where countless other prisoners, reaped by the legions over the course of preceding generations, had similarly stood: Britons and Gauls, Syrians and Greeks, Spaniards and Carthaginians. It was a telling measure of the scale of Rome's conquests that more slaves were to be found in Italy than anywhere else in the world. They constituted perhaps a quarter of the population.[40] Quite as much as all the other fruits of empire — exotic cooking ingredients, rare marble, fantastical flora — they illustrated the sheer range and sweep of Rome's dominion. More than that, however, they served as living lessons in civic virtue: in the value of liberty.

That, of course, was not the only purpose of slaves. They existed to do whatever their master might require of them, whenever he might require it. For many this meant ceaseless toil. On farms and agricultural estates, where a majority of the slaves in Italy lived, most were worked so hard that most of them, after spending dawn to dusk out in the fields, could think only of food and sleep. Others laboured in mines, 'wearing out their bodies by day and by night, deep below the earth',[41] others in quarries, others on the building of harbours, or tunnels, or any number of infrastructure projects. Vespasian, in the wake of his conquest of Galilee, had sent six thousand of the strongest prisoners to Nero, who promptly set them to digging out a canal. Yet work like this, suited to slaves though it might be, was not exclusively the province of slaves. Free men as well toiled in fields and on building sites. Miners and their apprentices enjoyed contracts which specified their right to quit. These were the class of men, not slaves, who were known by the elites as *operae*: labourers. Lack of work was such a scourge precisely because there existed across Italy so many men desperate to be hired, to bend their backs, to strain their muscles, to sweat in the sun. Slavery was not a solution to any shortage of cheap labour. Quite the opposite. Slaves were, as one philosopher put it, 'hirelings for life'.[42] Work, however, was not necessarily what defined them in the eyes of their masters. Rather, it was their status as commodities: human beings who, by consenting to live as property rather than to perish as free men or women, served to affirm the honour, the dignity and the superiority of those who owned them.

Caveat emptor. Since slaves, by definition, constituted the lowest class of humanity, the risk was always that this inferiority, rather than making them the serviceable tools of their master, might actively serve to damage his interests. A man content to submit to servitude, so it seemed to the Romans, was a man all too likely to prove a liar, or a thief, or a layabout. Conversely, a slave who accepted himself for what he was, acknowledging that he was destined never to have any status save that derived from his master, or be ascribed any virtue save loyalty, might well prove a treasure. Investing well in a slave was often a matter of luck. Not exclusively, however. Magistrates, well aware of the reputation of slave-dealers for cheating, went to great lengths to regulate the market. Attempts to disguise physical ailments were strictly forbidden. In a similar vein, merchants were obliged to declare everything in a slave's character that might have the effect of lowering his price: a tendency to wet the bed, for instance, or to run away, or to attempt suicide. Nor were these drawbacks the only ones to bear in mind. As with horses, so with slaves: form counted for a great deal. Only a fool would buy a Briton, for instance, to perform anything but the most menial of tasks. Gauls made the best herdsmen. Doctors, teachers, secretaries: here were jobs ideally suited to Greeks. People from Asia, so connoisseurs tended to agree, were the best suited of all to slavery. Naturally, these considerations affected price. Bargains were always to be had; but at the very top end of the market, where potential buyers were strictly limited to the ranks of the elite, quality was quality.

Nowhere was it more evident than in a rich man's household that slaves served not as necessities, but as status symbols. The more specialised a role each domestic had, the better it reflected on the master. Expecting the young man appointed to direct a drunken senator's penis over a chamber pot also to clean his teeth, or a masseuse to double as a hairdresser, was the height of vulgarity. Inevitably, the competitive instincts of Rome's greatest men being what they were, one-upmanship was a relentless driver of fashion. One market in the capital, alert to the demand for novelty, went so far as to specialise in slaves with deformities: 'the legless, the armless, the three-eyed, the slave with a tiny head'.[43] Dealers were even rumoured to confine children in cramped cages, with the aim of stunting their growth, so as to satisfy the craze for dwarfs.[44]

These, however, were always recherché tastes. The surest premium was set on beauty. By law, human chattels were as subject to their master's sexual needs as they were to any other demand that he might lay upon them. The fashion among interior decorators for portraying scenes of rape on frescoes served as a constant reminder to slaves of both sexes and of every age that their bodies were not their own: their owners could use them exactly as they pleased. Inevitably, then, an attractive attendant served as a status symbol much as a racehorse or an antique statue might. The success of a dinner party was quite as dependent upon the good looks of the waiters as it was on the quality of the food. Guests assigned ugly slaves would grumble about it. There was nothing like physical perfection in an attendant to inspire what every man of taste, every snob, every trendsetter most dreamed of inspiring: the jealousy of his peers.

The absolute cutting edge – as exemplified by the transformation of Sporus into Poppaea Sabina – was a boy as beautiful as the most beautiful of girls. Nero, of course, had pushed this particular fashion to a level that no one could possibly hope to rival; but the basic principle of it was, for all that, not novel. Indeed, it went with the grain of how every Roman viewed slavery: as an institution bound, by its very nature, to feminise every male subjected to it. When even an aged slave might be called 'boy' by his master, it was hardly any great scandal to keep a genuine boy smooth, to doll him up with make-up, to have his long hair crimped and teased into feminine curls. *Delicati* – pretty boys, pets – were a common sight in the palaces lining the Bay of Naples; but they were to be found as well in less exclusive surroundings. A *delicatus* bought to impress dinner guests in Pompeii was hardly likely to compare for beauty with boys owned by the wealthier habitués of Baiae; but even so, he could serve his master as a statement of aspiration. The lifestyles of the elite had always been grist to the fantasies of the upwardly mobile. Only the craze for eunuchs – the expense of which put them beyond the reach of any but the most fabulously rich – tended to be viewed askance. This was due not to any particular concern for the victims of the gelding knife, but rather to the opposite: anxiety about the influence they might come to exercise over the mighty. Pliny, whose eye for such details was unerring, noted that the most expensive slave of all time had been a eunuch: a shameful waste of money. It was noted as well by traditionalists afraid of Titus that he had a particular taste for eunuchs. Nervousness about what this might portend for his rule as emperor was hardly surprising. The fear was that Rome might end up like some oriental monarch's court: decadent, debased, the plaything of twittering slaves who failed even to rank as male.

In truth, there was more to this dread of eunuchs than met the eye. It spoke – for all that moralists liked to cast it as the manly repudiation of a sinister foreign custom – of a much deeper anxiety.

Slaves were mere property, creatures who existed to affirm their owners' superiority: but was that all they were? Not necessarily. A *delicatus*, if he had wit, charm and intelligence, might well inspire in his owner something more than simple desire. A telling instance of such a possibility was provided by the career of a slave once owned by Vitellius: not a eunuch, but a boy with whom the future emperor had become hopelessly infatuated. The relationship had proved as tempestuous as it was, on Vitellius' side, passionate. Asiaticus – named after the region of the world believed by the Romans to breed the most naturally submissive slaves – had shown himself the very opposite of submissive. As insolent as he was irresistible, he was forever thieving, absconding, pushing his master's devotion to the limit. When Vitellius, resolved to end the relationship once and for all, sold Asiaticus to a gladiator school, he only had to attend a show in which his favourite was fighting to buy him back immediately. Who, then, was the master, who the slave? In due course, after his appointment by Galba to the command of Lower Germany, Vitellius had set his beloved free. Then, on the very day he was hailed as emperor, he had raised Asiaticus to the rank of equestrian. This promotion, a shocking illegality, had been viewed by Vitellius' enemies as a blot on the honour, not just of the emperor, but of the Roman people themselves. It had been compounded by his insistence on employing Asiaticus as his closest advisor. In due course, following the implosion of Vitellius' regime, Mucianus had known precisely how to clear up the mess. Asiaticus was sentenced not as a freedman, still less as an equestrian, but as a slave. He perished on a cross.

Such, at any rate, was the account pushed by Flavian propagandists. Vitellius, notorious for his gluttony, had been a monster of appetite. Yet there was in this excoriation of the fallen emperor more than an element of hypocrisy. Vespasian, too, had been devoted to a one-time slave. Antonia Caenis, celebrated for her intelligence, prodigious memory, and familiarity with the innermost workings of the house of Caesar, had served Claudius' mother as a secretary. Even though, as a former slave, she was forbidden to marry a Roman citizen, she had lived with Vespasian as his wife in all but name: a relationship that, in the opinion of many, had redounded at least as much to the benefit of Caesar as to that of Caenis herself. She was, after all, a woman who knew where numerous bodies lay buried.

Emperors, no matter what they might say in public, had long recognised the indispensability of slaves raised in the imperial household. Not only were they blessed with a fuller understanding of how the empire functioned than many senators; they were also likely to be fiercely intelligent. Granting freedom to such slaves enabled them to serve Caesar openly as his agents. Some, once set on the ladder of advancement, had gone on to reach startling heights. A notorious example was Antonius Felix, who – like Caenis – had originally been a slave of Claudius' mother: sent out to govern Judaea, he had pulled off the remarkable feat of marrying none other than a sister of Herod Agrippa.* Claudius himself, as the emperor responsible for such arrant social climbing, had been widely mocked as the dupe of his freedmen; but Vespasian had known better. He had appreciated just how efficiently Claudius' sponsorship of former slaves had improved imperial administration. Early in his career, he had benefited from their backing. Now, as an upstart emperor, he depended on their advice and service. Caenis was not the only one to have helped him shoulder the burden of rule. There were many others, too. To a few of them – although, naturally, this had done nothing to ease the condemnation of Vitellius for having done precisely the same – Vespasian had even granted the rank of equestrian.

Here was something to infuriate every class of society. The plebs could resent the spectacle of foreigners who had once ranked as their legal inferiors enjoying wealth beyond their wildest dreams; the elites could fulminate that the country was going to the dogs. Petronius, the senator whom even Nero had acknowledged as the most stylish man in Rome, had satirised the trend with spiteful brilliance. A

---

* Even more remarkably, he had already been married to a princess: the daughter of the former king of Mauretania.

208

writer of fiction as well as an arbiter of fashion, he had conjured out of the great swirl of Roman snobberies a memorably feline satire on the nouveaux riches. Trimalchio, he had named his billionaire freedman. The backstory given to his creation was a telling one. Like Asiaticus, Trimalchio had originally been a *delicatus*, a sex toy for his master, and for his mistress as well; unlike Asiaticus, however, he had made his fortune as a freedman by going into business: 'In one voyage I made a cool ten million. Immediately I bought back all my master's old estates. I build a mansion, I buy slaves and beasts of burden; everything I touched, it turned to gold.'[45]

If these boasts evoked the spirit of anywhere, then it was that of Puteoli: the port where Asiaticus, making his first escape, had headed to work in a bar. Nowhere else – perhaps not even Rome – quite so embodied the flux and churn of the age. Only in Puteoli were there fortunes to be made readily from nothing; and only in Puteoli were there opportunities to spend them in the vulgar manner of a Trimalchio, on luxuries freshly imported from across the globe, all jumbled up together, without decorum or taste. Pliny, across the bay, might labour at cataloguing the immense diversity of everything beneath the sun, and ordering it into neat categories; but his efforts were mocked by the wharves of the great port, where foodstuffs, and treasures, and peoples all constituted one promiscuous mix. This was why, in an age when slaves could end up as equestrians, and Syrians Romans, it was Puteoli that seemed to offer elites a particularly terrifying glimpse of the future: a world in which every accepted distinction of hierarchy had been dissolved to nothing, and the only thing that truly mattered was money.

There was, however, another way of framing the rise to prominence of freedmen: not as a menace to tradition, but as its perpetuation. The fact that Romans were so willing to set their slaves free had always astonished outsiders. Back in the days of Augustus, a Greek historian had noted in astonishment that it was 'one of their most sacred and unalterable customs'.[46] A people who originally, according to legend, had been recruited by Romulus from among shepherds, outlaws and fugitives, they had never claimed to possess a distinctive bloodline, or to have sprung from their city's soil. 'What idiocy it is, when you are willing to grant liberty to such slaves of yours as merit it, then to envy them the rights of citizenship.'[47] So, back in ancient times, one of Rome's kings — a man who had himself begun life as a slave — was reported to have told his people. It was a lesson the Romans had never forgotten. If slaves out in the fields or the mines were unlikely ever to be freed, then those in close contact with their owners — the accountant who handled his master's business, the maid who dressed her mistress's hair — might indeed hope, as a reward for long and loyal service, one day to receive their freedom. Naturally, the shame of their term of servitude would never entirely fade. Chalk, once it had been used to whiten feet, could never wholly be dusted off. A citizen whose body had been used to satisfy the sexual needs of another man would always be stained by the insoluble disgrace of it. Freedmen, for this reason, were excluded by law from standing for office. No such restriction, however, was imposed on their sons. No wonder, then, that senators, jealous of their breeding, should have been so ready to wrinkle their noses at anything that smacked of 'the wealth and spirit of a freedman'.[48] They knew all too well where it might ultimately lead.

Already, in the towns of Campania, there were men serving as decurions whose forebears in the time of Augustus had ranked as slaves. Most of these forebears — like Petronius' Trimalchio — had made a fortune in business, then promptly invested it in land. A magistrate in Puteoli or Pompeii from such a background might still suffer the whisperings of colleagues from more established families; but service as a decurion was, for all that, an accepted way for the upwardly mobile to wash reputations, to push skeletons into closets. When the son of Umbricius Scaurus ran for office as a duumvir, he did not draw attention to the fact that he was heir to a fish-based condiments empire — and, sure enough, he won election. In a similar manner, it was perfectly possible for the descendants of freedmen to veil their ancestry: either by disguising anything in their names that might smack remotely of servility, or by discarding them altogether. This was not, however, the course adopted by most. A freedman, by law, belonged to the family of his master; and this association, in the long run, might provide his descendants with opportunity. Life, in a city like Pompeii, was precarious. Death, even for the elites, was a constant risk. A dynasty like the Epidii might be able to trace their origins back many centuries; but this was unusual. A family that had furnished Pompeii with magistrates for two, three, four generations might well, the vagaries of fortune being what they were, find itself one day without an heir. Better, in such circumstances, for the descendant of a freedman to inherit its name, its wealth, and its status than to let it go extinct altogether. Everything must change, such a family would reassure itself, so that everything could stay the same.

Emperors might come and go, earthquakes bring temples crashing down, the descendants of slaves come to rank among the elite – but Pompeii, that ancient city, founded centuries previously by Hercules, would always be Pompeii.

The Giants Awaken

For several days the Bay of Naples had been troubled by earthquakes. Pliny's nephew, who was staying with his mother at Pliny's villa in Misenum, made sure to keep track of them. Although he was only eighteen, the younger Pliny had already imbibed from his uncle both a fascination with the wonders of the natural world and a commitment to taking notes. An earnest and dutiful young man, he had once been told off by Pliny for walking rather than taking a litter: for by taking a litter he would have had the opportunity to read a book. 'All time is wasted which is not devoted to study.'[49] Such was Pliny's maxim.

His encyclopaedia served as a monument to a stirring principle: that there was no occurrence so remarkable, no wonder so unsettling, that it might not become for a Roman a legitimate object of enquiry. Earthquakes, for all the terror they might generate, were as susceptible to methodical enquiry as all the other objects of his prodigious research. Pliny, detailing the many times they had convulsed the world, did not blame them on buried giants, or – as some other scholars had done – on air trapped underground, but on winds. 'For the earth never shakes except when the sea is deathly calm,' he wrote, 'and the sky so still that there is not a breeze on which a bird can take wing, and all the breath of wind is exhausted; and this only ever happens after it has been particularly gusty, doubtless because all the winds end up enclosed in the veins and hidden caverns of the sky.'[50] So much for the theory. But Pliny had been attentive as well to the practicalities. Many were the observations he had listed: that earthquakes were most frequent in the spring and autumn; that they were often accompanied by tidal waves, and by noises that sounded like shouting or the clash of weapons; that the safest place to stand in a tottering building was directly below an arch. To Pliny, the earthquakes that shook Campania day after day were something more than an inconvenience: they were phenomena that promised a better understanding of the world.

Elsewhere, not surprisingly, perspectives tended to be rather different. In Pompeii, seventeen years after the great earthquake that had brought so many of its buildings crashing to the ground, the recovery was still incomplete. To arrive at the city by sea, and pass into it through the gate that led from the harbour, was immediately to be struck by this. The temple of Venus, raised on a vast artificial platform just across the main road from Scaurus' mansion, and visible from far out at sea, was the largest in the city. Originally built to mark its inauguration as a colony, and dedicated to the goddess who presided as its patron, it served as a monument to almost two centuries of Pompeian history. Yet although parts of the complex had been restored, most of it was still one enormous building site. Deep trenches scored the courtyard; large building blocks were massed along its sides; piles of debris and chippings lay scattered everywhere. No one working on the temple needed Pliny to tell them how much damage an earthquake could do. Nevertheless, the sheer scale of the project, immense as it was, did not bear witness solely to Pompeii's vulnerability. It testified as well to something more: a faith in its future. Venus, arrayed in the gold and jewellery presented to her by Poppaea Sabina, had not abandoned her city; nor had those labouring to restore her sanctuary to the goddess. All of them, whether through their benefactions or their labour, were committed to raising a temple bigger, richer, more resplendent than the one that had stood there before. Its restoration would symbolise the rebirth of Pompeii itself.

Naturally, as tremor after tremor shook the city, day after day after day, people worried what these convulsions might portend for the project. It was noted with alarm that springs on the slopes above Pompeii had dried up, and that men of an unnatural size – 'such creatures, in fact, as the giants are supposed to have been'[51] – were to be glimpsed, sometimes on Vesuvius, sometimes out in the countryside, sometimes even in Pompeii itself, striding overland, or else pacing the sky. Yet life went on. Some, fearing the worst, might have chosen to pack up and leave; but there were plenty who had no intention of abandoning the city. It was, after all, their home. And so most Pompeians stayed put.

Decorators in the city – skilled by now at filling in cracks, repairing damaged details, touching up frescoes – certainly had no lack of work to keep them busy. Others, too, from high to low, continued with their daily routines. Decurions met with their clients, attended to their business interests, consulted with their peers; slaves, obedient to the rhythms of their owners' demands and requirements, led such lives as they were forced to lead. In the city itself, there were still plenty of springs to satisfy the people's needs. Near the Forum, on the city's main commercial street, water continued to splash from the mouth of Fortuna, the goddess of plenty. Fittingly, the fountain stood not far from the mansion of Epidius Sabinus, the man whose prospects – with the death of Maius – were now more golden than anyone else's in the city. Not that the blessings of Fortuna were confined to Epidius. Beyond his house, the venerable bath complex that had been so severely damaged in the great earthquake had been upgraded to splendid effect, so that visitors could now enjoy state-of-the-art facilities: heated floors, running fountains, a swimming pool. Elsewhere on the street, people had work to do: deliveries to make, shops to staff, food to prepare for inns and bars. In a bakery two blocks down from the baths, a pair of donkeys turned a mill. Dogs barked. Lizards flickered over stones. Grapes in the vineyard at the very far end of the street grew fat and sweet in the sun.

And then, abruptly, everything changed, utterly and for ever. It was an hour after midday. In Misenum, twenty miles across the bay from Pompeii, Pliny was digesting his lunch. Lying on a couch, he was — inevitably — reading a book. Even so, when his sister interrupted him with news of a remarkable cloud that had appeared in the sky, he did not hesitate to call for his sandals and hurry to a suitable vantage point. Gazing out over the Bay of Naples, Pliny saw that his sister had not been exaggerating. The cloud was like nothing he had ever seen before. His nephew would later recall it in vivid terms: 'In appearance and shape it most closely resembled a pine-tree, for it had a column of great length and height, as though it were a trunk, over-topped by a number of branches.'[52] Others, perhaps, might have described it as a mushroom cloud. Pliny, a man as well qualified as anyone in the world to appreciate just what a fascinating opportunity for enquiry into nature's workings it promised, could not have been more excited. Resolved to investigate the phenomenon more closely, he ordered a galley to be readied for him. He ordered it to head towards the cloud.

From Misenum it was impossible to identify the mountain from which it was rising. People across the bay, however, had no such problem. There, at the base of Vesuvius, the violence of the eruption could be felt in tremors so convulsive that walls, just as they had done seventeen years before, were buckling and collapsing, and it seemed that the entire mountain 'was imploding into ruin'.[53] In Herculaneum, west of Vesuvius, people gazed up in stupefaction at the column of ash and rock as it towered above them. Only minutes after the eruption had been heralded by a deafening crash, the cloud already reached miles into the sky, blotting out the sun. Then, after about thirty minutes, a faint drizzle of pumice and ash began to fall. A sound like trumpets was heard, and people began to cry that the giants, long buried beneath the mass of the mountain, had risen in rebellion, and were to be glimpsed amid the smoke. Those in the streets fled into their homes; those in their homes out into the streets. Many, desperate to escape Herculaneum altogether, hurried to the harbour, or else out along the road that led towards Naples: for that way not only were they leaving Vesuvius behind them, but they had the wind in their faces. The pumice and ash, borne on the wind's breath, was slowly drifting eastwards: away from Naples, and towards Pompeii.

Here, although it was still early afternoon, it might as well have been night. Only to the south and east, along the line of the horizon, did there remain so much as a hint of the sun, like the faintest and feeblest of dawns. Otherwise the darkness was total. Pompeians who wished to witness the ruin that was being visited on their city had no choice but to rely on lamps and torches. Holding them up as they waded through the pumice that was already starting to clog the streets, they saw roofs straining under the weight of their loads, and increasingly, as the hours passed, giving way. The more this happened, so the more nervous people became about taking shelter in their homes, and the likelier they were to attempt escape. A stream of people and pack animals, loaded down with such belongings as could be transported, left through the city gates and took to the open roads. Yet here too there was peril. Intermixed amid the pumice were rock fragments, 'charred and cracked by the heat of fire'.[54] Ripped from the summit of Vesuvius by the force of the eruption and blasted high into the air, these were now, like irregular but deadly hailstones, crashing to the ground: a hard rain indeed. The pumice as well, although too light to inflict bodily harm, was falling in sufficient quantities to make the roads that led from Pompeii challenging to negotiate – and certainly impossible for wagons. Those looking to escape by boat found the harbour choked by debris: the pumice, floating on the water, had formed a scum so thick that vessels were unable to force a way through to the open depths. 'Filled with the rubble of the mountain, the waters along the coast had in no time at all become mere shallows: impassable.'[55]

Similarly baffled by the challenge of this was the admiral of the Misene fleet. Pliny, despite his original aim of taking ship to investigate the mushroom cloud, had rapidly broadened the scope of his mission. He had been prompted to do this by the arrival, just as he was about to set sail, of a letter. It had been sent by a woman from a villa on the shore directly below Vesuvius. Written a few hours before the eruption – and evidence, therefore, of just how terrifying the portents of looming disaster, from the earthquakes to the phantoms of giants, had been for those who experienced them – it had opened Pliny's eyes to a pressing responsibility: the need to organise a mass evacuation. This was why, setting sail from Misenum, he had done so at the head of a fleet. With the wind in his sails, he and his galleys had made good time; but even so, when they reached the waters below Vesuvius they found themselves no more able to pull into harbour than the people stranded on the shore were to leave it. Briefly, Pliny wondered whether to turn back; but the winds were against him, and he scorned to show what might be misconstrued by his men as fear. Accordingly, he continued eastwards along the coast, aiming for Stabiae. Here, where the rain of pumice was much lighter than it had been directly in the shadow of Vesuvius, he and his fleet were able at last to make land. In the harbour, Pliny found a friend of his, a senator by the name of Pomponianus, who was frantically trying to make his escape, and in despair that the winds were against him. Pliny, taking his friend in his arms, comforted him, and then – partly to demonstrate his own lack of concern at the situation, and partly because he was streaked with ash – proposed taking a bath. Pomponianus, whose villa stood above the harbour, ordered his slaves to carry the admiral to the bath-house. Then, once Pliny had completed his ablutions, he joined his host for dinner in perfect spirits – 'or at least with a show of good spirits that was, under the circumstances, no less remarkable than genuine good spirits would have been'.[56]

Meanwhile, fifteen miles along the coastline from where Pliny was enjoying Pomponianus' hospitality, death was preparing to claim Herculaneum. All afternoon and evening it had seemed to the people still in the town that they might be spared the worst. The winds continued to blow from the north-west, and such pumice as fell was very light. But then, some three or four hours before midnight, the anger of the giants, freed from the bonds that for so long had kept them imprisoned, reached a new pitch of horror. A jet of red fire began to rise from the summit of Vesuvius. Not all the billowing clouds obscuring it were enough to veil the ominous glow from the view of those who had gathered at the foot of the mountain. Lightning flared sheetwise through the ash, and jagged bolts of flame. 'So pitch was the night that their blaze seemed all the more brilliant for it.'[57] Midnight came and went. Then, twelve hours after the initial eruption, spectators in Herculaneum watching the lightning shimmer and stab above them noticed something new. They did not have long to process the sight: a glowing red cloud that, emerging from the column of ash, had begun to flow down the side of Vesuvius directly towards them. In terror, people broke and ran. Those who could threw themselves into the sea; those who couldn't – mothers with babies, young children, the elderly – huddled in the vaults where they had already taken shelter. All perished equally. The avalanche of ash, pumice and gas, moving at ferocious speed, overwhelmed the entire city in a matter of minutes. No living creature could survive the terrible heat. Skin was vaporised, intestines boiled. Brains, bursting through skulls, dissolved on the passage of the fiery cloud. Heads were knocked off statues. Beams, tiles, walls: all were sent flying. The entire city was left buried. The entombment of Herculaneum had begun.

That something terrible had happened was evident to everyone along the Bay of Naples. It was still night, and the mushroom cloud, which by now had reached an almost impossible height, blotted out the moon and the stars. The change in the mountain's behaviour could be felt in the air. Pliny, in Stabiae, had sought to downplay the lightning display over Vesuvius and insisted on retiring to bed; but there were few who joined him in going to sleep. Although, in Pomponianus' villa, no one could make out the precise details of what was happening fifteen miles away, it was evident enough that the eruption, menacing though it had been from the very start, was entering a new and ominous stage. The fall of pumice was now so thick that if Pliny had not been woken up by anxious attendants, he would have been trapped in his bedroom, while the tremors had become so violent that it seemed the entire villa might come tumbling down around them. An anxious consultation was held. Was it safer to take shelter in some basement, or to head down to the harbour and trust to the sea? Eventually — because the villa seemed on the verge of being shaken loose from its foundations — Pliny and Pomponianus decided that the least worst option was to make for the ships. First, to guard against the rocks that were raining down now in increasing numbers, they and their attendants tied pillows around their heads; then, lighting torches, they began to pick their way down the slope. By now the sun was rising, but the dawn might as well have been the dusk. The winds remained contrary, and so there was nothing for it but to wait on the shore. An attendant spread out a sheet. Pliny, wheezing heavily, lay down on it. He called for a cup of water. Then he called for a second. The breezes still blew in his face. The ash and pumice continued to fall.

It was not only downwind of the eruption, however, that people dreaded they might be trapped. On the far side of the Bay of Naples, in Naples itself, and in Puteoli and Baiae, panic was mounting. The devastating tremors that accompanied the destruction of Herculaneum had, for the first time, brought home to people living along the coastline west of Vesuvius that they, too, might be in danger. Earthquakes, unlike clouds of pumice, did not depend on winds to spread chaos and death. In Misenum, the convulsions that had led Pliny to abandon Pomponianus' villa had simultaneously jolted both his sister and his nephew from their sleep. The pair of them, uncertain what to do, went out into the courtyard of their house. There, at least there was no roof to fall on their heads. They sat down. The younger Pliny, ever his uncle's nephew, unrolled a volume of history and started taking notes.

But then, with the coming of dawn, the violence of the earthquake grew worse. Even the younger Pliny was obliged to accept that the time for study had passed. He duly ordered carts to be loaded; then he and his mother left their house and made their way to the heaving streets. Others began to follow them, and soon everyone in the city seemed to be fleeing. The younger Pliny, once he and his mother reached open ground, sought in vain to stabilise his carts, which were rolling backwards and forwards ever more violently; but even so, distracted by supervising his slaves as he was, he could not help but keep glancing over his shoulder at the expanse of the bay behind him. There lay a scene of awful wonder. Dry land stretched where previously the sea had been. Marine creatures, left stranded by the retreating waters, littered the sands. In the distance, the great mushroom cloud, although still many miles tall, no longer reached the heights it had before. Vesuvius itself, the source of this terrifying spectacle, was crowned by flames. Pliny, in his encyclopaedia, had marvelled at how, across the world, 'in a vast range of locations, and in an immense number of ways, fire will blaze up naturally from the earth'.[58] The younger Pliny, nervous as he was for his uncle, and resolved not to flee the bay until his return, at least had the consolation of knowing that the great encyclopaedist had been proven right.

'They swallow cities whole, burying them beneath earth so that not a trace of them is left.'[59] So Pliny, writing about earthquakes, had noted. Had he been able, in the first light of dawn, to inspect the site of Herculaneum, he would have glimpsed, through the faint drizzle of pumice, a sight sufficiently terrifying to merit an entire new chapter. Earthquakes, it turned out, were not the only natural phenomena capable of burying a city. Hour after hour, high above Vesuvius, the column of ash and rock — which at one point had seemed ready to brush the very heavens — had been collapsing. Periodically, following in the wake of the first avalanche to descend on Herculaneum, more avalanches of fire-edged dust had overwhelmed the city. Ash, pumice and rock; trees uprooted from the side of the mountain; rubble from toppled walls; tiles from demolished roofs: all had been borne on the repeated surges, burying the city and spilling out into the sea, so that by dawn every last trace of habitation had vanished beneath almost a hundred feet of rubble. The shoreline lay transformed beyond all recognition. Nothing remained of Herculaneum. In place of the famous city founded long centuries before by a triumphant Hercules, there was only desert. The giants had claimed their revenge.

In Pompeii, by contrast, sunrise seemed — however tentatively — to promise an easing of the nightmare. For the first time since the initial eruption, the downpour of debris had begun to ease. True, many of those who had opted to shelter in their homes rather than fleeing had perished: trapped beneath immense accumulations of pumice, and either asphyxiated or crushed beneath fallen masonry. But many remained alive. Some, held captive by rubble, sobbed and cried out for help. Others, afraid to risk the open, cowered where they lay. Dogs howled, frantic with hunger and fear. It seemed that the very city, like a crippled beast, was moaning in pain. Those who dared to emerge from their hiding places, stepping out into the spectral light and picking their way over the rubble, did so as quickly as they could. Although all but the topmost storeys of buildings lay buried beneath pumice, the fugitives still found pathways through what used to be streets to make an escape. They headed for various city gates, men leading their families, slaves lugging heavy sacks, children holding hands as they ran. A doctor, clutching his box of medical instruments, prepared to venture out from his refuge beside the amphitheatre; a temple servant carefully bundled up the particular treasures of his shrine and struggled not to spill them as he bore them away; a woman fleeing with some twenty other fugitives hugged to herself a tiny statue of Fortuna.

But there was no help to be had from the gods. The giants, who had already claimed one of the two cities founded by Hercules for their vengeance, were not to be denied. When the black cloud of gas and molten rock descended on Pompeii, it moved too fast to be escaped, killing every living creature in its path. The woman who, falling to her knees, pressed in vain a piece of cloth to her mouth. The slave shackled in a villa just outside the city, whose fetters were fused to his bones. The dog, tethered by the entrance of his master's house, writhing in its death throes as its lungs filled up with concrete. Ash fell on them, and on all the dead. Everyone, and everything, was buried. Epidius would never now attain the honour that had seemed, in the wake of Maius' death, so tantalisingly within his reach. The repairs to the temple of Venus would never be completed. The donkeys in the bakery would forever be chained to the mill. 'All lay sunk in flames and dismal ash.'[60]

The surge that buried Pompeii was on a fittingly monstrous scale. Terrible though the avalanches had been that descended on Herculaneum, they could not compare for fury with the final flow, the black and fiery cloud that completed the devastation visited on the sites where the two ancient cities had stood. The great column of ash that ever since midnight had been subsiding in fits and starts was now, after almost twenty hours, in its terminal state of collapse. Like a great wave it burst over the Bay of Naples. Pliny's nephew, watching from Misenum as it spilled out across the sea and swallowed up landmark after landmark, took his mother by her hand and sought to outpace the cloud. But the cloud was moving too fast. On the storm of ashes came 'a dense blackness that swept ever onwards, spilling over the earth in a great flood'.[61] The dark, when it descended, was like that of a deep prison that has never known light. Small children sobbed; parents screamed for lost sons and daughters; some wept for themselves, some for the world. 'For if there were many who raised their hands to the gods, then there were many others who declared the gods to be no more, and that the darkness would last for ever, and the world was at its end.'[62] Hints of fire glimmered in the

221

distance. Then blackness returned, and the ashes fell more thickly. The younger Pliny and his mother, feeling themselves in danger of suffocation, sought desperately to brush them off. To both it seemed that an eternal night had claimed them, along with all of Misenum and Campania, and everything beyond them. But then came the faintest glimmering, a hint of light. The darkness began to dissipate. The smoke became visible as smoke. The sun, blood-red, shone dully through the veil of black cloud. Misenum still stood, and Baiae beyond it, and Puteoli, and Naples. Shrouded in ash though they were, and though thousands of their inhabitants had perished, they had been spared the fate of the two cities founded by Hercules. The world, after all, had not been brought to an end.

Meanwhile, on the far side of the bay, the same black cloud that engulfed Misenum had reached Stabiae. Pliny and his party, sitting amid the rain of pumice, had failed to see it coming. But they had glimpsed, coming from the direction of Vesuvius, the faintest flickering of something: a glow of fire. Then, borne on the wind, had come a stench like sulphur. Pliny's party had risen to their feet in panic. Most had turned tail. Two slaves, rather than abandoning Pliny, who by now was gasping for breath, had helped him to his feet. Immediately the old man had collapsed again. The sulphur-like smell had worsened. The clouds of ash had grown thicker. Thicker and thicker they had blown. The darkness soon was total.

Two days later, by which time the skies were clear again and the full scale of the destruction visited on Campania had been made horrifyingly clear, a search party returned to the spot where Pliny had last been seen. He was found dressed just as he had been on the morning of his attempted escape. No animal had disturbed him. No fragment of rock had hit him as he lay. His body suggested not a corpse at all, but someone deeply, dreamlessly asleep.

V

THE UNIVERSAL SPIDER

The Greatest Show on Earth

One day, standing on the quays at Puteoli and watching freighters unload their cargo, Mucianus had observed a most unusual sight: a troupe of elephants walking backwards down a gangplank. It had not taken him long to fathom the reason for this behaviour: the giant beasts, nervous about the gap between the ship and the land, had turned round 'so as to give themselves a false estimate of the distance'.[1] Mucianus had always been a great admirer of elephants. As a connoisseur of nature's wonders, he was bound to be. The largest animals to walk the face of the earth, they were also renowned as the most intelligent. Mucianus himself had noted that one particularly educated elephant could write in Greek; another one, more backward than its companions, was reported by Pliny to have spent its nights solemnly practising the tasks that its instructor had set for it during the day. Size and brainpower: no other creature could boast such a winning combination.

Unsurprisingly, then, elephants had become great favourites of the Roman people. While enthusiasm for watching them write in Greek might be limited, they could be taught as well a whole range of crowd-pleasing skills: to walk tightropes, to perform as gladiators, to hurl weapons with their trunks. When, a year after becoming emperor, Titus decided to celebrate the completion of the Flavian Amphitheatre by staging *munera* of unprecedented brilliance, the world's largest and smartest quadrupeds were naturally given centre stage. Coins minted in gold and silver to celebrate the occasion were stamped with the image of a particularly martial-looking elephant.

Colossal, wondrous, awe-inspiring: it served as an emblem of the Flavian Amphitheatre itself.

Elephants, like most of the beasts exhibited in the arena, tended to flourish beyond the limits of Caesar's rule. That wild beasts, no less than barbarians, should be taught to respect Roman courage, and to dread punishment for trespassing where they were not wanted, was a tried and tested principle. This was why, when Rome embarked on its conquest of Africa, lions that presumed to menace the cities of the new province had been crucified. Centuries on, the presence of such ferocious beasts in the Flavian Amphitheatre served as a public tribute paid by nature to the capital of the world. Whether a rhinoceros from the depths of Africa, or 'a padding tiger, shipped in a golden cage'[2] from India, or a bear from the northernmost wilds of Britain, there was no creature so outlandish, so fearsome, so exotic that it might not illustrate Rome's global reach.

Yet wild beasts, for all the premium that was inevitably set on their capacity to provide entertainment, were not used merely as exemplars of ferocity. Lions, so Pliny had noted, were 'alone among animals in showing mercy to those who begged for it'.[3] In Mauretania, in the forests that bordered the Atlas Mountains, elephants would descend to a river every full moon, and there, sprinkling themselves with water, perform a ritual of purification. Many other such examples of admirable behaviour might be adduced from the animal kingdom: from the gazelles that, whenever they saw the Dog Star, would stand facing it as though in worship, to the snake that had once, so it was reported, rescued a small boy from bandits. Crowds in the amphitheatre might cheer as wild beasts were speared for their entertainment; but they might weep at the spectacle too. Just as the courage and skill of gladiators served as a reminder to the Roman people of their own ancestral prowess, so might a wild animal, even one brought to their city from the very ends of the world, move them, and stir them, and prompt them to a contemplation of their own noblest qualities. When, during one of the beast shows staged to inaugurate the Flavian Amphitheatre, an elephant knelt before Titus, offering him reverence, the episode assured everyone who witnessed it that Caesar, Rome and the natural world were all joined in a common harmony. 'Trust me, that devout and suppliant elephant is moved by the same breath of the divine as are we are.'[4]

It was a comfort to believe this. Only a few months had passed since the eruption of Vesuvius, and only a few years since the very empire had seemed on the verge of collapse. Dread as to whether these disasters were the expression of some universal convulsion was only natural. The fear had to be that the heavens were tugging on the affairs of the earth to malign effect. Just as the waxing and the waning of the moon were known to influence the motion of tides, the organs of shrews, the thickness of oyster shells, the capacity for hard work in ants, and the behaviour of lunatics, so perhaps, in the comet that had heralded Titus' accession to the rule of the empire, there had been the marker of some fateful slipstream that had the world caught up in its wake. The annals of Roman history, which recorded many natural disasters, many signs of cosmic anger, contained nothing remotely comparable to the vomiting of fire from the bowels of Vesuvius. The Bay of Naples was not some isolated region inhabited by peasants and bandits, after all, but the playground of the world's elite. The very admiral of the fleet had perished in the eruption. So, too, had the son of Antonius Felix: the nephew of Herod Agrippa, no less. Meanwhile, resorts along the length of the Campanian coastline – Naples, Puteoli, Cumae – were crowded with refugees.[5] Other fugitives from Pompeii and Herculaneum had migrated to Ostia, bringing first-hand accounts of the disaster to the very doorstep of the capital. Even before the arrival of eyewitnesses, people across the Mediterranean had been looking to the skies, and shuddering at what they saw there. Clouds of ash, drifting on the breezes, had cast Rome into darkness, as well as lands much farther afield: Africa, and Egypt, and Syria. 'And the people in these places, ignorant of the cataclysm and unable to imagine what might have happened, were no less ready than those who had experienced it directly to believe that the whole world was being turned upside down, the sun extinguished, the earth borne up to the sky.'[6]

225

Titus was grimly aware of how badly such portents might play. Ten years before the eruption of Vesuvius, in the dying days of the year of four emperors, the burning of the Capitol had provoked consternation across the empire. In Rome, it had threatened to undermine the legitimacy of the Flavians before their regime could even be established; in Gaul, it had fed the flames of civil war. Unsurprisingly, in the aftermath of the cataclysm visited on Campania, Titus had done all he could to show himself a father to his suffering people. While there was no helping Pompeii and Herculaneum, both of which were left to their tombs of pumice and ash, other cities in the region received substantial relief. Funds supervised by former consuls were provided to help their citizens repair damaged buildings, clear the detritus deposited on them by Vesuvius, and build sufficient infrastructure to cope with the influx of refugees. No one would say of Titus that he had fiddled while Campania choked.

Yet it was not enough merely to clean up after the disaster. The heavens had to be appeased. The Romans, ever a practical people, took for granted that any disturbance of the natural order, any incident out of the ordinary, ranked as the equivalent of a bailiff's dun. There was no alternative, when debts were owed the gods, but to pay them. The call was to retrenchment: to repair a fractured order, to renew abandoned customs, to return things to the way they had been in ancient times. Titus, a man notorious as an enthusiast for eunuchs, and viewed with deep suspicion by conservatives as potentially a second Nero, might have seemed an unlikely standard-bearer for such a programme. In the event, however, his talents proved well suited to the mood of crisis. Presume not, he might have said, that I am the thing I was.

Certainly, as emperor, he knew what was required of him. Steely, cynical, and possessed of a ready charm, he displayed a previously unsuspected genius for posing as a model citizen. Ostentatiously, and to widespread approbation, he presented himself as partner equally of the senate and the people of Rome. Senators he wooed by relaxing the security apparatus that he himself had only just stopped heading, and by refusing to countenance any charges of treason; the plebs by making it clear that he delighted in both their company and their pastimes. Titus, conscious of the high seriousness demanded from him by the anger of the heavens, did all he could to oblige. Accepting the office of *pontifex maximus* – the most distinguished priesthood in the gift of the Roman state – he declared himself motivated by one thing, and one thing only: a desire never to pollute his hands with blood. Lying at dinner one evening, and realising that he had done nothing all day to help anyone, he lamented his failure with words redolent of an antique hero: 'My friends, I have wasted a day.'[7] Sentiments like these, even as they redounded splendidly to Titus' credit, were calculated to remind everyone in Rome of the ancient dues of civic responsibility that had won the city its greatness. The Roman people, if they were truly to flourish, and keep the gods on their side, had an obligation to be true to their own best selves.

The Flavian Amphitheatre – vast on a scale appropriate to the vastness of Rome's empire, wondrous in a manner that eclipsed every other wonder – loomed as a stupefying monument to this conviction. The crowds that flocked to the inaugural staging of *munera* in its arena knew themselves to be much more than spectators. Just as, in ancient times, the Roman people had assembled in centuries to vote for their magistrates or to prepare for military service, so now, climbing staircases and taking their seats, were they moving to rhythms as venerable as Rome itself. That every citizen should be ranked according to his wealth and status remained, in the age of the Flavians, what it had been back in the earliest days of the republic: the organising principle of the Roman state. Unlike the parkland of the Golden House, which had permitted a promiscuous mixing of rich and poor, of senator and plebs, the Flavian Amphitheatre stood as one great census fashioned out of stone. Titus, who had served as censor only six years before, knew that a people without order were merely a rabble. Taking his place in the amphitheatre, he offered himself up to the gaze not of a mob, but of his fellow citizens. Beside him were senators; above him, segregated punctiliously according to wealth, and profession, and tribe, and dress, and sex, everybody else. It was, for anyone anxious that the Roman people might have forfeited their ancient dower of civic cohesion, a most satisfying sight: a living, breathing, cheering demonstration that they remained a community. 'Rome is restored to herself.'[8]

The assurance of this gave, to the one-hundred-day extravaganza with which Titus opened his great amphitheatre, an unprecedented resonance. Certainly, the crowds were entertained; but they were not merely entertained. Spectators had never before taken their seats in a building so colossal that it seemed to scrape the very sky. To enter it was to enter a dimension of myth. Dim though the origins of *munera* in the funerary rituals of Campania were, it would have been hard for anyone, watching gladiators stain the world's largest arena with their blood, not to reflect on just how many corpses, denied every ritual owed the dead, had lately come to litter the Bay of Naples. It was not enough, however, to appease their restless shades: there were the gods to appease as well. It was here that Titus, as the son of a god himself, had a particular role to play. When he had informers – men he personally had employed in his role as head of security – hauled into the arena, and beaten with cudgels and whips, it was a more effective declaration of policy than any number of speeches. Not only was he publicly turning his back on his past misdemeanours, but he was also summoning the spectators to reflect on their own obligations. A city united was a city with no place for those who would set citizen against citizen. Caesar, senate and people: all were joined in a common purpose.

Yet all this, in an age that appeared caught in the toils of a universal disharmony, still threatened to prove inadequate. The elephant that knelt before Titus, like the other beasts in the arena that similarly came to offer the emperor obeisance, served as a reminder to the Roman people of an order that existed beyond their daily lives: an order in which the anger of the gods, and the rhythms of the natural world, and the demands of a cosmic justice, had recently manifested themselves to terrifying effect. Would they do so again?

To feel the shadow of divine power was to experience, amid the swirl and snarl of daily life, an intimation of ancient legend. This, as Nero had brilliantly understood, provided scope for excitement as well as dread. The toppled emperor himself, posing as a hero of tragedy, had literally taken centre stage; but this was not the strategy Titus chose to adopt. His aim was very different: not to defy the gods, but to identify himself, and all the Roman people, with their celestial vantage point. The opportunity in the arena to recreate the wonders and the terrors of myth was infinitely greater than it was on a stage. Under Nero, it was the emperor himself who had played the role of tragic hero; under Titus, it was criminals. Stagecraft of an unparalleled sophistication and precision was combined with a whole menagerie of beasts imported from around the world. The result was spectacle of such an order that even the humblest members of the crowd, as they watched, might well have felt divine. The intestines of a man chained by his wrists were gnawed at by a bear; a woman was mounted by a bull. Episodes such as these, the themes of Greek mythology, had never before so vividly been brought alive. 'Let decrepit antiquity boast all it likes. Whatever has been rendered famous by song, Caesar, has been reproduced in the arena for you.'[9]

Yet events, despite the emperor's best efforts, continued to slip his grasp. The terrors of myth, the manifestations of divine potency, the sense of a cosmos governed by capricious forces beyond mere mortal comprehension: these, in the final reckoning, were not to be contained within the limits of an arena. The walls of the Flavian Amphitheatre, colossal though they might be, vast beyond the wildest imaginings of previous generations, proved inadequate to restrain them. A year after coming to power, while on a visit to the scenes of destruction in Campania, Titus was brought devastating news. For the second time in barely a decade, fire had laid waste the Capitol. The temple to Jupiter, which he and his father had restored with such effort and dutiful intent, had once again been reduced to smoking rubble. Nor was it the only monument left in ruins. The fire had swept across the Campus for three days and nights, destroying everything in its path: temples, theatres, bath-houses. Even the Pantheon, that famous shrine to all the gods built back in the early days of Augustus' supremacy, had gone up in flames. Then, in the wake of fire, came pestilence. Disease, in crowded cities, was a constant hazard; but the plague that swept Rome in Titus' reign 'was of a severity rarely witnessed before'.[10] The emperor began to despair. Two years after coming to power, sitting in the Flavian Amphitheatre, he wept so bitterly that everyone in the stands could witness his tears. Then, heading for the Sabine estate where his father had died, he was struck down by fever. Thunder, sounding from a clear blue sky, had already warned the Roman people to expect the worst. Sure enough, a day after falling ill, Titus breathed his last. Briefly though he had ruled – just over two years – he had come to be viewed by his fellow citizens as a man 'adored and doted upon by the whole of humanity'.[11] And now this favourite of the world was dead.

To many it seemed a body blow. A dynasty could not hope to perpetuate itself without heirs, and Titus had no son. Two wives, back in his youth, had come and gone. The second of these – a woman of commendable pedigree, whose sister was married to Trajanus – he had divorced when her father fell into disfavour with Nero: a separation that did not seem to have caused him any particular regret. As dashing as he was cynical, Titus had made a natural playboy. Indeed, prior to his elevation to the rule of the world, he had been notorious for it. His affair with Berenice, begun in Judaea and continued in Rome, had caused particular scandal, for it was widely felt that a Caesar had no business consorting with a foreign queen. This was why, on his father's death, Titus had made a point of sending his mistress packing: a signal to the Roman people of his intention to rule responsibly and well. Doubtless, then, had he remained alive, he would have taken a wife, fathered an heir, and secured his line. As it was, however, he had signally failed to do as Vespasian had done and provide an heir presumptive. Now that Titus had breathed his last, there was no one steeled for rule as Titus himself had been: on the battlefield, in the Praetorian camp, in the senate house. And so many in Rome, conscious of how perilous a moment the death of a Caesar might be, hugged themselves against the future, and dreaded the worst.

The Flavian dynasty was not entirely extinct, however. There was always Domitian. Titus' younger brother, although granted plenty of honours by Vespasian, had never been given responsibility. His attempts to secure military experience for himself had consistently been rebuffed, his hopes of meaningful office blocked. Only in one field for advancement had he been able to forge his own path: for early in his father's reign, and without Vespasian's permission, he had succeeded in seducing the daughter of Corbulo, Domitia Longina, and persuaded her to leave her husband. Domitia had provided not just a marital link to a war hero, but a whole circle of useful contacts: a better dynastic pairing, to be sure, than anything that Titus had managed. Otherwise, however, it had seemed – certainly while Titus was alive – that Domitian was doomed forever to be supernumerary. His sense of resentment and frustration had festered. A notorious loner, he lacked his brother's easy charm. 'Always,' so it was said of him, 'he dwelt in the shadows and dealt in secrets.'[12]

Rather than stay in Rome, where his lack of meaningful responsibility was inevitably felt as something raw, Domitian had preferred to closet himself away some twenty miles south of the capital, in a lakeside villa set amid the beautiful Alban Hills. Here he had seduced Domitia, written poetry, and practised archery by shooting arrows through the outstretched fingers of a slave boy. Back in Rome, where a craving for solitude was viewed at best as eccentricity, and at worst as evidence of secret deviancies, gossips had enjoyed a field day. All kinds of dark rumours about his unsociable nature were reported: that even the most innocent mention of baldness was viewed by him as mockery of his own receding hairline, and taken as a mortal insult. That rather than staying with his guests after a meal, he preferred to head out for a solitary walk. That alone in his study he would stab flies with a pen.

The malevolent quality of this last rumour – at once unforgettable and unverifiable – spoke clearly of the dread that Domitian, even in his Alban seclusion, was capable of inspiring. Nevertheless, he was the obvious, the only choice to succeed Titus as emperor. No one, of course, appreciated this more readily than Domitian himself. Even before the senate had confirmed him in his dead brother's titles and privileges, he had made sure to head to the Praetorians' camp, and there secure the soldiers' backing with a lavish donative. Although both Vespasian and Titus had denied him substantive responsibility, Domitian had not spent twelve years at the heart of the imperial court for nothing. He had penetrated to the very heart of its functioning. His understanding of how power operated in Rome was pitiless and without sentiment. Unlike Vespasian, who had emerged to greatness from the ranks of the senate, or Titus, a man who all his life had found it easy to be loved, Domitian was a natural outsider. It mattered nothing to him what senators might think of him. He aimed to rule as an absolute monarch, and had no intention of pretending otherwise. Augustus, founding his rule amid the rubble of the republic, had picked his way carefully through the ruins, nervous about what might give way beneath him, what teetering buildings were still at risk of falling; but a century had passed since his establishment of the monarchy, and the ruins were long since stabilised. There was, in Domitian's impatience with the pretensions of the senate, his scorn for their specious slogans, a brute and abrasive honesty. He did not object, as Augustus had done, when people addressed him as 'master', or even 'god'.[13] Why should he? It might not have been diplomatic; but it did, in Domitian's opinion, suggest something precise about his role.

When poets hailed him as Jupiter's deputy, 'commanded to rule the happy earth in the god's stead',[14] they were not indulging in mere literary flights of fancy. The new emperor, a man of stern and exacting piety, had no doubt that he had indeed been entrusted with a divinely mandated charge. No less than Titus, he felt himself in the shadow of a cosmic crisis. For two years the heartlands of the empire had been afflicted by a relentless sequence of disasters: first great clouds of ash, then fire, then pestilence. Who was to say, were the gods to be left unappeased, what further calamities might not be visited on the world? Domitian's scorn for the senate as a superannuated talking-shop implied no contempt for the traditional values of the Roman people. Quite the contrary. It was precisely because he experienced the obligation laid on him by the gods as a personal burden, as his own exclusive responsibility, that it never crossed his mind to share it. In his youth, twiddling his thumbs, Domitian had written poems on the ruin of famous cities: the annihilation of Jerusalem, the burning of the Capitol. Now, as emperor, it was his aim not to destroy, but to build. If he was to succeed in the great task that had been laid upon him, and redeem mankind from the threat of further calamity, then he had no choice but to attend to every aspect of the Roman state. Not a detail of its functioning could be overlooked. The need was for punctilious micromanagement. His enemies might mock him as a bald Nero; but Domitian was no Nero. Not since Augustus, indeed, had an emperor been possessed by such a sense of moral mission. Domitian took his responsibilities, both to the gods and to the Roman people, very seriously indeed.

Unsurprisingly, of course, the idea of him as an arbiter of morality was greeted by many with snorts of derision. When, dusting down laws originally brought in by Augustus, the emperor sought to toughen the penalties for adultery, the spectacle of him presiding in solemn state with Domitia Longina wrote its own satire. So, too, did his attempt to regulate a particularly notorious marker of depravity. Domitian, like his older brother, had a taste for top-end slaves. Attending the games, he would invariably be accompanied by a small boy dressed in scarlet, 'to whom he would chat away, often in a tone of great seriousness'.[15] This attendant was distinguished by a feature that marked him out as unmistakeably a purchase from one of Rome's most exclusive slave markets: a tiny head. No less close to Domitian's heart was a second boy, a fabulously beautiful eunuch named Earinus, who served the emperor as his cup-bearer: 'a bright star of incomparable beauty'.[16] Inevitably, when Domitian passed a

law banning the castration of children – and even, with his characteristic eye for detail, imposed price controls on the sale of slaves who
had already been made into eunuchs, so as to prevent dealers from
capitalising on the contraction of supply – the hypocrisy, to many,
seemed glaring. Yet this was not altogether fair. When Earinus came
of age, the emperor freed him. Here was an attempt by Domitian not
only to make amends for the wrong done his cup-bearer as an infant,
but to signal his own obedience to the stern demands of ancestral
morality. Haters were going to hate; but Domitian, when he expelled
from the senate a man for dancing, or degraded an equestrian for
remarrying a woman he had already divorced as an adulteress, or
banned courtesans from using litters, he was not behaving like a
tyrant. He was behaving like a censor.

It was, in Domitian's opinion, the honour – or the shame – of each
individual citizen that provided the surest measure of his record as
ruler. There was, however, a more public one as well: the face of Rome
itself. No more sobering evidence for the anger of the gods could be
imagined than the scarring that everywhere disfigured the capital.
As ever, Domitian's concern with detail was remorseless. Order was
all that mattered. Every last obligation had to be satisfied. When
Domitian sponsored the construction of additional passageways
beneath the Flavian Amphitheatre, facilitating yet further prodigies
of stagecraft, he also made sure to toughen up the prescriptions on
where each class of citizen might legally sit. Reminded that Nero,
in the wake of the great fire, had vowed to erect altars to Vulcan – a
promise 'long-neglected and unfulfilled'[17] – he painstakingly set
about fulfilling it. Conscious that without a full treasury no repairs
could be completed, no new projects embarked upon, he took his
father's concern for sound money to predictably obsessional extremes.
Unlike previous emperors, Domitian did not even try to pretend that
coinage might still rank – as in ancient days – as the responsibility of
the senate. Rather than leaving the treasury to run itself, he dismissed
from office the freedman who had served both his father and his
brother in the post of financial secretary. When, anxious to reverse the

debasement of the currency that had been a feature of every emperor's reign since the time of Tiberius, he restored the amount of silver to the level that it had held under Augustus, no one had any doubt whose policy it was. Even the appearance of the coins themselves — the titles, the portraits, the choice of gods on the obverse — proclaimed the startling truth: that there was no detail of policy so insignificant that Domitian might not busy himself with it.

'I beg my readers to remember that I am in a rush to cover everything in the cosmos.'[18] So Pliny, midway through his encyclopaedia, had apologised to his readers. Domitian was hardly a man to issue apologies; but he, too, neurotically conscious as he was of the vastness and complexity of the empire he ruled, could not help but feel the pressure of serving as a universal monarch. It was the burden of Caesar, as well as his glory, to have global horizons. There was nothing he did so finicky that it might not reverberate far and wide. Income left uncollected on a fountain in Rome might diminish his ability to order the world. This was why Domitian, rather than seeing the management of the capital's water rentals as beneath his dignity, attended to it with the same intensity that he brought to every other aspect of policy. The more rent was collected, the fuller the treasury became; the fuller the treasury, the better he could fulfil his awesome responsibilities. To restore the temples lost to fire. To renew Rome, so that its beauty and splendour might reflect back to the gods the blessings they had bestowed on its people. To raise by a third the pay of the legionaries, those valiant and steel-forged warriors who stood guard over civilisation itself. And if, by emblazoning his name on inscriptions across Rome, and by healing the capital of its scars, and by securing for himself the undying loyalty of the legions, Domitian was able to render his own rule more stable and secure, then that as well, of course, was nothing if not in the interests of the Roman people. 'Who is this I see as I recline?' So a poet, invited to dine with Domitian on the Palatine, exclaimed in wonder. His answer was the only one possible. 'Sovereign of every land, great parent of a world subdued, humanity's hope, favourite of the gods!'[19]

Thule Tide

Late summer, AD 83. A thousand miles and more from the imperial capital, corpses littered the site of the northernmost victory ever won by Roman arms. Pliny, writing in his encyclopaedia only a decade before, had noted that the remotest reaches of Britain, shielded as they were by a mighty forest, had never been penetrated by the legions. The Caledonians, as the inhabitants of these distant lands were known, ranked as barbarous even by the standards of other Britons. Large-boned and orange-haired, they subsisted without any of the comforts afforded by civilisation: wine, central heating, baths. On one side of their settlements stretched bleak mountains; on the other, the heaving ocean. When, at the opening of the Flavian Amphitheatre, a bear from Caledonia had been exhibited feasting on a criminal, the spectacle of it had conveyed to the Roman people an important and timely lesson: that the nursery of such a monster, its claws fearsome, its jaws sticky with blood, was not easily subdued.

Which was precisely what made the challenge of attempting it so deserving of Roman courage. Britain was a theatre of war in which the Flavian dynasty had a personal stake. Vespasian, at the head of one of the three legions assigned by Claudius to the conquest of the island, had played a key role in the invasion, winning thirty engagements against the enemy and storming twenty of their strongholds. Titus, after his initial tour of duty in Germany, had served there as a junior officer. Then, after the civil war, Vespasian had entrusted Britain to his son-in-law. Fresh from stabilising the Rhine and pacifying the Batavians, Cerialis had arrived in the province with a mandate to resume the northwards advance of Roman arms. As token of this charge, he had brought with him an extra legion, raising the number under his command to four: an intimidating concentration of power. Britain, it had been made clear, was to serve the Flavians as a distinctively dynastic trophy.

Cerialis' initial target had been the Brigantes, a formidable people who lived on either side of the Pennines, and who, under the

236

Britain

N

SHETLAND

ORKNEY

Moray Firth

O c e a n

Inchtuthil

Tay

Firth of Forth

Firth of Clyde

Tyne

BRIGANTIA

Eboracum

Pennines

B R I T A I N

| 0 | 50 | 100 | 150 miles |

| 0 | 50 | 100 | 150 | 200 kms |

leadership of their queen, Cartimandua, had served the Romans as generally loyal allies. Factions among them, however, had chafed against this subordination, and periodically sought to reverse her policy. Batavian auxiliaries appointed to garrison the frontier with Brigantia had repeatedly been drawn into skirmishes with rogue warbands. Civilis' nephew, that loyal servant of Rome, had preserved the memory of battle-honours won against them in his very name: Briganticus. Then, during the year of the four emperors, Cartimandua had been toppled from her throne, and a mixed force of legionaries and auxiliaries, sent to rescue her, had found themselves drawn into a full-blown war. Cerialis, arriving in Britain, had prosecuted this conflict with gusto. Remorselessly, he had hunted down warband after warband. A new legionary base – Eboracum, the future city of York – had been planted in the heart of Brigantia. Forts had come to dot the Pennines, and roads, like the cords of a net, to stretch over moors and fells. Still, however, there was more to conquer. First under Cerialis, and then under his successors as governors, the legions had continued their advance towards Caledonia. By the time of Domitian's accession to power, they stood poised on its very frontier: 'the narrow neck of land'[20] separating what today we call the Firths of Clyde and Forth. Back in Rome, in the chambers of power where Caesar, 'gazing west and east, scanning the south wind and the wintry north',[21] kept watch on the limits of the world, a brilliant triumph seemed close at hand: the conquest of the entire island of Britain. Alert to the swelling mood of excitement, poets could recognise the prospect of the fulfilment of a distinctively Flavian destiny. One of them, not content with imagining the subjugation of Caledonia, went so far as to portray Vespasian as offering to his sons an even more fabulous victory: 'the conquest of unknown Thule'.[22]

The opportunity to lead a Roman army on such an adventure was rare and precious: conjured up from ancient annals, it might almost have seemed. The man entrusted with the expedition could hardly have been better qualified for the task. Gnaeus Julius Agricola, a senator from southern Gaul, had studied in the ancient Greek city of

Massilia: a port from which, four centuries before, an explorer named Pytheas had set out for the Ocean. Far beyond Britain he had gone, sailing for six days until he had seen, mist-veiled and set in waters dotted with ice, the mysterious island of Thule. Agricola, although he had hardly ventured as far as Pytheas, had similarly made a name for himself beyond the Ocean. Time after time he had been posted to Britain. He had served in the war against Boudicca. He had commanded a legion under Cerialis. Finally – the climax of his career in the island – he had been appointed by Vespasian as its governor. By 82, the year in which he finally led an expedition across the Firth of Forth, he had already been in office for five years: an impressively long term. His men, battle-hardened by the campaigns that had seen them fight their way up the length of Britain, enthusiastically shared in his sense of mission. Marines from the fleet that Agricola had commissioned to shadow the advance of his army, when they landed and spoke of their experiences – the screaming of gales in their ears, the glistening of black rocks before their gaze – would boast of having conquered the Ocean. Legionaries ambushed by the enemy, rather than panicking, would steel themselves, rout the barbarians, and scorn any talk of withdrawal. 'Such was their fortitude, they declared, that nothing could stop them. They would plunge ever deeper into Caledonia, they would fight and fight again until they had reached the outermost limits of Britain.'[23]

And they were as good as their word. Agricola's great victory in the late summer of 83, during the seventh year of his governorship, was a triumph not just over the barbarians, but over Caledonia itself: its remoteness, its savagery, its terrible weather. Repeatedly, confronted by Roman steel, the Caledonians had melted away into bogs and woods, as insusbstantial, so it seemed to the frustrated invaders, as the cloud that veiled the highland peaks; but now at last they had been brought to battle. Agricola's fleet, raiding the length of the coastline, had successfully goaded the barbarians into a determination to seek revenge; and his army, advancing to the foot of a mountain named Graupius, had there found a great clamorous mass of warbands, yelling, chanting and cheering their chieftains as they rattled up and down in chariots. It was the Batavians, burnishing anew the reputation for loyalty to Rome so recently tarnished by Civilis, who had taken the lead against the enemy; and the cavalry that had finished them off. The next day at dawn, Agricola sent horsemen out to reconnoitre the wilds that for so long had been the haunt and the refuge of the barbarians; but he need not have worried. 'The silence of desolation reigned on all sides: the hills were abandoned, distant homesteads put to the torch, and not a soul was to be seen by our scouts.'[24]

Still, the great mission of Agricola's term as governor remained incomplete: to strive, to seek, to find, and not to yield. Summer was fading, and Agricola himself, taking hostages as he went, was ready to head south; but first, before he went, he commanded the bulk of his troops to overwinter in Caledonia. There, he instructed them, they were to construct a great network of forts, stretching all the way up the eastern flank of the Highlands as far as the Moray Firth. It was to the fleet, however, that he entrusted the most challenging and heroic task: to circumnavigate Britain. No Roman had ever attempted this; and so it was, for Agricola's sailors, a journey into the unknown. The wildness of the sea, the savagery of the coastline, the gathering violence of the autumn gales: all combined to render it a fearsome voyage. Its successful completion ranked as a triumph almost on a par with the victory at Mount Graupius.

Yet it was neither of these feats, when Agricola's dispatch arrived in Rome, bringing news of the year's campaigning, that most vividly captured the public's imagination, but rather an even more epic achievement. The Roman fleet, sailing past the northernmost point of Britain, had paused in its voyage to subdue the islands that lay just north of the mainland: Orkney. Beyond them in turn, intimidatingly far out to sea, lay a further constellation of islands: the archipelago that today is known as Shetland, and which Pliny, in his account of the world's geography, had named the Acmodae. The Roman fleet, obedient to orders they received from Domitian himself, had sailed sufficiently far north to catch a glimpse of them on the distant horizon; and then, because winter was approaching, and the fleet had been instructed not to make land, turned and headed back southwards. A remarkable accomplishment; and yet the Acmodae, as a destination, were not nearly mysterious or haunting enough to resonate in the imaginings of Rome. This was why, when Agricola reported the sighting in his dispatches, he opted to call them by a very different name. His inspiration was Pytheas, that ancient mariner who, sailing far beyond the bounds of Britain, had reached an ocean of ice, and seen there a land which ever since, in the imaginings of all civilised peoples, had served as a byword for impossible distance. A fleet obedient to the orders of Caesar, so Agricola insisted, had caught sight of a veritable wonder of wonders: the island of Thule.

'The furthest limits of the world have surrendered, around which the ebbing floodtide roars.'[25] The victories won by Roman arms against the Caledonians and the Ocean ranked as victories won by Domitian, and were hailed as such by exultant poets. The news from Britain set the seal on what had been, for the new emperor, a year of brilliant achievement. Thirteen years before, travelling to Gaul in the immediate wake of the Flavian seizure of power, the young prince had found his hopes of winning martial glory blocked by Mucianus; but now there was no one to stymie his ambitions. Alerted that in the depths of Germany, beyond the immediate reach of Roman arms, a particularly warlike people named the Chatti were growing restless, Domitian had executed a model campaign. First, returning to Gaul, he had lulled the barbarians into a false sense of security by pretending to conduct a census; then, advancing across the Rhine from Mogontiacum, he had taken them wholly by surprise. When the Chatti, attempting to fight back, employed their customary hit-and-run tactics, Domitian had ordered his cavalry to track them down, and then, rather than allowing the barbarians to retreat into the woods, to dismount and follow them on foot. Slaughter had resulted on a formidable scale.

This splendid victory, which had expanded the reach of Roman arms by some fifty miles, enabled Domitian to tighten the infrastructure of occupation his father had begun to develop on the eastern bank of the Rhine. Beyond Mogontiacum there stretched a tract of particularly fertile farmland; and beyond this farmland there loomed the Taunus, a range of low but eminently fortifiable mountains. Domitian, demonstrating that he was not Corbulo's son-in-law for nothing, ordered his legionaries to get to work with pick and shovel. Roads leading out from Mogontiacum began to score the approaches to the Taunus; forts and watchtowers to line the crest of the mountains themselves. Domitian, meanwhile, trailing clouds of glory, had returned to Rome, there to celebrate a triumph and adopt a new name: 'Germanicus'. When the dispatches reached him from Agricola, he was able to receive them not as he had been when he first became emperor, as a man without experience of warfare, let alone a record of victory, but as an authentic *imperator*: a conqueror fit to be ranked alongside his father and brother at last.

And perhaps even above them. In the early months of 84, Domitian marked his defeat of the Chatti by issuing a new design of coin. On one side was stamped a stylish portrait of the emperor himself, crowned with laurel and lacking so much as a hint of baldness; on the other the image of a woman seated on a long barbarian shield, her head bowed in mourning. The slogan: *GERMANIA CAPTA*. The echo, of course – unmistakeable and unavoidable – was of the slogan that Flavian moneyers were still, fourteen long years after the sack of Jerusalem, busily recycling: *IUDAEA CAPTA*. Glorious though the defeat of the Judaeans had been, Domitian had no intention of basking forever in the reflected glory of his predecessors. The Chatti, unlike the Judaeans, had authentically lain beyond the bounds of the empire. Their defeat had enabled Domitian to tighten his grip on territory that – in contrast to Judaea – had not previously been subject to the direct rule of Rome. Fittingly, the coins that proclaimed the capture of Germany were weightier than any minted by Vespasian or Titus. To hold one in the palm of the hand was to feel just how solid it was, how reassuring its heft, how pure its silver. Domitian, ever alert to detail, knew precisely the message broadcast by such a coin to the Roman people. That the anger of the gods was appeased. That prosperity was restored. That Germany had been made captive for good.

As had Britain, too, of course. Domitian, assured by Agricola that the entire island was now 'peaceful and secure',[26] certainly saw no reason to doubt him. The governor, his job done, was recalled to Rome, there to be welcomed with signal honours, including a statue in the forum of Augustus, alongside those of the city's greatest heroes. Yet Rome's rule of the world did not depend on victory in battle alone. The more barbarous a land, the greater the long-term challenge of pacification. In Caledonia, as in the Taunus mountains, soldiers busied themselves sawing wood, shovelling earth, fitting stone. They cut roads through the heather. At the foot of a glen, at a site now known as Inchtuthil, beside the river Tay, they built a legionary base large enough to house five thousand men. Never before had the markers of Roman order and discipline been stamped on such barbarous terrain.

The investment of effort was immense; and so, too, the expense. Four legions were required to hold the entirety of Britain; and legionaries did not come cheap. Domitian's willingness to fund the pacification of Caledonia was an expression of faith – not just in Agricola's record as governor, but in his own as Caesar. Like a spider at the heart of a mighty web, one so tirelessly and expertly woven that it spanned the world, he knew there was no thread so distant but that it reached back ultimately to him. Everything was interconnected. The soldier digging a ditch in Caledonian drizzle needed to be paid in coin that he could trust. The mines, the roads, the harbours, the vineyards, the estates, everything that sustained the Roman peace, depended on the protection of the legions, and without it would be lost. The success of the legions, and the prosperity of the empire, depended, in turn, on the favour of the gods. Domitian, three years after coming to power, could be well pleased with his achievements: he had set the empire, previously tottering before repeated and indubitable manifestations of divine anger, back on firm foundations. Yet the task had been a wearisome one. It had required ceaseless attention to every last detail of the empire's functioning. Nor was there anywhere – from the marble-clad slopes of the Capitol to the dankest reaches of Germany – that might not need his presence. No wonder, then, to Domitian's admirers, that the work demanded of him and his ministers should have seemed crushing: 'a weight almost beyond endurance'.[27] Others might sleep – but not the emperor. His gaze was relentless, unblinking – for it had to be.

Yet even Domitian could not keep watch everywhere. Distracted as he was by his reordering of the defences along the Rhine, he had failed to attend to a menace that had long been building beyond a second mighty river: the Danube. Sixteen years previously, during the year of the four emperors, the embroilment of legions from across the empire in civil war had served to expose, by weakening Rome's defences, precisely where the threat from would-be invaders was most pressing. Germans were not the only barbarians to have taken advantage of Roman distraction. So, too, had the Dacians. Mucianus, pausing in his march from Syria to Italy, had forced the invaders back from Moesia; but the threat to Rome's provinces in the Balkans remained. Now, just when it seemed that the world had been returned to peace and order, Dacian warbands once again began flooding across the Danube. Two legions, marching out to meet them, were cut to pieces. Among the dead was the governor of Moesia. This was humiliation almost on a Varian scale.

Domitian, ever hands-on, headed at once for the scene of the debacle. With him – due acknowledgement of just how alarming the situation was – he took his most trusted military henchman. Cornelius Fuscus, a Flavian loyalist appointed by Domitian to the command of the Praetorians, had previously been a governor in the Balkans: a record of service ideally suited, so it seemed to the twitchy emperor, to the task of taming the Dacians. Sure enough, with Fuscus at his back, Domitian rapidly succeeded in stabilising the situation. After only a few months' campaigning, the emperor felt sufficiently confident in the state of the Danubian defences to head back to Rome, and there celebrate a second triumph. Fuscus, meanwhile, rather than returning with his master to the capital, prepared to invade Dacia. It had never been the Roman way to leave barbarian impudence unpunished; and Domitian, ever sensitive to his own and the empire's dignity, felt duty bound to ensure that the Dacians were taught a lesson. So over the Danube Fuscus went. In the event, however, it was not the barbarians who were given the caning. No sooner had Fuscus and his men crossed the Danube than the Dacians began to stalk them. The ambush, when it came, was murderous. The entire expedition was wiped out. The Praetorians lost their standard. 'Dacian vultures fed on the guts of Fuscus.'[28]

Rip a hole in a spider's web, and the wound will send tremors reverberating through every last filament. When news of Fuscus' defeat reached Rome, the shockwaves were sufficient to alarm Domitian into hurrying back to Moesia, there to resume the wearisome labour of patching up the province's defences. But they were felt as well far from the capital, in the northernmost reaches of the empire, in distant Caledonia. There, where the construction of military infrastructure had been proceeding with great efficiency since the victory at Mount Graupius, orders arrived from the emperor that Agricola's conquests were to be abandoned. Brilliant achievement though the annexation of Caledonia had been, its continued occupation was a luxury that Rome could no longer afford. With its ability to hold the line of the Danube now hanging perilously in the balance, the very security of the empire was at stake. Domitian, desperate to plug the gap left by the loss of two armies to the Dacians, had no choice but to source manpower from Britain. He duly reduced the island's garrison of legions by a quarter. The great base raised up with such effort and care at Inchtuthil was not merely abandoned, but disassembled. Buildings were demolished; the flagstones of the bath-house dug up; an entire storehouse of nails buried, to prevent the barbarians from melting them down and turning them into swords and spearheads. Forts spanning the entire length of Agricola's northwards advance were levelled and burnt. The retreat from Caledonia was total.

Agricola himself, a living reminder to everyone in Rome of conquests won and squandered, knew better than to complain. The emperor was not a man to take criticism lightly. Domitian's jealousy of anyone who might dare to infringe his prerogatives was a fearsome and potentially lethal thing. Like his brother, he had initially made a show of banishing informers. 'The princeps who fails to punish them,' he had ringingly declared, 'is only spurring them on.'[29] Yet it did not take Domitian long to change his mind. A strain of paranoia came naturally to him. Treason was treason, no matter the rank of those who might talk it. As such, it needed sniffing out. Such came to be Domitian's settled opinion. Already, only a couple of years after succeeding Titus to the rule of the world, he had shown himself perfectly ready to execute senators convicted of conspiring against him. Well, then, might Agricola have opted to hold his tongue.

Even so, to his admirers, it seemed a grievous affront that Rome's greatest general, at a time when news from the Balkans was all of military disasters, should be lying low. Prominent among those who felt this was his son-in-law, a brilliant orator and scholar who, although from an equestrian background, had already entered the senate, and was ambitious to scale the ladder of advancement: a young man named Publius Cornelius Tacitus. To be sure, astute as he was, and reluctant himself to court the attention of informers, he did not presume to blame Agricola. Any undue show of independence, Tacitus knew, was likely to prove not merely fatal but futile. Agricola was a citizen authentically worthy of the noblest traditions of his city: living evidence that 'men, even under an evil princeps, can be great'.[30] Yet the general who had defeated the savage Caledonians in open battle, and sent a fleet to glimpse distant Thule, had found Rome an infinitely more treacherous place to negotiate than the outer limits of the world. To Tacitus, it appeared self-evident that Domitian's reluctance to employ Agricola in Moesia was prompted by dread of the great name that he had won for himself. 'Britain, no sooner conquered, was given up.'[31] Such was Tacitus' damning verdict on the withdrawal from Caledonia. It was, as a take on the situation in the province as a whole, as inaccurate as it was unfair. Nevertheless, it did characterise, in its mordancy and bitterness, how many in the senate viewed the abandonment of Agricola's conquests: as an unconscionable humiliation, a blot on the honour of Rome.

In truth, there was no senator who could feel the sting of it as painfully as Domitian himself did. It went without saying that the emperor – who had personally sanctioned the annexation of Caledonia – had no wish to see his legions in retreat. Britain was not just a Roman trophy, but a Flavian one. The crisis struck at the very basis of the emperor's authority and prestige. Every aspect of his reputation for competence stood in the balance. Domitian had prided himself, for instance, on his strict control of Rome's mints: on his redemption of the gold and silver coinage from what, until his coming to power, had seemed an inexorable process of debasement. Briefly, he had restored its purity to the standard it had enjoyed under Augustus – but then the disaster of the Dacian invasions had intervened. 'The sinews of war,' as Cicero had once famously put it, 'are limitless money.' But what to do when the supply of money ran out? The cost of levying fresh troops had left the emperor with little choice but to license a debasement of his own. True, it had not been a precipitous one. Domitian's coins remained far more solid than those of either his father or his brother. Even so, the financial retreat forced on him by the debacle on the Danube was far more evident to the Roman people than the withdrawal from a few forts and watchtowers in distant Caledonia had ever been. They could feel it in their purses; they could feel it in the palms of their hands. To shop with gold or silver was to be alerted to the full scale of the emperor's defeat.

Unsurprisingly, rather than risk the embarrassment of a further debasement, Domitian set himself to defending the purity of his coinage as resolutely as though it were the Danube or the Rhine. Since it was self-evidently unthinkable either to cut the pay of his soldiers or to economise on his renovation of Rome, he opted instead to tighten the screws on his tax base. When a tribe in Africa named the Nasamonians, oppressed by Domitian's exactions, sought to rebel, and were massacred for their pains, the emperor, addressing the senate, declared, with baleful satisfaction, 'I have forbidden the Nasamonians to exist.'[32] The joke, grim as it was, prompted only the wannest of smiles. It had not escaped the attention of senators that the fate visited on the Nasamonians was not a million miles from the ruin visited on several of their own number. The penalty for treason, as they were all too painfully aware, was not only death but confiscation of property. This, to an emperor in the toils of a financial crisis, constituted an irresistible temptation. So, at any rate, it appeared to many members of the super-rich. Since the eruption of war against the Dacians, a growing number of senators – a nephew of Otho, a governor of Britain, several former consuls – had been put to death. Spies, it seemed, might be everywhere. The wealthier the citizen, the more he had to be on his guard.

Nor was treason the only crime that Domitian's informers were employed to sniff out. In the first year of the war against the Dacians, at about the same time the currency was being devalued, the emperor had declared himself *Censor Perpetuus*: Censor for Life. No longer, as had previously been the case, was the census to be conducted at periodic intervals. Instead, it was to be a continuous, never-ending process. The Roman people were to imagine the eye of Caesar as fixed perpetually upon them, penetrating the innermost recesses of their homes, keeping track of their most private activities. Domitian, faced by irrefutable evidence that the gods, despite all his previous efforts, remained in a state of anger with the Roman people, had doubled down on his determination to appease them. More intrusively than ever before, he aimed to regulate and punish infractions of Rome's time-hallowed morality. 'It is the concern he has for mankind that prompts him to exact such retribution: for without it the duty we should properly show to the gods, that dread of every evil, will never again be seen on earth.'[33]

Here, for members of the elite, was yet a further tightening of Domitian's stranglehold: now he had the right to dismiss them from the senate whenever he pleased. Resentment of their 'Censor and Master'[34] was intense, and the stories told in hushed tones about his hypocrisy vituperative. It was claimed that he liked to depilate his concubines with his own hand; that he had a taste for frolicking in swimming pools with the cheapest street-whores; that he had conducted an adulterous affair with his own niece, and then, having got her pregnant, caused her death by forcing her to have a series of abortions. Yet such talk, by implying that Domitian's obsessive censoriousness was merely a cloak for his depravity, was a woeful misreading of his character. Whatever his private failings — and who could vouch for the truth of any of the gossip whispered about him? — Domitian was not a man given to duplicity. He cared little what the elites might think of him. His readiness to offend even the most eminent senators in the cause of regulating the morals of the Roman people was as unflinching as it was unapologetic. His duty was not to the senate, but to the empire as a whole. His responsibility: nothing less than to keep the world at peace.

And most people, even those who most bitterly hated him, appreciated it. On 1 January 89, twenty years to the day since Caecina's mutiny in Mogontiacum, rebellion erupted again in the great legionary base. Its leader was the governor of Upper Germany: a former consul by the name of Antonius Saturninus. Domitian, for all the efficiency of his security apparatus, was taken by surprise. For two and a half years, ever since Fuscus' defeat, he had been focusing on the need to put the Dacians back in their box. The emperor had displayed commendable patience in working to achieve this. Rather than launch a headlong attack and risk Fuscus' fate, he had opted to bide his time: mustering manpower, repairing destroyed infrastructure, handing out bribes to the more biddable among the barbarians. By the summer of 88, no fewer than six legions had come to be stationed in Moesia. The governor of the province, licensed at last by Domitian to cross the Danube, had inflicted a most promising defeat on the Dacians. Domitian himself, keen to press home the advantage, felt ready to renew the campaign in person.

But then the news of Saturninus' mutiny reached him. No wonder that he was thrown into panic. The only forces he had with him in Rome, the Praetorians, were a shadow of their former selves: for they still bore the scars from their mauling at the hands of the Dacians. The nearest available legion, VII Gemina, was stationed in Spain. True, its commander was a distant relative of the Flavians by marriage – the son and namesake of Marcus Ulpius Trajanus, the man known by us as Trajan – and this, so Domitian had to trust, was sufficient to ensure its reliability; but still, it was a long way from the Rhine. Even as the emperor sent Trajan a desperate summons, he knew he could not rely on VII Gemina joining him in time. Heading northwards to confront Saturninus, he found himself fearing the worst: the fate of Nero, the fate of Otho.

Yet in the event he need not have worried. Trajan, who marched as fast as he could to join Domitian, was not the only man to demonstrate his loyalty. So did Lappius Maximus, the governor of Lower Germany. Other legates, too, including the commander of Vindonissa, refused to join Saturninus' mutiny. By the time the emperor reached Mogontiacum, the rebellion had already been crushed. Oppressive though many in the Roman elite found Domitian's rule, they knew the alternative was worse. Saturninus, making his pitch to become Caesar, had recruited the Chatti as allies; and only the fortuitous thawing of the Rhine had prevented them from crossing the river while it was still frozen, and spilling into Gaul. A close shave – and a reminder to everyone that civil war was not the only threat to the peace of the empire. Domineering and censorious Domitian might be; but anyone with experience of the Rhine or the Danube, and of the peoples who lurked beyond them, could appreciate his efforts to strengthen their defences. Better an autocratic Caesar than provinces open to the depredations of barbarians. Better the stability that the Flavians had restored to the world than the chaos that had preceded their rule. Better, in the final reckoning, tyranny than anarchy.

Certainly, Domitian did not lack for a sense of duty. No sooner
had he arrived in Mogontiacum, and made sure of the situation
there, than he was on his way back to the Danube. With him he took
one of the two legions that Saturninus had persuaded to mutiny:
for he was resolved never again to permit the existence of a double
legionary base. The effect of this measure was to diminish for good
the potential for rebellion in both Upper and Lower Germany; and
this, combined with the punitive measures already taken against the
Chatti, served to bring a new and enduring stability to the Rhine.
The Danube, it was true, remained more unsettled; and Domitian
was obliged to work hard to endow the Balkans with anything like
the sense of security he had brought to Gaul. At one stage he was
absent continuously from Rome for almost a year. By 92, however,
he had succeeded in his primary goal: bringing peace to the limits
of the Balkans. The Dacians laid down their arms. They formally
acknowledged Roman supremacy. A Dacian prince received a crown
from the emperor's own hands.

Admittedly, Domitian's victory was not as glorious as it might
have been: for he was obliged, as part of the peace treaty, to slip
the Dacians subsidies, and to help them improve their capital, the
impregnable stronghold of Sarmizegetusa, by supplying them with
craftsmen. These were details that the emperor opted not to trumpet
in Rome. Nevertheless, his achievement was considerable. His critics
might sneer at him as a man who had stooped to negotiate with
barbarians; but Domitian had calculated the costs of breaking the
Dacians to Rome's will, and decided that they were simply too high.
The expense of blood and treasure threatened to bleed the empire
white, and plunge it back into chaos. Compromise, to Domitian, was
not necessarily a dirty word. The prize he had won by negotiating
terms with the Dacians was very great. The entire length of the
empire's northern reaches, from the Ocean to the Black Sea, stood
at peace at last.

Order, in a world darkened by the gods' anger, was not easily
kept. Domitian knew this, none better. It took resolution, and

sleeplessness, unblinking and unsparing, and an attention to detail so implacable as to verge on the merciless. If these were qualities such as the gods themselves might be expected to display, then Domitian did not deny it. His task was of a more than mortal order: the task indeed, as poets might put it, of a master and god.

World City

It was no surprise that Gaius Suetonius Tranquillus should have been present in court to witness the shocking scene. Young as he was, and ambitious to make a name for himself as both an orator and a man of letters, he knew that lectures on rhetoric would never provide him with the complete education that he had come to Rome in the hope of obtaining. Only the spectacle of its workings could do that: the pleading of rival advocates, the cut and thrust of their repartee, the murmuring of appreciative crowds as they listened to a particularly devastating prosecution, a particularly dazzling defence. In Rome, the law still provided audiences with what it had given them back in the days of Cicero: a ready source of drama and excitement. The chance to take a rival to court lingered on in the capital as one of the last civic freedoms to have survived from the days of the republic. Suetonius, although born in Hippo Regius, a decidedly provincial *colonia* on the north coast of Africa, came from a family that was not without influence in Rome.[35] His grandfather, back in the days of Caligula, had enjoyed contacts on the margins of the imperial household; his father, an officer under Otho, had been with the emperor when the fateful news arrived of the defeat outside Cremona. Suetonius himself, although barely twenty, was familiar enough already with the workings of power to keep an eye open for their more unexpected manifestations. And so it was, in a crowded courtroom, that he found himself gawping at a most unexpected sight: a financial officer inspecting the penis of a ninety-year-old man to see if he had been circumcised.

This, even by the standards of Domitian's attention to detail, struck Suetonius as obsessional. Never before had an emperor sought to boost revenue by licensing officials to inspect the genitals of suspected tax evaders. The roots of this initiative lay, as the roots of Flavian initiatives so often did, in the foundational achievement of the new regime: the defeat of the Judaeans. Vespasian, alert to how soon after the incineration of the Capitol that of the great temple in Jerusalem had been, had recognised in this coincidence the unmistakeable hand of fate. A law had duly been passed obliging Judaeans to pay to Jupiter the tribute they had previously been paying to their own god. Domitian, as grasping as he was pious, had found in this measure an exquisite licence for extortion. Splendidly though Vespasian had restored the Capitol, the fire that swept it during Titus' reign, for the second time in barely a decade, had provided scope for an even more extravagant refurbishment. So glittering was the new temple raised by Domitian to Jupiter, so ornate, so grandiose, so vulgar, that critics compared the emperor to Midas, the king whose touch, according to legend, had turned everything to gold. The hill that had once served the Roman people as the great shrine to their collective past was now, under Domitian, transformed into something very different: a monument to Caesar. This was why, behind his back, people might cast his building programme as the expression not of duty to the gods, but a mortal sickness: 'a lunatic desire to build'.[36] And it was why, when Suetonius came to witness a suspected Judaean stripped naked before a crowded court, he felt sympathy for the old man rather than contempt, and shock at just how far the emperor's exactions might be taken.

Naturally, fellow-feeling for Judaeans had its limits. Hostility towards them, and suspicion of what Romans viewed as their atheistical practices, had only been intensified by the events of the preceding thirty years: the rebellion in Judaea, the destruction of Jerusalem, the relentless showboating by the Flavians. After the ruin visited on their homeland, large numbers of Judaeans had made their way to Rome to scrape a precarious living as best they could, or else to join the ranks of beggars thronging the capital's streets. The sense of a city overrun by foreigners, which traditionalists had been grumbling about ever since Rome had embarked on its rise to power, had become, under the Flavians, a defining characteristic of the age. To many, the influx of Judaeans that had followed the great victory won by Vespasian and Titus was one side of a coin that had on its other the crashing of wagons laden down with marble, the hammering and chiselling from building sites across the capital, and all the various clamorous markers of Domitian's building programme. Nowhere, it seemed, was peaceful or venerable enough to be spared. Even the spring beside the Porta Capena, where in ancient times Rome's second king, Numa Pompilius, had consorted with a nymph, was no longer what it had been. Workmen employed by Domitian to renovate the area had covered the grass with stone, and Judaean squatters now filled the grove surrounding the fountain. Both alike, the pomposity of the marble and the ugliness of the shanty town, seemed to disgruntled conservatives a betrayal of the timeless holiness of the place: a 'desecration'.[37]

Judaeans, however, were not the only objects of Roman disdain. The more dyspeptic class of chauvinist loathed every kind of foreigner. A satirist who urged his readers to defecate on statues of Julius Alexander ('pissing on them isn't enough!'[38]), condemned the erstwhile prefect not as a Judaean, but as an Egyptian. Syrians, a people notorious for their mingled obsequiousness and avarice, not to mention their extravagant use of pomade, were spoken of with particular vituperation. Most resented of all, perhaps, because the most envied, were Greeks. A subject people they might be, but they remained what they had been back in the age of Plato and Aristotle: suspiciously, alarmingly clever. 'Quick wit, shameless nerve, a fluency readier than that of a trained orator':[39] such were the qualities that seemed the markers of a Greek. How was the honest Roman to compete? The question nagged at every social class, from top to bottom. Senators proud of their deep roots in Rome's past were obliged to watch as Domitian raised magnates from notoriously epicene cities

Fermented fish guts: the making of Aulus Umbricius Scaurus. (Sophie Hay)

Titus. (Tom Holland)

Domitian. (Tom Holland)

A scene such as Mucianus, the great lieutenant of Vespasian, might have seen on the quays of Puteoli. (Wikipedia)

The Flavian Amphitheatre. (agefotostock/Alamy Stock Photo)

The cityscape of Rome: arches, temples and — second from the left — the great amphitheatre we know today as the Colosseum. (Sophie Hay)

Coins minted by Domitian and Titus respectively to celebrate the tribute paid by nature to the Roman people. (Tom Holland)

The northernmost legionary base ever built: Inchtuthil in Scotland. (Wikipedia)

Nerva.
(Tom Holland)

The best of emperors.
(© Kenneth Garrett)

Auxiliaries on campaign in Dacia present a complement of severed heads to Trajan.
(Collection of the National History Museum of Romania © MNIR 2013)

Sarmizegetusa: the mountainous stronghold of Decebalus, the Dacian king. (Tom Holland)

Hadrian.

(Wikipedia Creative Commons)

Hadrian's Wall: clinging to crags, bristling with forts, running from coast to coast. (Peter Barritt/Robert Harding/agefotostock)

Antinous.
(Sue Clark/Alamy Stock Photo)

Hadrian's great villa outside Rome: 'built for him in a marvellous manner, so that he was able to give to its extensive range of features the names of various provinces and places'. (© NPL – DeA Picture Library/Bridgeman Images)

The great dome surmounting Hadrian's reconstruction of the Pantheon. (Nikretas/Alamy Stock Photo)

in Greek-speaking Asia — Sardis, Pergamon and other such flesh-pots — to the consulship, and gave them the governorship of key provinces. Meanwhile, down among the social dregs, where people employed in Rome's most shameful professions — prostitution, acting and the like — subsisted, Romans might find themselves no less beset by competition. Greek whores were prettier, wittier; Greek actors more convincing at playing women. 'A pretty pass, when someone who from childhood has breathed in the air of the Aventine, been nourished by Sabine olives, should find himself put in the shade by such people!'[40]

Such complaints, however, betrayed assumptions that were already badly out of date. The definition of a Roman had long ceased to be someone who, all his life, had breathed in the air of the Aventine, or snacked on the homely produce of Sabine farms. Trajan, the legate Domitian summoned to rescue him from the mutiny in Mogontiacum, had been born in Spain; Agricola, the conqueror of Caledonia, on the southern coast of Gaul. Even someone who might have been born on the Aventine was most unlikely to be descended from a long line of forebears who could say the same. What to other peoples seemed the prodigal generosity of the Romans with their citizenship had always given the city a mongrel quality. Ever since the founding of Rome, immigrants from beyond its walls — first from Italy, then from the Mediterranean, and then from the whole world — had been adding to the swirl of its crowds. Some had been granted citizenship as a gift or reward; others, by far the majority, by virtue of winning their freedom from servitude. Slavery had served for many as a pass to becoming Roman. It was rare, generations on, for the descendant of a captive brought to Italy during the course of Rome's rise to global rule, whether from Syria, or Greece, or Spain, to be distinguishable from native Italians. All alike ranked as citizens; all alike belonged to the Roman people.

This process of change rarely occasioned much comment. For the most part, the immigrants blended in, rendering the demographic changes almost invisible. True, there were some who stood out: the exceptions who proved the rule. Born in regions far to the south or north of Rome, their hair and skin – rather than resembling that of people who lived on the shores of the Mediterranean – bore unmistakeable witness to the climatological extremes of their homelands. 'For it is beyond question', as Pliny had noted in his encyclopaedia, 'that Ethiopians, because they live so close to the sun, are burnt by it, and so are born looking scorched, with curly beards and hair; while the skin of peoples from the opposite end of the world is white like frost, and their hair yellow and straight.'[41] This was why, had Domitian obliged, say, the Britons to fund the temple to Jupiter on the Capitol, they would have found it impossible to disguise themselves: northern barbarians, with their pale complexions and blond locks, looked nothing like Romans. Judaeans, however – because in appearance they resembled all the other peoples who inhabited the shores of the Mediterranean – found it a simple matter to deny their identity. There was only the one giveaway. Just as an Arab might invariably be recognised by the holes bored in his ears, so no Judaean could ever hope to grow back his foreskin. And this, for Domitian's tax inspectors, was giveaway enough.

Yet if there were Judaeans in Rome who, traumatised by the disasters and humiliations visited on them, had despaired of their god, repudiated all that rendered them distinctive, and sought to pass as Roman, then there were others who refused to see the two identities – Judaean and Roman – as incompatible. 'The Romans, such is the astounding quality of their generosity, have allowed almost everyone else a share in their name – entire nations as well as individuals.'[42] So wrote the one-time rebel commander originally known as Yosef ben Mattityahu, but who, since sailing from Judaea with Titus, and receiving a grant of citizenship from Vespasian, had come to be called Flavius Josephus. In the capital he ranked as a significant figure: the prophet who had foretold the rise of the Flavians to power. Although he had not been invited to stay on the Palatine, Josephus had been given rooms in one of the houses owned by Vespasian back when the emperor had been a private citizen: licence enough, for a man as ready to blow his own trumpet as Josephus, to boast of having met 'with every provision from Caesar'.[43] Further marks of Flavian favour had followed. A history of the Judaean war, in which Josephus naturally made sure to give himself a starring role, had been personally approved by Titus. Copies of it had been placed in Rome's public libraries. The author had even been honoured with a statue. Josephus, more than anyone else in the capital, provided living proof that a man might rank as a loyal citizen of Rome and at the same time remain a devout and unapologetic Judaean.

Even so, for many of his compatriots Josephus was the epitome of a traitor. Although Titus had granted him estates in his native land, he never returned from Rome to claim them: the hostility towards him in Judaea was too seething, too dangerous. To Judaeans mourning the sheer scale of the ruin that had been visited on them, the notion that the Romans, who had destroyed God's sanctuary and paraded His treasures past cheering mobs in their accursed capital, might in any way have been His agents, as Josephus argued, was blasphemy. Yet there was a ready response to this criticism. Josephus had only to point out the disasters that the rebels against Rome had brought down upon their fellow Judaeans. There was no alternative to interpreting the destruction of Jerusalem as God's punishment on an errant people, save to abandon trust in Him altogether. This – despite the fact that in Rome Josephus was surrounded by compatriots who had indeed abandoned trust in their god – he refused to do. More than that, he was resolved to explain to his Roman audience that the Judaeans, far from ranking as a contemptible people, were, in their piety, and their courage, and their martial prowess, a people not dissimilar to the Romans themselves. A people who fully merited respect.

The circle was not an easy one to square, and Josephus, struggling to reconcile his awe for the divinely appointed supremacy of Rome with his identity as a proud Judaean, was never less than conflicted. Nowhere, perhaps, was this more evident than in his account of the climactic episode of the Judaean war: an episode that had occurred a full two years and more after his departure for Italy. X Fretensis, the legion left behind by Titus to garrison the ruins of Jerusalem, had stirred itself at last from its base, marching southwards into the desert. Its mission: to clear three fortresses of bandits. This was, in its essentials, a routine police operation. The Judaeans who had fled to the desert — women and children as well as men — were refugees, not freedom fighters.[44] For seven or eight years, ever since the start of the war, they had been hiding from the Romans in the wilderness. They were no threat to the provincial authorities; but they were fugitives from Roman rule, and therefore could not be permitted to remain in their bolt-holes indefinitely. And so X Fretensis had set to work, scouring the desert clean.

The last of the three fortresses to be stormed was Masada, the remote palace built on a mountaintop by Herod. The operation had been briskly executed. A siege; the construction of the inevitable earthworks; the elimination of the inhabitants. Nevertheless, there was a hint in the governor's dispatches to Vespasian, just a hint, that not everything had gone quite as smoothly as it might have done. Some of the bandits, shortly before the Romans succeeded in storming the citadel and breaking through its fortifications, were reported to have killed one another rather than face death at the hands of their conquerors. The truth of the matter, admittedly, was sketchy, for no Roman had actually witnessed the scene. Nor were communications from the front necessarily to be taken at face value. After all, had the siege ended amid more squalid circumstances — perhaps, say, with the violation of a pledge of safety to the bandits, and a general massacre — then the details were bound to have been discreetly veiled.[45] Whatever might have happened at Masada, however, the gist of the governor's dispatches provided Josephus with the perfect opportunity to fashion a narrative of stirring drama. And so that, in the climactic section of his great history of the Judaean revolt, was precisely what he did.

In Josephus' version of the siege of Masada, the summit had been occupied not by refugees, but by the same breed of armed rebel as had already brought Jerusalem to ruin. Hours before the final Roman assault on the summit, all of them – men, women and children – had perished in the equivalent of a suicide pact. 'Never will we be slaves – and so we choose death.'[46] These words, ascribed by Josephus to the rebel commander at Masada, articulated a course of action that Josephus himself had very notably not taken. A course of action that had proven ruinous, lunatic, suicidal indeed; and yet which Josephus, despite his contempt for it, could not help but endow with a certain patina of glory. The ambivalence was one that others, too, might have recognised in themselves: the Batavian auxiliaries who, loyal to their oath, had helped to suppress Civilis' revolt; the Brigantian noblemen who, obedient to the policy of their queen, had refused to take up arms against the legions. Accommodation to the might of Caesar was the only sane policy; and yet, for all that, deep within the hearts of those who understood this, and scorned defiance of Rome as the policy of madmen, there lay a shadow of awareness that the sanest policy was not always the most heroic one.

Yet Josephus, certainly, was no coward. His insistence on the dignity of his people and their customs, expressed in his voluminous writings and aimed squarely at the imperial elites, took courage. Rome under Vespasian and his sons was not, for any Judaean, a comfortable place to be. Never before had a subject people been the objects of such systemic vituperation. Flavian self-glorification had amplified, for two decades and more, a message that could not have been more unsettling to Josephus. That the customs of the Judaeans were barbarous. That the worship of their god was mere superstition, discredited and overthrown. That to live as a pious Judaean was incompatible with being a Roman. Josephus, by very publicly denying all these propositions, was offering not merely a subtle defiance of Flavian propaganda, but also a public reassurance to his compatriots that such defiance was possible. In the capital, where the glittering temple to Jupiter squatted monstrously over the city, funded by a tax without precedent in Roman history, one deliberately calculated to rub the noses of every Judaean in the brute fact of their god's humiliation, Josephus' bravery could hardly help but serve as an inspiration.

And not only, perhaps, to Judaeans. 'Our laws need no written defence,' Josephus insisted, 'for they manifest themselves through the behaviour of those who live by them: a demonstration not of impiety, but of the truest piety to be seen anywhere in the world.'[47] The appeal of Judaean customs – as Josephus himself, who had met Poppaea Sabina as a young man, well knew – had reached to the very summit of Roman society; nor, even after all the calamities that had overwhelmed the Judaeans under the Flavians, had this appeal been entirely diminished. This became shockingly apparent when, in the summer of 95, an accusation of atheism – 'a charge on which many who had drifted into Judaean ways were condemned'[48] – was brought against Caesar's own two closest relatives. Titus Flavius Clemens was the grandson of Flavius Sabinus, Vespasian's elder brother, and had just served four months with Domitian as consul when he was charged and convicted; Flavia Domitilla, Clemens' wife, was Domitian's cousin. Their downfall reverberated through the imperial court like a thunderclap. Clemens was put to death, Domitilla exiled to a tiny island off the Italian coast. The seriousness with which Domitian took his role as the guardian of Rome's traditional morality could not have been made more clear. Crimes against it would be punished, no matter the rank of the perpetrator. Domitian's primary responsibility was neither to his family nor to the nobility but to the gods. He was censor, pontifex maximus, the father of his country. What hope for the Roman people if they could not depend on him to do his duty?

Josephus, defending the laws inherited by the Judaeans, never ceased to make play with their antiquity: to insist that even the Greeks and the Romans could accept them as just because they were ancient. Domitian, similarly, scorning the whispered accusations levelled against him of tyranny, cast the sternness with which he might deliver sentence as the expression not of cruelty, but of the respect that was owed the past. In 91, four years before the execution of Clemens, he had demonstrated this with a display of justice red-olent of the very severest days of the republic. In the Forum there stood a temple to Vesta, the goddess of the hearth; and here, ever since the days of Numa Pompilius, priestesses consecrated to virgin-ity had served as the guardians of an eternal flame. The privileges bestowed upon these virgins were of a formidable order: they enjoyed the use of a two-wheeled carriage; could free a slave or a condemned criminal simply by gracing him with their touch; sat in the front row alongside senators at the games. No women could rival them for sanctity: for the flame they guarded was the hearthfire of Rome itself. This in turn, however, ensured that the Vestals' chastity was an issue of national security: for the hearthfire, unless it were guarded by virgins, might be extinguished, and threaten the ruin of the state. Such, at any rate, was what ancient custom decreed.

Increasingly, however, under the rule of the Caesars, it had come to be moderated by displays of leniency. Under Vespasian and Titus, certainly, the rules that protected the sanctity of Rome's hearthfire had been more honoured in the breach than in the observance; and even Domitian, although he had imposed the death penalty on three errant Vestals, had been gracious enough to permit them to choose their own method of execution. No such mercy, however, had been shown Cornelia, the chief Vestal convicted in 91 of sleeping with numerous lovers. Domitian, after trying her in the privacy of his Alban villa, and dismissing her frantic protestations of innocence, had sentenced her to the full horror of the penalty demanded by tradition. Placed in a litter, gagged and bound with straps, she had been carried in solemn procession through the Forum and onwards, to an underground chamber beside the city walls, within which, as her friends and family wept for her, she was walled up alive. Her lovers – all save one, who had prudently confessed his crime before the inquisition began – were caned to death beside the Lapis Niger. So shocking was the episode that it would long endure in the collec-tive memory of the city. The genius of the Flavians for spectacle had reached, with Cornelia's entombment, a macabre apotheosis.

By the time Clemens, four years later, came to meet his fate, it was evident that no one at court, no matter how close he might be to Caesar, or how high his rank, or how devoted his record of service, could reckon himself truly secure. Generally loathed in the senate though Domitian was, the emperor had always kept about him a council of particularly valued senators, men whom he cherished as his *amici*, his 'friends'. Mutual trust was the foundation of their relationship. A man such as Cocceius Nerva, whose record of service to the Flavians reached back decades, well before Vespasian's rise to power, was typical of the breed of senatorial advisors on whom Domitian, like his father and brother, had always depended. Yet even Nerva, marking the mood of his master, might have been brought to feel a certain degree of nervousness. The sense of a lapping tide was becoming ever more difficult to ignore. Clemens was not the only eminent figure to be executed in 95 on a charge of impiety. Also put to death that year was one of the more distinctive of Domitian's *amici*: a senator of distinguished family and prodigious strength by the name of Acilius Glabrio. Summoned by Domitian to participate in a festival in the Alban hills, he had demonstrated his Herculean qualities by fighting a giant lion, and dispatching it without sustaining so much as a scratch. Rumour had it that it was this feat, by provoking Domitian's envy, which had doomed him; but Glabrio's peers may well have had their doubts on that score. Certainly, Nerva and his fellow *amici* were not alone in having reason to feel twitchy. Four years before his death, Glabrio had been consul alongside a man whose very marks of distinction – an impressive military record, a distant relationship by marriage to the Flavians – had come to seem ever more perilous. Trajan, no less than Nerva, had good cause to worry about the limits of the emperor's friendship.

'How wretched is the lot of a princeps.' So Domitian liked to observe. 'For the only time that people believe him when he reports the uncovering of a conspiracy is if he ends up actually murdered.'[49] Domitian had always been conscious of the shadow of death. Notoriously, he had once staged a banquet in which the dining room, the pageboys and the food were all coloured black; each guest had a slab laid next to him inscribed with his name like a gravestone; and no one spoke but Domitian, whose talk was of nothing but slaughter. As a result, 'it seemed to all those in attendance that they were already in the realm of the dead';[50] and so they dreaded that their host was set on dispatching them to the underworld for good. In the event, however, their lord and master proved to have been toying with them: for after a night spent in a state of the utmost terror, they found themselves not just spared execution, but lavished with gifts. The joke, however, had been on Caesar as well as on his guests. Domitian, whose sense of humour was never less than grim, understood himself well enough to make play, on occasion, with his own darkest fears. The more Rome came to serve him as a stage for the display of his power, his supremacy, his greatness, so the more, away from the people's gaze, did he seem haunted by a dread of how insubstantial they might prove to be. In the Forum, dominating that most historic of the city's public spaces, there loomed an immense equestrian bronze of the emperor, one predicted by his admirers 'to endure as long as the earth and the heavens shall last'.[51] Meanwhile, in his palaces, Domitian had ordered the colonnades lined with reflective stone, 'so that he would be able to see reflected in its gleaming surface everything that might be happening behind his back'.[52] A decade and a half after his coming to power, the rhythms of his paranoia were quickening. Seamlessly, his fears had fused with his censoriousness and his obsession with moral grandstanding. The result: a ready licence for judicial murder.

Nor were Flavians the only members of his court who might be made to serve the Roman people as a lesson. So, too, might freedmen. Domitian, who had sacked his father's treasurer early in his reign, had never hesitated to put his secretaries in their place. Some, over the course of his reign, he had removed from office altogether, replacing them with equestrians. Any hint of inappropriate behaviour in their ranks was brutally punished. When one freedman raised a funerary monument to his sons, and used stones intended for the temple of Jupiter to build it, Domitian had ordered the tomb demolished, and the bones and ashes flung into the sea. The most pointed of all the warnings he delivered to his freedmen, however, came in 95. Even as Clemens was being convicted of atheism, so were charges being brought against Epaphroditus, the secretary who, almost three decades before, had assisted Nero in committing suicide. The message was one that no freedman in the imperial court could possibly mistake. Even though Epaphroditus had acted in obedience to Nero's orders, the crime he had committed in compassing a Caesar's death was beyond the pale. And so Domitian had ordered him put to death.

It was possible, however, to draw from his execution, and from the executions as well of Clemens and Glabrio, lessons other than the one intended. On 18 September 96, just before noon, Domitian was murdered in his bedroom on the Palatine. His assassins were freedmen, court officials who, as one post-mortem put it, 'had lost all their affection for him, some because they were facing trial on an assortment of charges, and others because they anticipated being charged'.[53] That same day, Nerva was hailed as emperor by the Praetorians.[54] Once a loyal servant of Nero, then a partisan of Vespasian and Titus, and for a decade and a half the most distinguished among the *amici* of Domitian, there was no more seasoned survivor in the entire ranks of the senate house. Smoothly, Nerva purchased the loyalty of the Praetorians with the customary lavish bribe, and presented himself – since he knew that the soldiers loved Domitian – as the heir and avenger of the murdered Caesar. Then, just as smoothly, he proceeded to address his fellow senators. Here, before a meagrely attended assembly, he assured them of his loathing for the murdered tyrant. The following day, presented with a fait accompli, the senators duly followed the Praetorians in proclaiming their erstwhile colleague emperor. Nerva, to win their support, signalled his approval for the erasure of the tyrant's memory. The senate, erupting in feverish jubilation, needed no second invitation. The giant equestrian statue of Domitian in the Forum was promptly toppled to the sound of exultant cheering; so, too, across the city, were all his many other statues. Those made of gold and silver were melted down. Some senators, in their excitement, even ordered ladders to be brought, so that temples might be cleared of every last trace of the tyrant. 'What a pleasure it was to smash those arrogant faces, to raise our swords against them, to hack at them ferociously with our axes, as though our blows might inflict pain or draw blood.'[55]

Yet all this, of course, even as it delighted Nerva's colleagues in the senate, risked infuriating the Praetorians; nor, despite the new emperor's best efforts, could he stop the guards' resentment from continuing to bubble away. No matter how many coins he might issue proclaiming his sense of concord with them and the legions, he knew – as only a man who had lived through Nero's downfall and the year of the four emperors could know – just how sharp a sword was hanging over his head. Finally, a year after his coming to power, the moment of crisis came: the Praetorians marched on the Palatine, laid it under siege, and took Nerva, who had been vomiting with terror, hostage. The emperor, humiliated but unharmed, bought his freedom by handing over to his captors the ringleader of Domitian's assassins: a freedman whom the Praetorians first castrated, then tore to pieces. Not that the wretched object of the guards' fury was their only victim, of course. Nerva's prestige too had suffered a grievous blow. His entire regime appeared emasculated and eviscerated.

Yet Nerva, despite the devastating nature of the assault on his authority, was resolved not to permit the empire to slip into anarchy because of it. Doing as Galba had done almost three decades previously, but with infinitely greater success, he adopted an heir. His new son was the commander of Upper Germany, a man on whose fortieth birthday – by a perhaps telling coincidence – Domitian had been assassinated: Trajan. As token of this decision, Nerva sent his newly designated successor a diamond ring. His choice, popular both with the military and the senate, was the obvious one. Perhaps, indeed, Trajan's elevation had been the plan all along. If so, then it was not only Trajan himself who benefited from it. When, a mere sixteen months after Domitian's assassination, Nerva caught a fever and died, there was no crisis, no collapse into civil war. The new emperor, brought the news of his accession in Colonia, that great nerve centre of Roman power, felt no need to hurry back to the capital. Stationed as he was in Germany, he could see for himself how stably the empire stood. The Rhine defences were formidable. The legions were battle-trained. The treasury was full. The coinage was strong. The provinces were prosperous. The Roman world lay at peace.

Although Trajan would never admit it, he owed much to Domitian.

VI

THE BEST OF EMPERORS

Bread and Circuses

Early winter, AD 101. Rome had been desperate for news for months. Everyone knew that far distant, in strange and barbarous lands, great deeds were being performed; but all the Roman people had to go on was rumour. Now at last, with the arrival of a young officer in the senate house, their curiosity could be satisfied. Hadrian had ridden directly from the wilds of the Balkans bearing dispatches from Caesar. In Dacia, a great war was being fought. The emperor himself, who had left Rome on 25 March and not returned to the city since, remained on the front. His plan was to winter beside the Danube, so that come spring he would be ready to resume campaigning the moment weather permitted. Superbly though the legions had performed, there remained much to be done. The Dacians were a hardy, obdurate and treacherous foe. This was why preparations for their defeat required Caesar's personal attention. Already, fresh legions had been summoned from across the empire: the Rhine, Vindonissa, the eastern provinces. Auxiliaries too – including even, from distant Britain, the governor's personal bodyguard. Never before had a Roman commander mustered such an enormous and variegated force. Trajan, when he rode to war, did so as the master of the world.

The senators themselves, men recruited from across the Mediterranean, served as living witness to this. So too did Hadrian. Not just a messenger, he was the son of Caesar's cousin, and as a child had been his ward. When snobs, behind Trajan's back, sneered at the emperor as a 'Spaniard' and a 'foreigner',[1] they were sneering at Hadrian too: for the young man, like Trajan himself, came from Italica. It was a telling marker of the times. How global the name of 'Roman' had become when it was possible for the closest relative of a princeps to rank as the member not of a dynasty, celebrated in ancient annals, or even of a line of Sabine farmers, but of a family that had for generations lived in the sweltering plains of Baetica. Hadrian, certainly, was alert to his good fortune. He knew the dazzling prospects that his guardian's rise to supreme power had opened up to him. This was why, alerted to the news of Nerva's death, he had made sure to outpace the official emissary, and be the first to announce it to Trajan. Already, he had put his relationship with Caesar to good use, shamelessly capitalising on it to run up extravagant debts. At the same time, in his attention to the workings of power, he had shown himself cool, clear-sighted, proficient. To his audience, he served as a reminder of just how fast the world was changing: of how, even as it became ever more Roman, so Rome itself was becoming far removed from its own past. Standing before the senate, Hadrian did so as the face of the city's future.

To the Romans themselves, who viewed novelty and change with the utmost suspicion, this might easily have seemed sinister. That it did not owed much to the fact that Hadrian, a man born and raised in the capital, and deeply steeped in its history, understood perfectly the part he had to play. His role was to cast Trajan as an emblem not of innovation but of renewal. It helped that, in attempting to meet this responsibility, Hadrian was able to go with the grain of his audience's hopes and expectations. Trajan, to senators cowed by Domitian's megalomania, appeared a reassuringly old-fashioned figure. The qualities he put on public display – plainness and self-discipline, affability and lack of pretension – were pointedly not those of a monarch. In everything he did, he had been guided by one overriding objective: to avoid any hint of behaviour that might smack of his murdered predecessor. Three years into his reign, he could reckon this policy an outstanding success. Whether in the effusions of senators or in inscriptions chiselled by grateful plebs, Trajan was coming to be saluted in terms less appropriate to a mortal than to Jupiter. The more he affected the modesty and seemliness characteristic of an antique hero, so the more – by a paradox calculated to torment Domitian's embittered shade – he was hailed by the people as *Optimus*: the 'Best'.

'He is neither a god nor divine, and it would be ludicrous to flatter him by claiming that he is; no tyrant but a fellow citizen of ours; not our master but our parent.'² So Pliny's nephew, a year before Hadrian's arrival from Dacia in the senate house, had told his colleagues. In the decades since his uncle's death, the younger Pliny had enjoyed a brilliant career. Like his hero, Cicero, he had become the first man from his family to attain senatorial rank. In 89, the year of Saturninus' mutiny, he had served Domitian as Hadrian was now serving Trajan: as the magistrate charged with reading out Caesar's communications to the senate. He had brought and won various high-profile prosecutions. In 100, when he delivered his commendation of Trajan to the senate, it had been to mark his elevation to the consulship: an honour that he had attained, as he delighted in pointing out to his friends, 'at a much earlier age than Cicero did'.³

Naturally, when the younger Pliny – or Pliny, as we shall call him from now on – delivered his panegyric, it had been shadowed by a certain awkward fact: that the new consul had not only begun his career as Domitian's spokesman, but consistently been promoted by him. Yet if everyone knew this, no one cared to dwell on it: for the entire senate was guilty of a similar hypocrisy. Six hours Pliny had spoken in praise of Trajan, and every last breath of it had been heartfelt. Unlike Domitian, that unapologetic autocrat, the new emperor offered senators the chance to indulge in a welcome illusion: that Rome might simultaneously be ruled by a monarch and yet be true to its most venerable traditions. To praise such a man was to show patriotism, not to grovel like a slave. Hadrian, arriving in the senate house to report on wars fought in the cause of the Roman people, might have been a messenger sprung from the antique past. Pliny, only the previous year, had put it well: 'Our enemies see now that Rome has an emperor fit to rank with her heroes of old.'[4]

This impression was enhanced by the fact that the Dacians, Trajan's recent adversaries, themselves seemed to have been conjured up from the annals of the ancient republic. Much as the Samnites had done, back in the days of Rome's conquest of Italy, they combined peasant backwardness with martial sophistication, bizarrely barbarous customs with a fascination for Greek culture, a predatory restlessness with brooding, stone-built strongholds. Of all the northern peoples who dwelt beyond the limits of Roman power, they were the most fearsome. Back in ancient times, a Greek historian had noted of the barbarians who inhabited the banks of the Danube that, 'were they only to share a single ruler or a common purpose, they would be invincible, and put every other nation deep in their shadow'.[5] The Dacians, by coming together under the leadership of a formidably able king named Decebalus, had demonstrated just how shrewd this judgement had been. His capital, Sarmizegetusa, was no compound of savage huts, but a citadel fashioned out of monstrous blocks of stone, sited on the heights of a mountain, and guarded along the road that led to it by fortresses built on precipitous crags. Barbarians the Dacians might be, but their aptitude for warfare was of an almost Roman order.

The fearsome quality of their reputation did not derive, however, merely from their mastery of arms. Raised on the plateau where Decebalus' bristling capital stood were temples and a great circle fashioned out of blocks of timber, constructed as an image of the heavens. The reputation of the Dacians for occult wisdom was venerable and well merited: they believed it was possible, thanks to rituals taught them in ancient times by a peculiarly enigmatic god – a deified slave by the name of Zalmoxis – for them all to become immortal. So it was that they marked birth with grief and death with joy, and threw themselves onto the spears of an enemy 'more readily than others might embark on a journey'.[6] They were, in short, an adversary fully worthy of Roman arms, strange, menacing and terrible: men who wielded scythes in battle as though they were cutting corn; who bore standards shaped in the form of dragons that screamed as the wind blew through their lupine jaws; who wrote messages on giant mushrooms. If senators, listening to Hadrian report on these alarming foes, could feel themselves transplanted to a more distant and heroic age, then so, too, once the news of it had been more generally reported, could everyone else in the capital. A mood of excitement such as the Roman people had not known for a long while swept the city. 'For under the rule of sluggish emperors, they seemed to have grown old and enfeebled, but now, under the rule of Trajan, they were stirring themselves afresh, and – contrary to every expectation – renewing their vigour as though their youth had been restored to them.'[7]

Unlike Domitian, who had paid subsidies to keep the Dacians quiet, the new emperor had marched directly into their homelands, defeated them in open battle, and returned to winter quarters laden down with plunder. Out in the field, he had readily shared in the hardships of his men, mingling his sweat with theirs, comforting them when they were weary, tearing up his cloak to bind their injuries when they were wounded. Yet his dispatches, while conveying to the assembled senators a vivid sense of the heroism his men had shown, also conveyed something more: the sheer excitement of it all. The scenes of warfare in Dacia were ones that Trajan wanted brought alive for his fellow citizens, so that they might be reminded of what it was to be truly a Roman. The forts on the Danube filled with provisions and provender; torches blazing from watchtowers; barges laden down with supplies, straining against the currents of the mighty river. The legionaries, led by Trajan, advancing into Dacia: crossing the Danube over twin pontoon bridges; cutting paths through woods; fording rivers while carrying their armour over their heads. The auxiliaries, making a gift to Trajan of severed heads. Barbarian warriors, defeated in battle, fleeing Caesar's armies, suing for terms. Barbarian fortresses, surmounted by dragon standards and the skulls of Domitian's soldiers. Barbarian women, torturing prisoners. War, to the Roman people, had always been a dimension of wonder, of terror, of epic, of legend. And now it was so again.

Not that the narrative, if it were to have the appropriate ending, could be hurried. Trajan's audience back in Rome, hungry though they were for news of victory, were familiar enough with the rhythms of their city's wars back in the days of the heroic past not to feel overly impatient. They knew, for instance, that it had taken the legions half a century to subdue the Samnites; and that the pacification of a land like Dacia, fierce as it was, and even more savage than Samnium had been, would require all of Caesar's martial talents. They knew as well, however, that Trajan could be relied upon to finish the job – and so it proved. In the end, not one war had to be fought against Decebalus, but two. The story of how the Dacians were brought at last to utter defeat was as full of thrilling episodes, heroic feats, and brilliant accomplishments as any in Roman history: 'a theme so rich in poetry', as Pliny enthused, 'that it seems almost a thing of fable – although every detail of it is true'.[8]

Many had been the dispatches brought to the senate. As in the report delivered by Hadrian on the first season of the war, so in the reports that followed: Trajan had been anxious to make the details come alive. Scene after scene had been painted in vivid colours. The emperor, crossing the Danube in the spring of 102, and carrying all before him. The standards lost by Fuscus recaptured. Decebalus, coming into Trajan's presence and humbly suing for terms, ceding territory, acknowledging himself Caesar's vassal. It seemed that the war was won: for Dacian envoys, much as ambassadors back in the days of the Samnite wars would have done, had come before the senate, laid down their arms, and 'placed their hands together, as though they were manacled prisoners'.[9] The senate, exceedingly gracious, had accepted their submission and returned to them their arms. Trajan, set as he was on bringing order to the Danube, appeared to have triumphed where Domitian had consistently failed. The Dacians had made their surrender. The Pax Romana had been upheld.

Yet it was rarely the nature of barbarians to accept an enduring peace – not unless they had first been brought to utter defeat. Decebalus proved no exception. As treacherous as he was implacable in his hatred of Rome, the Dacian king had refused to abide by the senate's terms. Late in 105, Caesar had duly found himself returning to the Dacian front. Back on the banks of the Danube, he had commanded a great bridge to be built across the river, one fashioned not of wood but of stone, to stand as a mighty witness to the permanence of Roman power. Designed by Apollodorus, an engineer from Syria renowned as the greatest architect of his day, it stunningly fulfilled Trajan's ambition for it: to intimidate and stupefy. All winter it had taken the legions to complete it. Then, in the spring of 106 – having survived an attempt sponsored by Decebalus to assassinate him – Trajan had closed in for the kill. Over the great stone bridge he had gone. Slowly, painstakingly, remorselessly, he had advanced into the savage depths of Dacia. He had captured every last stronghold, stamped out every last bushfire of resistance. Sarmizegetusa, that holy and impregnable fortress, had been taken without so much as a fight. Then the *coup de grâce*: Decebalus, who had fled into the remotest fastnesses of his kingdom, was cornered by a squad of Roman cavalry. Rather than be taken prisoner to grace his conqueror's triumph, he killed himself. His severed head, delivered to Trajan, was sent onwards to Rome, there – before the gaze of the assembled people in the Forum – to be flung onto the Steps of Mourning. Meanwhile, down in the senate house, Caesar's dispatches had been delivered to the conscript fathers. They were read out, as they had been five years previously, by Hadrian.

Not since Julius Caesar's conquest of Gaul had there been a feat of arms quite so glorious, so gore-sodden, so lucrative. Hadrian, who had commanded a legion during the final stages of the war, had witnessed for himself the full scale of his cousin's accomplishment. For the first time since the retrenchment of Roman power in the wake of the Varian disaster, an entire new province had been carved out of the wilds beyond the Danube and the Rhine. The ruin Trajan brought to Dacia had been on an awesome, a stupefying scale. Vast numbers of the natives had been either slaughtered or enslaved; settlement after settlement put to the torch; the aristocracy exterminated. The survivors, forcibly expelled from their homeland, had been replaced by colonists from Moesia. Decebalus' kingdom had been wiped from the face of the earth. Not just its lands but its mineral wealth were now Trajan's to do with as he pleased. He had always banked on his conquest of Dacia – brutally expensive though it had been – to pay for itself: for deep in its mountains there lay extensive gold and silver mines. More spectacularly, however, there was the fabulous treasure amassed by generations of Dacian kings, and which Decebalus, in the dying days of the war, had sought to put forever beyond Trajan's reach. This he had done by using Roman prisoners to divert the course of a river, burying the treasure in the drying mud of the bed, and then, after covering the channel with stones, bringing the river back so that it flowed again along its original course. Inevitably, however, with Decebalus' flight from Sarmizegetusa, the secret had been betrayed. The gold, the silver, the goblets, the plate: all fell into Trajan's hands. No emperor since Augustus had won himself such a hoard. It certainly put the Flavian bragging about Judaea into perspective.

There was no need, when Trajan returned to the capital in the summer of 107, for him to display anything in his triumph that had not authentically been sourced from Dacia. The occasion was as dazzling as the triumph celebrated by Vespasian and Titus had been gimcrack. Of the gold and silver carted back from Sarmizegetusa, and the half a million or so prisoners taken over the course of the wars, only a fraction could be displayed to the cheering people. Rome, that great stage for the celebration, stood healed of the wounds of fire and civil war. Never in its history had it looked more sumptuously the capital of the world. There was, however, only the one cynosure. This – it went without saying – was the returning hero himself:

Imperator Caesar Nerva Trajanus Augustus. Tall, broad-shouldered and weather-beaten after the many months he had spent under canvas, he exuded a quality of *virtus*, of manliness, such as a Roman from the most primitive days of the city, one raised on turnips and acorns, might readily have saluted. Even his receding hairline, rather than nagging at him in the way that baldness had nagged at Domitian, seemed to his admirers yet another marker of his greatness. It was surely, so Pliny suggested with his customary suavity, a gift from the gods: bestowed on Caesar 'so as to enhance the majesty of his appearance'.[10]

Trajan's hairstyle — straight, short, a soldier's cut — marked him unmistakeably as what he was: a *vir militaris*, a military man. It was a look that could hardly help but seem to the plebs, no matter how much they might cheer him, as a reproach. The Roman crowds liked their princes stylish; but Trajan, by scorning to have his hair teased into an elaborate mane of curls (as even the follicly challenged Domitian had sought to have done), was making plain that he cared nothing for their taste. Everyone in Rome knew that Trajan preferred military life to the metropolis. That much was evident from how little time he had spent in the city. As emperor, he had waited almost two years before returning from the northern limits of the empire to the capital. He had spent over half his reign on the Danube. Attention to the needs and desires of the Roman people had transparently mattered less to him than the love of battle and the pursuit of fame. But now, with Dacia conquered and peace universal, there was no call for him to go and fight distant barbarians. Rome demanded his attention. At issue was whether a Caesar who had shown himself peerless as a conqueror could similarly, now that his sword was sheathed, demonstrate prowess as the father of his people. The time had come for Rome to serve as the emperor's stage.

A comparison between a land infested with menacing savages and the capital of the world was not entirely far-fetched. Such, at any rate, was the opinion of those who — secure in their rank and privilege — literally looked down on the teeming masses. To live in Rome as a member of the elite was, by and large, to live on a hill. If Caesar had come to monopolise the Palatine, that most exclusive of all residential neighbourhoods, then there were plenty of other heights that might offer refuge from 'the restless rumble of great Rome'.[11] Below the senator in his hilltop mansion, where the breezes were cool and fresh, there stretched the most astonishing urban landscape on the face of the planet. For miles it extended, an immense agglomeration of marble and brick: clamorous, mephitic, wreathed in smoke. No other city in history had ever been as vast as Rome was now.

Over a million people lived there, crammed into a few square miles – more than the entire population of Dacia. Few of them passed their days as senators did, surrounded by gardens, and fountains, and the very latest in interior decoration. The demand for accommodation was too relentless, too predatory for that. The property market in Rome was an exercise in exploitation. 'Nowhere does a squalid room cost more.'[12] The rent charged on the tenement blocks that furnished most of the plebs with their accommodation was graded with a ruthlessly exacting precision. The higher a floor, the likelier tenants were to find their rooms shaking as waggons rumbled by below, or collapsing in the event of an earthquake, or cut off from the street by fire. The crash of falling buildings was one of the most distinctive sounds of the city. So, too, the sound of mourning: for many were the neighbourhoods in which 'the wailing for the departed is a constant noise in the background'.[13] To live in Rome, that capital of a peerless and peaceful empire, was to live in the shadow of death.

Even to walk the city was, for many Romans, to take their lives into their hands. The streets were greasy and slippery, and many of them – despite Nero's attempt to improve the urban infrastructure – were as crooked and narrow as they had ever been. The rich, borne in their litters above the press of the crowds, resembled ships heaving in a storm; the poor, elbowed here, knocked by crossbeams there, knew that any slip, amid the general crush, might easily prove fatal. Even on the Capitol it was not unknown for people to be trampled to death. Down in more insalubrious quarters, where carts piled high with building material were forever struggling to negotiate the winding streets, traffic jams brought particular risks. 'For suppose an axle were to snap under the weight it was carrying, and an avalanche of marble to descend on top of the dense crowd, what then would be left of the bodies? What limbs, what bones would be distinguishable?'[14]

There was no legislating against such accidents. Even though heavy-goods vehicles had long been banned from Rome during daylight hours, it was impractical to ban the transport of building material: both the renovation of the city and the employment of the plebs depended on it. Yet even the legislation that did exist only created its own problems. The crashing of waggons throughout the night ensured that Rome was a city that never slept. This, in turn, brought its own perils. As night fell, and shops were boarded up, and dogs fell quiet, so the rhythm of the streets became darker in every sense. A great man, wrapped in his scarlet cloak, and guarded by a long retinue of heavies, all bearing flaming torches, had nothing to worry about; but not everyone could afford such protection. The mood in Rome was often threatening, and after sunset especially so. Such was the notoriety of the seamier reaches of the capital, where gambling and prostitution flourished, that Nero and Otho, as young men, were said to have haunted them, just for the fun to be had in beating up passers-by. Muggers, however, might lurk anywhere; nor were street brawls confined to taverns and brothels. Dawn would invariably bring to light corpses littering the capital's streets, lying in puddles of blood. Sometimes they would be collected by those who had loved them, to be mourned and cremated; and sometimes they would remain where they had fallen, to be swept up with the rubbish.

Jupiter himself had decreed that corpses, like excrement, should be deposited beyond the sacred limits of the city. Cleanliness was next to godliness. This, ever since Numa's meeting with Egeria, had been an enduring maxim of the Roman people. Inevitably, the challenge of keeping the streets swept, of furnishing sewers capable of serving the entire city, of ensuring that water never stood stagnant, but instead flowed fresh and clear wherever it might be needed, bubbling up from fountains, pouring out from pipes, was a relentless one. Rome's largest drain had been constructed back in the days of the kings, and its most iconic aqueducts built under the republic. The city's most impressive infrastructure, however, was of more recent origin. A succession of Caesars, ruling a city that seemed forever in peril of buckling under the explosive growth of its population, had sponsored engineering projects on a truly titanic scale. 'Calculate accurately just how much water flows to public buildings, baths, swimming pools, canals, private residences, gardens and suburban estates; consider how far the water has to flow before reaching its destination; contemplate the rows of arches, the tunnels through mountains, the bridges running level over deep valleys, and we are left with no choice but to acknowledge that there is nothing in the entire world more remarkable.'[15]

When Pliny's uncle, towards the end of his encyclopaedia, delivered this opinion, he did so with the authority of a man who had drawn up lists of every wonder in the cosmos. Yet the aqueducts – unexampled though they certainly were – did not reach everyone in the city. The plebs in their crowded tenements had to carry water up to their lofts, and then cart their waste down to covered cisterns. No matter how carefully urine might be decanted into jars, for use by fullers in the treatment of cloth, and no matter how assiduously the gangs of public slaves might nightly transport excrement out into the fields beyond the capital, for use by farmers as fertiliser, the stench of it was never entirely banished from the city limits. Mingling with dust, sweat, the incense offered to the gods, the brown smoke from workshops, and the scents from countless multitudes of cooking fires, it was so much a part of Rome that to live there was barely to notice it. Only in times of plague and fever, when the city stood wreathed in miasmas, would the stench become unbearable. The more diarrhoeas there were, the more corpses; and the more corpses, the more miasmas. Then the people would look to Caesar; and Caesar would look to the gods. Dread of the responsibility laid upon his shoulders had driven Titus to an early grave, and had been crucial in determining the entire tenor of Domitian's rule. Rome, vast and infinite and unfathomable, was rife with peril for any emperor – even the very best of them. Trajan, returning to the capital, was not oblivious to what it furnished him: no less worthy a setting for the display of his greatness than Dacia had been.

And as on the Danube, so in Rome: he had profited greatly from the labours of his murdered predecessor. 'A terrible emperor, but one who had excellent friends.'[16] So, with gnomic wit, Trajan was said to have acknowledged his debt. By raising temples to the gods and tending to the morals of the Roman people, Domitian had readied the stage for his heir in Rome no less surely than he had done in Dacia by fortifying the line of the Danube. The threat of plague and fire had been banished. The capital was stable. This did not mean, of course, that Trajan could afford to relax. Danger still threatened. The greatest risk of all, as it had ever been, was of famine. Trajan was alert to this on a more global scale than any of his predecessors. His concern was for the people, not just of Rome, but of the empire as a whole. Pliny, in his six-hour eulogy of the emperor, noted this admiringly: how ready Trajan had been to 'divert and direct the earth's abundance now here, now there, as the moment and necessity demanded, supplying aid and sustenance to peoples across the sea. Indeed, it is almost as though they were to be ranked among the plebs of Rome!'[17]

Pliny's tone of surprise was due reflection of just how heavily the obligation to keep the capital fed had weighed on Caesar after Caesar. Trajan, no less than Augustus, or Claudius, or Nero, was a devout supplicant of Annona. His return from Dacia, laden with plunder, had enabled him to demonstrate this in the most conclusive manner possible. Shortly after Trajan's triumph, Pliny wrote in wonder of the barges and breakwaters that were to be seen some thirty miles north of Ostia, 'where a bay is being converted into a harbour'.[18] This, however, was only one of a whole number of engineering projects along what had previously – with the exception of Ostia itself, and Claudius' upgrade of it – been a featureless coast. Trajan's goal was both simple and breathtaking in its ambition: to ensure the absolute security of Rome's corn supply. No longer was Puteoli to serve the capital as the only harbour capable of furnishing anchorage to the very largest corn ships. Berths were to be provided at last beside the mouth of the Tiber. Centrepiece of this development was a vast mooring, joined by a narrow channel to Claudius' port, in the shape of a hexagon. The labour, and the expense required to fund it, were immense; but so, too, once it had been completed, was the glory that accrued to its sponsor. The name of the complex, broadcast to all who visited it by an immense statue of the emperor placed opposite its entrance: the Harbour of Trajan the Fortunate.

It was not enough, however, for Caesar to keep the capital fed. Seasoned analysts admired Trajan for penetrating to the heart of what the plebs expected from him: not just bread but circuses.[19] Entertainment, as it had ever been in Rome, was a serious business. Trajan, emulating Titus, had used the Flavian Amphitheatre during his first appearance in the capital as emperor to issue a manifesto, to proclaim his bona fides, to win the hearts and minds of the people. Informers had been paraded before the baying crowd, then led down to the Tiber, forced onto ships, and set adrift. 'The sight was an unforgettable one: a whole fleet of the wretches thrown on the mercy of the winds.'[20] So Pliny had gloated. The real extravaganza, however, had come eight years later, with the *munera* that were staged to celebrate Trajan's final victory in the Dacian wars. Every kind of spectacle, every kind of expense, was served up to the Roman people. The great conqueror's ambition – one funded with the plunder from Dacia – was to leave his predecessors trailing in the dust. Rather than stage sea-battles in the arena purpose-built for them by Domitian, he built his own from scratch. The previous arena, once it had been disassembled, furnished material for his improvements to the Circus Maximus. Most sumptuous of all was an enormous complex of baths – so vast that a new aqueduct had to be inaugurated just to keep it supplied with water – built on peculiarly symbolic foundations: a stretch of the Golden House that had been filled up to its ceilings with rubble. This it was well and truly to bury Nero.

To parade disapproval of self-indulgence while simultaneously sponsoring the largest bath-house in the world was quite the manoeuvre. Trajan, model of discipline and modesty that he was, had no patience with luxury. His only vices were those appropriate to an honest soldier: alcohol and boys. Certainly, there was no place in his building programme for palaces. Harbours, arenas, bath complexes: these were all projects that served, not Caesar, but the Roman people. And yet Trajan, despite his show of seriousness and frugality, was a builder in a long line of builders, a showman in a long line of showmen. When, flush with his Dacian loot, he commissioned Apollodorus to design him a forum appropriate to the full massive scale of his victory, the complex ended up larger in area than those built by Augustus, Vespasian and Nerva combined. Libraries were counterpointed with statues; shopping centres with friezes, arches and triumphal columns.

Indeed, so monumental was Trajan's forum, so overwhelming in its impact, that it set the seal on a programme of building begun more than a century before: the transformation of the city centre from an expanse of brick into one of marble. Augustus had embarked on the progamme, and Domitian had refined it; but it was Trajan, that stern and rugged captain of the legions, who brought it to its ultimate fruition. Surrounding his forum there rose a wall as high as it was blank. Beyond it, amid smoke and clamour, the contents of chamber pots continued to be flung from attic windows, and gangs of public slaves to farm excrement from cisterns, and the victims of muggers to lie bleeding in squalid side-alleys, and beggars to sit in huddled clusters beside bridges, and miasmas to creep up from the Tiber. But Rome, for all its horrors, was like nowhere in the world – or indeed like anywhere that had ever been. Trajan, that best of emperors, had met the challenge set him by the gods: of ensuring that the Roman people had a capital at last that was truly worthy of their greatness.

Levelling Up

In Prusa, a city at the foot of Mount Olympus, very few people had been to Rome. The journey, for those without the money or contacts to facilitate it, was a challenging one. The roads were long, the seas dangerous, the inns expensive. Even the governor's messengers, practised riders who could rely on fresh horses supplied to them at regular posting stations, took two months to reach the capital. Vaguely, of course, the citizens of Prusa were aware of Rome as the mistress of the world. They knew that she was the seat of Caesar. That she was dressed in purple and scarlet, and glittered with gems and pearls. That the columns lining her shopping centres were fashioned out of purest gold. The world, however, was full of cities, and no one could hope to see them all. Most people in Prusa were perfectly content to be bounded by limited horizons: for they knew that those horizons contained within them great wonders and resources of their own.

The best place to survey them was from the heights of Olympus. The mountain, although not quite as towering as its namesake in Greece – identified by tradition as the home of the gods – commanded spectacular views. Looking northwards, the adventurous climber could see, at the foot of the mountain, the city of Prusa, and then, some fifteen miles farther north, beyond a plain rich in vineyards, orchards and olive groves, an expanse of water called the Propontis. Its shipping lanes were as busy as anywhere in the Roman world: for it joined Asia to Europe and linked the Aegean to the Bosphorus, the narrow channel that led onwards to the Black Sea. From Olympus, on a clear day, it was just about possible to make out Byzantium: an ancient Greek city that commanded the entrance to the straits. Not just Byzantium but the entire region was of immense strategic significance: the hinge that joined Anatolia to the Balkans. The people who lived there might feel themselves far distant from Caesar, but the eye of Caesar was certainly fixed on them.

Bithynia, it was called: a land which bore the stamp of various

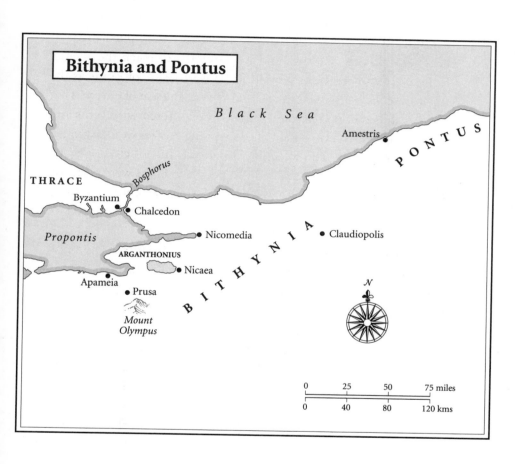

Bithynia and Pontus

Black Sea

Amestris

THRACE

Bosphorus

PONTUS

Byzantium

Chalcedon

Propontis

Nicomedia

Claudiopolis

ARGANTHONIUS

B I T H Y N I A

Apameia

Nicaea

Prusa

Mount Olympus

N

0	25	50	75 miles
0	40	80	120 kms

peoples, barbarian, and Greek, and Roman. The name of the region derived from a tribe distantly related to the Dacians; but so enthusiastically had the Bithynian elites come to adopt Greek culture that their native language – rather like Oscan in Campania – had been put irreversibly into eclipse. By 74 BC, when their last king, alert to the way the wind was blowing, had left Bithynia in his will to Rome, their four leading cities – Prusa, Nicomedia, Apameia and Nicaea – were Greek in both character and appearance. Although Prusa and Nicomedia had both been named after kings, and Apameia and Nicaea after, respectively, a queen and the wife of an upstart autocrat, all four cities boasted strong elements of self-government. The wealthy served on a council, a *boule*, and provided the magistrates; the masses constituted an assembly, an *ecclesia*, and made sure that not even the snootiest dignitary could afford to close his ears to their opinions and demands. It was all very reminiscent of Greece.

But then had come the Romans. Pompey, the plenipotentiary charged with restructuring Bithynia to serve Rome's ends, had no patience with democracy. He viewed it as rackety, destabilising and a menace to Roman order. What Prusa and the various other cities of Bithynia needed was, in Pompey's opinion, administration by the kind of institution that he himself represented: a senate. And so that, to all intents and purposes, was what he had forced on them. Almost two centuries on, the council of Prusa preserved its Greek name of *boule*; but in other ways, rather as the Order of Decurions in Pompeii had done, it bore a palpable resemblance to the senate of Pompey's day. *Timetai* – the equivalent of censors – sternly patrolled its membership rolls. Only magistrates and men of the very best families were permitted to belong to it. Meanwhile, the assembly, banned from initiating legislation, ranked as an impotent talking shop. The Roman governor, if he so chose, could suspend it altogether. As on the Bay of Naples, so in Bithynia: responsibility for the administration of a city lay with its great and good.

Some cities, it was true, had greater freedom of manoeuvre than others. Apameia, some fifteen miles from Prusa on the coast, had been re-founded by Julius Caesar as a *colonia*, and had never let anybody in Bithynia forget it. Other cities, ones particularly honoured by the Romans, ranked as *civitates liberae*: settlements spared the obligation to pay tax. This was the freedom that Nero had granted the entire province of Greece, and that Vespasian had then rescinded; and it was a status, of course, that was highly prized. Byzantium had been graced with it; so, too, the people of Chalcedon, a city on the Bithynian side of the Bosphorus, famous for its jasper, and for a breed of tiny crocodile that lived in one of its springs. Prusa, however, ranked neither as a *colonia* nor as a *civitas libera*; and so the members of its council, like the members of councils across the vast expanse of the Roman world, had no choice but to raise and pay imperial taxes. Their resentment at this was directed not at Caesar himself, however, but at their near neighbours in Apameia: a city which served them as their port, was smaller and less wealthy than Prusa, and would have been nothing without the timber and other raw materials exported from the slopes of Mount Olympus — and yet which, thanks to its status as a *colonia*, enjoyed a quite infuriating preponderance of bragging rights.

Jealousy, rivalry, ambition: these were emotions that, like the wildfires that sometimes ripped through forests and fields during the hot summer months, had long been at risk, wherever the Greeks had cities, of blazing out of control. The Romans knew this as well as anyone: for it had been the failure of the various Greek states to swallow their differences and fight as one that had facilitated their subjugation. Centuries on from their absorption into Rome's empire, cities such as Prusa knew better than to push their mutual rivalries too far. Just as the senate had come down hard on the Pompeians for brawling with sports fans from a neighbouring city, so, out in the provinces, were the imperial authorities brutally impatient with any hint of civic disorder. The days when the citizens of a Greek city, embroiled in a disagreement with a neighbour, could strap on their armour, pick up their spears, and go marching off to war were long gone. The Roman peace was maintained at the point of a sword. Every governor exercised a strict monopoly of violence. Roman rule might have deprived the Greeks of their liberty, but it had bestowed on them a condition that they had never enjoyed while they were free: an enduring and universal peace. This it was, under the rule of the Caesars, that had enabled them to flourish. Yet the Roman authorities, with the cynical pragmatism that had always been characteristic of their approach to Greek affairs, did not stamp out every show of independence. Quite the opposite. The governor responsible for Bithynia relied on the council in a city like Prusa to do the vast majority of his work for him: not just to collect taxes, but to administer justice in cases that did not merit his personal attention; to uphold security on the streets of the city; to maintain roads; and to furnish horses for the imperial post. The balance to be struck was a delicate one: permitting a city like Prusa the illusion of autonomy, while making sure the illusion never shaded too far into reality. The Pax Romana depended on its successful maintenance.

Ambition, then, in Prusa, was not only licensed by the provincial authorities but positively encouraged: the ambition of the city itself to be more celebrated, more beautiful, more esteemed than its neighbours; the ambition of its leading men to put their rivals in the shade, and win a renown that would echo down the ages. Prusa itself was not the only stage on which the most able of its citizens might aspire to make names for themselves. Roman chippiness towards Greek high-achievers bore witness to the sheer range and scale of their success. Under Trajan, the most celebrated dynasts of Anatolia — the grandson of a king deposed by Vespasian, the leading noblemen of, respectively, Galatia and Cilicia — had come to be awarded the greatest honour in Caesar's gift: the consulship. No one from Bithynia, it was true, could say as much; but an ambitious nobleman coming of age in Nicomedia or Nicaea, plotting out the course of his career, could know that the consulship was not an impossible aspiration. The summit of Roman achievement lay within his reach. He could dare to dream.

Service in the senate was, of course, only ever a prospect for the absolute *crème de la crème* of Bithynian society. There were, however, for those who did not belong to the nobility but were ambitious still to win golden opinions in the broader world, other options. 'Bithynia', a scholar from the neighbouring region of Pontus had noted back in the time of Augustus, 'has produced numerous men notable for their learning':[21] philosophers and physicians, orators and mathematicians. A century on, and it was a man from Prusa who most famously exemplified this tradition. Dio Chrysostom – 'the Golden-Tongued' – was an intellectual who embodied every stereotype held by the Romans about the Greeks. A philosopher, historian, political analyst and literary critic, equally at home offering advice to emperors on the art of kingship and giving playful eulogies of parrots or gnats, his powers of oratory were hypnotic – even when his listeners were not entirely sure what he was talking about. 'I don't really understand you,' Trajan was said once to have told him, 'but I love you as I love myself.'[22]

Favour of this order, shown to a man of not particularly distinguished pedigree, from a not particularly distinguished city, in a not particularly distinguished corner of the world, was due reflection of the opportunities that might, with fortune's blessing, open up in Rome to the eloquent and the brilliant. Bluff, no-nonsense soldier though Trajan was, he valued Dio as the kind of advisor that an emperor with aspirations to rule wisely should properly have at his side, and was even said to have offered the philosopher a ride in his triumphal chariot. Yet Dio, a man who might readily have secured for himself a comfortable retirement in Rome, and was a habitué of the richest and most sophisticated urban centres in the Greek world, only ever loved one place as home. 'Yes,' he acknowledged, 'Prusa may not be the largest of cities, and it may not be the oldest – but it is more highly rated than many, as even outsiders will confirm, so that its citizens, when ranked in competition against the men of other cities, come not last, nor third, nor even second.'[23] Cosmopolitan Dio might be – but he was nothing if not a patriot.

Yet if his career demonstrated the opportunities open to men hoping to better both themselves and their native cities, then so it also illustrated the perils of ambition. Potential elephant traps lay everywhere. This was especially the case for a man like Dio, whose status in Prusa was not as stable as he would have liked it to be. For all that his mother was the daughter of a Roman citizen, a woman from one of the leading families in the city, his father was an altogether more disreputable figure: a moneylender, a property speculator, an arriviste. Dio, painfully sensitive to this, had done all he could to identify himself with the values and aspirations of the municipal elite. He had run for civic office; he had shown himself a public bene-factor. When, however, he followed in his father's footsteps by buying a plot of land, and building a shopping centre on it, he provoked a riot. Prusa at the time was in the grip of famine; and Dio's commercial speculation had alerted everyone to the fact that he was richer than previously appreciated. A crowd of starving people, convinced that Dio was hoarding corn, marched on his house. The city magistrates were barely able to dissuade the mob from stoning him and burning his mansion to the ground. Their concern was less for Dio himself than about what the breakdown of public order might signal to the Roman authorities. The poor, who had long since been deprived of any stake in running the city, had nothing to lose by staging a riot; but the rich, whose administration of Prusa was conducted entirely on Roman sufferance, were frantic not to give the governor any excuse to impose direct rule. The young Dio, bundled into the local theatre by the city fathers, and obliged to justify his behaviour over raucous jeering and catcalls, had been given a brutal crash course in the realities of civic politics. Only with difficulty had he managed to exculpate himself, and wriggle out of his baying audience's demands that he fund Prusa's entire corn supply. The boundary between self-betterment and ruin might sometimes be very thin.

The ordeal had left permanent scars. A city, Dio would repeat-edly argue, was happiest when it was most like a hive of bees, a heap of ants, a flock of birds: ordered, harmonious, hierarchical. Such a philosophy, which he taught in cities across the Greek world, was one on which civic elites — cast by Dio as leaders of the hive, the antheap, the flock — were unsurprisingly keen; but it had appeal as well for a Roman audience. 'On what does the security of a household depend, if not harmony between the master and the mistress, and on the obedience of their slaves? And yet just think how many times a household has been brought to disaster by conflict between master and mistress, and by the treachery of their slaves!'[24] Here was a reflection as relevant to a Caesar as to the members of a Bithynian council. Dio's popularity with emperors and governors was hardly surprising. A philosopher who could provide high-minded sanction for his patrons' self-interest was invariably valued; and Dio could furnish the Roman elite with justification for nothing less than the Pax Romana.

Yet Rome, like Prusa, was rife with peril. Just as Dio, in the theatre of his native city, had narrowly avoided being torn to pieces, so in the capital of the world his intimacy with leading figures at Domitian's court had proved almost fatal. The patronage of great men, for a provincial looking to make a name for himself in Rome, might easily prove a double-edged sword. Dio, over the course of his career, had formed associations with some very great men indeed. So intimate had he been with Marcus Cocceius Nerva, the future emperor, that he was known in Rome as 'Cocceianus'. Not all his patrons, however, had been as careful how they trod as Nerva. One of them, charged by Domitian with treason, had duly been convicted and put to death.[25] Dio, caught up in the wake of the scandal, had been sentenced to exile. Years later, in a speech to the people of Athens, he would joke that his fate had been like that of 'the cup-bearers, and cooks, and concubines of a barbarian king, who are buried alive with their master when he dies'.[26] Banished both from Italy and Bithynia, he had roamed from city to city, impoverished by the loss of his property, physically broken by the demands of his peripatetic lifestyle. For years the dread had haunted him that he might never see Prusa again.

Yet philosopher that he was, Dio had refused to succumb to despair. Just as he had drawn valuable lessons from his youthful experience of bread riots, so had he sought to benefit from the opportunity to see the world. 'For I came to appreciate that exile is not entirely bad news, nor entirely without profit.'[27] When, in due course, Domitian was murdered, and Nerva, coming to power, restored to his client both his civic rights and his property, Dio did not immediately abandon his wanderings. Instead, alert to the rumours of war, he made repeated trips to Dacia, gathering material there for a history, and witnessing with the detached gaze of a philosopher the full awesome might of Trajan's legions. 'It was as a man unqualified to participate in military matters, that I arrived among soldiers who, although no fools, did not have the time for listening to speeches – for they were like racehorses at the starting-barriers, highly strung and tense, impatient with delay, and in their excitement and eagerness pawing at the ground with their hoofs. There were swords everywhere, and armour, and spears, and the entire camp was filled with horses, with weaponry, with armed warriors.'[28] When Dio returned from the Dacian wars, it was as a man who could offer commentary on Trajan's achievements that drew directly on personal experience; and when he headed onwards to Prusa, like some hero of myth returning in triumph from his wanderings, it was as a man who could boast the personal friendship of Caesar.

Inevitably, now that he was a man of wealth and status, Dio did what any Greek in his situation would have done: he commissioned lots of showy buildings. This was done, of course, with the aim of promoting himself as a civic benefactor; but also in a spirit of patriotism. Dio, over the course of his wanderings, had visited many famous cities, and seen for himself just how ferocious the competition between them to rank as the most beautiful, the most impressive, the most cultured had become. Colonnades, temples, libraries: these, in the richest and most famous centres of the Greek world, were going up at a furious rate. Dio had been despondent, on his return from exile to Prusa, to discover just how shabby his own city looked by comparison. Its baths were old and dilapidated; once splendid mansions had crumbled into ruin; it lacked even the most basic amenities. Dio, who had made sure to obtain written backing from Trajan for his plans, aimed at a full-scale programme of urban renewal. His ambition was not merely to beautify Prusa, 'by equipping it with colonnades and fountains',[29] but to renovate its fortifications and boost its transport links. This programme, originating as it did with Prusa's most famous son, was greeted with widespread enthusiasm. Many citizens offered financial contributions of their own. Dio, earmarking a particularly squalid stretch of town for renovation, aimed to clear its ruins and run-down workshops, and build a gleaming new portico and library. He even climbed Mount Olympus to source marble for the development. The sense of excitement in the city was palpable.

But so, too, was a mood of resentment. The return of the exiled hero had not been greeted with universal approbation. There were many prominent figures in the city whose noses had been put badly out of joint by Dio's arrival, and who scoffed at his claim to be a favourite of Trajan. If he were really such an intimate of Caesar, they sneered, then why had he not obtained for Prusa the status that every Greek city most craved – that of a *civitas libera*? A pointed question: for Dio had indeed sought to obtain freedom from taxation for his native city, and been rebuffed. True, he had secured other privileges – a boost to Prusa's judicial status, an increase in the number of councillors permitted to serve on the *boule* – but his failure to win the city a status equivalent to that of Byzantium or Chalcedon was a sore point with him, and his enemies knew it. They knew as well that between Dio and Caesar, now that the philosopher had left Rome, there extended many layers of provincial administration. It was far easier for Dio's enemies to bend the ear of the governor than it was for Dio to bend the ear of Trajan. Various charges began to circulate. That Dio, in his ambition to rebuild Prusa, was acting like a tyrant by 'tearing down all its shrines'.[30] That he was fleecing the subscribers to his development, which was nothing but a scam. That he had erected a statue of Trajan next to where his wife and son were buried – a flagrant case of treason. Cumulatively, these accusations added up to one single, damning smear: that Dio had transformed Prusa into a sink of malfeasance and impiety.

Yet if this patently spelt trouble for Dio himself, so also did it spell potential trouble for his accusers. They had adopted a dangerous tactic: an upper-class equivalent of a riot. By inviting the governor to poke his nose into the affairs of their city, they had knowingly put the entire basis of their autonomy at risk. In truth, the danger was greater than they appreciated. Prusa was not the only city that seemed to the Roman authorities to be in a state of mounting chaos. Nicomedia and Nicaea were at daggers drawn. Corruption and peculation were rife. Councils everywhere were riddled with debt. There was barely a city in Bithynia that seemed on a stable footing.

Perhaps, had the provincial authorities themselves displayed a record of competence, the risk to stability in the region might have been manageable; but a succession of governors, rather than working to ease the crisis, had only contributed to it. For a century and more, Bithynia and Pontus – paired by Pompey into a single provincial unit – had suffered from notoriously incompetent administrations. Both of the governors appointed to the province in the wake of Dio's return to Prusa had indulged in blatant displays of extortion. Both, brought to trial before the senate, had managed to escape the full sanction of the law. Both, despite their obvious guilt, had been able to rely for their defence on an orator who, as the self-appointed heir of Cicero, cast himself as the spokesman for principle, propriety and tradition. To Pliny, it seemed clear that, in the trial of a senator 'possessed of noble birth and official distinction',[31] the precise details of what he might or might not have done in some distant province counted for little when weighed in the balance against his breeding. In private, Pliny was perfectly capable of acknowledging that the occasional peccadillo might perhaps have been committed – but his responsibility was to wink at it. The health of the provincial administration in Bithynia, the right of the natives not to suffer oppression, the good name of Roman justice: all of these certainly mattered. It was just that, in the final reckoning, they mattered less than the prestige of the senate.

Pliny had particular reason to believe this. Two decades previously, in 93, he had won his first case in the senate by successfully prosecuting a corrupt governor of Baetica. The victory, however, had proven a pyrrhic one. The governor's conviction had set in train an escalating sequence of prosecutions and counter-prosecutions – one that, fatally, had ended up embroiling Domitian himself. Some of the most distinguished members of the senate had perished amid a blaze of book burnings. Pliny himself had not been complicit in this bloodbath – but the memory of it haunted him, even so. 'When we first became senators, we found ourselves tainted by the evils of the age, and then for many years afterwards were both spectators and victims of those same evils.'[32] Pliny, like Tacitus, and like many others of his generation, was all too painfully conscious of the shame that such collective passivity had brought on Rome's most august and venerable body. Sensitivity to the charge of collaboration made him only the more determined, now that the tyrant was toppled, and a happier age inaugurated, to see the dignity of the senate restored.

Meanwhile, however, Trajan had other priorities. The whiff of corruption drifting across the sea from Bithynia was a much greater cause of alarm to the emperor than it was to Pliny. That the interests of the senate should take priority over the stability of a distant province was a perspective dependent on a certain insularity. Pliny, to a degree unusual among the leading men of his age, had little personal experience of the empire's outer reaches. Although, in his youth, he had served with a legion in Syria, he had otherwise passed his entire career in Italy. The senate, the law courts, the salons where the very latest works of literature were discussed: these constituted his natural habitat. To speak in the ancient cockpit of Roman affairs, to hone the arts of oratory that Cicero had honed, to furnish a colleague like Tacitus with material for a history, or to serve as patron to a promising young man of letters like Suetonius: such were the activities, in Pliny's opinion, appropriate to a man of eminence. He might never have supervised the finances of Baetica, or ventured across the Danube, or braved the midges of Caledonia; but that did

293

not mean he was parochial. Quite the opposite. Italy was the richest, the most prosperous, the most cultivated of lands. To know it as Pliny knew it was a precious thing.

He was familiar with Rome, of course; but there was more to Italy than Rome. Pliny understood this as only someone with an immense portfolio of properties could understand it. He had played host to famous writers in his villa on the coast, welcoming them to his dining room with its spectacular views of the sea, and to enjoy his heated swimming pool. He had tended to his Umbrian estates, keeping track of the harvests, insisting that his slaves not be chained as they laboured, helping out local dealers when the grape harvest failed. He had travelled to his native Comum, revelling in how the glories of its architecture complemented the natural beauty of its setting, and endowing it with a quite fabulously expensive library. He was, in short, a man of taste and learning, with a concern for the propriety of things that did not necessarily preclude him from occasional displays to his inferiors of graciousness and clemency. And this, perhaps, was why, when Trajan was deliberating about who should be sent to Bithynia and Pontus, to attend to the chaos brewing there, and set the province back on a stable footing, he should have settled on Pliny.

'These Greeks in their little towns — how they do love a gymnasium!'[33] The emperor's joke, written in a letter sent by express courier to Bithynia, was one that he knew would bring a wry smile to the lips of the man appointed there as his personal legate. Pliny, while travelling to his province, had not been immune to a sense of excitement. Rounding the southernmost cape in Greece, he had broken rhapsodically into Greek; visiting the ancient city of Ephesus, on the Aegean coast of Asia, he had seen monuments there so fresh and splendid that they would not have disgraced a town in Italy. Bithynia and Pontus, by contrast, offered nothing but disappointment. Pliny found his province the very definition of provincial. Even cities blessed by their natural setting or graced with impressive architecture inclined towards the squalid. In Claudiopolis, a small town on the main military road, famous for its cheese, the locals had made such a hash of a development sponsored by Trajan that Pliny wrote in despair to the emperor, warning him that the entire complex might need to be levelled, and a new one begun from scratch. In Amestris, one of the more handsome cities of Pontus, the central street was disfigured along its entire length by an open sewer, 'a disgusting eyesore which gives off an appalling stench'.[34] Pliny, wrinkling his nose, made sure that sufficient funds were provided to have the drain covered; but this was a gesture of benignity that was simultaneously, and very obviously, a mark of reproach. Dio, even as he petitioned Trajan to bestow favours upon Prusa, and sought to reshape his native city in accordance with the most sophisticated fashions, had lived in dread of precisely such Roman contempt. 'The marks of distinction on which you set such store', he had once warned the people of Nicomedia, 'provoke the scorn of every person of discernment, and in Rome especially, where people laugh at them, they are known – humiliatingly – as "Greek failings"!'[35] The arrival in Prusa of a plenipotentiary like Pliny, a man of exemplary and intimidating taste, personally appointed to his commission by Caesar, and unafraid to make a show of his metropolitan airs and graces, was for Dio a nightmare.

But the joke was on Pliny as well. Had Trajan, when he appointed his legate to Bithynia, smiled at the thought of a man so habituated to the glories and splendours of Italy travelling from provincial backwater to provincial backwater, demanding accounts from recalcitrant councils, investigating drains? Pliny had been given the commission in the expectation that he would do a good job – and so he did. Where there was maladministration to be found, he sought to find it. 'How on earth have they managed to waste so much money screwing this up?' Trajan erupted, when informed by Pliny that the people of Nicomedia had managed to build two expensive aqueducts in succession, neither of which worked, and were gearing up to build a third. Yet even as the governor pored over fraudulent accounts, sniffed out bogus expense claims, and chased after stolen furniture, he was painfully aware of just how much more remained to be done. No one in either Bithynia or Pontus thought to offer armed resistance to Pliny; but neither was everyone dutifully submissive to him. As governor, he had the authority to intrude into the murkiest crannies of any city he might choose to investigate; but he lacked the resources to do this on a comprehensive scale. He knew, and the various councils in his province knew he knew, that the exercise of Roman power could never be dependent on Roman power alone. Without the backing of leading provincials, its entire functioning would fall to pieces. When Dio warned the people of Nicaea or Nicomedia not to squabble or riot, in case they should attract the attention of the governor, he was acknowledging Roman impotence as well as might: for it implied just how simple a matter it was for a city to keep the imperial authorities in the dark. The might of Rome was dazzling, intimidating, terrifying; but it was simultaneously a thing of smoke and mirrors.

When Pliny arrived in Prusa, he showed neither the city nor its most famous son any special favour. 'I am examining the public expenditure, revenue and outstanding debts owed the state,' he wrote to Trajan. 'The more I look into the accounts, the more necessary such an investigation comes to seem.'[36] It was tribute to Dio's international prominence that Prusa should have been Pliny's first stop on his tour of duty; and testimony to just how complex the legal wrangling there had become that even the new governor, for all his experience of legal matters, struggled to make sense of it. First he sat in judgement on the case in Prusa; then in Nicaea; then he wrote to Trajan for advice. The reply was brisk and to the point. The notion that Dio might have committed treason was dismissed out of hand; so, too, the prospect that he might have concealed or fabricated his accounts. The eye of Caesar, which like a mighty beam of light was forever sweeping and scanning the vastness of the globe, had penetrated to the heart of a case that for years had baffled Greek and Roman alike. It was no cause of shame for Dio to acknowledge this; nor for Pliny either. The profound differences between the two men – that one was being judged and the other was the judge, that one had thoughts only of Prusa and the other cherished Italy, that one identified with the glories and traditions of Greek culture and the other with the dignity of the Roman senate – had, thanks to Caesar, been successfully reconciled. In Bithynia, as elsewhere across the Greek world, the governor might despise the provincial, and the provincial might despise the governor; but both could find in the empire's helmsman an assurance that it was being held to a steady course. 'To do the greatest good to the greatest number of people':[37] so Dio, addressing Trajan, had defined the task of a properly godlike ruler. Distant though Caesar was from Bithynia, it was possible for Greek and Roman elites alike to bathe in the warmth of his gaze, and be grateful for it. Here was the measure of his greatness: that ruler and ruled alike could acknowledge him as *Optimus Princeps*, the Best of Emperors, and feel that the world was one.

A Passage to India

Dio, despite the favour shown him by both Nerva and Trajan, had never been much interested in the city of his patrons. Such indifference was not necessarily characteristic of Greek scholars. There were plenty, over the years following Rome's rise to greatness, who had written extensively about their new mistress. They had analysed her constitution; traced the course of her history; written biographies of her leading men. Dio viewed attention to such ephemera as beneath his dignity. Philosopher that he was, he aimed to trace patterns and articulate verities that transcended such mundane details as how the Roman state might actually function. Addressing Trajan, advising him on how best to govern, Dio made no mention of senators, or equestrians, or freedmen. 'What enables a king best to maintain the prosperity of his lands is less his wealth, or his armies, or any other manifestation of his strength, but rather the loyalty of his friends.'[38] This was a maxim which philosophers, back in the days when the

Greeks still had their own kings, had tended to take for granted. Rather than analysing whether such a prescription might be applicable to the very different functioning of Roman monarchy, Dio simply assumed that it was. A ruler, he solemnly instructed Trajan, was only as wise as the wisest man who had his ear.

As to who the wisest man among Caesar's circle of acquaintances might be, Dio was too modest to say. His audience, even so, would have found it hard to miss his drift. Repeatedly in his addresses to Trajan, Dio compared the emperor to the most famous conqueror in history. Almost half a millennium after blazing a comet-trail from Greece to India, Alexander the Great remained the archetype of military genius. 'As everyone knows,' Dio told Trajan, 'he was the most ambitious of men, possessed of the most inexhaustible love of glory.'[39] There was no one, not in Persia, not in India, not anywhere in the world, whom Alexander had feared. His fame had come to sound not only among Greeks and barbarians, but among the birds of the air and the beasts of the mountains. In Rome, some of the most celebrated men in the city's history had been fired by his example. Pompey, whose very quiff was inspired by the great conqueror's hairstyle, had never ceased to ape him; Julius Caesar, prior to embarking on his own career of conquest, had stood before a statue of Alexander and wept hot tears of envy.

It was hardly to be wondered at, then, that Trajan, who keenly admired Caesar's achievement in pacifying Gaul, should also have betrayed a certain fascination with the man who had inspired him to weep. Dio, by name-checking Alexander in his speeches, was making knowing play with this. But he was also doing something more. As a boy, Alexander had been taught by Aristotle, no less. Repeatedly, over the course of his career of conquest, he had sought out the company of philosophers. Philosophers, in turn, had repeatedly guided, cajoled and upbraided him. Here was an example from which any great ruler might learn. Even as Dio offered guidance to Trajan on how best to rule the world, he also presumed to remind the emperor that ambition for ambition's sake was undeserving of the wise ruler.

The true conquest that any king was obliged to make was not over barbarians, but over himself. Otherwise, as one notoriously acerbic philosopher, quoted by Dio, had put it to Alexander, there could be no true glory. 'No, not even were you to swim across the ocean, and vanquish a continent vaster than Asia.'[40]

Trajan, listening to this, had not remotely taken offence. In part, this reflected the delicacy with which Dio had made sure to frame his argument. Alexander had been headstrong, and selfish, and young – whereas Trajan, of course, was none of these things. So obvious, indeed, was this point that Dio had not even bothered to make it. There was, however, another reason why Romans would be unlikely to raise an eyebrow at criticism of Alexander: they were predisposed to agree with it. That Pompey and Caesar, the two great warlords of the dying republic, should have admired a king notorious for his vanity and ambition had only confirmed, for many Romans, a suspicion of the great conqueror that was deeply rooted in their past. The story was told in Rome that Alexander, sitting in judgement on a captured pirate, had demanded to know what drove the man to sail the seas, robbing and terrorising the innocent. 'The same', the pirate answered, 'as drives you to rob the whole world.'[41]

It was important to Trajan – for all that Dio might address him as 'king' – that he fought wars not as some royal conqueror, but as an *imperator*, a general who stood in a long line of generals reaching back to the early and virtuous days of the republic. In 107, when even the loot of Dacia proved inadequate to the full titanic scale of his plans for renovating Rome, and he was obliged to debase the currency that Domitian, with such care and effort, had sought to keep stable, he veiled the embarrassment of it by making his distinctively Roman pedigree explicit. Some of his coins were stamped with the portraits of Caesars who deserved honour: Julius Caesar himself and Augustus; Tiberius and Claudius; Galba, Vespasian, Titus and Nerva. Others, however, bore witness to more distant reaches of time. Gold and silver won from the Dacians, turned into coin, were adorned with the images of heroes from the heyday of the republic, and of

Rome's oldest buildings, and of the gods who, ever since the foundation of the city, had watched with a special care over the fortunes of the Roman people. Trajan might have won conquests fit to compare with those of Alexander, and he might stand at the head of an empire as vast as any in history; but he was certainly no king. He ruled as the father of his people: as the heir of all the men and women who, over the centuries, had made Rome great.

'Now at last our spirit revives.'[42] Tacitus, writing a memorial to his father-in-law early in Trajan's reign, had hailed the banishment of shadow from the senate house. By 112, when he travelled to the province of Asia to serve as its governor, the entire empire seemed radiant with the brilliance of a golden age. It was evident, almost half a century on from the death of Nero, that the collapse of Rome into civil war during the fateful year of the four emperors had been only a temporary spasm. The peace brought by Augustus to the world had not been seriously damaged. The sinews that joined market to market, city to city, province to province still held. Everywhere, whether in the Bay of Naples, or on the Propontis, or across the entire vast span of the Mediterranean — named by the Romans, proprietorially but accurately, 'our own' — the sea lanes teemed with shipping. Never before had the world been so connected. Trajan's new port beside Ostia, a vast concrete complex where previously there had been only mud and reeds, fuelled the appetites of the capital, already voracious, by ensuring that there was no demand, no fantasy, that might not be satisfied. To those who contemplated Rome's greatness it appeared a wonder and a miracle: that 'all who had ships at sea grew rich by her wealth'.[43]

The capital was not alone in benefiting from the unprecedentedly vast market established by Roman power. The transport of food stuffs, raw materials and luxury goods, conducted across vast distances on a scale never witnessed before, had enabled cities everywhere in the empire to flourish. Some — Alexandria, Carthage, Antioch — had grown immense on a scale that would have seemed inconceivable to previous generations; but even the most flyblown

300

settlement might boast a library. What had been notable about the famine that gripped Prusa during Dio's youth was less its severity than that it had happened at all. Corn, however, was not the only product to be transported, traded, consumed. The sophisticated framework of laws, the network of agents, the shipping, the harbours, the warehouses – everything that over the course of the previous century had enabled Annona to bestow her blessings on the Roman people – served the interests as well of countless merchants. The Scauri of Pompeii, purveyors of the finest garum not just to Campania but to markets as far afield as Gaul, had not been alone in treating the great sea as their lake. Merchants, cities, entire regions: all could afford to specialise. There seemed no limit to what might be shipped: 'gold, silver, jewels and pearls, fine linen, purple, silk and scarlet, all kinds of scented wood, all articles of ivory, all articles of costly wood, bronze, iron and marble, cinnamon, spice, incense, myrrh, frankincense, wine, oil, fine flour and wheat, cattle and sheep, horses and chariots, and slaves'.[44]

This list of the commodities transported to Rome, compiled by a Judaean resident in the province of Asia, was not intended to flatter. The city, to those who hated Rome and yearned for its downfall, seemed like a monstrous parasite swollen with blood and gold. Such a perspective, among those who scorned the claim of Caesar to the rule of the world, was hardly surprising. It was not only Judaeans, however, who were capable of looking askance at the wealth of the age. Tacitus, appointed by Trajan to the governorship of Asia, had been given responsibility for the province that, ever since its annexation more than two centuries previously, had been a byword among the Romans for spectacular extravaganzas: its chefs, its sex manuals, its statues made out of gold. 'It was the conquest of Asia', Pliny's uncle had recorded in his encyclopaedia, 'that first introduced luxury into Italy.'[45] Ever since, the baneful effects of this development had been a running theme of Roman moralists. Tacitus, an orator of great distinction, a former consul, a man who had devoted much of his career to the service of Rome, was no less a patriot for dreading that the very prosperity of the empire might portend its downfall. When, shortly after Domitian's murder, he wrote a laudatory biography of Agricola, he could not help but wonder whether his father-in-law, exemplary governor though he had been, might not have done the provincials under his stewardship more harm than good. Perhaps, by introducing to the savage Britons all the various refinements of Roman life – baths, fine dining, swanky architecture – he had only debased them, exactly as the Romans themselves had been debased. 'For what in their naivety the Britons termed "civilisation" was in reality a mark of their enslavement.'[46]

The fruits of conquest for the Roman people had been manifold: glory, power, wealth. But what if the fruits of these in turn had been servitude and decadence? The question was one that Tacitus, over the course of his illustrious career, had never ceased to brood upon. Like Pliny, he had owed his early advancement to Domitian; like Pliny, he had felt tainted and compromised as a result. How was it that the senate had lost its ancient dower of liberty? Tacitus, in his attempt to make sense of this question, had never ceased to cast his gaze backwards, to contemplate the rise of the Caesars from the beginning. He did not, as Pliny did, imagine that the senate could ever have its dignity restored. The shadow of autocracy lay too dark. Liberty was nothing but a slogan. Augustus, who claimed to have restored freedom, *libertas*, to the republic, had been motivated in all he did by a spirit of subtle tyranny. Vespasian, who had stamped *libertas* on his coins after securing the monarchy, had soon erased it. Tacitus had studied the history of Augustus' dynasty and the Flavians with close attention, and he never doubted what they had constituted: a revolution. Trajan, stamping his coins as Vespasian had done with the slogan *libertas*, could not alter that. 'The ancient, untouched character of the Roman people was gone.'[47]

Or was it? In the early years of Trajan's rule, Tacitus had looked to the vast expanses of Germany, where there were none of the luxuries that had so corrupted and softened the Roman people, and dreaded the worst. For two centuries and more the Germans had preserved their freedom against the full might of the legions. The Caesars, who initially had sought to subdue them, had abandoned the attempt. Limits had been set on the advance of Roman arms. The victories claimed by Domitian, so Tacitus had noted sourly, 'were little more than excuses for celebrating triumphs'.[48] But that, under Trajan, had changed. The conquest of Dacia had demonstrated that Rome's ancient quality of martial valour might not, after all, be completely dead. Was it possible that at last, under a bold and puissant *imperator*, Rome might be ready to resume its career of conquest, and fulfil the destiny ordained it by the gods? Tacitus, in his province, was alert to tremors that might have been imperceptible to him had he still been in Rome. He knew that Hadrian, Trajan's cousin, had been sent east. He was alert to a brewing succession crisis in Armenia, the mountainous kingdom that Rome had been content to tolerate as an independent state, but which periodically — as in the time of Corbulo — had demanded intervention. He could sense, very faint but unmistakeable, the shaking of the earth, as legions from across the eastern provinces were subjected to ferocious drills, forced marches and new bases. It did not require a man of Tacitus' shrewdness to fathom what this portended. War was brewing. Trajan, who for five years had been devoting himself to the needs of the capital, was growing restless. When he next left Rome, however, it would not be for the Danube or the Rhine. The example of Alexander blazed before him. Where to look for fresh conquests, fresh glory, if not the East?

'The liberty of the Germans is a greater menace than the despotism of the Arsacids.'[49] So Tacitus, comparing the two most dangerous peoples on the borders of Roman power, dismissed the dynasty that ruled the Parthians. Only a man more familiar with the Rhine than with Syria could ever have expressed such a sentiment. The Arsacids did not, like German chieftains, stand at the head of a mere tribe; nor did they lurk amid forests and bogs. The lands subject to Parthian rule were wealthy, fabled and extensive. Beyond Syria, flanked on either side by two great rivers, the Tigris and the Euphrates, lay Assyria and Babylonia, lands studded with famous cities already ancient when Romulus was born. Mesopotamia, these kingdoms were called by the Greeks: 'the lands between the rivers'. Here, amid dreary mudflats, stood the great seat of Arsacid power, Ctesiphon; but the homeland of the Parthians lay even farther east, beyond a mighty wall of mountains on the upland plateau of Iran. These were lands, rich in palaces and stores of glittering treasure, that Alexander had conquered: a feat that ever since had served to brand the peoples of Mesopotamia and Iran as inveterately womanish. Such, at any rate, was the opinion of the Greeks. For many centuries they had clung to it. Even as the subjects of Caesar they had continued to look down on the Parthians as slavish and effeminate.

This prejudice was one that the Romans had readily come to share. The Arsacids wore eyeliner, platform heels, and ringlets in their hair. Their subjects, approaching the royal presence, would kneel like slaves and press their foreheads to the floor. Their warriors, rather than standing and fighting as legionaries did, like men, would instead wheel and wheel again on fast-galloping horses, firing arrows over their shoulders as they sped away. All the more disgraceful, then, that twice the Parthians should have routed a Roman invasion force. The first, launched in the final decade of the free republic, had been annihilated outside a city named Carrhae. Crassus, its commander, had lost thirty thousand men, seven eagles, and his own head. Two decades later, when Mark Antony led a second attempt to subdue the Parthians, he had managed to survive the ensuing debacle with his head still on his shoulders – but again lost thirty thousand men. Augustus, preferring diplomacy to war, had negotiated the return of Crassus' lost eagles and an enduring peace, a treaty that a long succession of Caesars had been content to uphold. Nevertheless, the stain of Carrhae had never entirely been wiped away. The Arsacids remained awkward and untrustworthy neighbours. In the decades following Nero's suicide, they had played host to a number of imposters claiming to be the dead emperor. They persisted in meddling in Armenia. The very existence of their empire, a dominion barely less immense than that ruled by Caesar himself, was a standing reproach to the claim of the Romans to be the masters of the world. All these factors, to a man of Trajan's stern and fearless cast of mind, were bound to furnish matter for thought.

Glory, vengeance, the elimination of Rome's only true geopolitical rival: here, it might have been thought, were reasons enough for him to contemplate war with Parthia. Yet there was, perhaps, glimmering on the margin of his reflections, a more fantastical motivation. To follow in the footsteps of Alexander was inevitably to dream of reaching, as Alexander had done, the ends of the earth. Beyond the limits of Parthian power lay the land that by common consent was the farthest from Rome and the closest to the rising of the sun. India, for the Romans, was the very epitome of the exotic. 'No land anywhere can rival it for wonders.'[50] So Pliny's uncle, a man whose fascination with distant marvels was limitless, had written. His opinion was not, however, original to him. Greek scholars who, in the wake of Alexander's expedition to India, had been able to report on it first-hand, and provide a detailed portrait of that fantastical land, had left no one in any doubt that it was indeed a realm of superlatives. There were eels that grew to twice the length of a warship, locusts the size of dogs, snakes that dropped out of trees and swallowed oxen whole. There were forests taller than any mortal could shoot an arrow. There were war elephants in the stable of every king. Pliny's uncle, despite his ambition to describe the entire globe, had confessed himself defeated by the sheer teeming immensity of India. 'It contains peoples and cities beyond number.'[51] Even so, he had persisted in attempting to list its marvels. The magnetic mountain beside the Indus. The philosophers who immolated themselves alive. The people ruled exclusively by queens. So extraordinary were such reports that they might have seemed, to those who heard them, the invention of a poet rather than details appropriate to an encyclopaedia. Yet in the wake of Trajan's great victory over the Dacians, the Roman people had been able to witness with their own eyes the appearance in the capital of ambassadors from India. This embassy, sent to offer congratulations to the emperor on his victories in Dacia, had created a sensation. Clearly,

---

if the thunder of Trajan's greatness had reverberated as far away as India, there was nowhere that lay beyond the reach of Roman arms. Who was to say, then, that Alexander might not be surpassed?

In truth, there was no need for Trajan to surrender to wild fantasies of venturing to the ends of the earth for him to take an interest in India. Cool, hardheaded pragmatism demanded it as well. A land that from the perspective of Rome might seem fantastically distant and exotic had a very different look when viewed from Egypt. There, in Alexandria and in ports along the Red Sea, there were plenty of mariners who were more than familiar with its coastline. If India was a land of wonders, then so also was it a land of quite spectacular luxury goods. The diamond set in the ring presented by Nerva to Trajan had come from India. So, too, in the expert opinion of Pliny's uncle, did the world's best pearls. Shipmasters from Egypt, borne on the monsoons that blew eastwards across the Ocean every spring, would brave reefs, storms and pirates to source them. In Muziris, a port in southern India hailed by the elder Pliny as the greatest emporium in the country, merchandise of every description was to be found piled high. There seemed almost nothing that might not be bought there.

Some products, indeed – the most exotic ones – had been transported there from the very limits of the world. Silk, a shimmering fabric woven from a mysterious wool that grew on trees, and as popular with trendsetters in Rome as it was shocking to moralists, derived either from a people called the Seres, noted for their 'golden hair and blue eyes',[52] or else from a place called China – a land in every other way unknown. Most of the commodities on sale in Muziris, however, came from the port's immediate hinterland. There was ivory, and tortoise-shell, and malobrathrum, an aromatic plant used in top-end hair products. Above all, there was pepper, a black berry which grew on vines guarded by poisonous snakes, could only be harvested by monkeys, and was ground up to provide a culinary seasoning. In Rome, food snobs tended not to rate it highly. 'The only thing to recommend it is a certain pungency.'[53] So sniffed the elder Pliny. Nevertheless, in the wake of Augustus' conquest of Egypt, enthusiasm for pepper among every class of Roman had become a mania. Demand was voracious. Every spring, vast ships would sail from Berenice, a port on the Red Sea that had originally been built to enable the import of elephants, and was the only harbour along Egypt's Red Sea coast capable of providing vessels of their gargantuan size with anchorage. The arrival of the merchants from Egypt in these ships — 'perfect and wonderful constructions', as one Indian poet hailed them, 'churning the white surf'[54] — was celebrated in Muziris as a great spectacle. Thousands of tons of pepper, gathered into sacks stamped with the image of a tiger, were exchanged for chests loaded with Roman gold. It was, for all concerned, a most lucrative venture.

It was not only the merchants who made a profit, however. So too did Caesar. The customs duties levied on the trade with India provided the treasury with a sizeable chunk of its annual income. Every item imported into Egypt, and every item exported onwards to the rest of the empire, was subject to tax. It was a measure of just how much income this might raise that the private contractors appointed by the imperial government to administer it — the *arabarchs* — were notorious even in Rome for their wealth. This was the business that had enabled Julius Alexander's father, the Alexandrian who gilded the gates of the Temple in Jerusalem, to make his fortune. Even after he had served as prefect of Egypt, Julius Alexander himself continued to be mocked as 'the Arabarch'.[55] It was not Judaean loot that had kept the Flavian regime afloat, but duties imposed on the trade in Indian commodities: Vespasian, simultaneously grasping and contemptuous of conspicuous consumption, had not hesitated to raise them to eye-wateringly high levels. Trajan, conscious of his responsibilities as the *Optimus Princeps*, and anxious not to price pepper out of the reach of the average citizen, had lowered the rates again, and done all he could to expedite the flow of merchandise from India. Not every legion in the eastern half of the empire was in training for war against Parthia. Even as Hadrian was summoning an immense expeditionary force to join him in Antioch, soldiers from the great base outside Alexandria were busy at work digging a canal between the Nile and the Red Sea.[56] It mattered to Trajan that elites across the empire, and especially in Rome, should enjoy the fruits of improved access to the treasures of the East. Pearls and diamonds were not idle luxuries, but trophies appropriate to the dignity of the masters of the globe. And soon, if all went to plan, and fortune continued to smile on the best of emperors, there would be even more trophies from the eastern limits of the world for the Roman people to enjoy.

Trajan arrived in Antioch early in 114. Hadrian had assembled three legions in the city; but these only hinted at the full scale of the task force with which his relative was intending to settle the Parthian question once and for all. That spring, just as Corbulo had once done, Trajan headed northwards from Antioch for Armenia. At Satala, a base on the frontier garrisoned by a legion originally transferred by Vespasian from the Rhine, he completed a rendezvous with two huge contingents drawn respectively from Syria and the Danube. Then, at the head of some eighty thousand men, he crossed the border. Briskly, he deposed the Armenian monarch, reduced Armenia itself to the status of a Roman province, and summoned the nobility to pay him homage. The local princes, knowing better than to ignore this command, scurried to obey; one of them, alert to Trajan's ultimate ambitions, brought him a horse that had been trained to kneel on its forelegs and lower its head to the ground, as though it were in the presence of a Parthian king. The senate, more attuned to Roman tradition, opted to confirm him in the name *Optimus*: the honour in which – 'because it bore witness to his character rather than to his military prowess'[57] – the emperor took the greatest pride of all.

Once already under Trajan's leadership, the Roman people had thrilled as their ancestors had done, to the news of great victories won by the legions over barbarous peoples, and of the sweep of the eagles over distant lands. Now they did so a second time. The portrait of Caesar's exploits on the eastern front was painted for them in brilliant, primary colours. As in any epic worthy of the

308

Parthian Empire

Caspian Sea

Black Sea

ARMENIA

• Satala

IRAN

A S S Y R I A

Selnus

• Carrhae

• Antioch

SYRIA

MESOPOTAMIA

Hatra
•

Tigris

Euphrates

Mediterranean Sea

B A B Y L O N I A

• Ctesiphon

Babylon •

JUDAEA

• Jerusalem

Persian Gulf

N

Red Sea

| 0 | 50 | 100 | 150 | 200 miles |

| 0 | 100 | 200 | 300 kms |

name, there were perils as well as triumphs. Late in 115, after two seasons of campaigning that had secured for Roman rule a great arc of mountainous territory directly north of Mesopotamia, Trajan arrived in Antioch. The winter months were marked by ominous portents. Thunderstorms rolled over the Syrian capital. Winds howled through the city's streets. Then, abruptly, there came a great roar, like a bellow of pain rising up from the earth, and everything began to shake. Trajan, trapped in his room, was led to safety by a mysterious entity of giant stature; but few in the city were as fortunate. Multitudes were killed, either crushed by collapsing masonry, or else by starving to death beneath fallen stone and timber. Among the casualties was a consul. Only a few of those caught in the earthquake were rescued. There was one woman who had managed to sustain both herself and her baby with her breast milk, and another infant who was found suckling at her dead mother's breast; otherwise Antioch was left a city of corpses. And even the peaks of the mountains that lay beyond it were toppled, and hills flattened, and rivers set on entirely new courses.

Yet Trajan, rather than seeing in the annihilation visited on Antioch a warning from the gods, interpreted it as encouragement. Mesopotamia awaited, and the great conqueror was not to be baulked of his prize. That spring of 116, he embarked on his third season of campaigning. He invaded, subdued and annexed Assyria, where Alexander had won his greatest victory. Then, on a flagship with a sail embroidered in gold with his name and titles, Trajan embarked on the conquest of Babylonia. Down the Euphrates his great fleet sailed. He did not, however, continue all the way. Some fifty miles north of Babylon, the fabulously ancient city where Alexander had died, he ordered his ships transported on rollers across the mudflats to the Tigris. Here, on the far bank, stood Ctesiphon. The city had been abandoned. Chosroes, the Parthian king, had fled. Rather than defending his capital, he had opted for the womanish option: retreat behind the mountainous frontier of Iran. Trajan, entering Ctesiphon unopposed, could feel at last that his great labour of conquest was done. The land of two rivers was his. Chosroes' humiliation seemed complete. His palace lay in Roman hands. His daughter was a captive. His golden throne, before which his subjects had so often prostrated themselves, was a trophy of the victorious Caesar. Trajan, ready at last to celebrate the consummation of three hard years of campaigning, accepted the title of 'Parthicus', awarded him a year earlier by the senate, and ordered a coin minted to proclaim his achievement. Its slogan: *PARTHIA CAPTA*.

Still, though, he had not reached the limits of Mesopotamia. Beyond him lay the Persian Gulf, with its shipping lanes to India. Trajan, who had already commissioned a canal to join the Red Sea to the Mediterranean, had now, with his eastern conquests, taken an even more decisive step to facilitate the flow of global commodities into the empire: pepper and diamonds, pearls and tortoise-shell, malobrathrum and silk. Pliny's uncle, in his encyclopaedia, had noted the drain of Roman gold to the East with alarm; but Trajan, tireless as he was in his service to his fellow citizens, had not conquered Dacia and Mesopotamia merely to fret over that. Luxuries were not mere luxuries, but tokens of Roman greatness. What were the treasures of India if not due tribute paid to the mistress of the world?

So it happened that once Trajan had secured Ctesiphon, he was filled with a longing to see what lay beyond it. Sailing onwards down the Tigris, he arrived at the Persian Gulf. 'And as he stood beside the ocean, and was briefed about its nature, he saw a ship departing for India. "I should certainly have crossed to India myself," he commented, "if only I had been younger." Whereupon he fell to contemplation of the Indians, and expressed curiosity as to how they conducted their affairs. And he reckoned Alexander to have been a lucky man.'[58]

VII

I BUILD THIS GARDEN FOR US

Frontier Spirit

No sooner had Trajan achieved the unprecedented feat of capturing Ctesiphon and carrying Roman arms to the very shores of the eastern ocean than all his labours failed him. He had reached too far, too fiercely, after greatness. Fortune, whose favourite he had been all his life, had abruptly abandoned him. He learnt this in Babylon, a city that had once, many centuries before, ruled as the capital of the world, but of which little now remained save for mounds of crumbling mud-brick. The palace in which Alexander had died, a complex still topped with Greek roof-tiles but otherwise a ruin, was where Trajan made sacrifice to the great conqueror; and it was also where he learned that Mesopotamia had risen in rebellion. Immediately, he set himself to stamping out the bushfires. Already, his legates had gone on the attack. Joining forces with them, the emperor defeated a Parthian army on the outskirts of Ctesiphon, then for a second time entered the capital in triumph. His situation, even so, remained precarious. Recognising that his plan to administer Mesopotamia as a province would temporarily have to wait, he opted to make the best of a bad job by crowning a renegade son of Chosroes as king and installing him as a puppet. A more damaging blow to the imperial prestige was soon to follow. Withdrawing from Ctesiphon to Syria, Trajan paused en route to besiege Hatra, a citadel that commanded the road between Assyria and Babylonia, and was notorious for the impregnability of its walls, the aridity of its setting, and the swarming of its flies. Confronted by these challenges, the emperor found himself unable to take the city before the approach of winter; and so, cutting his losses, he withdrew to Antioch. Here, exhausted by the demands he had placed on his ageing body, he fell ill; but even so, partially paralysed by a stroke though he was, he refused to rest. There was, after all, a fourth campaigning season to plan.

The need for this was very pressing. More was at stake than the maintenance of Roman rule in Armenia and Mesopotamia. The immense force assembled for the destruction of the Parthian monarchy had left Rome's military apparatus with minimal spare capacity. Three years Trajan and his army had been absent on the eastern front; and in that time the monopoly of violence habitually exercised by the legions within the limits of the empire had begun to fray. Whether in the wilds of northern Britain, or along the Danube, or in Mauretania, the westernmost of Rome's African possessions, a lack of ready reinforcements threatened entire provinces with a breakdown of civil order.

Nowhere, however, was the situation more perilous than in the region that ranked as the jewel in the imperial crown: Egypt. Here, Alexandria had always been a sectarian tinderbox. The Roman authorities, stripped of the reserves that would normally have enabled them to police the city, had found themselves impotent to suppress running battles in the streets between Greeks and Judaeans. The rioting had blazed out of control. Entire stretches of the city had gone up in flames. Meanwhile, farther along the African coast, in Libya, the ancient Greek city of Cyrene had already been devastated by a full-blown Judaean uprising. Temples had been attacked and burnt; statues smashed; a menorah carved into the main road that led out of the city. By 116, even as Trajan was advancing on the Persian Gulf, Judaeans across much of the eastern Mediterranean – not just in Egypt and Cyrenaica, but in Cyprus and Judaea as well – were in open revolt. Hair-raising reports from the scenes of carnage, brought to the emperor, left him in no doubt as to that. It was claimed that Roman captives – those who, supposedly, had not been eaten by the rebels or skinned to provide their captors with cloaks – were being thrown to wild beasts or forced to fight as gladiators. The humbling by the insurgents of their erstwhile masters was pointed and deliberate. The retribution visited decades previously by the Flavians on the Judaeans was now being visited by the Judaeans on the Romans themselves.

To the emperor – whose father had played such a key role in Vespasian's campaign – the insult was personal. Although Nerva had sought to ease the burden of the exactions laid on the Judaeans, Trajan, like Domitian, preferred to keep the sack of Jerusalem and the humiliation of the Judaean god fully before the gaze of the Roman people. Yet this, now that he had embarked on the conquest of Mesopotamia, stood revealed as an unwise policy. Long before, back in the time of Caligula, a governor of Syria had advised against needlessly insulting the Judaeans. 'For unlike other peoples,' he had warned, 'they are not confined within the limits of a single region, but have spread across the entire face of the earth, so that they are to be found in every continent, and resident on every island.'[1] In every empire, too, he might have added – for there had been Judaeans settled in Babylonia, the subjects of the Parthian monarchy, for centuries. These, now that Trajan had come to Mesopotamia, had joined their compatriots in rising up against the legions. The emperor, during the course of his counter-insurgency operations, had targeted them with particular savagery. His most brutal general, a Mauretanian prince named Lusius Quietus, had been instructed 'to extirpate them from the province'.[2] Quietus, whose service in Dacia had already seen him elevated from the rank of auxiliary commander to senator, had needed no second invitation. The slaughter he inflicted on the Judaeans of Babylon in the summer of 116 had been something terrible. Trajan, certainly, had been thoroughly impressed. That winter, as he drew up his plans for the campaigning season to come, he granted the barbarian chieftain the status of a consul and bestowed a startling promotion on him. Lusius Quietus was appointed governor of Judaea.

The coming of spring, however, did not see Caesar return to his own saddle. Even as insurgency blazed across the Roman world, from Babylonia to Brigantia, the empire found itself facing an additional crisis. Trajan, semi-paralysed and convinced that he had been poisoned, decided he had no choice but to convalesce in Rome. Only a few days after leaving Antioch, however, his condition took a turn for the worse. His ship pulled into Selinus, an obscure and shabby port on the southern coast of Anatolia. Here, in early August, the *Optimus Princeps* breathed his last. Unlike Nerva, he had not made it clear who was to succeed him. Meanwhile, back in Syria, where Trajan had appointed Hadrian to the command of the eastern front, a dramatic development had taken place. On 9 August, a letter had been made public to the people of Antioch. It had been written – so Hadrian claimed – by the *Optimus Princeps* himself, and proclaimed his full adoption by the emperor. Two nights later, Trajan's new son dreamed that a bolt of fire had descended from the heavens and struck him twice in his neck, but neither frightened nor harmed him. Then, the following morning, came the news that the *Optimus Princeps* was dead. Hadrian at once reported it to his legions. They enthusiastically hailed him as *imperator*. The empire had a new Caesar. But there were many, both in Rome and elsewhere, who narrowed their eyes at this hurried chain of events. Hadrian, so his enemies whispered, had been playing dirty. He and his partisans in Trajan's entourage had put words into a dying man's mouth, bribed his freedmen, faked his correspondence. Hadrian was not the legitimate emperor. He had staged a coup.

Talk like this, in the midst of an emergency such as Rome was facing, was perilous in the extreme. A disputed succession, a Judaean insurgency, trouble on the Danube: here were precisely the circumstances that had contributed, almost half a century before, to the catastrophe of the year of four emperors. Yet even as his rivals conspired against him, Hadrian could cite manifold proofs of his legitimacy. He was Trajan's closest living male relative. His wife, Sabina, was the dead emperor's great-niece. On his finger he wore the very diamond ring that Nerva, shortly before his death, had bestowed upon Trajan. Hadrian's claim to the rule of the world did not depend, however, solely on his family connections. His entire career had been preparation for the role. Like Trajan, he had profited from an unusually long apprenticeship with the legions. He had served on both the Rhine and the Danube, distinguished himself in the conquest of Dacia, been entrusted by the dying emperor with the command of the Parthian war. He was physically tough, always went bare-headed, no matter the heat or the cold, and never demanded anything of his men that he did not demand of himself. A stickler for discipline, he was simultaneously adored by the legions. Like Trajan himself, he was properly an *imperator*.

Yet Hadrian, steeled by years of military service though he was, had never been simply a soldier. More than any Caesar since Tiberius, he ranked as an intellectual. While still a boy, his devotion to philosophy had been such that he was nicknamed *Graeculus* – the little Greek. The passion for it had never left him. Indeed, to a degree that his peers found faintly suspicious, Hadrian was interested in everything: from music to geometry, from antiquities to architecture, from poetry to the functioning of the tax system. Unsurprisingly, many of his contemporaries found it hard to make sense of him. That he was a Caesar unlike any other was evident from his chin. The new emperor, in contrast to his clean-shaven predecessors, sported a beard. This gave him the look of a common soldier, a legionary serving in some base far distant from elite circles in Rome – or was it, perhaps, the look of a Greek? Ambiguity came naturally to the new emperor. Hadrian, to those who studied him, appeared nothing but paradox.

'By turns stern and affable, severe and playful, hesitant and headstrong, mean and generous, deceptive and straightforward, merciless and merciful, he was a man whose character was impossible to pin down.'[3] Certainly, in the early days of his rule, as he sought to master his perilous inheritance, Hadrian's capacity to do the unexpected stood him in excellent stead. Swiftly, subtly, ruthlessly, the rumblings against him in the senate house were silenced. There was no need for the emperor himself, who was still in Syria, to leave any fingerprints at the scene. Trajan had recently promoted Hadrian's former guardian, a native of Italica by the name of Acilius Attianus, to the command of the Praetorians; and once Attianus returned from Selinus to Rome, he played Mucianus to Hadrian's Vespasian. The city prefect was dismissed from office; two particularly distinguished senators were strong-armed into exile; and four men of consular rank were put to death on charges of treason. A purge, in short, of which Domitian might have been proud.

Notable among its victims was Lusius Quietus. His elimination served a double purpose. First, it demonstrated to legates across the empire that Hadrian would tolerate no rogue elements within his command structure. Second, it signalled to Judaeans in Judaea itself that there might be the possibility of a rapprochement with Rome. It was the carrot, not the stick, that proved most effective in inducing them to lay down their arms. Some went so far as to hail the new emperor as a deliverer. Perhaps, they dared to hope, he might license the rebuilding of Jerusalem. Quietus, during his brief term as governor, had installed a shrine to Proserpina on the blackened rock where the Temple had once stood – but this he had done as a legate of Trajan. Hadrian, unlike either his adoptive father or the Flavians, had no personal stake in keeping Jerusalem a ruin. What, then, was to stop him from granting permission for the Temple to be rebuilt? Why should the perfumes of sacrifice not rise once again over Jerusalem? Who was the new Caesar, some Judaeans dared to wonder, if not the favourite of the Holy One Himself, and the redeemer of His Chosen People?

Hadrian, however, had other priorities. With Armenia and Mesopotamia a quagmire, much of the eastern Mediterranean in flames, and the Balkans menaced yet again by barbarians from beyond the Danube, the stakes could hardly have been higher. The entire infrastructure of Roman rule appeared in danger of collapse. Hadrian, applying the pitiless gaze of a pathologist to the tissue and sinews of the empire, did not hesitate to arrive at his diagnosis. Trajan, best of emperors though he might have been, had advanced

317

too far beyond the natural limits of Roman rule. The strain on the empire's resources had been too great. It was not only Trajan who had suffered a stroke. So had Rome itself. The treatment, then – brutal though it might be – prescribed itself. Days after coming to power, Hadrian ordered all of Trajan's conquests in Armenia and Mesopotamia evacuated. Forces that had already been committed to the suppression of the Judaean uprising were reinforced. Now at last the full murderous professionalism of the legions could be brought to bear on the rebels. The slaughter was terrible. By the time order was finally restored, the Judaean populations in Cyrenaica and Cyprus had effectively been eradicated, and in Alexandria reduced to a ghostly shadow.

Meanwhile, as autumn turned to winter, Hadrian himself was heading for the shores of the Propontis. Here, midway between the eastern theatre of war and the Balkans, he spent his first winter as Caesar. By spring he had arrived on the Danube. The need for his presence was urgent. As had been the case in Armenia and Mesopotamia, major surgery was required. Hadrian had not hesitated to perform it. Large stretches of territory to the west of Dacia, only recently secured by the *Optimus Princeps*, were abandoned. The celebrated stone bridge designed by Apollodorus was demolished, to impede potential incursions. So shocking a betrayal of Trajan's legacy did this seem to many observers that Hadrian was widely rumoured to have planned the evacuation of Dacia itself, and only with difficulty been dissuaded. The wide currency given to this story was due reflection of just how unpopular the policy of retrenchment was. The abandonment of Trajan's conquests by his successor ensured that they blazed even more brilliantly than they would otherwise have done in the memory of the Roman people.

Hadrian himself, shrewd and alert to public opinion, perfectly understood this. When at last, almost a year after the death of his adoptive father, he entered Rome for the first time as Caesar, he made sure to tread with a cat-like care. Tact and cynicism, seamlessly fused, characterised his every policy. He counterpointed the high-handed lavishing of bribes on the masses – donatives, a remittance of debts – with a manner ostentatiously reminiscent of a private citizen. Appearing before the senate, he solemnly denied all responsibility for the deaths of the four senators purged by Attianus; then, having dismissed his old guardian from the Praetorians, he coolly raised him to the rank of a consul. Perhaps the most impressive display of Hadrian's ability to face two ways at once came with the celebration of his predecessor's victories in Parthia. This, of course, had always had the potential to cause him embarrassment; but Hadrian, rather than attempting to draw a veil over the matter, insisted instead that the dead Trajan be awarded a triumph. A statue of the by now deified *Optimus Princeps* was loaded onto a chariot and drawn through the streets of Rome. His ashes, which had been brought with mournful ceremony from Selinus, were buried beneath the great column in his forum. *Munera* were staged to celebrate his victories in Mesopotamia: the 'Parthian Games'. As for the role played by Hadrian in withdrawing from the provinces Trajan had won, and bringing the supposedly triumphant war to an end, no mention was made of it.

There were many among the Roman elite – the sceptical, the weary, the disillusioned – who scorned to be fooled by this. Tacitus, who had dared to hope that Trajan's wars of conquest, reminiscent as they were of the heroic days of the republic, might mark a return of health and vigour to Rome, found no cause for optimism in the new Caesar's character. The mirror that the past held up to the present was a sombre one. It was no problem, for a scholar of Tacitus' learning and temperament, to identify an ominous parallel to Hadrian in the line of his predecessors. Tiberius, Augustus' heir, had been rigorously schooled in war and possessed of immense intellectual gifts, but moody, suspicious, impossible to fathom. His coming to power had prompted a number of shadowy crimes. Four senators had been put to death on a charge of treason. Meanwhile, for all the battle-honours Tiberius had won as the legate of Augustus, he had refused, on becoming princeps himself, to sanction the advance of

Roman arms. To be sure, he had presided over an age of peace – but a sterile, stagnant one, devoid of all glory and polluted by blood. Rome, once the city of a free people, had become a despotism. The empire had sunk into lethargy. The ancestral virtues of its citizens, the very qualities which had served to win them the world, had been lost to decay and corruption. This it was that had enabled Tiberius to rule as a tyrant – and after him Caligula, Nero and Domitian. Who, then, was to say that the new Caesar would prove any different? Tacitus did not dare to pose the question openly; but he did, by embarking on a history of Tiberius and his successors just as Hadrian came to power, presume to float it. Certainly, the senate had good reason to regard its new master with suspicion – and also to veil its suspicion. Tacitus, writing about the mood in Rome during the early days of Tiberius' rule, understood the instinct well. 'The higher the rank of a man, the more urgently he felt the need to dissemble what he thought.'[4]

Hadrian himself, meanwhile, was no less scornful of his critics than they were of him. As well read in history as in everything else, he had no need to rely on sour and malevolent senators to interpret the past for him. It was not Tiberius to whom he compared himself, but Augustus. This was why, when he sealed his communications, he did so with a signet ring engraved with the head of the first princeps. It was why, when his chief secretary, the man responsible for managing his correspondence, came across a bronze of Augustus as a boy, complete with antique lettering, the official made sure to present this rare and precious find to the emperor himself. Suetonius had risen far. His eye for a useful patron had proven unerring. Although Pliny had died shortly before the invasion of Parthia, a friend of his, a man 'reliable, frank and trustworthy'[5] by the name of Gaius Septicius Clarus, had taken Suetonius under his wing, adopting him as a protégé. In 119, when Septicius was appointed to the command of the Praetorians, the post Attianus had recently vacated, Suetonius' position at the heart of the imperial establishment appeared assured. Alert to Hadrian's self-identification with the first princeps, and taking full advantage of the ready access he enjoyed to the imperial archives, he embarked on a lengthy life of Augustus. Although, once he had finished it, he dedicated the biography to Septicius, the patron he really aimed to please was the emperor himself. Suetonius' portrait of Augustus bore an unmistakeable resemblance to Hadrian. 'Never did he make war on a people without just and pressing cause, nor was he a man to lust after any expansion of the empire, or his own renown as a conqueror.'[6] This, as a description of the warlord who had annexed Egypt, completed the pacification of Spain, and repeatedly sought to subdue the Germans, was not, perhaps, as accurate as it might have been; but as a mission statement for Hadrian it served very well.

Certainly, to claim sanction for change from the example of Augustus was no mere antiquarian eccentricity. Radicalism, in the opinion of the Romans, was sinister by its very nature. The phrase *novae res* – novel enterprises – was convenient shorthand for everything destructive of the settled order. This was why Augustus himself, even as he was constructing a monarchy, had insisted that he was restoring the republic. Hadrian, confronted by the task of setting the empire back on a stable footing after Trajan's disastrous invasion of Mesopotamia, had little choice but to parade his devotion to the first princeps. In reality, however, he was forging policies that were distinctively his own. The challenge facing Hadrian was twofold. First, he needed to project an image of himself as the heir to Trajan's martial prowess, as an *imperator* in deed as well as name, while simultaneously undoing much of what his predecessor had attempted. This in turn, however, served to commit him to a far more fundamental programme of reform. If, as Hadrian had come to believe, expeditions beyond the natural limits of Roman rule threatened the entire fabric of the empire with collapse, then it followed that the venerable dream of a dominion without limit, one that might authentically span the world, was a fantasy. Such a conclusion, to moralists in the capital, was naturally anathema; but Hadrian, who had spent much of his life on the limits of Roman rule, was able to embrace it precisely because his horizons were so expansive and broad. This, of course, inevitably imposed demands. Hadrian had no hope of imposing a radical restructuring of Rome's military apparatus from the capital itself. Only by touring the rivers, the mountains and the deserts that delineated the limits of the empire could he hope to push through such a policy. Fortunately, Hadrian had a taste for travel. 'Such was his wander-lust that he only had to read about some distant region to be filled with a long-ing to learn more about it first-hand.'[7] So it was that three years after his arrival in the capital as emperor, he set off on a tour of the Roman world.

Taking the road northwards from Rome to Gaul, the *imperator* was accompanied by leading members of his court. Sabina, his wife, was with him. So, too, representing the imperial secretariat, was Suetonius. The administration of the world never took a holiday, after all. Correspondence still needed to be handled, whether Caesar was in the Palatine or out on the open road. Hadrian's primary con-cern, however, was not with civilian matters. The initial object of his journey was the Rhine. Arriving in Mogontiacum, touring the Taunus, wintering 'amid German snows',[8] he drilled the legions as though a great war with the barbarians might be brewing. Bearded and bare-headed, he made a point of setting the legionaries a per-sonal example. If there were twenty-mile marches in full armour to be done, he would do them. If there were basic rations to be eaten, he would eat them. If there was rough wine to be drunk, he would drink it.

Yet even as Hadrian scorned to fasten his cloak with jewelled clasps or to carry a fussily decorated sword, he never let anyone forget that his rank was that of a commander-in-chief, heir to the noblest traditions of Roman arms. This was why, at his back, he had both a detachment of Praetorians, led by Septicius, the prefect, and a thou-sand Batavian horsemen. It was why as well, even as he made sure that he knew every soldier's name, he was implacable in correcting even the slightest hint of ill-discipline. No one was to say, when he gave orders for the limits of Roman rule in Germany to be marked by a continuous palisade, fashioned out of massive oak posts and cross-beams, that he was permitting his men to go soft. Quite the opposite. The excellence of the soldiers' discipline, together with the stupefying scale of the palisade they were engaged in building, signalled to Roman and barbarian alike that the proficiency of the legions was as formidable as it had ever been: lethal, irresistible, terrifying. The truest show of contempt that Hadrian could display towards the Germans, however, was not to launch punitive expeditions against them, but to fence them off altogether. What concern was it to the lord of a spreading garden, after all, that outside its walls, squatting in filth and scratching at their sores, there might lie beggars, envious of the fountains, the fruit trees, the flower beds from which they were barred?

'If Hadrian trained his soldiers as though conflict were imminent, then it was because he was eager not for war, but for peace.'[9] There were few, during his tour of the Rhine, who felt that this redounded to his discredit. Germany, after all, had been in a settled condition for many decades. Beyond the Ocean, by contrast, it was a different story. In the spring of 122, Hadrian sailed for a province that seemed positively to demand the attentions of a warlike and conquering Caesar. Britain, during the dying days of Trajan's rule, had been convulsed by uprisings. The legions stationed in the province had suffered heavy casualties. Only with difficulty had order been restored. Yet even after several years of campaigning, Rome's command of the Ocean remained circumscribed. The northern reaches of Britain, conquered by Agricola, abandoned by Domitian, were still lost to barbarism. Had Trajan travelled to the island as Hadrian was now doing, he would never have tolerated such a situation. He would have embarked on a campaign of reconquest, and brought the entire island back under Roman rule. All his admirers believed this – and Hadrian knew they believed it. The challenge of how best to order the limits of Roman power, and 'to separate the barbarians from the Romans',[10] was, then, a much more awkward one to meet in Britain than it had been in Germany. The risk for Hadrian was that he might compromise his entire project of stabilising the empire: that by spurning the chance to emulate Trajan, he might cast himself in the eyes of the Roman people as a new Domitian.

Agrippa, camped beneath Mount Graupius, had dispatched a fleet to glimpse distant Thule. Hadrian, touring the northernmost limits of Roman power, surveyed the line that a great stone wall was to take, clinging to crags, bristling with forts, running from coast to coast. The emperor's enterprise was quite as much an expression of assertiveness as the governor's had been. To explore the limits of the world was one thing; but to dismiss them as unworthy of conquest ranked as an altogether more imperious display of self-confidence. When Hadrian made sacrifice to the Ocean beside the Tyne, he was not doing so as a hapless supplicant, frantic to stabilise his position. Quite the opposite. The emperor had brought substantial reinforcements with him to Britain: some fifty thousand men, a tenth of his entire military force, were now stationed in the province. The commitment to garrisoning the reaches of the island that had merited subjugation, and to constructing a wall fashioned entirely out of stone to mark its limits, only emphasised the worthlessness of those barren reaches left unsubdued. To march into the lands of barbarians, to defeat them in battle, to bring them the benefits of rule by the Roman people: here, it went without saying, were actions worthy of a Caesar. But to pen them up, to leave them to their own savagery, to make clear to them with walls and palisades their irrelevance: this, too, was a course of action that might redound to an emperor's glory. Rome's destiny was not, as had long been claimed, to rule the limits of the world; rather, it was to rule the limits of those lands that merited its rule.

Six years after Hadrian, standing on the banks of the Tyne, had mapped out his plans for a great wall, he arrived in Africa. No emperor had ever set foot there before – not even Augustus. Suetonius, diligent in his researches, had noted that it ranked alongside Sardinia as one of only two provinces the first princeps had not visited – although Suetonius himself, who had travelled with Hadrian through Gaul, Germany and Britain, was no longer in the imperial train. His term of office in the secretariat had been brought to a scandalous end after he and Septicius, his patron, had been accused of indecorous behaviour in the presence of Sabina. Hadrian, a man sensitive to every slight, did not approve of improprieties. Discipline was all. As in Germany and Britain, so in Africa: this was the message the emperor had come to instil. There was just the one legion in the entire province; but this only made its responsibilities the more important. Lambaesis, its base, was not an appealing destination. Situated in a location barely more hospitable than the northern wilds of Britain – ferociously hot in summer, freezing cold in winter – it was only half complete. This did not put off Hadrian. Arriving at Lambaesis, he did so, as ever, bareheaded. A mile and a half west of the base there stood a parade ground; and here, after watching manoeuvres, Hadrian delivered a series of addresses. Praise was given, and advice, and the occasional admonishment. Units expert at building walls out of stone, and cutting ditches through tough gravel, were singled out for special commendation. The horseman proficient with a javelin, the legionary proficient with a pick: such were the men who prevented the world from falling apart. It was to show his respect for them and their fortitude that Hadrian had travelled to Lambaesis. His aim was not to lead them into battle, but to steel them in their responsibility as guardians of the Roman peace. 'Soldiers, I salute your spirit!'[11]

Meanwhile, beyond the olive groves that extended for a hundred miles south of Lambaesis, beyond a range of mountains, and beyond the scrub that marked the beginning of endless desert, there stretched a wall fashioned out of mud-bricks, punctuated by watchtowers, and garrisoned by auxiliaries. Along the southern reaches of the world, as along the northern ones, the limits of civilisation were marked by the apparatus of Roman power. Beyond them lay nothing, behind them everything that made life worth living.

What, after all, was a garden without a wall?

The Glory That Was Greece

Once, during the term of exile Domitian had imposed on him, Dio of Prusa was roaming the wilds of southern Greece. Above Olympia, the sanctuary to Zeus where Nero had raced his chariot and won first prize, the philosopher had found himself hopelessly lost. Stumbling through rugged woodland, he saw, on the crest of a hill, 'a clump of oaks that looked like a sacred grove'.[12] Sure enough, once he had clambered his way up to inspect it, Dio found a shrine fashioned out of crude stone. The skins of various animals were hanging from it, together with a number of clubs and staffs. Sitting nearby was a peasant woman, grey-haired but still strong and handsome despite her advanced years. The shrine, she informed Dio, was sacred to Hercules. She herself, she revealed, had been blessed by the gods with the gift of prophecy. She fixed Dio with her stare. His exile, she told him, would not last for ever. He was destined once again to mix with the high and mighty. 'For the day will come when you meet with a man so powerful that lands and peoples without number will be subject to his sway.'[13]

Sure enough, in time, Dio did meet with such a man. Standing before Trajan, he mentioned the anecdote. It might almost have been calculated to appeal to a Roman audience. Rare was the senator so hard-headed that he did not cherish the notion that somewhere, in groves of ancient trees or on the slopes of mountains, the wondrous might still be stumbled upon. In landscapes measured out by surveyors and divided up into immense estates, even the most sophisticated plutocrat might cherish reminders of a more primitive but god-haunted age. Pliny, staying outside Comum, had noted how, during the harvest, huge crowds would descend on an ancient temple to Ceres that stood on his estate. He had been much moved by this spectacle of devotion to the goddess. It had perturbed him, however, that the temple was crude and cramped, and the people who gathered there 'lacked shelter from the rain and the sun'.[14] Accordingly, in a spirit of mingled piety and paternalism, he had commissioned a refurbishment. Let the temple be supplied with marble for its columns and floors, he had instructed, the wooden statue of the goddess replaced with one carved from stone, and a portico built to provide shelter. It had been Pliny's ambition that his tenants should enjoy the best of both worlds: a site of worship still hallowed by its antiquity and rural setting, but given a splendid upgrade, in accordance with the very latest in architectural fashion.

Dio, giving his speech to Trajan, had aimed to pull a similar trick. Redolent of a vanished age of myth though the old woman was, she had soon revealed herself, in her conversation with the philosopher, to be startlingly familiar with the currents of the age. When she talked of Hercules, the divine hero to whom the rough-hewn shrine was dedicated, she might almost have been describing Caesar. 'Not merely the king of Greece was he, but lord over every land from the rising to the setting of the sun.'[15] Yet Hercules, godlike and glorious though he was, could not rule the world unguided. He first had to be shown the path to true wisdom. His father, Zeus – the name by which the Greeks knew Jupiter – had duly arranged for this to happen. Hercules, brought before a mountain with twin peaks, had been instructed to climb each summit in turn. On one he found enthroned a woman wearing a malignant scowl, surrounded by a train of attendants: Cruelty, and Lawlessness, and Insolence. Tyranny she was called – but few who heard Dio describe her would have failed to recognise in her something of Domitian. Meanwhile, on the other peak, sat a woman as radiant and lovely as her sister had been ugly and forbidding. Royalty, this queen was called; and the names of her ladies-in-waiting were Civic Order, and Law, and Peace. Of these three, it was Peace who was the fairest: 'for she was exceedingly beautiful, exquisitely dressed, and with the very loveliest of smiles'.[16] All this the old peasant woman had narrated to Dio; and Dio, in turn, had narrated it to Caesar.

Trajan, of course – although flattered by the oration – had paid no attention to its key recommendation. That a man as muscularly Roman as the conqueror of Dacia would ever have allowed himself to be guided in his policy by a philosopher was a notion so far-fetched that he had doubtless failed even to realise he was being asked to entertain it. Dio, while perfectly alert to what the Roman elites wanted from him, had never thought to make sense of the brute reality of their power except in terms that were determinedly, defiantly Greek. This approach was one that had long tended to characterise the perspective of philosophers on their Roman masters. Chauvinist and naïve in equal measure, it derived from an age when the world had been ruled, not by Caesar, but by the heirs of Alexander.

Increasingly, however, to a new generation of the Greek upper classes, it was coming to seem badly out of date. If wealth and status offered the nobility of a province such as Bithynia the chance, as it had always done, to study philosophy and play the intellectual, then so also, unexpectedly, thrillingly, dazzlingly, had it begun to offer them the prospect of careers at the very summit of the Roman state. The first senator from the province, an equestrian promoted by Vespasian, had come from Apameia; but already, in Dio's own lifetime, Bithynians were starting to arrive in the senate as well from cities that had never ranked as *coloniae*. Why, then, should an ambitious young man from Nicomedia or Nicaea, of good family and education, imagine that the only way to win influence with Caesar was to play Aristotle to his Alexander? Why should he not aim to be a consul as well as a philosopher, a commander of armies as well as a chronicler of their deeds, a Roman as well as a Greek?

Such questions spoke of a new sense of identity among the Bithynian elites. Dio, for all his Roman citizenship, had never had any wish to become a Roman. Visiting the island of Rhodes, he had been appalled to discover that when the locals wished to flatter a visiting dignitary, they would chisel his name onto an ancient statue, thereby erasing the very identity of the hero to whom it had originally been dedicated. This, it had seemed to the philosopher, was the fate awaiting any city that betrayed its own heritage by slavishly apeing Roman manners: the erasure of its past. Yet even as Dio was making this argument, the ground was shifting beneath his feet.

Ambitious young noblemen from cities like Prusa saw no contradiction between devotion to the glories of their native culture and
commitment to the demands of Roman public life. The distance
between Bithynia and the imperial capital was starting to shrink.

No one illustrated this better than a brilliant intellectual from
Nicomedia: Lucius Flavius Arrianus. Some forty years younger than
Dio, Arrian combined a resolute pride in his native land with horizons as broad as the Roman empire itself. He had studied philosophy
in Greece with Epictetus, a former slave universally honoured as the
most brilliant philosopher of the age; composed poetry; written a
life of Alexander the Great. Simultaneously, he had been entrusted
by Trajan with the command of a particularly rugged corner of
Armenia; gained promotion from Hadrian into the senate; governed
Baetica, the province which boasted the home town of both of his
imperial patrons. Over the course of his career, he would chart the
coast of the Black Sea and the tributaries of the Danube; marvel at the
Caucasus and the Alps; witness African nomads hunting on horseback. He was a Greek, he was a Roman, he was a citizen of the world.[17]

A man better qualified to strike a chord with Hadrian it would
have been hard to imagine – and so it had proved. The two men
had met a few years before Trajan's great war against Parthia, when
Hadrian, dispatched from Rome to prepare the ground for the invasion, had paused a while in Greece, and sat at the feet of Epictetus. The
friendship forged by the two students of the great philosopher was to
prove an enduring one. It helped that they had numerous interests
in common: philosophy, yes, and literature and history, but also –
and perhaps especially – hunting. It helped as well that Hadrian,
with his beard, his preference for Greek over Roman poetry, and his
insatiable appetite for travel, displayed a readiness unprecedented
among his predecessors to meet a provincial like Arrian halfway. If
the Bithynian, in his ambition to attain a consulship, had little choice
but to take on Roman manners, then the emperor, devoted as he
was to the legacy of Greece, had few compunctions, while touring
the eastern half of the empire, in adopting the manners of a Greek.

Hadrian visited Arrian's homeland in 123, on the second leg of the same expedition that had already taken him to Germany and Britain. As in the west, so in the east, his aim was to tend to the wounds recently inflicted on the empire and make an attempt at healing them. In Cyrenaica, he had ordered the restoration of monuments 'destroyed and burned down in the Jewish distur-bances';[18] on the banks of the Euphrates, he had held a summit with Chosroes; in Antioch, he had graced the still shattered city with a bath-house and an aqueduct. Bithynia, although it had been spared war and rebellion, had also demanded Hadrian's attention: for, like the Syrian capital, it had recently been devastated by an earthquake. Nicomedia, Arrian's home town, had suffered particular damage. Even though Hadrian had been preparing to depart for the German frontier when the disaster struck, he had responded with notable generosity. Unsurprisingly, then, when he finally arrived from Syria in Nicomedia, he received an ecstatic welcome. Crowds lined the streets to cheer. Civic dignitaries hailed him as their saviour. Coins portrayed him raising the city from its knees.

Why had Hadrian been so ready with a helping hand? The funds lavished on restoring Nicomedia could certainly be justified in cool, strategic terms: the Propontis, as the *imperator* well knew, was key to the command of both the Euphrates and the Danube. That, after all, was why he had spent his first winter as Caesar on its shores. Yet when he sponsored the beautifying of a city such as Nicomedia, he had more than the defences of the empire on his mind. His friendship with Arrian reflected not just personal compatibility, but admiration for much that the Greek upper classes represented. Unlike Trajan, who had dismissed them as *Graeculi*, 'little Greeks', Hadrian himself had once been mocked as a *Graeculus*. Now, though, he was Caesar, and the wealth of the empire was his to do with as he pleased. By restoring the monuments of an ancient city, by sponsoring its festivals, by grac-ing its leading men with the proofs and marks of his favour, he aimed not just to revive its cultural glories, but to appropriate them to the greater glory of Rome and its empire. The beauty and the eeriness of myth, which had once hallowed every reach, every corner of the Greek world, were to be redeemed from oblivion by Caesar's patronage. Past was to merge with present; the local with the cosmopolitan. Such was the garden that Hadrian wished to tend: one that, like him, was 'various, infinite, possessed of many forms'.[19]

Dio, addressing Trajan, had evoked a world in which the dimensions of myth and the imperial court shed light on each other. To come from Bithynia, perhaps, was to take for granted that Hercules might serve as a point of reference for a Caesar. Gaze out from Prusa, and the view was not just of the Propontis, that vitally strategic seaway, but of a mountainous promontory named Arganthonius. Here it was, during a voyage bound for the Black Sea, that Hercules had landed with his attendant: a boy of exquisite beauty by the name of Hylas. Disaster had quickly followed. Climbing the side of the mountain in search of water, Hylas had come across a spring. Gazing into the waters that rose from it, he had found himself staring into the face of a beautiful nymph. Seeing her arms rise up to seize him, feeling her reach for him with her lips, he had cried out in alarm – but it had been too late. Hylas had vanished, swallowed up by the water. Hercules, although he had roamed the mountainside for days, bellowing in anguish, had searched for the boy in vain. 'And still to this day the people of Prusa commemorate his bereavement, taking to the mountain in a kind of festival, marching in procession, crying out for Hylas.'[20]

Trajan – whose passion for boys was such that an Assyrian king, looking to win the emperor's favour, had secured it by getting his son to perform 'some barbaric dance or other'[21] – might well have been intrigued by such a custom, had Dio only thought to report it. Hadrian, touring Bithynia, was certainly alert to the allure of the region's myths: the way in which they touched the landscape with their radiance, the mirror they held up to human existence. A glimpse of the divine in a boy's smooth cheek: here was something which merited the attention of Caesar no less than roads and docks. Why, after all, labour at keeping a garden secure, only to ignore its blooms? Hadrian embraced every aspect of the empire that he ruled. 'He was an explorer after all things fascinating.'[22]

Which was why, much travelled though he might be, there was one destination more than any other which he clasped to his heart. Bithynia had its attractions, to be sure, and so too did many other reaches of the Greek world. Nowhere, however, could begin to rival the legacy — mythological, historical, poetical, architectural, philosophical — of one particular city: Athens. Six hundred years had passed since the founding of its democracy and the glories of its golden age, when it had ranked as both the bulwark and the school of Greece; and two hundred years since a Roman task force, breaching the city's walls and pillaging it with brutal abandon, had brought a definitive end to its independence. Since then Athens had subsisted as a shadow of its former self: somnolent, provincial, impotent. The Athenians, once the trendsetters for the entire world, now flocked to the foot of the Acropolis to cheer on gladiators. There, in the very shadow of the Parthenon, the Theatre of Dionysus — where Sophocles had staged his tragedies and Aristophanes his comedies — was washed with blood. Yet Roman tourists, for all the mild contempt they might feel for the Athenians as a people reduced to parasitism on their own ancestors, could not help but thrill to the sheer glorious immanence of the past in the city's streets. Even Cicero, a man of obdurate chauvinism when it came to foreign travel, had acknowledged it. 'Wherever we tread in the city, we tread on hallowed ground.'[23] To walk where Pericles had walked; to sit where Plato had sat; to speak where Demosthenes had spoken: here, even for the most philistine tourist, was a moving, stirring experience.

And for Hadrian, very heaven. He had first visited Athens in 112, shortly after his spell of study with Epictetus. He had arrived in the city as a figure of already menacing rank: Trajan's relative and heir presumptive, charged with laying the groundwork for war with Parthia. The Athenians, flattered to find such a powerful man so obviously smitten by their city, had heaped honours on him: citizenship, a senior magistracy, a statue in the Theatre of Dionysus.

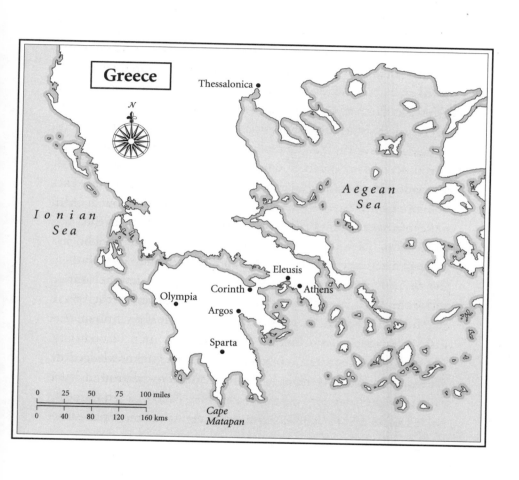

Greece

N

Thessalonica •

I o n i a n
S e a

A e g e a n
S e a

Eleusis
Corinth •   • Athens
Olympia •

Argos •

Sparta •

| 0 | 25 | 50 | 75 | 100 miles |
| 0 | 40 | 80 | 120 | 160 kms |

Cape
Matapan

But these were not the only benefits Hadrian had derived from his visit to Athens. While in the city he had met with a living embodiment of the future: Gaius Julius Antiochus Epiphanes Philopappus, a grandee whose formidable array of names bore splendid witness to his status as a one-man melting pot. Descended from one of Alexander the Great's generals, he was the grandson of the last king of Commagene, a small realm in northern Syria that Vespasian had annexed in 72. Philopappus' father, the first of his line to become a Roman citizen, had fought for Otho at Cremona and with Titus at Jerusalem. Philopappus himself was the grandson of a king who had been raised to the consulship by Trajan. He had also – just for good measure – served as the chief magistrate of Athens. Fabulously rich, fabulously well-connected, fabulously civilised, he was hailed by the philosophers and scholars who profited from his patronage as 'a man of immense generosity, magnificent in the rewards he handed out'.[24] His sister, Julia Balbilla, who lived with him in Athens, was a celebrated poet. The presence there of such a pair of siblings – dynasts simultaneously Greek, Syrian and Roman – was tribute to the enduring hold of the city on the world's imagination. Hadrian was prompted by it, perhaps, to a momentous reflection: that Athens might not, after all, be as irredeemably provincial as the Roman elite had always tended to assume.

Certainly, by late 123, when he first visited Athens as emperor, Hadrian had come to imagine a future for the city as something more than a tourist trap. He based himself there for almost a year and a half – and in that time he lavishly repaid the Athenians for the honours they had granted him a decade previously. With sensitivity and grace he displayed respect for their traditions. When he attended the Theatre of Dionysus, it was not to cheer on gladiators, but to preside over one of the city's most sacred festivals. Taking his seat at the foot of the Acropolis, he did so in Athenian dress. It was not his intention, however, to wallow in nostalgia. Profound though his respect for the glories of the Athenian golden age might be, Hadrian wished to renew the city, not preserve it in aspic. That he celebrated the legacy of Athens' past did not prevent him from commissioning a massive project of urban renewal. Even as he left the Acropolis well alone, he lavished infrastructure on the city appropriate to a modern capital: baths, aqueducts, reservoirs. This, even by the standards of his generosity to Antioch or Nicomedia, was largesse on a prodigious scale. It was almost as though the city were being founded a second time.

Nothing, perhaps, better exemplified Hadrian's plans for Athens, the manner in which he was obsessed simultaneously by the antique and the cutting-edge, than his single most spectacular *grand projet*. For almost six and a half centuries, in a building site south-east of the Acropolis, a colossal temple of Zeus had stood unfinished. Such was the scale of its design that even an ancestor of Philopappus – a king of Syria, no less – had failed to complete it. Now, under Hadrian, the builders returned to work. Vast columns began to rise where previously there had been only foundations. A wall half a mile long was built to enclose the site. A statue of Zeus fashioned out of gold and ivory, surpassed in size only by the Colossus in Rome, was readied in a nearby workshop. At once an ancient monument and a masterpiece of modern design, the temple was an unmistakeable statement of the emperor's vision for the Greek world: one that prompted Greeks themselves to hail him as 'the benefactor of his subjects – and especially of Athens'.[25]

By late 128, when Hadrian returned to his favourite city, the temple of Olympian Zeus – the Olympeion – was nearing completion. Also taking shape were his plans not just for Athens, but for the entire Greek world. Earlier that year, standing on the dusty parade ground at Lambaesis, Hadrian had been inspecting the defences of the empire, and testing the mettle of those who stood guard over them. Now, arriving in Athens, he was labouring still to keep the world in order. Those who knew him well had long appreciated this. 'Observe the profound peace that Caesar has procured for us.' So Epictetus had marvelled. 'There are no wars or battles, no bandits or pirates, with the result that we may travel as we please, and sail from east to west.'[26] The philosopher had a long memory. He was old enough to remember the year of the four emperors, and to be grateful that the world was no longer being trampled beneath the tread of rival warlords. Born a slave, and disabled from an early age, Epictetus had no illusions as to how brutal life might be. The value he placed on the Pax Romana was neither wishful thinking nor sycophancy. It was the considered judgement of a man widely viewed as the wisest in the world.

Yet Epictetus had spoken not only as the world's most distinguished intellectual but as a Greek. He knew — just as Arrian, who recorded his words, knew — that the history of Greece before the coming of Rome had been ceaseless conflict. Cities that now profited from the Pax Romana had once, back in the days of their liberty, forever been tearing chunks out of each other. Did this mean, then, that conquest by Rome had been for the Greeks' own good? There were many, unsurprisingly, who shrank from acknowledging this. Even as Dio lamented the inability of Greek cities to live in harmony with one another, he had seen the attentions of Roman governors as something to be feared. Addressing the people of Nicomedia, whose rivalry with the Nicaeans was notorious, he had urged them to recognise just how damaging their squabbling was, and how demeaning. To appreciate this, they had only to look to history. The Athenians, back in their golden heyday, had flaunted their predominance, thrown their weight around, put other cities in their shadow. By doing so, they had roused the envy of the one power in Greece that could compare with Athens for greatness: the fearsome warrior state of Sparta. The two cities had ended up going to war. The consequences had been ruinous for both — and for all the Greeks. It was what had led, in the long run, to their conquest by Rome. 'At least, however, when Athens and Sparta fought, a genuine empire was at stake, not just some vain conceit.'[27] Dio, urging Nicomedia and Nicaea to bury the hatchet, had done so on the assumption that it was the surest way for them to uphold their mutual dignity. Only by living in harmony would they be able to avoid the more intrusive manifestations of Roman rule. Such a message, coming from a powerless intellectual, was one that the people of Nicomedia had felt no particular obligation to heed. Now, a generation on, the most famous cities in Greece were waking up to a similar exhortation. The idea that they might all be joined in a single confederation – a Panhellenion – was no longer the fantasy of philosophers. It was the policy of Caesar himself.

Although Athens was the particular focus of Hadrian's attentions, the city was not the only one for which he had plans. In 128, just as he had done four years previously, he headed into southern Greece. His destination: Sparta. The city, which in ancient times had been the dominant power in southern Greece, existed, like Athens, as the ghost of its own greatness. To the Romans, the Spartans served as the epitome of *virtus*: manliness. Back in its heyday, when Sparta had challenged Athens for the rule of Greece, education in the city had been famously exacting. Boys had been kept in barracks, regularly flogged, and trained never to show any pain; girls had been taught to wrestle. Sparta's commitment to military excellence was viewed by Roman moralists as a tradition quite as admirable as anything to be found in Athens. It was true, of course, that the Spartans, a people who had not been to war for three centuries, no longer had cause to breed a race of heroes – but this had cut no ice with their Roman admirers. Pressure on the city's inhabitants to live up to the example of their ancestors had become ever more irresistible. So it was that the ancient ways of doing things had come to be dusted down. 'Wrestling grounds and displays of exertion renewed their popularity with the young; the barracks were restored; Sparta was herself again.'[28] Nero, ever the showman, had imported girls from Sparta to put on displays of wrestling for the entertainment of the Roman people. Tourists who could afford to travel to the city itself would thrill to the spectacle of boys being lashed to a bloodied pulp, and never once letting out a whimper. Those with a particular relish for history might join the Spartans in their barracks and nibble at their notoriously revolting food.

To Hadrian, these displays of 'Spartan self-discipline and training'[29] appeared wholly as authentic as if they derived from unbroken tradition. The marks of favour with which he graced the city were signal, and appropriate to the city's past as a military hegemon. He made various gifts of land, including two islands, to Sparta, and granted it the right – hitherto exclusive to Rome – to source wheat from Egypt. Its most distinguished citizen, a cousin of Philopappus, was awarded the command of a legion. Just as the Athenians, under Hadrian's patronage, had been restored to their ancient dignity, so were the Spartans restored to theirs. The two most famous cities in Greece, whose rivalry had once been so calamitous, were now, under the benignant rule of Rome, joined in amity. With Athens and Sparta at its head, the Panhellenion was fast taking shape. When Hadrian, in the spring of 129, departed Greece for Asia, it was in the full expectation that he would soon be back. Although the Olympeion was still covered in scaffolding, it would not take long for the great temple to be completed. It was to serve not just as a gift from Caesar to his favourite city, but as a monument to his many labours in the cause of peace: as the headquarters of the Panhellenion.

'No ruler has done more for the glory of Zeus, and for the happiness of his subjects.'[30] The more familiar Greeks were with their own history, the more remarkable a figure did Hadrian come to seem. It was not just the ancient rivalry between Athens and Sparta that the Panhellenion aimed to heal. There was also the scarring left by Hadrian's own people: the Romans. Their conquest of Greece had been brutal. Multitudes had been enslaved. The looting had been wholesale. Most devastating of all had been the destruction of an entire city. Corinth, situated beside the narrow isthmus which joins northern to southern Greece, had been celebrated for its wealth, its industry, its sophistication, its temples, its philosophers, its whores. None of which had been sufficient to save it. In 146 BC a Roman general had razed the city to the ground. A century later, when Julius Caesar re-founded Corinth as a *colonia*, it had served as the headquarters for the governor of the province: an island of Romans amid a sea of Greeks. The settlers had all come from Italy; they spoke Latin; they lived in a city designed in imitation of Rome. Corinth, a metropolis which once had redounded to the glory of Greece, had become an emblem of the opposite: Greek prostration, Greek humiliation. Yet now, under the rule of Hadrian, it seemed as though even this very deepest of wounds might be healed. 'Colonists sent from Rome':[31] so, ever since the founding of the *colonia*, Greeks had referred to the Corinthians. Yet for how much longer would that distinction apply? The boundary between natives and colonists, between Greeks and Romans, was increasingly uncertain. This blurring, it seemed, had the sanction of Caesar himself. Certainly, alongside Athens, alongside Sparta, alongside Argos, and Rhodes, and Thessalonica, Corinth too appeared on the roster of the Panhellenion.

There were, of course, beyond the Greek world, many other cities, many other lands. These could not, by definition, be permitted to join the Panhellenion. The Greeks were a distinctive people, and Hadrian's plans for them depended on him treating them as such. Nevertheless, there was inspiration to be had, perhaps, from the remarkable bloom, simultaneously Roman and Greek, that had sprung from the ashes of the original Corinth. The torching of famous cities by the legions was not mere ancient history, after all. In the spring of 130, Hadrian arrived in a province that, within living memory, had witnessed the utter annihilation of its metropolis: Judaea. The ruins of Jerusalem remained the base of X Fretensis, and the emblem of the wild boar still stood guard over what had once been the Judaeans' holiest city. A second legion, originally recruited by Trajan, and transferred from service in Parthia following the emperor's death, occupied a base in Galilee. The continued presence of two legions in the province, over a decade after the suppression of the revolt that had darkened Hadrian's first months in power, bore witness to an enduring undercurrent of unrest. The Judaeans had been given little cause to identify themselves with Rome.

Nevertheless, to an emperor who had repaired the disaster of Trajan's eastern war, built a wall across the wilds of Britain, and succeeded in joining the Greeks in a common brotherhood, the task of bringing peace to Judaea seemed far from insurmountable. In Syria, as the emperor was making sacrifice on the summit of a mountain outside Antioch, a thunderbolt had incinerated his offering: irrefutable evidence that his efforts at ordering the world enjoyed divine favour. Hadrian had no reason to doubt, as he rode towards what had once been the Judaean capital, that his intentions for the ruined city would be as fruitful as all his other plans. Just as he had brought peace to Britain, and Africa, and Syria, so now he would bring peace to Judaea. Not just the site of Jerusalem but the entire province was to be set on a new and more stable footing.

That Hadrian's visit promised splendid things was the hope of many Judaeans too. Looking at his record, comparing him to his predecessors, it was still possible for them to reckon him 'an excellent man, whose understanding spans all things'.[32] In Athens, Hadrian had displayed his respect for the ancient greatness of the city, and sponsored its restoration; why, then, should he not do so in Jerusalem? Six decades had passed since the destruction of the Temple, six decades in which the Judaeans had been unable to perform the rituals prescribed by their scriptures. Blackened rubble littered the rock where the Holy of Holies, the shrine of the Most High God, the dwelling place on earth of the Divine Presence Itself, had once stood. How long, Judaeans wondered, in mingled anguish and expectation, could the Almighty tolerate such a desecration? Once before, in ancient times, in the wake of the storming of Jerusalem by the king of Babylon, a foreign emperor — a Persian by the name of Cyrus — had permitted the Temple to be rebuilt. Judaean scripture commemorated him as a *christos*: a messiah. Perhaps, now that the emperor of Rome had arrived in Judaea, a second messiah was riding to Jerusalem? Surely, once Caesar arrived before the Temple Mount, and beheld the sight of the desolation there, he would command the rubble cleared, the shrine to Proserpina raised by Quietus removed, and the House of God at long last restored?

But the Judaeans were to be disappointed. Hadrian had no interest in playing a second Cyrus. It was Corinth, that *colonia* planted on the ruins of an ancient and famous city, that provided him with a readier example from history: the evidence of how it had consolidated Roman authority over a people initially alien and resentful, but then, over the long run, reconciled to their subordination. Hadrian, arriving at the camp of X Fretensis, did indeed – as the Judaeans had been hoping he would – order the clearing of rubble from the site of Jerusalem; but not because he intended the restoration of their capital. Instead, he ordered that an entirely new city – a *colonia* – be built. As with similar such foundations across the empire, it was to be thoroughly Roman: in its language, in its layout, in its gods. On the great rock where the shrine of the Judaean god had stood, Hadrian commanded the construction of a temple to Jupiter. The name he gave his new city – Colonia Aelia Capitolina – bore witness both to his forebears, the Aelii, and to the hill in distant Rome where Jupiter's greatest temple stood. The Judaeans, a people inveterately rebellious, had shown themselves unworthy to have their metropolis restored to them. Better for all concerned, then, that the very name of Jerusalem be consigned to oblivion. Such, in Hadrian's opinion, was the surest way to guarantee an enduring peace.

And so it was, having ordered the affairs of Judaea to his own satisfaction, that the emperor and his party continued on their way, along the road that led to Egypt.

Pantheon

Late October, AD 130. The body of a young man – still not twenty – was found floating in the Nile. Hauled out from the river, dragged through the silt left by the retreating floodwaters, the corpse was brought to dry land. It was clear that the drowned man had been a figure strikingly out of the ordinary. His body was gym-toned. His proportions were perfect. His face possessed a heart-stopping, almost supernatural beauty. Who was he? A foreigner, clearly. Yet the stretch of the Nile in which he had drowned was hardly the haunt of glamorous foreigners. Alexandria lay far to the north. Although there was an ancient temple, adorned with squat pillars and the carvings of a forgotten pharaoh, looming over the flow of the waters, the building did not feature prominently in the roster of Egypt's tourist attractions. Nothing stood beside it save a scruffy village. Yet here, to this obscure and rural spot, Caesar himself had come – Caesar, who ruled in Egypt as pharaoh, at once king and living god. His barge, together with a great flotilla of other vessels, stood moored in the shallows by the temple. Clearly, the young man found in the Nile could only have been of his party. And so it proved.

The drowned youth was the beloved of Hadrian. His name was Antinous. The emperor, informed of what had happened to his favourite, was overwhelmed by grief. 'He wept like a woman.'[33] Such an extravagant display of emotion was seen as unworthy of a man; but this did not mean that taking a concubine was itself regarded as scandalous. Quite the contrary. Men, including emperors, had needs, after all, and whether on a prostitute or a slave, a woman or a boy, they were expected to satisfy them. Most citizens, gazing on Antinous, would only have envied the emperor his good fortune. 'Such beauty had never before been seen.'[34] On this, everyone was agreed. Domitian's ban on eunuchs, upheld both by Nerva and by Hadrian himself, had done nothing to diminish the widespread passion for *delicati*. If anything, indeed – by drying up the supply – it had made the competition in elite circles for boys of lustrous beauty only the more intense. Antinous was not a slave – but neither was he a citizen, and therefore, by the stern standards of Roman law and morality, he qualified as fair game. He came from Claudiopolis, the small town in Bithynia famous for its cheeses and not much else.* As well as beautiful, he was smart. 'His heart was wise,' Hadrian wrote in praise of his beloved, 'his intelligence that of a grown man.'[35] Even Sabina – whose relationship with her husband had long been

---

* Presumably – although it is nowhere stated explicitly – Hadrian first set eyes on Antinous in 123, while on the road that led from Syria to Nicomedia. If so, Antinous would have been around twelve years old at the time.

difficult – found Antinous a sufficiently mollifying influence that she had agreed, when Hadrian embarked on his tour of the eastern Mediterranean, to accompany him. The emperor, sailing up the Nile, had done so with both his wife and his concubine by his side.

To a Roman, a free citizen, submission to the advances of another man, even a Caesar, would have been a cause of undying shame. Vitellius, who as a boy was said to have been used by the elderly Tiberius, had been stuck ever after with the nickname 'Sphincter'. Even more shocking – because more credible – was the gossip that Mucianus, Vespasian's ally in the winning of the world, had enjoyed being treated in bed like a woman. 'At least', so Vespasian had once muttered, after Mucianus had been particularly rude to him, 'I am a man.'[36] A reputation stained by the disgrace of such talk could not hope to be washed clean, of course. Yet even as Romans scorned males who actively consented to penetration as the very worst of deviants, they were aware that such a perspective was not necessarily universal. 'In Greece,' they noted, 'it is the custom to praise a young man for taking plenty of lovers.'[37] The knowledge of this had fostered a sense both of moral superiority and of titillation. The figure of an adolescent who was not merely beautiful but shimmeringly and seductively Greek obsessed the Roman erotic imagination. Playboys, pornographers, poets: all delighted in the fantasy. It was why *delicati* were so often given Greek names. That Antinous was not a slave but a free-born Bithynian – a native of the very land in which Hylas, Hercules' exquisite pageboy, had met his watery doom – only compounded his allure. Hadrian, by taking such a lover, was merely doing what many a red-blooded Roman would have leapt at the chance to do. He was living the dream.

Hadrian's own dreams, however, were peculiarly complex and rich. Antinous offered something more than just a pretty face. He offered love – and love, what was more, of a distinctively Greek kind. It served to blur the erotic with the poetic: to cast Antinous as a Hylas, and Hadrian as a Hercules. What in Rome might seem a perfectly conventional relationship, that of a master and his concubine, carried a very different charge in Greece. When the emperor appeared before the gaze of the Athenian people accompanied by a freeborn son of the Greek world, they took it not as an insult, but as a compliment. When he arrived in Alexandria, the presence of Antinous beside him reassured the citizens of that turbulent city that Caesar held their traditions in respect. There were many ways for an emperor to display his superiority, and not all of them were Roman. Hadrian positively relished the opportunity to meet the philosophers and poets of Alexandria on their own terms. Convening the city's leading scholars, he put a battery of questions to them before triumphantly providing all the answers himself. Then, informed that a ferocious lion was roaming the deserts beyond Alexandria, he resolved to play the part of Hercules. The hunt was an adventure of which even that most famous of lion-slayers might have been proud. Poets, tipped off by Hadrian as to the precise details of the expedition, made sure to record it all in song. Fire had come from the lion's eyes, showers of foam from its ravening jaws. Hadrian and Antinous, paired in the battle against the monster, had demonstrated their proficiency not only as huntsmen but as lovers. Just as Hercules had sought to train Hylas in the skills required of a hero, so had Hadrian deliberately missed the target with his spear, so that Antinous might display his prowess; and then, when Antinous' horse was brought down by the lion, saved the life of his beloved by dispatching the monster with a single, muscular thrust. A scene not merely Greek, but heroically, mythically so.

Yet the dimension of myth, even for Hadrian, was potentially treacherous. Egypt was an ancient land, and the Nile a mysterious river. The imperial party, setting sail on their cruise, had witnessed for themselves how its waters, every late summer and autumn, would rise and flood the parched earth. This inundation enabled Egypt to serve as the world's breadbasket: for the waters, as they retreated, would leave behind black mud of a miraculous fertility. It was not only the Egyptians who obsessed over this phenomenon. So, too, did the Greeks. Even before the founding of Alexandria, they had been fascinated by the Nile, and by the primordial wisdom of Egypt's priests, who had long since fathomed the true history of the gods. By Hadrian's time, Greek scholars were as familiar with the great narrative of how and why the Nile had come to flood as they were with the stories of the Trojan War. The story had come to seem almost their own.

Once, so the report went, the god Osiris had ruled as pharaoh. Isis, his sister, had ruled as queen. But then their brother Typhon, who was cruel and savage and red, like the desert that stretched on either side of the Nile, tricked Osiris by sealing him up in a coffin, drowning him in the great river, and leaving his body to drift out to sea. Isis, ever faithful, searched the world for her husband's corpse and redeemed it; and when Typhon, stealing back the body, dismembered it and scattered the pieces far and wide, she found every last missing part – all, that was, except for the penis, which had been devoured by the fish of the Nile. 'And so Isis made a replica of it, and endowed it with a potent and awful power.'[38] Osiris, brought back to life by his queen, passed to the realm of the dead, there to rule for eternity; but even though he no longer sat enthroned on earth, he continued to serve humanity as the model of all that was best and most just. Such was the lesson taught by the flooding of the Nile: for its water was nothing less than the seed of Osiris, and the earth drenched by its flood-surge the body of Isis, his queen.

There were many ways of gauging the truth of this story. To the peasants who, late every October, as the river began its retreat, sowed the black soil, it was evident in the annual flourishing of their fields. Scholars such as Hadrian's secretary, a learned freedman by the name of Phlegon, might bring a parallel perspective. Corroborating an observation made by Pliny the Elder, that 'drinking the waters of the Nile boosts fecundity',[39] he noted the example of 'a woman from Alexandria, who had four pregnancies, and delivered twenty children'.[40] There was no need, however, to live in Egypt, nor to study its birth statistics, to sense the sheer potency of the ancient tale. That Osiris was the mightiest of the gods, and Isis the mistress of the elements, initial begetter of the ages, supreme of divine powers, was a conviction that had become accepted across the Greek world.

And even in Rome. Not by everyone in the capital, of course: for the priests of Isis, with their shaven heads and their temples decorated with animal-headed gods, could hardly help but strike many Romans as sinister in the extreme. During the dying days of the republic, the senate had even voted to topple the goddess's altars and demolish her temples. Yet this suspicion of Isis – although conservatives might still sniff at her as foreign – had faded. A century on from the collapse of the republic, a Roman could worship her and feel that she was not so foreign after all. In the ecstatic opinion of her devotees, Isis was the queen not merely of Egypt but of every land. The Romans knew her as Juno, the Sicilians as Proserpina, the Cypriots as Venus. 'People across the entire globe – albeit that they may worship me in any number of ways, and call me by any number of names – all acknowledge me as holy, transcendent, unique.'[41] A goddess capable of such imperious self-confidence was one that even a Caesar might respect. Domitian, fleeing the Capitol as it was being stormed by Vitellius' supporters, had done so disguised as one of her priests; Vespasian and Titus, the night before their triumph, had stayed in her temple on the Campus Martius. Like a slave transported from some distant land to the capital of the world, and there, after lengthy service, granted her freedom, the Queen of Egypt had become a Roman.

Nevertheless, there were certain opportunities that even Rome could not provide. To a man as relentlessly curious as Hadrian, the chance to sail the waters of the Nile at full flood had been irresistible. Everyone in his entourage, as his flotilla made its way up the river, would have been alert to the significance of the spectacle around them: hills transformed into islands, the Nile itself into a sea. They would perfectly have understood what this portended for the security of the empire: for a flood that failed meant a ruined harvest, and a ruined harvest spelt danger for Egypt, for Rome, for Caesar.[42] The stability of imperial rule still depended, as it had always done, on the successful provision of corn to the Roman people.

It was not Annona, however, who ranked as the queen of the heavens. The great drama of Isis and her love for Osiris, manifest in the very waters that Hadrian was sailing that late October, revealed more profound truths. It opened up for those with eyes to see the deepest mysteries of the cosmos: a place in which the patterns of death and life, hatred and love, extinction and resurrection, might be distinguished by those with the wisdom to discern them. A fateful day dawned: 24 October. It was the date on which Osiris, thrown into the river by Typhon, had drowned. That night, to mark it, small boats took to the Nile, ablaze with lamps. The sounds of music and revelry drifted from settlements along the banks. On Caesar's barge, men and women of learning reflected on the anniversary and pondered what its true meaning might be. Philosophy suggested the truest answer. 'For the soul of Osiris, so the legend has it, is immortal and imperishable; and although Typhon may repeatedly dismember his body, and make it disappear, yet Isis will always search the world for it, and piece it back together. For that which is true and good is always superior to destruction and change.'[43]

It was shortly after the anniversary of Osiris' death, in the final week of October, that the discovery of Antinous' body was made.[44] The tears shed by Hadrian were the least of the scandal. Speculation as to how and why Antinous might have perished was soon feverish. According to Hadrian himself, it had all been an accident: 'He fell into the Nile.' Others, however, proposed a more sinister explanation: 'He was the victim of a sacrifice.'[45] The notion that a Caesar, fearful of death, might seek to prolong his own life by offering up to the underworld the life of another mortal was certainly not unprecedented. Suetonius, dismissed in disgrace from Hadrian's service, and busy back in Rome adding sequels to his biography of Augustus, would cite in his life of Nero a particularly telling example. A comet – 'which is commonly held to presage the death of great rulers' – had appeared in the skies. Nero, informed 'that it was standard practice for a king to counter a portent like this by having some important figure killed, thereby diverting the danger from the king's own head onto that of someone else high-ranking, decided that he would have the leading nobles in Rome put to death'.[46] Antinous, admittedly, was hardly of noble rank; but otherwise the parallels were suggestive. For once again, blazing in the skies, a new star had appeared. What did it signify? The Nile was a perfect place to ponder the question. Nero's own astrologer had once sailed its waters. An equestrian by the name of Balbillus, steeped in the lore of Egypt, he had served as Egypt's prefect. Balbillus himself might be long dead – but his granddaughter was not. Julia Balbilla, the sister of Philopappus, was present on the Nile with Hadrian. Mourning the recent death of her brother, she had accompanied the emperor as Sabina's companion. Here, for those minded to detect a conspiracy, were clues enough, perhaps.

Yet there were other possibilities. Perhaps Antinous, aware that he was passing into adulthood, and all too painfully conscious of the contempt in which a hirsute catamite was conventionally held, had drowned himself. Perhaps Hadrian, a man normally possessed of iron self-control, but capable of the occasional violent outburst, had lashed out in a fit of murderous rage. Perhaps Sabina, envious of Antinous' hold over her husband, had disposed of him. Perhaps some prominent figure in Hadrian's train, as suspicious of the emperor's favourite as a previous generation had been suspicious of Asiaticus, the favourite of Vitellius, had done the deed.[47] Perhaps the truth was destined never to be known. One thing, however, was certain: the titanic scale of Hadrian's grief. Whatever the cause of Antinous' death, he appeared, in the days and weeks that followed, broken by it.

Nevertheless, the travel plans of Caesar could not lightly be rearranged. Rather than leave the Nile, Hadrian continued with his journey upriver. As he sailed, so he brooded darkly on his loss. In Egypt, reminders of death, of mourning, of resurrection, were never hard to find. Mooring at Thebes, a village clustered around a stupefyingly vast temple complex, Hadrian and his party crossed the river to the western bank, there to visit two colossal statues of a hero who had died and been brought back to life. Memnon, son of the Dawn, had perished before the walls of Troy; but Zeus, moved by his mother's tears, had raised him from the dead. The two colossi of the hero, enthroned amid lonely scree, were as celebrated as any landmark in Egypt.* Generations of Roman sightseers had visited them – among them Suedius, who had served in Pompeii as Vespasian's agent. It was not the statues themselves that drew tourists, however, but rather a remarkable property of the base on which the right-hand colossus sat: for periodically, when touched by the first light of dawn, it would make a noise 'like a lyre when a string is broken'.[48] Ominously, when the members of Hadrian's imperial party paid their first visit, the statues kept their silence. Only when Sabina and Julia Balbilla returned without Hadrian did they sing. Over the course of their stay in Thebes, the two women made repeated visits to the colossi. Four poems by Julia were inscribed on Memnon's left leg. Hadrian, meanwhile, returned only once. Memnon, on this occasion, did sing to him; but the emperor otherwise kept away. Fascinated though he normally was by memorials to heroes, he had an even greater wonder on his mind. For Antinous had appeared to him.

'Because of a revelation he was honoured as a god.'[49] Many details converged to convince Hadrian that his dream, in which Antinous had revealed his resurrection, was authentic. He had delivered oracles that Hadrian, putting into verse, had made sure to promulgate. Astrologers, studying the new star as it blazed in the heavens, assured their imperial master that, far from portending doom, 'it had actually resulted from the spirit of Antinous'.[50] Most haunting of all, and the key to Hadrian's understanding of his favourite's fate, was the fact that he had perished in the same way, in the same river, and at the same time of year as Osiris. Could this just be coincidence? Already, only a few days after Antinous' death, Hadrian had decided that it was not. A city, he decreed, was to be built from scratch beside the

---

* In reality, the twin statues portrayed Amenhotep III, whose long reign in the fourteenth century BC had marked the apogee of Egyptian wealth and power.

very stretch of river on which the fateful accident had occurred, and it was to be dedicated to a new god: Osirantinous.

That winter, back in Alexandria after his voyage up the Nile, Hadrian developed his plans. The new city, Antinoopolis, was to be a sumptuous monument to Greek urban planning; but its central temple, in which the deified Antinous would 'listen to the appeals of those who invoke him, and heal the sick among the needy poor', was to be of Egyptian design.[51] In the new year, messengers were dispatched far and wide to proclaim the good news: that Antinous, risen from the dead, had ascended to the heavens. Across Egypt they went, and to Greece, and to his homeland of Bithynia. A Greek from the Propontis, the favourite of Caesar, drowned in the Nile as Osiris had been, and risen to eternal life: Antinous was a flamboyantly multicultural god.

But Hadrian — however much he might have wished to devote himself solely to the memory of his beloved — still had the rule of the world as his responsibility. Leaving Egypt, the land that had brought him so much grief, he resumed his travels. From Alexandria he sailed to Syria; from Syria he headed overland to the shores of the Aegean. By winter he was back in Athens. Great things awaited him there. The scaffolding had come down from the completed temple of Olympian Zeus, the great wall that enclosed it was complete, and its forecourt was crowded with statues. At its dedication in the spring of 132, cities from across the Greek world each donated a portrait of the emperor; the emperor himself donated a snake brought from India. The Panhellenion, approved by official decree of the senate, was inaugurated amid splendid festivities. Athens was ready at last to take her place on the throne that Caesar had prepared so assid-uously for her.

For Hadrian himself, it marked a moment not just of celebration but of awful solemnity. The joining of the most famous cities of Greece into a common union was no light achievement. Amity had been forged where previously, for many centuries, there had been only mutual hatred. Greece, maimed and drained of its life blood, had been brought back from the dead. This was why, in Hadrian's opinion, Athens so richly merited the tribute of other cities: for her glory it was, every year, to celebrate the possibility of resurrection, the triumph of life over death, in a rite more awesome than any other in the world. Eight and a half years had passed since the emperor's initiation into the mysteries at Eleusis; three and a half since he had attended them again in the company of Antinous. Now, by meeting in 'the most brilliant city of the Athenians', the Panhellenion was itself sharing in 'the fruit of the Mysteries'.[52] It bore witness to the possibility of redemption from past sufferings and miseries. It proclaimed that brotherhood might come from fratricide, peace from war, order from chaos.

Meanwhile, in the heavens, the star that signified the elevation of Antinous to the ranks of the immortals blazed over all the lands of the world. Even as Hadrian presided over the inauguration of the Panhellenion, he had not neglected to foster the worship of his beloved. In Athens, he instituted an annual festival, the Antinoeia, in which youths on the cusp of manhood were to compete for athletic and artistic prizes; in Eleusis, where he sponsored a similar series of contests, a statue was erected in the sanctuary portraying the divine Antinous as a divine physician, healer of the broken and the wounded. Not since the funeral of Poppaea Sabina, almost seventy years before, had a Caesar made such a public display of his grief. Yet Hadrian, by deifying a Greek, a provincial who was not even a citizen, had displayed a disregard for the traditions and proprieties of the Roman people that might have given even Nero pause. Never before had a Caesar added to the ranks of the immortals a mortal who was neither an emperor nor a member of an emperor's family. When Nero had mourned his beloved, he had used the Forum as his stage; but Hadrian was using the world. Rather than obtaining the senate's sanction for his elevation of Antinous to the halls of the gods, he had not even bothered to return to the capital. When provincials in Egypt, or Asia, or Greece gazed into the face of the preternaturally beautiful young man who – so it was rumoured – had died that

Caesar might live, they did not see expressed there the might and distant majesty of Rome. They saw themselves.

That the cults as well as the luxuries of the east might ultimately corrupt the Roman people had been a cause of dread to moralists in the senate ever since the city's first rise to greatness. It was why, back in the days of the republic, they had viewed the worship of Isis with such stern disapproval. The danger was always that, in a world where Greeks, Egyptians and Syrians were able promiscuously to mix, their superstitions might come to mix as well. Most dangerous of all, of course, were the superstitions of the Judaeans. The dark strain of fanaticism that they fostered, and that twice in living memory had inspired rebellion against the Roman peace, had shown itself alarmingly prone to mutation. Tacitus, whose contempt for it was sombre and profound, had noted a particularly egregious example: a sect founded by a Judaean named Christ, a criminal who had been put to death by Pontius Pilate. These 'Christians', as people termed them, had already, by the time of Nero, established themselves as a notable and sinister presence in Rome. This, perhaps, was no great surprise. Rare was the foreign cult that could not be found polluting the city's slums. The capital, as Tacitus observed, was a sink into which 'everything monstrous and degraded drains'.[53]

Alarmingly, however, Christians were also to be found even in obscure reaches of the empire. Travelling through Pontus during his term as governor, Pliny had discovered them 'infecting with their wretched superstition not merely the towns, but the villages and fields as well'.[54] Christ, whom they believed to be divine, was the only god they acknowledged. Commanded by Pliny to make offerings to Jupiter and to Caesar, they had refused. The sacrilege of this had been self-evident. It was one thing for the Judaeans – who were, after all, an ancient people – to behave in such a manner; but no upstart sect could be granted a legal sanction to flaunt such arrogance and impiety. Once Pliny was satisfied that the Christians brought before him were obdurate in their superstitions, he had duly had them put to death. When Trajan was asked to confirm the justice of this ruling, he had done so; as, in due course, had Hadrian. Sacrilege, it went without saying, was beyond the pale. Christians, like Druids, like the devotees of any superstition that promulgated practices and doctrines noxious to morality, were an offence to Roman order. No Caesar could possibly have thought otherwise.

Nevertheless, it was possible to think as well that the aggressive persecution of any section of society was an unattractive policy. Trajan, writing to Pliny, had warned him to pay no attention to anonymous informers. 'These create the worst kind of precedent, and are not at all in keeping with the spirit of our age.'[55] The perspective of Caesar was inevitably broader than that of a senator. Trajan had been in the midst of preparations for the invasion of Parthia when Pliny had written to him about the Christians, and he had no wish to convulse a region like Pontus by purging a sizeable proportion of its population. Hadrian, who had responded to an enquiry from a governor very similar to Pliny's while he was touring Britain, had been equally alert to the perils of stirring up civil unrest. The empire, he knew, had enemies enough already beyond its walls. Distasteful though he naturally found the Christians, he was not a man to feel greatly threatened by the range and variety of Rome's subject peoples. Certainly, he had little patience with the chauvinism of senatorial traditionalists. This was why he had scorned to obtain their approval for his deification of Antinous. That cities and peoples across the vast span of the empire had greeted the new god with a quite startling degree of enthusiasm, so that even Hadrian himself had been surprised, demonstrated conclusively that he was right. It was not the fusty and antique traditions of Rome that had won the provincials' love. These were inadequate to inspire the loyalty of the whole world. The new star blazing in the sky, the star that proclaimed the immortality of Antinous, proclaimed as well a new order: an order in which multiple traditions, multiple loyalties, might be reconciled, and all the empire joined in devotion to its leader, Caesar.

What, though, of traditions, of loyalties that could not be reconciled? There were many ways, after all, to read the heavens. 'A star shall come out of Jacob, and a sceptre shall rise out of Israel.'[56] So it was prophesied in the scriptures of the Judaeans. The star, their scholars taught, was the messiah; and now, some of these scholars dared to hope, a star had come.* Even as Hadrian, in Athens, was establishing festivals in honour of Antinous, messengers were speeding from his legate in Aelia Capitolina with devastating news. The Judaeans, yet again, had risen in revolt. For years, it turned out, they had been stockpiling weapons, preparing strongholds, excavating underground refuges and tunnels. The banditry long endemic in Judaea had escalated, almost without the Romans noticing it, into a full-blown insurgency. Only after they had found their supplies and communications cut off had they come to realise the full scale of the crisis confronting them. Even as Hadrian, summoned back to war, sought desperately to marshal reinforcements, the entire Roman position in Judaea appeared in danger of collapse. Decades later, it would still be vividly remembered in Rome 'just how many soldiers were slaughtered by the Judaeans'.[57] One of the two legions stationed outside Alexandria, dispatched to the war zone, suffered such grievous casualties that it had to be cashiered.[58] Meanwhile, in the badlands south of Aelia Capitolina, a brigand chieftain named Simeon proclaimed himself the prince of a reborn Judaean kingdom. On his coins were stamped ringing slogans: 'For the Liberty of Israel', 'For the Redemption of Israel'. Bar Kokhba, Simeon was nicknamed: Son of the Star.

To the Greeks, a people honoured by Hadrian as no foreign people had ever been honoured by a Caesar before, the emperor himself appeared to be a prince of peace, a leader whose supreme genius was for the sponsorship of civic amenities, the restoration of antiquities, the inaugurating of festivals. 'He never willingly went to war.'[59] Yet Hadrian, whose drilling of the legions would serve as a model for generations to come of how best to whip an army into shape, was a man with a grim appetite for pushing his soldiers to the limit. It did

---

* Specifically, according to Jewish tradition, Rabbi Akiva.

not take him long to fathom the correct strategy for dealing with Bar Kokhba. The Roman forces, confronting the rebels' guerilla tactics, had been too ponderous, too muscle-bound. Clearly, the situation demanded a more agile approach. Hadrian sent for his ablest general, a former consul by the name of Julius Severus, whose experience in counter-insurgency had been honed during his governorship of Rome's most barbarous province: Britain. Severus, transferred from the distant Ocean, made brisk work of the rebels. His forces, divided up into mobile hit-squads, fanned out across the Judaean badlands, smoking out nest after nest of Bar Kokhba's men. No respite was offered. No mercy was given.

Such was the slaughter, Judaean scholars would later claim, that horses almost drowned beneath the blood, and a great wall, measuring eighteen miles by eighteen miles, was raised by Hadrian entirely out of corpses. Exaggerated or not, such stories spoke of ruin on a scale that was capable of appalling even Roman observers. 'Almost the whole of Judaea was left a desert.'[60] Those Judaeans who did manage to escape death or enslavement fled to Galilee. Here, because the Galileans had not joined the revolt, refugees were able to evade the vengeance visited on Judaea. Over the decades that followed, Judaean communities would succeed in building a new life for themselves in the region, a new sense of identity, a new understanding of their scriptures and the purposes of their god. Of their original homeland, however, not even the name was preserved. What was once Judaea had become, by imperial decree, the province of Syria Palaestina. Meanwhile, in the city once called Jerusalem, on the very site of the demolished Temple, a giant statue was raised of Hadrian, armoured and victorious, seated on a horse, riding as though to trample down every last memory of what Aelia Capitolina had originally been.

In Rome, the celebrations were muted. Although Severus was granted honours appropriate to his achievement, Hadrian was in no mood to hold a triumph. It was not his wish to draw attention to Bar Kokhba's revolt. The war, which had taken him wholly by surprise, might almost have been designed by the gods to humiliate him, and make a mockery of all his dreams of peace: a squalid, inglorious business. Certainly, settled back in the capital after his many travels, the ageing emperor appeared exhausted, embittered, disillusioned. If Antinous, by plunging into the waters of the Nile, had indeed won his lover a new lease of life, then it had brought Hadrian little joy. His mood, darkened by bereavement and disappointment, increasingly alarmed his friends. Many, like Arrian, kept well away from the emperor. Again and again, senators whom Hadrian had particularly admired ended up the objects of his hatred, envied and detested for the very qualities that had once led him to consider them potential successors. Ever darker stories were told of his mood swings. It was claimed, for instance, that when Apollodorus, the great engineer who had designed Trajan's bridge over the Danube, presumed to criticise Hadrian's plans for a temple, he was put to death. 'A man in command of thirty legions must always be reckoned more learned than anyone else.'[61] This, an observation by a scholar explaining why he had ceded a point of literary criticism to Hadrian, had once been taken as a joke. No longer. Senators, speaking in hushed tones, dreaded the worst. Meanwhile, Hadrian had fallen ill. Unable to travel the world, he retreated to an immense villa beyond Rome, 'which had been built for him in a marvellous manner, so that he was able to give to its extensive range of features the names of various provinces and places'.[62] Here, the much-travelled Caesar might imagine himself back in Alexandria, or in Athens, or in the vale below Mount Olympus. Masterpieces garnered from across the empire – paintings, fittings, bronzes – stood everywhere. So too did statues of Antinous.

Below the vast expanse of the villa – the reception halls, the dining rooms, the pavilions, the water features – there stretched an underground chamber designed to simulate the realm of the dead. It was glimmering, cold, unlit. Hadrian had no happy expectations of the afterlife. There would be no laughter there, no jokes. Nor, however, did the ailing Caesar find much joy any more in the land of

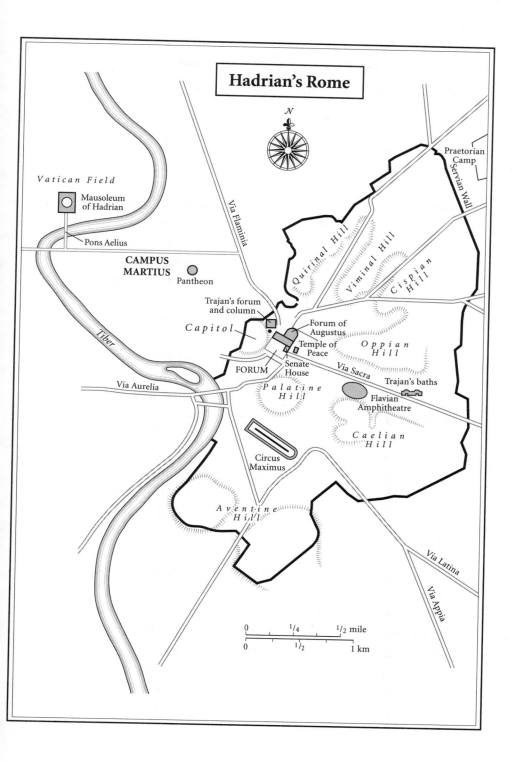

Hadrian's Rome

N

Vatican Field

Mausoleum of Hadrian

Pons Aelius

CAMPUS MARTIUS

Pantheon

Tiber

Via Flaminia

Trajan's forum and column

Capitol

FORUM

Via Aurelia

Forum of Augustus

Temple of Peace

Senate House

Via Sacra

Palatine Hill

Quirinal Hill

Viminal Hill

Cispian Hill

Praetorian Camp

Servian Wall

Oppian Hill

Trajan's baths

Flavian Amphitheatre

Caelian Hill

Circus Maximus

Aventine Hill

Via Latina

Via Appia

0		1/4		1/2 mile

0		1/2		1 km

the living. Sick and paranoid, he attempted a bungled suicide, forced his elderly brother-in-law to kill himself on a charge of conspiracy, had his great-nephew put to death for plotting a coup. Yet Hadrian – even as the talk in the senate was all of a new reign of terror, of a return to the dark days of Nero or Domitian – had not abandoned his responsibilities. 'My faculties', he insisted, 'are unimpaired.'[63] He had no intention of permitting the empire to implode on his death into civil war, nor for his statues to be toppled by vengeful mobs. Accordingly, on 24 January 138 – his sixty-second birthday – Hadrian summoned the leading men of the senate to his sickbed. There he announced to them a plan for the future of the empire designed to preserve its stability for many decades to come. First, he proclaimed his intention to adopt a man universally admired for 'his nobility of character, his mildness, his compassion, his prudence, who was neither young enough to do anything rash nor so old as to be neglectful of his duties':[64] a senator by the name of Titus Aurelius Antoninus. Antoninus in turn, the emperor decreed, was to adopt the most cherished of Hadrian's great-nephews, a young man of immense promise named Marcus Annius Verus. After taking a few days to decide whether he felt equal to the challenge of ruling the world, Antoninus accepted Hadrian's proposal. He was duly adopted on 25 February, becoming Titus Aelius Hadrianus Caesar Antoninus. Marcus Annius, after his own adoption by Antoninus, became Marcus Aurelius.

That July, when Hadrian died in Baiae, the succession was seamless. Antoninus, fully justifying his soubriquet of 'Pius', met all his adoptive father's expectations of him: he protected Hadrian's memory from vengeful elements within the senate, had him elevated to the ranks of the gods, and conducted his funerary rites in strict obedience to the dead man's wishes. Work had begun on Hadrian's mausoleum a full decade previously. Situated on the far side of the Tiber from the Campus Martius, in an undeveloped neighbourhood named the Vatican Field, the structure had been designed on such a massive scale that Hadrian's ashes were only finally interred there in 139, a full year after the emperor's death. Located as it was within eyesight of Augustus' tomb, sealed forty years previously, after Nerva's ashes had been laid there, Hadrian's mausoleum was designed both as homage to Rome's greatest emperor and as a declaration of independence. It would, of course, have been sacrilege for any Caesar to withhold honour from the man who had redeemed the Roman people from ruin and ensured their greatness for all eternity. Equally, it was fruit of the very peace established by Augustus that Rome, Italy and the empire were no longer what they had been.

Hadrian's mausoleum, however, was not the most stunning monument raised by the emperor to this seeming paradox. That was to be found on the opposite side of the Tiber, in the heart of the Campus Martius. Here stood the Pantheon: the great temple to all the gods originally built under Augustus, and then restored by Domitian. Hadrian had rebuilt it again. This, to anyone approaching the temple, was not immediately obvious. The portico, the inscription, the roof: all appeared much as they had originally, back in the time of Augustus. Only when the visitor passed into the main body of the temple was it possible to appreciate just how radically, just how brilliantly, Hadrian had redesigned it. Never before had there been so immense, so sublime a dome. It appeared, to those who gazed up at it in stupefaction, less a ceiling 'than the very heavens'.[65] The Pantheon was just as it had always been; but it was also utterly transformed.

Such was the time-honoured Roman way of managing change. The phrase *novae res* – 'novel enterprises' – remained what it had always been: a warning, a nightmare, a curse. Yet Rome, a city once bounded by the limits of seven hills, now ruled a dominion stretching from Caledonia to Arabia. It was a measure of just how incomparably great the empire of the Roman people had become that the entire world, under the benign and placid rule of Antoninus Pius, seemed blessed by peace. It was as though history itself had come to an end. The bloodline of Augustus might be no more, but seventy years on from the civil war that had followed Nero's death, a Caesar still ruled over Rome. When a senator from Athens – both a consul and a tutor to Marcus Aurelius — appropriated the grove where Egeria had once spoken to Rome's second king, and turned it into a water feature, for the delectation of visitors to his garden, the spring continued to chatter just as it always had. When soldiers in remote provinces marked out the limits of Roman rule with timber, turf or stone, the existence of such fortifications in no way implied any diminishment in their martial ardour. Quite the opposite. Antoninus Pius himself might never once, over the entire course of his career, have experienced military service; but Rome's armies, stationed along the Rhine or the Danube, in darkest Britain or Africa, remained as proficient as they had ever been. Universal though the Pax Romana reigned, no one ever doubted what it was founded upon. Peace was the fruit of victory — eternal victory. It was a soldier in the wilds beyond Palestine, scratching on a rock face, who put it best, perhaps: 'The Romans always win.'[66]

TIMELINE

753 BC:	The foundation of Rome.
509:	The expulsion of the monarchy, and the establishment of the Republic.
340:	Manlius Torquatus executes his son for a breach of military discipline.
146:	The Romans destroy Corinth.
63:	Pompey captures Jerusalem.
53:	Crassus is defeated and killed by the Parthians at Carrhae.
50:	Julius Caesar completes the conquest of Gaul.
49:	Civil war breaks out between Caesar and his enemies in the senate.
44:	The assassination of Caesar.
43:	The murder of Cicero.
30:	The suicide of Antony. The annexation of Egypt.
10:	Herod the Great completes the Temple of Jerusalem.
AD 9:	The Varian Disaster.

14:	The death of Augustus. Tiberius becomes emperor.
37:	The death of Tiberius. Caligula becomes emperor.
41:	The assassination of Caligula. Claudius becomes emperor.
53:	Nero marries Octavia.
54:	The death of Claudius. Nero becomes emperor.
55:	The death of Britannicus.
58:	Nero falls in love with Poppaea Sabina.
59:	The murder of Agrippina. The Pompeians are banned from staging gladiator fights.
60:	Boudicca's revolt.
62:	Nero divorces, exiles and executes Octavia. He marries Poppaea Sabina.
64:	The Great Fire of Rome.
65:	The death of Poppaea Sabina.
66:	Outbreak of the Judaean revolt.
67:	Nero competes in the Olympic Games and marries Sporus. Vespasian pacifies Galilee.
68:	The rebellion of Julius Vindex. The death of Nero. Galba becomes emperor.
69:	(1 January): Mutiny on the Rhine.
	(2–3 January): Vitellius proclaimed emperor by the legions on the Rhine.
	(10 January): Galba adopts Piso.
	(15 January): Murder of Galba and Piso. Otho recognised as emperor by the senate.
	(March): Caecina crosses the Alps.

(14 April): The first battle of Cremona.

(16 April): Otho commits suicide.

(Late April): Vitellius arrives in Lugdunum.

(1 July): Vespasian proclaimed emperor in Alexandria.

(16 July): Vitellius enters Rome.

(Late July): Mucianus leaves Syria for Italy.

(Late August): Antonius Primus invades Italy.

(September): Civilis leads the Batavians against the Vitellian legions on the Rhine.

(18 October): Caecina switches sides from the Vitellians to the Flavians.

(24 October): The second battle of Cremona.

(26 October): The sack of Cremona.

(18 December): Vitellius tries and fails to abdicate.

(19 December): The storming of the Flavian positions on the Capitol and the murder of Flavius Sabinus.

(20 December): Antonius captures Rome. Murder of Vitellius.

(Late December): Arrival of Mucianus in Rome.

70: Mucianus establishes Flavian rule in Rome. Suppression of anti-Flavian factions in Gaul and along the Rhine. Titus captures Jerusalem. Vespasian arrives in Rome.

71: Vespasian and Titus celebrate their triumph.

73: Capture of Masada.

75: Dedication by Vespasian of the Temple of Peace.

79: Death of Vespasian. Titus becomes emperor. Death of Nigidius Maius. The eruption of Vesuvius.

80:	Inauguration of the Colosseum.
81:	Death of Titus. Domitian becomes emperor.
82:	Agricola invades Caledonia.
83:	Agricola defeats the Caledonians and sends a fleet past the northernmost point of Britain. Domitian campaigns against the Chatti.
86:	Defeat of Fuscus by the Dacians. Abandonment of Caledonia.
89:	Saturninus' mutiny.
91:	Execution of Cornelia, the chief Vestal.
96:	Assassination of Domitian. Nerva succeeds him as emperor. Dio of Prusa returns home from exile.
97:	The Praetorians march on the Palatine and take Nerva hostage. Nerva adopts Trajan.
98:	Death of Nerva. Trajan becomes emperor.
99:	Trajan enters Rome for the first time as emperor.
101:	Trajan embarks on the conquest of Dacia.
102:	Trajan celebrates a triumph over the Dacians.
105:	Trajan leaves Rome to resume the conquest of Dacia.
106:	The capture of Sarmizegetusa and the death of Decebalus.
107:	Trajan returns to Rome from Dacia.
110:	Pliny the Younger becomes governor of Bithynia and Pontus.
112:	Trajan dedicates his new forum and baths complex.
113:	Trajan leaves Rome for Parthia. Death of Pliny the Younger (?).

115:	Earthquake in Antioch.
116:	Trajan enters Ctesiphon and reaches the Persian Gulf. The outbreak of Parthian insurgency and Judaean revolt.
117:	Death of Trajan. Hadrian becomes emperor. He abandons Trajan's eastern conquests.
118:	Hadrian arrives in Rome for the first time as emperor.
121:	Hadrian leaves Rome for the Rhine.
122:	Hadrian arrives in Britain.
123:	Hadrian heads east. He visits Athens for the first time as emperor.
128:	Hadrian visits Lambaesis in Africa. He returns to Athens.
129:	Hadrian leaves Greece. He founds the *colonia* of Aelia Capitolina on the site of Jerusalem.
130:	Hadrian in Egypt. The death of Antinous.
132:	Hadrian inaugurates the Panhellenion in Athens. The Bar Kokhba revolt breaks out in Judaea.
136:	Suppression of the Bar Kockba revolt.
138:	Hadrian adopts Antoninus Pius. Antoninus Pius adopts Marcus Aurelius. Death of Hadrian.

DRAMATIS PERSONAE

The Beginnings of Rome

ROMULUS: Founder and first king of Rome.

NUMA POMPILIUS: Second king of Rome. Consorted with a nymph.

TARQUIN THE PROUD: The last king of Rome, expelled in 509 BC.

LUCRETIA: A noble virgin, assaulted by Tarquin's son.

MANLIUS TORQUATUS: A military hero, famed for putting discipline above family.

The Last Days of the Roman Republic

POMPEY ('THE GREAT'): The most powerful man in Rome during the last decades of the Republic.

CRASSUS: A fabulously wealthy power-broker who died fighting the Parthians.

JULIUS CAESAR: The conqueror of Gaul whose ambitions led to civil war and his own subsequent dictatorship. Assassinated in 44 BC.

CICERO: Rome's most famous orator. Murdered in 43 BC on the orders of Mark Antony.

MARK ANTONY: The rival of the future Augustus for the rule of the world.

Augustus and His Dynasty

AUGUSTUS: Great-nephew and adopted son of Julius Caesar. The founder of Rome's first imperial dynasty, and commemorated as the city's original emperor.

VARUS: Governor of Germany who lost three legions in the 'Varian disaster'.

TIBERIUS: Rome's second emperor.

PONTIUS PILATE: Prefect of Judaea under Tiberius.

CALIGULA: Rome's third emperor. Famously difficult to get along with.

CLAUDIUS: Rome's fourth emperor. The conqueror of Britain. Married his niece.

AGRIPPINA: Claudius' niece, Nero's mother.

BRITANNICUS: Claudius' son. Died under suspicious circumstances shortly after Nero had become emperor.

OCTAVIA: Claudius' daughter. Nero's first wife. Died under suspicious circumstances shortly after Nero had divorced her.

ANTONIUS FELIX: Upwardly mobile slave of Claudius' mother who ended up governing Judaea and marrying the sister of Herod Agrippa.

The Age of Nero

NERO: Emperor and showman.

ACTE: Nero's first love.

POPPAEA SABINA: Nero's second wife. The love of his life.

STATILIA MESSALINA: Nero's third wife. Did not resemble Poppaea Sabina.

SPORUS: Young boy castrated on Nero's orders. Did resemble Poppaea Sabina.

TIGELLINUS: Prefect of the Praetorians. Thuggish.

NYMPHIDIUS: Prefect of the Praetorians. Ambitious.

CALVIA CRISPINILLA: Nero's 'tutor in sexual depravity'.

PETRONIUS ARBITER: The most stylish man at Nero's court. Author of the *Satyricon*.

CORBULO: The greatest general of his age. Forced to commit suicide by Nero.

CESTIUS GALLUS: Governor of Syria. Incompetent.

GESSIUS FLORUS: Financial administrator of Judaea. Grasping.

CLODIUS MACER: Governor of Africa. Rebellious.

JULIUS VINDEX: Descendant of Gallic kings. Co-conspirator with Galba against Nero.

VIRGINIUS RUFUS: Commander of the Rhine. Defeats Vindex.

PETRONIUS TURPILIANUS: Commander of Nero's troops in Italy.

EPAPHRODITUS: Nero's secretary, later put to death by Domitian.

Galba's Rise and Fall

GALBA: Governor of Spain. Leader of a successful revolt against Nero. The first of Rome's emperors not to claim a dynastic link to Augustus.

OTHO: Former husband of Poppaea Sabina and friend of Nero. Joins Galba's revolt. Rules as emperor for three months.

CAECINA: Ambitious and inveterate trouble-maker.

CORNELIUS LACO: Galba's appointment as Praetorian prefect.

CIGONIUS VARRO: Ghost-writer who picks the wrong side.

LUCIUS CALPURNIUS PISO FRUGI LICINIANUS: Galba's adopted son. Does not last long.

Vitellius and the Northern Frontier

VITELLIUS: Commander of Lower Germany. Rules as emperor for eight months. Fond of pies.

GERMANICUS: Vitellius' son.

ASIATICUS: Vitellius' favourite and freedman.

HORDEONIUS FLACCUS: Commander of Upper Germany.

FABIUS VALENS: Colleague and rival of Caecina.

JULIUS SABINUS: Self-proclaimed emperor of Gaul. Supposedly a descendant of Julius Caesar.

The Flavians

VESPASIAN: Commander of the Roman forces in Judaea. The last emperor standing in the year of the four emperors.

TITUS: Vespasian's eldest son. The conqueror of Jerusalem. Remembered as a man 'adored and doted upon by the whole of humanity'.

DOMITIAN: Vespasian's youngest son, and Titus' heir as emperor. Not remembered as a man 'adored and doted upon by the whole of humanity'.

FLAVIUS SABINUS: Vespasian's elder brother. City prefect under Vitellius.

MARCUS ULPIUS TRAJANUS: Senator from Baetica. The commander of X Fretensis under Vespasian. The father of Trajan.

BASILIDES: Syrian prophet.

GAIUS LICINIUS MUCIANUS: Governor of Syria. Vespasian's plenipotentiary. A lover of wonders and elephants.

TIBERIUS JULIUS ALEXANDER: Prefect of Egypt.

MARCUS ANTONIUS PRIMUS: Commander of VII Galbiana. Fond of cutting corners.

JULIUS BRIGANTICUS: Batavian auxiliary commander.

QUINTUS PETILLIUS CERIALIS: Relative by marriage of Vespasian. Governor of Britain.

HELVIDIUS PRISCUS: Nostalgic for the lost days of the Republic. Put to death under Vespasian.

PLINY ('THE ELDER'): Equestrian, admiral, encyclopaedist.

LARCIUS LICINIUS: Governor of Spain, with a talent for giving offence.

Dramatis Personae

ANTONIA CAENIS: Secretary to Claudius' mother, much beloved by Vespasian.

DOMITIA LONGINA: Corbulo's daughter, Domitian's wife.

TITUS FLAVIUS CLEMENS: Grandson of Flavius Sabinus. Put to death by Domitian.

FLAVIA DOMITILLA: Granddaughter of Vespasian. Put to death by Domitian.

EARINUS: Eunuch owned and freed by Domitian.

AGRICOLA: Governor of Britain and conqueror of Caledonia.

CORNELIUS FUSCUS: Praetorian prefect.

ANTONIUS SATURNINUS: Governor of Upper Germany. Leads a mutiny against Domitian.

LAPPIUS MAXIMUS: Governor of Lower Germany. Refuses to join Saturninus' mutiny.

ACILIUS GLABRIO: Senatorial lion-wrestler. Put to death by Domitian.

Pompeii and the Bay of Naples

GNAEUS ALLEIUS NIGIDIUS MAIUS: The grand old man of Pompeian politics.

MARCUS EPIDIUS SABINUS: Pompeii's coming man.

AULUS UMBRICIUS SCAURUS: Garum tycoon.

CLODIA NIGELLA: Pig-keeper.

TITUS SUEDIUS CLEMENS: Centurion. Vespasian's agent in Pompeii. Tourist in Egypt.

POMPONIANUS: Senator with a villa in Stabiae. Friend of Pliny the Elder.

Kings and Queens

HEROD THE GREAT: Ruler of Judaea under Augustus.

HEROD AGRIPPA: Great-grandson of Herod the Great.

BERENICE: Herod Agrippa's sister. Titus' lover.

MITHRIDATES: Client king from Pontus overly fond of a joke.

CARTIMANDUA: Queen of the Brigantes.

DECEBALUS: King of the Dacians. Defeated by Trajan.

CHOSROES: King of the Parthians. Defeated by Trajan.

Rebels Against Rome

THEUDAS: Would-be Judaean miracle-worker.

'THE EGYPTIAN': Would-be Judaean miracle-worker.

BOUDICCA: British queen.

ELEAZAR: Judaean priest.

YOSEF BEN MATTITYAHU: Commander of the rebel forces in Galilee. Captured by Vespasian. Historian. Better known as Josephus.

VELEDA: German seeress.

MARICCUS: Gaul believed by his followers to be the son of a god.

JULIUS CIVILIS: Batavian auxiliary commander who may or may not have led a rebellion against Roman rule.

SIMEON BAR KOKHBA: Leader of the Judaean revolt against Hadrian.

The Age of Trajan

MARCUS COCCEIUS NERVA: Distinguished senator who briefly ruled as emperor following the assassination of Domitian.

TRAJAN: The best of emperors.

PLINY ('THE YOUNGER'): Nephew of Pliny the Elder. Owner of a large number of villas. Distinguished orator. Enthusiastic letter writer. Governor of Bithynia and Pontus.

TACITUS: Nephew of Agricola. Historian.

APOLLODORUS: Architect.

DIO CHRYSOSTOM: Philosopher.

LUSIUS QUIETUS: Mauritanian prince. Governor of Judaea.

The Age of Hadrian

HADRIAN: Trajan's heir as emperor.

SABINA: Hadrian's wife.

ACILIUS ATTIANUS: Hadrian's guardian and – briefly – Praetorian prefect.

SEPTICIUS CLARUS: Praetorian prefect in the wake of Attianus' dismissal. Patron of Suetonius.

SUETONIUS: Hadrian's chief secretary. Biographer.

PHLEGON: Freedman. Compiler of wonders.

ARRIAN: Senator from Bithynia. Historian, senator, governor of Baetica.

EPICTETUS: Philosopher.

PHILOPAPPUS: Fabulously well-connected mover and shaker in Athens.

JULIA BALBILLA: Philopappus' sister. Sabina's friend.

ANTINOUS: Hadrian's beloved. Drowned in mysterious circumstances. Became a god.

JULIUS SEVERUS: Governor of Britain. Appointed by Hadrian to pacify Judaea.

NOTES

Preface

1   Aelius Aristides. *Regarding Rome*: 13
2   C. E. Stevens, quoted by Breeze, p. xv
3   From an interview given by Martin in 2014: https://www.youtube.com/watch?v=bhpQwiz0Gq0
4   Rudyard Kipling, 'On the Great Wall', in *Puck of Pook's Hill* (London, 1906).
5   Gibbon, vol. 1, p. 103
6   Ibid: p. 31
7   Temin, p. 2
8   Revelation. 17.6
9   Ibid: 17.18
10   Ibid: 18.16–17
11   Matthew. 20.16
12   From a life of Saint Gregory the Great, written in the early eighth century by an anonymous monk of Whitby. Quoted by Vickers, p. 71
13   Origen. *Against Celsus*: 2.8
14   Quoted by Horbury, p. 15. 'The biblical and rabbinic title *nasi* used by Simeon bar Kosiba [the leader of the Jewish revolt against Hadrian] is also applied to the modern head of state, and is then rendered in English as "president".'
15   Florus. *Epitome*: 1.1

I. The Sad and Infernal Gods

1   Ovid. *Tristia*: 1.5.69–70
2   Cassius Dio: 53.16

3   Suetonius. *Life of the Deified Augustus*: 28
4   Plutarch. *Numa Pompilius*: 4.2
5   Livy: 1.59
6   Tacitus. *Annals*: 13.45
7   Ovid. *Tristia*: 4.4.15
8   Suetonius. *Life of the Deified Augustus*: 53
9   Cassius Dio: 53.19.3
10 Statius. *Silvae*: 5.211–12
11 Seneca. *On Consolation: To His Mother Helvia*: 10.4
12 From a papyrus fragment found at Oxyrhynchus in Egypt. Quoted by Capponi, p. 69
13 Tacitus. *Annals*: 16.6
14 Suetonius. *Nero*: 31
15 Martial. *Book of Spectacles*: 2.8
16 Ibid: 2.4
17 Cassius Dio: 63.22.1
18 Suetonius. *Nero*: 40
19 Cicero. *Against Verres*: 2.4.82
20 Ovid. *Black Sea Letters*: 4.9.68
21 Seneca. *On Benefits*: 4.28.2
22 From an inscription found in 1887 at Karditza, Greece. Smallwood (1967), p. 64
23 Sophocles. Fragment 837
24 Plutarch. *Romulus*: 11
25 Such at any rate is the most popular theory. See Lyes, p. 53
26 Varro, quoted by Macrobius. *Saturnalia*: 1.16.18
27 Suetonius. *Nero*: 49
28 Tacitus. *Histories*: 1.89
29 Ibid: 1.4
30 Ibid
31 Ibid: 1.73
32 That Calvia came from Africa is nowhere stated in our sources, but only a woman with substantial holdings and contacts there could possibly have influenced events in the way that she did in 69.
33 Tacitus. *Histories*: 1.5
34 Josephus. *The Judaean War*: 3.123
35 For this theory, see Morgan (2000), pp. 486–7
36 Suetonius. *Nero*: 16
37 The evidence for this derives from an inscription found on the site of the warehouses, and which had been set up in the autumn of 68.
38 Tacitus. *Histories*: 1.7
39 Ibid: 1.16
40 Ibid
41 Suetonius. *Otho*: 5

42 Ibid: 6
43 So, at any rate, Plutarch reports. According to Tacitus he was arrested, sentenced to exile on a remote island, and put to death before he could reach it.
44 Tacitus. *Histories*: 1.49

II. Four Emperors

1 Ausonius. 'On Bissula': 17–18
2 Tacitus. *Germania*: 4
3 *Res Gestae*: 3
4 Tacitus. *Histories*: 4.73
5 Livy: 22.38
6 For this explanation of the origin of the name – a thoroughly convincing one – see Bishop (1990).
7 Horace. *Odes*: 3.6
8 Tacitus. *Annals*: 4.4
9 Livy: 8.7
10 Suetonius. *The Deified Julius*: 24
11 Livy: 44.39
12 Josephus. *The Judaean War*: 3.83
13 Ulpian: 39.1.42
14 Ennius. *Annals*: 5
15 Such, at any rate, is the evidence from Vetera, which, like Mogontiacum, was a double-legionary base, but where – unlike in Mainz – the foundations of the first-century AD fortress have survived.
16 This was the report of Tacitus, our best and primary source for the events that led up to the proclamation of Vitellius as emperor. Suetonius, in a much more lurid account, has a posse of soldiers surprising him in his sleeping quarters, carrying him round Cologne on their shoulders, and then accidentally setting fire to his headquarters.
17 Tacitus. *Annals*: 1.62
18 Tacitus. *Histories*: 1.50
19 Ibid: 2.8
20 *Sibylline Oracles*: 4.119
21 Aristotle. *Politics*: 1327b
22 Josephus. *The Judaean War*: 1.65
23 Ibid: 2.278
24 Tacitus. *Histories*: 5.10
25 Ibid: 5.4
26 Ibid: 5.5
27 Ibid
28 Theophrastus. Quoted by Goodman (2007), p. 282

29   Seneca, as quoted by Augustine. *The City of God*: 6.11
30   Smallwood (1967). No. 370
31   Philo. 'Embassy to Gaius': 38
32   Pliny: 5.70
33   Josephus. *The Judaean War*: 2.390
34   Ibid: 2.362
35   So, at any rate, Suetonius reported (*Vespasian*: 4)
36   Tacitus. *Annals*: 13.35
37   Suetonius. *The Deified Vespasian*: 1
38   Ibid: 20
39   Tacitus. *Histories*: 2.78
40   2 Thessalonians. 2.4
41   Tacitus. *Histories*: 2.78
42   Suetonius. *The Deified Vespasian*: 4
43   Josephus. *Life*: 16
44   Josephus. *The Judaean War*: 3.401–2
45   Tacitus. *Histories*: 4.74
46   Strabo: 4.1.2
47   Pliny: 30.4
48   Tacitus. *Histories*: 2.32
49   Ibid: 2.46
50   Ibid: 2.47
51   Suetonius. *Otho*: 12
52   Tacitus. *Histories*: 2.89
53   Suetonius. *Vitellius*: 11
54   Dio: 65.10
55   Josephus. *The Judaean War*: 4.626
56   Daniel. 7.7–8
57   Tacitus. *Histories*: 2.84
58   Ibid: 4.61
59   Josephus. *The Judaean War*: 2.401
60   Isaiah. 11.4
61   Josephus. *The Judaean War*: 3.516
62   Ibid: 5.41

III. A World at War

1   Ovid. *Metamorphoses*: 15.209–11
2   Frontinus: 4.7.2
3   Velleius Paterculus: 2.100.2
4   Calpurnius Siculus: 7.43–4
5   Tacitus. *Histories*: 2.88
6   Dio: 64.13

7   Tacitus. *Histories*: 3.32

8   Pliny: 16.5

9   Dio: 61.3

10 Pliny: 16.3

11 Tacitus. *Germania*: 29

12 *ILS*: 2558. The inscription dates from Hadrian's time.

13 Tacitus. *Histories*: 4.22

14 Ennius. *Annals*: 247

15 Tacitus. *Histories*: 3.54

16 Ibid: 3.63

17 Tacitus. *Histories*: 3.67

18 Ibid: 3.68

19 Ibid: 3.70. Suetonius, for what it is worth, reports that Vitellius actively incited his men to attack the Capitol; but this seems – to put it mildly – improbable.

20 Ibid: 3.72

21 Ibid: 3.83

22 Tacitus. *Histories*: 3.85

23 So Suetonius reports (*Vespasian*: 7). In Tacitus' account of the incident, the second invalid had a withered hand (*Histories*: 4.81).

24 Tacitus, citing Flavian propaganda, reports that some of the legions did in fact take the oath of loyalty to Vespasian; but his subsequent narrative demonstrates the unreliability of this claim.

25 Tacitus. *Histories*: 4.54

26 The phrase appears in the third head of an inscription on a bronze tablet that survived thanks to its incorporation into an altar in the basilica of St John Lateran, and is now in the Capitoline Museum.

27 Dio: 66.2. The evidence for Mucianus' presence on the Palatine derives from lead pipes stamped with his name: 'the only ones found on the Palatine [in the first century AD] not mentioning a member of the imperial family'. (de Kleijn (2013), p. 437)

28 Tacitus. *Histories*: 4.86

29 Dio: 65.2. Suetonius (*Domitian*: 1) reports the same joke. Both men interpret it as an expression of Vespasian's foreboding that Domitian will prove a tyrant, and is already – even as a young man – plotting treachery; but this is plainly a misreading. Likewise, the claims made by Tacitus (*Histories*: 4.86) that Domitian, as an eighteen-year-old, was secretly plotting rebellion against his father tell us more about Tacitus himself, and the loathing he felt for the emperor that Domitian became, than about anything that is actually likely to have happened in the summer of AD 70.

30 Cicero. *Philippics*: 6.19

31 Josephus. *The Judaean War*: 3.248

32 Such, at any rate, is what Josephus claims to have witnessed during the siege that ended with his being taken prisoner by Vespasian (ibid: 3.246)

33 Ibid: 5.223

34 Virgil. *Aeneid*: 6.852–3

35 Josephus. *The Judaean War*: 5.353

36 Ibid: 5.515

37 Ibid: 5.451

38 Tacitus. *Histories*: 5.12

39 Josephus. *The Judaean War*: 6.285

40 Josephus reports that the Temple was torched 'in defiance of Caesar's wishes' (*The Judaean War*: 6.266). But since Josephus is constantly trying to square his devotion to the customs of his people with his status as a Flavian client, this probably tells us more about him than it does about Titus himself. Flavian propaganda certainly revelled in the burning of the Temple. In his account of its destruction, Dio reports that the legionaries were so nervous of despoiling it that Titus actually had to urge them to overcome their superstitious qualms (65.6).

41 Josephus. *The Judaean War*: 6.275

42 Ibid: 7.2

43 Dionysus of Halicarnassus: 2.34

44 Josephus. *The Judaean War*: 7.118

45 Statius. *Punica*: 3.596

46 Martial. *Book of Spectacles*: 2.11

47 Josephus. *The Judaean War*: 7.147

48 Quoted by Mason (2016), p. 4. His opening chapter, 'A Famous and Unknown War', is a brilliant example of recognising something that had always been staring historians in the face.

49 Pausanias: 7.17

50 From a fragmentary inscription written in Greek found at Ardea, just south of Rome, in 1947 (*L'Année épigraphique*: 1953.25)

51 Plutarch. 'On Love'

52 Suetonius. *The Deified Vespasian*: 14

53 Tacitus. *Histories*: 1.50

54 Pliny: 36.102. Pliny specifies that the Temple of Peace is one of the three most beautiful structures in the world – the other two being a basilica in the Forum and the forum of Augustus.

55 Suetonius. *The Deified Vespasian*: 23

56 Ibid

IV. Sleeping Giants

1 Strabo: 5.4.3

2 Ibid: 5.4.8

3 Petronius: 48.4. The speaker is a vulgar parvenu – a further refinement of the satire.
4 *Aetna*: 432
5 Pliny: 18.110
6 Vitruvius: 2.6.1
7 Martial, in one of his epigrams (11.80.1). It was also Martial who hailed Baiae as a princeps (6.42.7).
8 Strabo: 5.4.6
9 Pliny the Younger. *Letters*: 3.5.8
10 Pliny: Preface 14
11 Ibid: 14.2
12 Ibid: 7.130
13 Philo. 'On the Contemplative Life': 48
14 Suetonius. *Vitellius*: 13
15 Pliny: 7.6
16 Ibid: 3.39
17 Ibid: 3.42
18 Ibid: 10.135
19 The narrative has to be deduced exclusively from archaeological evidence, and particularly from inscriptions, edicts and graffiti preserved in Pompeii and Herculaneum. Poppaea's engagement with the area is evident from a wooden tablet discovered in Herculaneum that records her as the owner of some brick-works near Pompeii. It is likely as well – although not conclusively proven – that the great villa complex at Oplontis, some five miles from Pompeii, belonged to her. The thesis that Poppaea persuaded Nero to revoke the ban on gladiators draws on eight instances of graffiti around the town hall hailing the emperor's 'judgement', together with various other expressions of enthusiasm for the imperial capital scrawled across the city. The case is presented in forensic and convincing detail in James L. Franklin Jr., 'Middle to Late Julio-Claudians – Neropoppaeenes', in Franklin (2001).
20 *CIL*: X.1018
21 Cicero. *On the Manilian Law*: 3.7
22 Juvenal: 10.114–15
23 Murison (2003) convincingly argues that Nerva served Vespasian as a patron at Nero's court, and that he looked after Flavian interests while Vespasian and Titus were absent in Judaea.
24 The painting no longer survives. For a detailed account of what it looked like, and its significance, see Franklin (2001), pp. 263–4
25 Macrobius: 2.3.11
26 *CIL*: IV.1177b
27 Specifically, the inscription boasted that 416 gladiators had participated in the show. See Osanna, p. 290

28 Pliny: 31.24. Although Pliny does not say so specifically, it seems that Licinus died seven days after his visit to the non-flowing springs.
29 Cicero. *On Duties*: 1.151
30 Ibid
31 Cicero. *On Duties*: 1.151
32 Cited by Curtis, p. 561
33 Cited by Hemelrijk, p. 264
34 Valerius Maximus: 8.14.5
35 Suetonius. *The Deified Vespasian*: 18
36 Seneca. *Dialogues*: 7.24.3
37 Ibid: 12.12
38 *CIL*: 4.9839b
39 Gaius. *Institutes*: 1.3.9
40 Demographic estimates in ancient history are notoriously hazy. The servile population of Italy in the first century AD has traditionally been estimated at around a third of the total, but Scheidel (2005) convincingly argues that it was closer to a quarter.
41 Diodorus Siculus: 5.38.1
42 Chrysippus, quoted by Seneca in *On Benefits* (3.22.1)
43 Plutarch. *On Curiosity*: 520c. Literally, 'the slave with a head like a sparrow or an ostrich'.
44 So, at any rate, Longinus claims. *On the Sublime*: 44.5
45 Petronius: 76
46 Dionysus of Halicarnassus: 4.23.7
47 Ibid: 4.23.2
48 Seneca. *Letters*: 27.5
49 Pliny the Younger. *Letters*: 3.5
50 Pliny: 2.192
51 Cassius Dio: 66.22.2
52 Pliny the Younger. *Letters*: 6.16
53 Cassius Dio: 66.22.4
54 Pliny the Younger. *Letters*: 6.16
55 Ibid
56 Ibid
57 Ibid
58 Pliny: 2.239
59 Ibid: 2.194
60 Martial. *Epigrams*: 4.44
61 Pliny the Younger. *Letters*: 6.20
62 Ibid

V. The Universal Spider

1   Pliny: 8.6
2   Petronius. 119.17
3   Pliny: 8.48
4   Martial. *Book of Shows*: 17
5   Fugitives from Pompeii, it seems, migrated to Capua, and from Herculaneum to Naples. Puteoli played host to refugees from both cities. See Tuck (2020).
6   Cassius Dio: 66.23
7   Suetonius. *The Deified Titus*: 8
8   Martial. *Book of Shows*: 2
9   Ibid: 5
10 Suetonius. *The Deified Titus*: 8
11 Ibid: 1
12 Pliny the Younger. *Panegyric*: 48.5
13 Martial. *Book of Shows*: 5.8
14 Statius. *Silvae*: 4.3.128–9
15 Suetonius. *Domitian*: 4
16 Statius. *Silvae*: 3.4.26
17 *CIL*: 6.826
18 Pliny: 3.42
19 Statius. *Silvae*: 4.2.14–16
20 Tacitus. *Agricola*: 23. The Romans called the Clyde 'Clota' and the Firth of Forth 'Bodotria'.
21 Statius. *Silvae*: 5.1.81–2
22 Silius. *Punica*: 3.597
23 Tacitus. *Agricola*: 27
24 Ibid: 38
25 Statius. *Silvae*: 5.1.89
26 Tacitus. *Agricola*: 40
27 Statius. *Silvae*: 5.1.84
28 Juvenal: 4.111–12
29 Suetonius. *Domitian*: 9
30 Tacitus. *Agricola*: 42
31 Tacitus. *Histories*: 1.2
32 Cassius Dio: 67.5.6
33 Statius. *Silvae*: 5.2.91–3
34 Ibid: 5.1.42
35 Such, at any rate, is the evidence of an inscription found in Hippo and published in 1952. The ultimate origin of Suetonius' family was most likely Pisaurum, a colony founded on the Adriatic coast in 184 BC.
36 Plutarch. *Life of Publicola*: 15

37 Juvenal: 3.20
38 Ibid: 1.131
39 Ibid: 3.73–4
40 Ibid: 3.84–5
41 Pliny: 2.189
42 Josephus. *Against Apion*: 2.40
43 Josephus. *Life*: 423
44 For the archaeological evidence, see Reich.
45 See Cohen for the numerous implausibilities of Josephus' account of the siege, and the failure of the archaeology to square with his account of it. The possibility that the Romans may have violated a pledge of safety is suggested by Mason (2016), pp. 573–4.
46 Josephus. *The Judaean War*: 7.336
47 Josephus. *Against Apion*: 2.291
48 Cassius Dio: 67.14
49 Suetonius. *Domitian*: 20
50 Cassius Dio: 67.9
51 Statius. *Silvae*: 1.93
52 Suetonius. *Domitian*: 14
53 Cassius Dio: 67.15
54 Evidence that Nerva was proclaimed emperor on the same day as Domitian's murder is provided by an inscription from Ostia. Collins makes a convincing case that this 'refers to a proclamation of Nerva by the praetorian guard' (p. 100), and not – as others have argued – by the senate.
55 Pliny the Younger. *Panegyric*: 52.4

VI. The Best of Emperors

1 Cassius Dio: 68.4
2 Pliny the Younger. *Panegyric*: 2.3
3 Pliny the Younger. *Letters*: 4.8.5
4 Pliny the Younger. *Panegyric*: 12.1
5 Herodotus: 5.3
6 Julian the Apostate. *The Caesars*: 327.D
7 Florus: Prologue 7
8 Pliny the Younger. *Letters*: 8.4.1
9 Cassius Dio.
10 Pliny the Younger. *Panegyric*: 4.7
11 Statius. *Silvae*: 1.65
12 Juvenal: 3.165–6
13 Seneca. *On the Tranquillity of the Soul*: 11.7
14 Juvenal: 3.257–60

15 Pliny: 36.123
16 *Historia Augusta: Alexander Severus*: 65.5
17 Pliny the Younger. *Panegyric*: 32.1
18 Pliny the Younger, *Letters*: 6.31.15
19 The phrase was Juvenal's (10.81), who coined it with satirical intent. Fronto, altogether more admiringly, summed up Trajan's commitment to *annona et spectacula* – 'the supply of corn and spectaculars' – as 'the height of political wisdom' (*Principia Historiae*: 20).
20 Pliny the Younger. *Panegyric*: 35.1
21 Strabo: 12.4.9
22 Philostratus. *Lives of the Sophists*: 1.7.2
23 Dio of Prusa: 44.9
24 Ibid: 38.15
25 Dio nowhere gives the name of this patron. Traditionally, he has been identified with Titus Flavius Sabinus, the elder brother of the Titus Flavius Clemens who was executed in 95 on a charge of atheism. Harry Sidebottom (pp. 452–3) has plausibly suggested another candidate: L. Salvius Otho Cocceianus, a nephew of Nerva, who – according to Suetonius – was executed by Domitian for celebrating his uncle's birthday.
26 Dio of Prusa: 13.1
27 Ibid: 13.8
28 Ibid: 12.19
29 Ibid: 45.13
30 Ibid: 47.18
31 Pliny the Younger. *Letters*: 4.9.4
32 Ibid: 8.14.9
33 Ibid: 10.40.2
34 Ibid: 10.98.1
35 Dio: 38.38
36 Pliny the Younger. *Letters*: 10.17a.3.
37 Dio of Prusa: 1.65
38 Ibid: 3.86
39 Ibid: 4.4
40 Ibid: 4.54
41 The story is recorded by Augustine in the fifth century (*City of God*: 4.4), but the anecdote, it seems, was already being cited by Cicero.
42 Tacitus. *Agricola*: 3
43 Revelation. 18.19
44 Ibid: 18.12–13
45 Pliny: 33.148
46 Tacitus. *Agricola*: 21
47 Tacitus. *Annals*: 1.4

48   Tacitus. *Germania*: 37
49   Ibid
50   Pliny: 7.21
51   Ibid: 6.58
52   Ibid: 6.88
53   Ibid: 12.14
54   The *Akananuru*, quoted by De Romanis (2020), p. 115, n. 43
55   Juvenal: 1
56   Assorted papyri demonstrate that it was being dug between 112 and 114.
57   Cassius Dio: 68.23
58   Ibid: 68.29

VII. I Build This Garden for Us

1   Philo. *On the Embassy to Gaius*: 214. Philo was the uncle of Julius Alexander, the brother of the Arabarch who gilded the gates of the Temple in Jerusalem.
2   Eusebius, quoted by Jerome in his *Chronicle*: entry for the 223rd Olympiad
3   *Historia Augusta: The Life of Hadrian*: 14.11
4   Tacitus. *Annals*: 1.7
5   Pliny the Younger. *Letters*: 2.9.4
6   Suetonius. *The Deified Augustus*: 21
7   *Historia Augusta: The Life of Hadrian*: 14
8   Cassius Dio: 69.9
9   *Historia Augusta: The Life of Hadrian*: 10
10   Ibid
11   From an inscription found at Lambaesis detailing a number of Hadrian's addresses.
12   Dio of Prusa: 1.53
13   Ibid: 1.56
14   Pliny the Younger. *Letters*: 9.39
15   Dio of Prusa: 1.60
16   Ibid: 1.75
17   The biography of Arrian, whose life of Alexander is a key source for the great conqueror's military career, has to be pieced together from a wide variety of fragments – ranging from excerpts in Byzantine histories to inscriptions found in Cordoba – as well as from his surviving texts. This inevitably brings hazards. 'Erudite enquiry,' warns Sir Ronald Syme, 'has to seek after hints or traces in the writings, a seductive pastime but often hazardous and liable to deceive.' The outline of Arrian's life, however, is generally accepted – and such as it is, I have given it.
18   Smallwood (1966), p. 60
19   *Epitome of the Caesars*: 14.6

20   Strabo: 12.4.3

21   The story was reported by Arrian in his book on the Parthians.

22   Tertullian. *Apology*: 5.7

23   Cicero. *On the Ends of Good and Evil*: 5.5

24   Plutarch. *Table Talk*: 1.10

25   Pausanias: 1.3.2

26   Epictetus: 3.13.9

27   Dio of Prusa: 38.38

28   Philostratus. *Life of Apollonius*: 4.27

29   From a speech delivered by Hadrian in Cyrene. Quoted by Oliver, p. 122

30   Pausanias: 1.5.5

31   Ibid: 2.1.2

32   *Sibylline Oracles*: 5.48

33   Cassius Dio: 69.11

34   Clement of Alexandria, speaking with the full force of Christian
     disapproval, but articulating a tradition that had remained constant
     since Antinous' own lifetime. *Exhortation to the Greeks*: 4.

35   Inscription from an obelisk now standing in the Pincian Gardens in
     Rome, and almost certainly – although it is written in hieroglyphs –
     authored by Hadrian himself. Quoted by Lambert, p. 64.

36   Suetonius. *The Deified Vespasian*: 13

37   Cornelius Nepos. *Alcibiades*: 2.2

38   Plutarch. *Isis and Osiris*: 18

39   Pliny: 7.33

40   Phlegon. *On Amazing Things*: 28

41   Apuleius. *The Golden Ass*: 11.5

42   It is possible that the flood failed in both 129 and 130, the year that Hadrian
     sailed the Nile. The evidence for this, however, is sparse – deriving as it
     does principally from a lack of coins celebrating high flood waters dateable
     to the two relevant years. Nevertheless, for all that absence of evidence is
     not proof of absence, the possibility that Hadrian was confronting a crisis
     in the corn supply as he sailed upriver does add a further dimension to the
     mystery of Antinous' death. See Lambert, pp. 122–3.

43   Plutarch. *Isis and Osiris*: 54

44   For a measured survey of the reliability of this dating, see Vout, pp. 57–9

45   Cassius Dio: 69.11. Hadrian's claim that Antinous had drowned was
     derived by Dio from Hadrian's own autobiography.

46   Suetonius. *Nero*: 36

47   Speller (p. 289) offers a further possibility: 'that Antinous merely
     disappeared from the imperial entourage, possibly faking his own death'.

48   Pausanias: 1.42.2

49   From an Armenian version of Eusebius' *Chronicle*, quoted by Renberg,
     p. 173

50   Cassius Dio: 69.11

51   One of the hieroglyphic texts on the Monte Pincio obelisk in Rome.

52   From an inscription set up some time in the 130s to mark the admission
     of the city of Thyatira to the Panhellenion. Quoted by Spawforth (2012),
     p. 249

53   Tacitus. *Annals*: 15.44

54   Pliny. *Letters*: 10.96.9

55   Ibid: 10.97.2

56   Numbers. 24.17

57   Fronto. Quoted by Horbury, p. 331

58   The evidence, albeit sketchy, is widely accepted. The presence of XXII
     Deiotariana in Egypt is attested in 119, whereas an inscription from Rome
     dated to 162 omits it from an otherwise comprehensive list of the legions.
     This is the same inscription from which IX Hispana is similarly omitted.

59   Pausanias: 1.5.5

60   Cassius Dio: 69.14

61   *Historia Augusta: The Life of Hadrian*: 15.13

62   Ibid: 26.5

63   From a letter written by Hadrian to Antoninus Pius, preserved on a
     papyrus from Egypt. Quoted by Birley (1997), p. 299

64   Cassius Dio: 69.20

65   Ibid: 53.27

66   Quoted in Mattingly (1997), p. 185. The inscription was written by
     someone who signed himself 'Lauricius', in what is now southern Jordan.
     That he was a soldier seems by far the likeliest supposition – but it is also
     possible that he was a disgruntled provincial. Whoever Lauricius may
     have been, the point he was making still serves.

BIBLIOGRAPHY

Alcock, Susan, *Graecia Capta: The Landscapes of Roman Greece* (Cambridge, 1993)

Aldrete, Gregory S., *Floods of the Tiber in Ancient Rome* (Baltimore, 2007)

Allison, Penelope M., *People and Spaces in Roman Military Bases* (Cambridge, 2013)

Alston, Richard, *Aspects of Roman History 31 BC–AD 117)* (London, 2013)

Andrade, Nathanael J., *Syrian Identity in the Greco-Roman World* (Cambridge, 2013)

Andreau, Jean, *Banking and Business in the Roman World*, tr. Janet Lloyd (Cambridge, 1999)

Andreau, Jean and Raymond Descat, *The Slave in Greece and Rome*, tr. Marion Leopold (Madison, 2006)

Arnaud, Pascal and Simon Keay (eds), *Roman Port Societies: The Evidence of Inscriptions* (Cambridge, 2020)

Ash, Rhiannon, *Ordering Anarchy: Armies and Leaders in Tacitus'* Histories (London, 1999)

——'The Wonderful World of Mucianus', in *Essays in Honour of Barbara Levick* (Oxford, 2007)

Augoustakis, Antony and R. Joy Littlewood, *Campania in the Flavian Poetic Imagination* (Oxford, 2019)

Austin, N. J. E. and N. B. Rankov, *Exploratio: Military and Political Intelligence in the Roman World from the Second Punic War to the Battle of Adrianople* (London, 1995)

Badel, Christophe, *La Noblesse de l'Empire Romain: Les Masques et la Vertu* (Seyssel, 2005)

Ball, Warwick, *Rome in the East: The Transformation of an Empire* (London, 2000)

Barton, Carlin A., *Roman Honor: The Fire in the Bones* (Berkeley and Los Angeles, 2001)

Bartsch, Shadi, *Actors in the Audience: Theatricality and Doublespeak from Nero to Hadrian* (Cambridge, Mass., 1994)

Beard, Mary, *The Roman Triumph* (Cambridge, Mass., 2007)

——*Pompeii: The Life of a Roman Town* (London, 2008)

Bekker-Nielsen, Tønnes (ed.), *Rome and the Black Sea Region: Domination, Romanisation, Resistance* (Aarhus, 2005)

——*Urban Life and Local Politics in Roman Bithynia: The Small World of Dio Chrysostomos* (Aarhus, 2018)

Bennett, Julian, *Trajan:* Optimus Princeps (Abingdon, 1997)

Berlin, Andrea M. and J. Andrew Overman, *The First Jewish Revolt: Archaeology, History and Ideology* (London, 2002)

Birley, Anthony R., *Hadrian: The Restless Emperor* (Abingdon, 1997)

——'*Viri Militares* Moving from West to East in Two Crisis Years (AD 133 and 162)', in *The Impact of Mobility and Migration in the Roman Empire*, ed. E. Lo Cascio and L. E. Tacoma (Leiden, 2017)

Bishop, M. C., '*Legio V Alaudae* and the Crested Lark', *Journal of Roman Military Equipment Studies* 1, 1990

——*Handbook to Roman Legionary Fortresses* (Barnsley, 2012)

Boatwright, Mary T., *Hadrian and the Cities of the Roman Empire* (Princeton, 2000)

——'Women and Gender in the Forum Romanum', *TAPA* 141, 2011

Bosworth, A. B., 'Arrian in Baetica', *Greek, Roman and Byzantine Studies* 17, 1976

Boyle, A. J. and W. J. Dominik, *Flavian Rome: Culture, Image, Text* (Leiden, 2003)

Bradley, Keith, *Slavery and Society at Rome* (Cambridge, 1994)

Bradley, Keith and Paul Cartledge, *The Cambridge World History of Slavery: The Ancient Mediterranean World* (Cambridge, 2011)

Breeze, David J., *Hadrian's Wall: A History of Archaeological Thought* (Kendal, 2014)

Breeze, David J. and Alan Wilkins, 'Pytheas, Tacitus and Thule', *Britannia* 49, 2018

Brennan, T. Corey, *Sabina Augusta: An Imperial Journey* (Oxford, 2018)

Buttrey, T. V., 'Domitian, the Rhinoceros, and the Date of Martial's "Liber De Spectaculis"', *Journal of Roman Studies* 97, 2007

Bowman, Alan K., Edward Champlin and Andrew Lintott (eds), *Cambridge Ancient History X: The Augustan Empire, 43 BC–AD 69* (Cambridge, 1996)

Bowman, Alan K., Peter Garnsey and Dominic Rathbone (eds), *Cambridge Ancient History XI: The High Empire, AD 70–192* (Cambridge, 2000)

Campbell, J. B., *The Emperor and the Roman Army 31 BC–AD 235* (Oxford, 1984)

——*War and Society in Imperial Rome, 31 BC–AD 284* (London, 2002)

Capponi, L., 'Reflections on the Author, Context and Audience of the So-called Apotheosis of Poppaea (P.Oxy. LXXVII 5105)', *Quaderni di Storia* 86, 2017

Carradice, Ian, *Coinage and Finances in the Reign of Domitian* (Oxford, 1983)

Carroll, Maureen, 'Exploring the Sanctuary of Venus and its Sacred Grove: Politics, Cult and Identity in Roman Pompeii', *Papers of the British School at Rome* 78, 2010

Cartledge, Paul and Antony Spawforth, *Hellenistic and Roman Sparta* (Abingdon, 1989)

Champlin, Edward, *Nero* (Cambridge, Mass., 2003)

Chapman, Honora Howell and Zuleika Rodgers, *A Companion to Josephus* (Oxford, 1988)

Charles, Michael B., 'Nero and Sporus Again', *Latomus* 73, 2014

Choi, Junghwa, *Jewish Leadership in Roman Palestine from 70 CE to 135 CE* (Leiden, 2013)

Claridge, Amanda, *Rome: An Oxford Archaeological Guide* (Oxford, 2010)

Clarke, Katherine, 'An Island Nation: Re-reading Tacitus' *Agricola*', *Journal of Roman Studies* 91, 2001

Coarelli, Filippo, *The Column of Trajan* (Rome, 2000)

——*Rome and Environs: An Archaeological Guide*, tr. James J. Clauss and Daniel P. Harmon (Berkeley and Los Angeles, 2007)

Cobb, Matthew Adam, *Rome and the Indian Ocean Trade from Augustus to the Early Third Century CE* (Leiden, 2018)

——(ed.) *The Indian Ocean Trade in Antiquity: Political, Cultural and Economic Impacts* (London, 2019)

Cohen, S. J. D., 'Masada: Literary Tradition, Archaeological Remains, and the Credibility of Josephus', *Journal of Jewish Studies* 33, 1982

Coleman, Kathleen (ed.), *Martial: Liber Spectaculorum* (Oxford, 2006)

Collins, Andrew W., 'The Palace Revolution: The Assassination of Domitian and the Accession of Nerva', *Phoenix* 63, 2009

Collins, John J., *Seers, Sibyls and Sages in Hellenistic-Roman Judaism* (Leiden, 2001)

Cominesi, Aurora Raimondi, Nathalie de Haan, Eric M. Moormann and Claire Stocks, *God on Earth: Emperor Domitian* (Leiden, 2021)

Connors, Catherine, 'In the Land of the Giants: Greek and Roman Discourses on Vesuvius and the Phlegraean Fields', *Illinois Classical Studies* 40, 2015

Cooley, Alison E., *Pompeii* (London, 2003)

Cooley, Alison E. (ed.), *A Companion to Roman Italy* (Chichester, 2016)

Cooley, Alison E. and M. G. L. Cooley, *Pompeii and Herculaneum: A Sourcebook* (Abingdon, 2004)

Curtis, Robert I., 'A Personalized Floor Mosaic from Pompeii', *American Journal of Archaeology* 88, 1984

Dabrowa, A. (ed.), *The Roman and Byzantine Army in the East: Proceedings of a Colloquium Held at the Jageillonian Univeristy in September 1992* (Kraków, 1992)

D'Arms, John H., *Romans on the Bay of Naples: A Social and Cultural Study of the Villas and Their Owners from 150 BC to AD 400* (Cambridge, Mass., 1970)

——'Puteoli in the Second Century of the Roman Empire: A Social and Economic Study', *Journal of Roman Studies* 64, 1974

Darwall-Smith, Robin Haydon, *Emperors and Architecture: A Study of Flavian Rome* (Brussels, 1996)

Davies, Roy W., *Service in the Roman Army*, ed. David Breeze and Valerie A. Maxfield (Edinburgh, 1989)

De Carolis, Ernesto and Giovanni Patricelli, *Vesuvius, AD 79: The Destruction of Pompeii and Herculaneum* (Rome, 2003)

De la Bédoyère, Guy, *Praetorian: The Rise and Fall of Rome's Imperial Bodyguard* (New Haven, 2017)

De Kleijn, G., 'C. Licinius Mucianus, Leader in Time of Crisis', *Historia* 58, 2009

——'C. Licinius Mucianus, Vespasian's Co-ruler in Rome', *Mnemosyne* 66, 2013

De Quiroga, Pedro López Barja, 'Freedmen Social Mobility in Roman Italy', *Historia* 44, 1995

Den Hollander, William, *Josephus, the Emperors, and the City of Rome; From Hostage to Historian* (Leiden, 2014)

De Romanis, Frederico, 'Trajan's Canal and the Logistics of Late Antiquity India Trade', in *Interrelations Between the Peoples of the Near East and Byzantium in Pre-Islamic Times*, ed. V. Christides (Cordoba, 2015)

——*The Indo-Roman Pepper Trade and the Muziris Papyrus* (Oxford, 2020)

Dobbins, John J. and Pedar W. Foss, *The World of Pompeii* (London, 2007)

Earl, Donald, *The Moral and Political Tradition of Rome* (London, 1967)

Edmondson, Jonathan, Steve Mason and James Rives, *Flavius Josephus and Flavian Rome* (Oxford, 2005)

Edwards, Catharine, *Death in Ancient Rome* (New Haven, 2007)

Faulkner, Neil, *Apocalypse: The Great Jewish Revolt against Rome, AD 66–73* (Stroud, 2002)

Favro, Diane and Christopher Johanson, 'Death in Motion: Funeral Processions in the Roman Forum', *Journal of the Society of Architectural Historians* 69, 2010

Feldman, Louis H., 'Financing the Colosseum', *Biblical Archaeology Review* 27, 2001

Fink, Robert O., *Roman Military Records on Papyrus* (Ann Arbor, 1971)

Flohr, Miko and Andrew Wilson (eds), *The Economy of Pompeii* (Oxford, 2017)

Flower, Harriet I., *Ancestor Masks and Aristocratic Power in Roman Culture* (Oxford, 1996)

Fodorean, Florin, *The Topography and the Landscape of Roman Dacia* (Oxford, 2013)

Foley, Helene P., *The Homeric Hymn to Demeter: Translation, Commentary and Interpretive Essays* (Princeton, 1994)

Franklin, James L., 'Cn. Alleius Nigidius Maius and the Amphitheatre: "Munera" and a Distinguished Career at Ancient Pompeii', *Historia* 46, 1997

——*Pompeis Difficile Est: Studies in the Political Life of Imperial Pompeii* (Ann Arbor, 2001)

Galestin, M. C., 'Romans and Frisians: Analysis of the Strategy of the Roman Army in its Connections Across the Frontier', in G. M. Willems, W. Groenman-van Waateringe, B. L. van Beek and S. L. Wynia (eds), *Roman Frontier Studies 1995* (Oxford, 1995)

Gallia, Andrew B., *Remembering the Roman Republic: Culture, Politics, and History under the Principate* (Cambridge, 2012)

Gardner, Gregg and Kevin L. Osterloh, *Antiquity in Antiquity: Jewish and Christian Pasts in the Greco-Roman World* (Tübingen, 2008)

Gianfrotta, Piero A., 'Comments Concerning Recent Fieldwork on Roman Maritime Concrete', *International Journal of Nautical Archaeology* 40, 2011

Gibbon, Edward, *The History of the Decline and Fall of the Roman Empire* (3 vols) (London, 1994)

Goldsworthy, Adrian, *The Roman Army at War 100 BC–AD 200* (Oxford, 1996)

——*The Complete Roman Army* (London, 2003)

Goodman, Martin, 'Trajan and the Origins of Roman Hostility to the Jews', *Past & Present* 182, 2004

——*Rome & Jerusalem: The Clash of Ancient Civilizations* (London, 2007)

Grainger, John D., *Nerva and the Roman Succession Crisis of AD 96–99* (London, 2003)

Grenier, Jean-Claude, *L'Osiris Antinoos* (Montpellier, 2008)

Gruen, Erich S., *Rethinking the Other in Antiquity* (Princeton, 2011)

Grüll, Tibor and László Benke, 'A Hebrew/Aramaic Graffito and Poppaea's Alleged Jewish Sympathy', *Journal of Jewish Studies* 62, 2011

Gurukkal, Rajan, *Rethinking Classical Indo-Roman Trade: Political Economy of Eastern Mediterranean Exchange Relations* (New Delhi, 2016)

Hanson, William S. (ed.), *The Army and Frontiers of Rome* (Portsmouth, 2009)

Harris, B. F., *Bithynia Under Trajan: Roman and Greek Views of the Principate* (Auckland, 1964)

Helms, Kyle, 'Pompeii's Safaitic Graffiti', *Journal of Roman Studies* 111, 2021

Hemelrijk, Emily A., Women and Society in the Roman World: A Sourcebook of Inscriptions from the Roman West (Cambridge, 2021)

Hingley, Richard, *Conquering the Ocean: The Roman Invasion of Britain* (Oxford, 2022)

Hopkins, Keith and Mary Beard, *The Colosseum* (London, 2005)

Horbury, William, *Jewish War Under Trajan and Hadrian* (Cambridge, 2014)

Isaac, Benjamin, 'A Milestone of AD 69 from Judaea: The Elder Trajan and Vespasian', *Journal of Roman Studies* 56, 1976

——*The Limits of Empire: The Roman Army in the East* (Oxford, 1990)

——*The Invention of Racism in Classical Antiquity* (Princeton, 2013)

Isaac, Benjamin and Israel Roll, 'Legio II Traiana in Judaea', *Zeitschrift für Papyrologie und Epigraphik* 33, 1979

Jones, Brian W., *Domitian and the Senatorial Order: A Prosopographical Study of Domitian's Relationship with the Senate, AD 81–96* (Philadelphia, 1979)

——*The Emperor Titus* (Beckenham, 1984)

——*The Emperor Domitian* (London, 1992)

Jones, Christopher P., *The Roman World of Dio Chrysostom* (Cambridge, Mass., 1978)

Joshel, Sandra R., *Work, Identity, and Legal Status at Rome: A Study of the Occupational Inscriptions* (Baltimore, 2001)

——*Slavery in the Roman World* (Cambridge, 2010)

Bibliography

Joshel, Sandra R. and Lauren Hackworth Petersen, *The Material Life of Roman Slaves* (Cambridge, 2014)

Kamen, Deborah and C. W. Marshall, *Slavery and Sexuality in Classical Antiquity* (Madison, 2021)

Keay, Simon and Lidia Paroli, *Portus and its Hinterland* (London, 2011)

Knapp, Robert, 'The Poor, Latin Inscriptions, and Social History' (XII International Epigraphic Congress, 2002)

——*Invisible Romans* (London, 2011)

Köhne, Eckhart and Cornelia Ewigleben, *Gladiators and Caesars: The Power of Spectacle in Ancient Rome* (London, 2000)

Laehn, Thomas R., *Pliny's Defense of Empire* (Abingdon, 2013)

Lambert, Royston, *Beloved and God: The Story of Hadrian and Antinous* (London, 1984)

Lane Fox, Robin, *Pagans and Christians* (London, 1986)

Le Bohec, Yann, *Les legions de Rome sous le Haut-Empire* (Lyon, 2000)

Lepper, Frank and Sheppard Frere, *Trajan's Column* (Gloucester, 1988)

Levick, Barbara, *Vespasian* (Abingdon, 2017)

Lindsay, Hugh, 'Vespasian and the City of Rome: The Centrality of the Capitolium', *Acta Classica* 53, 2010

Luttwak, Edward, *The Grand Strategy of the Roman Empire: From the First Century AD to the Third* (London, 1976)

Lyes, Christopher J., 'Rethinking the Lapis Niger', *NEO* 1, 2017

MacKendrick, Paul, *The Dacian Stones Speak* (Chapel Hill, 1975)

Magness, Jodi, *Masada: From Jewish Revolt to Modern Myth* (Princeton, 2019)

Marks, Raymond and Marcello Mogetta (eds), *Domitian's Rome and the Augustan Legacy* (Ann Arbor, 2021)

Martyn, Rachelle, 'A Re-Evaluation of Manner of Death at Roman Herculaneum Following the AD 79 Eruption of Vesuvius', *Antiquity* 94, 2020

Mason, Steve, *Josephus, Judea, and Christian Origins* (Peabody, 2009)

——*A History of the Jewish War AD 66–74* (Cambridge, 2016)

Mattingly, David J. (ed.), *Dialogues in Roman Imperialism* (Portsmouth, Rhode Island, 1997)

——*An Imperial Possession: Britain in the Roman Empire, 54 BC–AD 409* (London, 2006)

——*Imperialism, Power, and Identity: Experiencing the Roman Empire* (Princeton, 2011)

Mattingly, Harold, *The Coinage of the Civil Wars of 68–69 AD* (New York, 1977)

McDermott, William C. and Anne E. Orentzel, *Roman Portraits: The Flavian-Trajanic Period* (Columbia, 1979)

McLaughlin, Raoul, *The Roman Empire and the Indian Ocean: The Ancient World Economy and the Kingdoms of Africa, Arabia and India* (Barnsley, 2014)

Meslin, Michel, *La fête des kalendes de janvier dans l'empire romain: Étude du'un rituel de Nouvel Ans* (Brussels, 1970)

Millar, Fergus, *The Roman Near East, 31 BC–AD 337* (Cambridge, Mass., 1993)

Morwood, James, *Hadrian* (London, 2013)

Mor, Menahem, *The Second Jewish Revolt: The Bar Kokhba War, 132–136 CE* (Leiden, 2016)

Morgan, Gwyn, 'Clodius Macer and Calvia Crispinilla', *Historia* 49, 2000
——*69 AD: The Year of Four Emperors* (Oxford, 2006)

Morgan, Llewelyn, '*Achilleae Comae*: Hair and Heroism According to Domitian', *Classical Quarterly* 47, 1997
——'The Eunuch and the Emperor', *History Today*, May 2016

Murison, Charles L., *Galba, Otho and Vitellius: Careers and Controversies* (Zurich, 1993)
——*Rebellion and Reconstruction: An Historical Commentary on Cassius Dio's Roman History* (Oxford, 1999)
——'M. Cocceius Nerva and the Flavians', *Transactions of the American Philological Association* 133, 2003

Murphy, Trevor, *Pliny the Elder's* Natural History: *The Empire in the Encyclopedia* (Oxford, 2004)

Olesen, J. P. (ed.), *Building for Eternity: The History and Technology of Roman Concrete Engineering in the Sea* (Oxford, 2014)

Oliver, J. H., *Greek Constitutions of Early Roman Emperors from Inscriptions and Papyri* (Philadelphia, 1989)

Oltean, Ioana A., *Dacia: Landscape, Colonisation and Romanisation* (Abingdon, 2007)

Opper, Thorsten, *Hadrian: Empire and Conflict* (London, 2008)

Osanna, Massimo, 'Games, Banquets, Handouts, and the Population of Pompeii as Deduced from a New Tomb Inscription', *Journal of Roman Archaeology* 31, 2018

Osgood, Josiah, *Claudius Caesar: Image and Power in the Early Roman Empire* (Cambridge, 2011)

Parente, Fausto and Joseph Sievers, *Josephus and the History of the Greco-Roman Period: Essays in Memory of Morton Smith* (Leiden, 1994)

Parker, Grant, *The Making of Roman India* (Cambridge, 2008)

Phang, Sara Elise, *Roman Military Service: Ideologies of Discipline in the Late Republic and Early Principate* (Cambridge, 2008)

Pigon, Jakub, 'The Identity of the Chief Vestal Cornelia', *Mnemosyne* 52, 1999

Poehler, Eric E., *The Traffic Systems of Pompeii* (Oxford, 2017)

Pollard, Elizabeth Ann, 'Pliny's *Natural History* and the Flavian *Templum Pacis*: Botanical Imperialism in First-Century CE Rome', *Journal of World History* 20, 2009

Popovic, Mladen, *The Jewish Revolt against Rome: Interdisciplinary Perspectives* (Leiden, 2011)

Rankov, Boris, 'A "Secret of Empire" (*Imperii Arcanum*): An Unacknowledged Factor in Roman Imperial Expansion', in Hanson

Reich, R., 'Women and Men at Masada: Some Anthropological Observations Based on the Small Finds (Coins, Spindles)', *Zeitschrift des Deutschen Palästina Vereins* 117, 2001

Renberg, Gil H., 'Hadrian and the Oracles of Antinous', *Memoirs of the American Academy in Rome* 55, 2010

Richardson, J. S., '*Imperium Romanum*: Empire and the Language of Power', *Journal of Roman Studies* 81,1991

Richardson, L., Jr, *A New Topographical Dictionary of Ancient Rome* (Baltimore, 1992)

Richmond, Ian, *Trajan's Army on Trajan's Column* (London, 1982)

Riggsby, Andrew M., 'Self and Community in the Younger Pliny', *Arethusa* 31, 1998

Rizzi, Marco (ed.), *Hadrian and the Christians* (Göttingen, 2000)

Roche, Paul, *Pliny's Praise: The* Panegyricus *in the Roman World* (Cambridge, 2011)

Romm, James S., *The Edges of the Earth in Ancient Thought: Geography, Exploration and Fiction* (Princeton, 1992)

Schäfer, Peter, *Judeophobia: Attitudes toward the Jews in the Ancient World* (Cambridge, Mass., 1997)

——*The History of the Jews in the Greco-Roman World* (London, 2003)

Scheidel, Walter, 'Human Mobility in Roman Italy, II: The Slave Population', *Journal of Roman Studies* 95, 2005

Schlude, Jason M., *Rome, Parthia, and the Politics of Peace: The Origins of War in the Ancient Middle East* (Abingdon, 2020)

Schwarz, Seth, *Josephus and Judaean Politics* (Leiden, 1990)

——*Imperialism and Jewish Society, 200 BCE to 640 CE* (Princeton, 2001)

——*Were the Jews a Mediterranean Society? Reciprocity and Solidarity in Ancient Judaism* (Princeton, 2010)

Shepherd, Si, *The Jewish Revolt AD 66–74* (Oxford, 2013)

Sidebottom, Harry, 'Dio of Prusa and the Flavian Dynasty', *Classical Quarterly* 46, 1992

Sigurdsson, Haraldur, Stanford Cashdollar and Stephen R. J. Sparks, 'The Eruption of Vesuvius in AD 79: Reconstruction from Historical and Volcanological Evidence', *American Journal of Archaeology* 86, 1982

Smallwood, E. Mary, *Documents Illustrating the Principates of Nerva, Trajan and Hadrian* (Cambridge, 1966)

——*Documents Illustrating the Principates of Gaius, Claudius and Nero* (London, 1967)

——*The Jews under Roman Rule* (Leiden, 1981)

Southern, Pat, *Domitian: Tragic Tyrant* (Abingdon, 1997)

Spaeth, Barbette Stanley, *The Roman Goddess Ceres* (Austin, 1996)

Spawforth, A. J., 'The Panhellenion Again', *Chiron* 29, 1999

——*Greece and the Augustan Cultural Revolution* (Cambridge, 2012)

Spawforth, A. J. and Susan Walker, 'The World of the Panhellenion. I. Athens and Eleusis', *Journal of Roman Studies* 75, 1985

——'The World of the Panhellenion. II. Three Dorian Cities', *Journal of Roman Studies* 76, 1986

Speidel, Michael P., *Emperor Hadrian's Speeches to the African Army – A New Text* (Mainz, 2006)

Speller, Elizabeth, *Following Hadrian: A Second-century Journey through the Roman Empire* (London, 2002)

Spencer, Diana, *The Roman Alexander* (Exeter, 2002)

Stefan, Alexandre, *Les guerres daciques de Domitien et de Trajan. Architecture militaire, topographie, images et histoire* (Rome, 2005)

Swain, Simon, *Dio Chrysostom: Politics, Letters and Philosophy* (Oxford, 2000)

Syme, Ronald, *Tacitus* (Oxford, 1958)

——'Pliny the Procurator', *Harvard Studies in Classical Philology* 73, 1969

——'Domitius Corbulo', *Journal of Roman Studies* 60, 1970

——'Partisans of Galba', *Historia* 31, 1982

——'The Career of Arrian', *Harvard Studies in Classical Philology* 86, 1982

——'Domitian: The Last Years', *Chiron* 13, 1983

Temin, Peter, *The Roman Market Economy* (Princeton, 2013)

Trentin, Lisa, 'Deformity in the Roman Imperial Court', *Greece & Rome* 58, 2011

Tuck, Steven L., 'Factors Contributing to the Dates of Pompeian "Munera"', *Classical Journal* 104, 2008/2009

——'Harbors of Refuge: Post-Vesuvian Population Shifts in Italian Harbor Communities', in *Reflections: Harbour City Deathscapes in Roman Italy and Beyond*, ed. Niels Bargfeldt and Jane Hjarl Petersen (Rome, 2020)

Udoh, Fabian E., *To Caesar What is Caesar's: Tribute, Taxes, and Imperial Administration in Early Roman Palestine* (Providence, 2006)

Van Buren, A. W., 'Cnaeus Alleius Nigidius Maius of Pompeii', *American Journal of Philology* 68, 1947

Varon, P., '*Emptio Ancillae/Mulieris* by Roman Army Soldiers', in Dabrowa

Vickers, Nancy J., 'Seeing is Believing: Gregory, Trajan, and Dante's Art', *Dante Studies* 101, 1983

Vout, Caroline, *Power and Eroticism in Imperial Rome* (Cambridge, 2007)

Wallace-Hadrill, Andrew, *Houses and Society in Pompeii and Herculaneum* (Princeton, 1994)

——*Herculaneum: Past and Future* (London, 2011)

Walsh, Joseph J., *The Great Fire of Rome: Life and Death in the Ancient City* (Baltimore, 2019)

Weaver, P. R. C., 'Epaphroditus, Josephus, and Epictetus', *Classical Quarterly* 44, 1994

Webster, Graham, *The Roman Imperial Army of the First and Second Centuries A D* (London, 1969)

Welch, Katherine E., *The Roman Amphitheatre: From its Origins to the Colosseum* (Cambridge, 2007)

Wells, C. M., '"The Daughters of the Regiment": Sisters and Wives in the Roman Army', *Roman Frontier Studies* 16, 1995

Wellesley, Kenneth, *The Year of the Four Emperors* (London, 2000)

Wells, Peter S., *The Barbarians Speak: How the Conquered Peoples Shaped Roman Europe* (Princeton, 1999)

Wilkinson, Paul, *Pompeii: An Archaeological Guide* (London, 2017)

Williams, Craig A., *Roman Homosexuality* (Oxford, 2010)

Wilmot, Tony (ed.), *Roman Amphitheatres and* Spectacula: *A 21st-Century Perspective* (Oxford, 2009)

Witt, R. E., *Isis in the Ancient World* (Baltimore, 1971)

Wolfson, Stan, *Tactius, Thule and Caledonia: The Achievements of Agricola's Navy in Their True Perspective* (Oxford, 2008)

Woods, David, 'Nero and Sporus', *Latomus* 68, 2009

Woolf, Greg, *Becoming Roman: The Origins of Provincial Civilization in Gaul* (Cambridge, 1998)

Yavetz, Zvi, 'Reflections on Titus and Josephus', *Greek, Roman and Byzantine Studies* 16, 1975

Yegül, Fikret K., 'The Thermo-Mineral Complex at Baiae and *De Balneis Puteolanis*', *Art Bulletin* 78, 1996

Zanker, Paul, *Pompeii: Public and Private Life*, tr. Deborah Lucas Schneider (Cambridge, Mass., 1998)

Zissos, Andrew (ed.), *A Companion to the Flavian Age of Imperial Rome* (Chichester, 2016)

INDEX

Acte (lover of Nero), 24, 34
Actium, battle of (31 BC), 12–13
Africa: canal between the Nile and the
  Red Sea, 308, 311; Carthage, 27, 38–9,
  42, 300; Cyrene (ancient Greek city),
  61, 313, 318, 330; Ethiopians, 256;
  grain ships from, 27, 38, 178, 279–80;
  Hadrian in (AD 128), 324–5; Lambaesis
  (army base), 325, 335; Macer revolt in,
  38–9, 42, 43; Mauretania, 208*, 224,
  313; Nasamonians massacred, 248;
  and Pliny, 183, 184; soldiers from on
  Hadrian's Wall, xvi; Suetonius born in,
  252; Vitellius as governor of, 70; wild
  beasts from, 223–5, 344
Agricola, Gnaeus Julius, 238–41, 242, 243,
  245–7, 255, 302, 323, 324
Agrippina (mother of Nero), 16, 17, 30, 69
Akiva, Rabbi, 354*
Alexander the Great, 73, 74, 104, 298–9, 303,
  304, 305–6, 310, 311, 312
Alexandria: grain ships from, 27, 104, 178;
  great legionary base outside, 83, 102,
  308, 354; Hadrian in (AD 130), 344, 350;
  immense scale of, 104, 300; Judaeans
  in, 80, 81, 101, 307, 313, 318; knowledge
  of India in, 306; Roman governors in,
  73, 74; slaughter of Judaeans in (AD 117),
  318; Vespasian in, 104, 123, 139
Amestris, city of, 295
Anatolia, 282–2, 293, 294–7, 301, 315; see also
  Bithynia
Annona (embodiment of the corn supply),
  27, 178, 279, 301, 347

Antinous, 341–4, 347–50, 351–2, 353, 356
Antioch, 73, 74, 80, 83, 300, 308, 310, 313,
  330; earthquake in (AD 116), 310, 330;
  Hadrian proclaimed emperor in, 315
Antoninus Pius (Titus Aelius Hadrianus
  Caesar Antoninus), xx, xxvi, 358,
  359–60
Antonius Felix, 208, 225
Antonius Primus, Marcus, 113–5, 119–22,
  123–4, 129; advance on Rome (late
  AD 69), 131–2, 135; invasion of Italy,
  114–16, 119–20, 129, 130–2; Mucianus as
  rival, 121, 133, 141, 142; and murder of
  Sabinus, 136–7, 141; victory at Cremona
  (24 October AD 69), 120–4, 130, 131;
  victory in Rome (19 December AD 69),
  137–8, 141
Apameia (Bithynian city), 284–5, 328
Apollodorus (engineer), 273, 281, 318, 356
arabarchs (tax administrators), 307
Arabic language, 187
Arganthonius (promontory), 331
Aristotle, 298
Armenia, 83, 101, 303, 304–5, 308, 318, 329
Arrian (Lucius Flavius Arrianus), 329–30,
  336, 356
Arsacids, 303, 304–5
Asia, province of, 73–4, 83, 207, 300, 301–2
Asiaticus (slave), 207, 209, 348
Assyria, 303–4, 310, 331
Athens: Eleusinian Mysteries, 29–30, 351;
  Hadrian in, xiii, 332–5, 344, 350–1, 354;
  Hadrian's renewal project in, 334–5,
  337, 338, 340, 350–1; material plundered

401

Index

Nero (Nero Claudius Caesar Augustus Germanicus): and city of Pompeii, 187, 194, 196; and death of Poppaea Sabina, 11, 14–15, 17–19, 351; extravagance of, 20–1, 75; 'Golden House' of, 20–1, 72, 73, 160–1, 168, 176, 178, 227, 280–1; legacy of, 37–8, 42–3, 44–5, 48, 72–3, 99–100, 160, 161; love of theatre/acting, 14, 29, 30, 42, 163, 229, 337; and the masses/plebs, 21, 72–3, 277; murder of his mother, 17, 30; Octavia as wife of, 16, 17, 45; orders suicide of Corbulo, 84; and Otho's exile, 44–5; and Piso's family, 49; popular nostalgia for, 72–3; portents following death of, 34; and the Praetorians, 17, 36–8; as *Princeps* (First Citizen), 11–12, 13, 14; promises after great fire, 32, 160, 234; racing of chariots, 29, 69–70, 326; rebuilding of Rome, 26, 45–6; remits Greek taxes, 29, 73, 164, 285; revolts against, 21–2, 32–3, 91, 97; as Sol, 14, 19, 20–1, 42; as son of Agrippina, 16; and spectacular entertainments, 21, 26, 118, 337; and Sporus (eunach), 24–5, 47–8; suicide of (AD 68), xxvii, 33–4, 264; and the supernatural, 14, 19, 20–1, 22–4, 26–32, 42, 47, 229, 347–8; use of death squads, 22, 42; visits Greece, 29–30, 76
Nerva, Marcus Cocceius: adopts Trajan as heir, 265–6, 268, 306, 315–16; ashes of, 359; background of, 193, 262, 264; as emperor, 264–6, 314; as patron of Dio, 289, 290, 297; and the Praetorians, 264, 265; in Vespasian's inner circle, 193
Nicaea (Bithynian city), 284, 286, 292, 296, 328, 336
Nicomedia (Bithynian city), 284, 286, 292, 295, 296, 328, 329, 330, 336–7
Nile, river, 27, 308, 341–2, 344–8
Numa Pompilius (second king of Rome), 7, 10, 26, 254, 261, 277, 360
Nymphidius Sabinus, Gaius, 36–40, 41

Obringa (river in Germany), 57, 57*
Octavia (daughter of Claudius), 16, 17, 45
Olympic Games, 29, 326
Olympus, Mount (Bithynia), 282, 285, 291
Orkney, 240
Oscan language/culture, 185, 186
Ostia, port of, 16, 27, 178, 225, 279, 300
Otho, Marcus Salvius: backs Galba's revolt, 43–4, 45, 48; coup against Galba, 50–3, 54–5, 72, 97–8; defeated at Cremona

(April AD 69), 95–6, 98–9, 116, 118–19, 120, 126; exile in Lusitania, 44–5; and Nero's legacy, 44–5, 48, 72–3, 160; not named as Galba's heir, 48, 50; in Rome (second half of AD 68), 45, 48, 58; suicide of (AD 69), 96–7, 98–9, 130; war against Vitellius, 71–2, 84, 88–9, 94–6; youthful friendship with Nero, 44–5, 46, 72, 277

Pannonia, province of, 114, 116
Parthians, 303, 304–5, 307–11, 312–13, 314, 319, 321
pepper, 306–7, 311
Persian Gulf, 311
Petronius (senator), 176, 208–9, 210
Petronius Turpilianus, 32, 33, 41
Philopappus, Gaius Julius Antiochus Epiphanes, 334, 348
Phlegon (Hadrian's secretary), 345
Pilate, Pontius, 80, 352
Piso Frugi Licinianus, Lucius Calpurnius, 49–50, 51, 52, 53, 142
Pliny (Gaius Plinius Secundus): account of world's geography, 240, 305, 306; and AD 79 eruption, 214, 216–17, 218, 219; commands Misene fleet, 179–80, 188, 197; death of (AD 79), 222, 225; encyclopaedia of, 180, 183, 184, 192, 197, 211–12, 219, 235, 236, 256, 278, 301, 311; and frontiers of knowledge, 179–84, 197–8, 199, 209, 211–12, 214; and India, 305, 306–7; observations of natural world, 184, 211–12, 219, 223, 224, 236, 345; observations of people, 182–4, 206, 256; social standing of, 179–80, 192, 197–8; study of earthquakes, 211–12, 219; villa in Misenum, 211, 214, 219, 221
Pliny the younger, 192, 197, 211, 269, 272, 326–7; and AD 79 eruption, 214, 219, 221–2; as centred on Rome/Italy, 293–4, 295; and Christians, 352–3; commendation of Trajan to senate (AD 100), 269–70, 275, 279, 280; as Domitian's spokesman, 269, 302; and prestige of the senate, 292–3, 302; as Trajan's legate in Bithynia and Pontus, 294–7, 352–3
Pompeii, city of: and AD 79 eruption, 214–17, 218, 219, 220–1, 225; archaeological remains of, xxvi; architecture/public buildings of, xviii, 185–6, 188, 196, 212–14; Clodia Nigella as 'public pig-keeper', 200; *colonia* status, 186, 190–2; earthquakes prior to AD 79 eruption, 211–14; *flamen*

409

Rome − *continued*
  Flavian refurbishment of, 160–2, 167–8;
  Hadrian's mausoleum, xiv, xx, 358–9;
  Nero's building programme, 20–1, 26,
  45–6; Nero's 'Golden House', 20–1, 72,
  73, 227, 280–1; Palatine hill, 3, 6–7, 12, 19,
  133, 276; the Pantheon, 18, 230, 359; Pons
  Aelius, xiv, xx; poor living conditions
  for masses, 21, 276–7, 278; Porta Capena,
  7, 254; property market in, 276; size of
  during Trajan's rule, 276; 'synagogue',
  79; temple of Libera (Aventine hill),
  25–6, 27–8, 31; Temple of Peace, 168;
  Trajan's building programme, 279–81,
  299–300; Trajan's column, xx, xxii,
  319; use of loot/plunder for building
  projects, 4, 12, 23, 28, 73, 161, 162, 279–81,
  299; warehouses south of the Aventine,
  46; water/sewage infrastructure, 277–8;
  see also Campus Martius (Field of Mars);
  the Capitol; the Forum
Romulus, 6–7, 9, 31, 158, 209–10

Sabina (wife of Hadrian), 315, 322, 325,
  342–3, 348, 349
the Sabines, 10
Sabinus, Flavius (brother of Vespasian), 85,
  99, 133, 134–6, 145, 260; murder of in
  Forum, 136–7, 141
Sabinus, Julius, 140, 144, 165–6
Samaria, 75–6, 80, 81–2, 106
Samnites, 184–6, 272
Sarmizegetusa (Dacian capital), 251, 270,
  273
Saturninus, Antonius, 249–51, 269
Scaurus, Aulus Umbricius, 199–200, 210,
  301
senate (council of elders): and Caligula,
  15; and Claudius, 16; decrees Vespasian
  emperor, 141; and Domitian, 232–3,
  246–7, 248, 249, 254–5, 262, 264–5, 268,
  293; under the Flavians, 193–4, 196; and
  Galba, 34–5, 40–2, 50, 51; and Hadrian,
  316–17, 319, 320, 351–2, 353, 356, 358;
  limited influence of, 35, 71; Mucianus
  as Vespasian's plenipotentiary, 141–2,
  144–6, 166, 190, 207; Nero's contempt
  for, 21–2, 35; and Nymphidius, 37,
  39–40, 41; and Otho, 71–2; Pliny and
  prestige of, 292–3, 302; and rule of
  Titus, 226–7; senators banned from
  Egypt, 102; senators from eastern
  provinces, 193–4, 254–5, 286–7, 328, 329;

Senatus Populusque Romanus (SPQR), 9–10;
  sentences Nero to death, 33, 34; size of,
  198*; and social structure, 198–200; and
  Tacitus, 302; and traditionalist image
  of Rome, 40–2; and Trajan, 267–70, 308;
  and Vespasian's autocratic rule, 166–7;
  wealth/land qualification for, 198
Sepphoris, Galilee, 111
Septicius Clarus, Gaius, 320–1, 322, 325
Severus, Julius, 355
sex: *delicati*, 206, 209, 342, 343; free citizens
  and homosexuality, 343; in Greek
  culture, 343–4; the Liberalia, 26; Nero's
  depravity, 24–5, 38; and Poppaea Sabina,
  11; rumours about Domitian, 249; and
  slaves, 205–6, 342; views on incest, 16
Shetland, 240–1, 324
Sibylline Books, 7, 30–1, 174
Sicily, 38
silk, 306
Simeon ('Bar Kokhba', Judaean chieftain),
  354–6
slaves, xxi; barred from legions, 64;
  eunuchs, 206–7, 233–4, 342; freed, 33,
  36, 39, 209–11, 234, 255, 263–4, 265;
  liberty-slavery duality, 10, 202–3, 204;
  market regulation, 204–5, 234; and
  peoples of Asia, 73–4, 205, 207; rise to
  power/influence of, 207–11; and sex,
  205–6, 342; slave auctions, 203; as status
  symbols, 205–6; work done by, 203–4
social structure: and army auxiliaries, 106;
  cives (citizens), 9, 18, 27, 57, 59, 64–5, 66,
  106, 199, 201–2, 255, 256–7; commercial
  classes, 198, 199–200, 301, 306–7;
  craftsmen, 201; decurions (third order
  of upper classes), 198–9, 210; destitute
  citizens, 201–2, 254; *eques* (cavalryman),
  35–6, 192, 197–8, 198*, 207, 208; freed
  slaves, 33, 36, 39, 207–11, 234, 255, 263–4,
  345; great families/aristocratic clans,
  9, 12, 35, 48–9, 193; link to deep past
  lost under Flavians, 193–4; the masses/
  plebs, 19, 21, 25–7, 41, 46–7, 48, 63, 200–2,
  208, 227, 269, 275–8, 280; and military
  service, 18, 59, 65–7; Nero's contempt
  for the *optimates*, 21–2, 35; the nouveaux
  riches, 208–9; *operae* (labourers), 204;
  optimates (best class), 9, 12, 15–16, 21–2,
  35; in Pompeii, 191–2, 194–7, 199–201,
  210–11; social calibration, 198–9,
  227–8, 234; wealth/status as organising
  principle of state, 227–8, 234